# Modeling the Distribution and Intergenerational Transmission of Wealth

Studies in Income and Wealth
Volume 46

National Bureau of Economic Research
Conference on Research in Income and Wealth

# Modeling the Distribution and Intergenerational Transmission of Wealth

Edited by James D. Smith

The University of Chicago Press

*Chicago and London*

JAMES D. SMITH is Senior Project Director, Institute for Social
Research, University of Michigan.

The University of Chicago Press, Chicago 60637
The University of Chicago Press, Ltd., London

87  86  85  84  83  82  81  80     5  4  3  2  1
© 1980 by the National Bureau of Economic Research
All rights reserved. Published 1980
Printed in the United States of America

*Library of Congress Cataloging in Publication Data*
Main entry under title:

Modeling the distribution and intergenerational transmission of wealth.

  (Studies in income and wealth ; v. 46)
  Includes indexes.
  1. Wealth—United States—Addresses, essays, lec-
tures. 2. Inheritance and succession—United States—
Addresses, essays, lectures. I. Smith, James D.
II. Series: Conference on Research in Income and
Wealth. Studies in income and wealth ; v. 46.
HC106.3.C714 vol. 46 [HC110.W4] 330s [339.2′2′0973]
ISBN 0-226-76454-0                         80-15537

Since this volume is a record of conference proceedings, it has been exempted from the rules governing critical review of manuscripts by the Board of Directors of the National Bureau (resolution adopted 6 July 1948, as revised 21 November 1949 and 20 April 1968).

# Prefatory Note

This volume contains the papers presented at the Conference on Modeling the Distribution and Intergenerational Transmission of Wealth held in Williamsburg on 8 and 9 December, 1977. Funds for the Conference on Research in Income and Wealth are provided to the National Bureau of Economic Research by the National Science Foundation; we are indebted for its support. We also thank James Smith, who served as chairman of the conference and editor of this volume.

*Executive Committee, December 1977*
Clopper Almon, Chairman
Laurits R. Christensen
Stanley Lebergott
Milton Moss
Jack A. Sawyer
Jack E. Triplett
Dorothy A. Walters
Burton A. Weisbrod
Allan H. Young
Joel Popkin, NBER representative

# Contents

# Introduction

James D. Smith

The papers in this volume are from the first meeting of the Conference on Research in Income and Wealth to be devoted primarily to the dynamics of the personal distribution of wealth. The meeting reflects a changing concern by economists from measuring the cross-sectional distribution of wealth to modeling the processes by which wealth is accumulated and transmitted through time to successive generations.

The relatively small share of the profession's resources devoted to issues of personal wealth prior to 1975 was almost entirely channeled into measuring cross-sectional distributions.[1] The history of these measurements in the United States dates back to the 1850 census, but only a handful of researchers were involved in such activities until after World War II.[2] The 1860 and 1870 censuses also included queries about asset holding, but none of the census data was ever published, and with the exception of house value, questions on asset values have never reappeared in the census.[3]

Following the census measurements, scattered attempts were made to estimate distributions of wealth. For instance, in 1927 W. I. King published estimates for 1921 (King 1927). The Federal Trade Commission published information from over forty-three thousand probated estates which permits some inferences about wealth concentration over the period from 1912 to 1923, but the sampling procedures are defective or nonexistent. There were attempts to estimate wealth by income capitalization and by combining data from several sources, such as social registers and income and estate tax tabulations in the thirties, but they too suffer from serious methodological flaws or inadequate data or both. Indeed, none of the estimates published before 1950 is satisfactory. Our knowledge of the history of U.S. wealth inequality has essentially been produced by contemporary researchers applying improved methodologies to old data carefully extracted in anthropologist-like fashion from their entombment in census manuscripts, probate records and tax files. Among others, Soltow (1971), Jones (1970), and Gallman (1969) have cast new light on the past by exploiting data that their predecessors had overlooked or ineffectively used. The production of historical wealth distributions has truly been a case of new bottles for old wine.

The 1950s were prelude to a relative explosion of activity measuring the distribution and concentration of personal wealth. Three significant events in that decade sparked the work of the next two decades.

First, the Survey Research Center of the University of Michigan, with funding from the Board of Governors of the Federal Reserve System, began measuring the assets of families in the Survey of Consumer Finances.[4]

Second, Horst Mendershausen applied the estate multiplier technique to federal estate tax data supplied by the Internal Revenue Service. The technique weights decedents' assets by the reciprocals of the death probabilities of persons their age to estimate the wealth of the living.[5] It has been the most effective tool for estimating the upper tail of the personal wealth distribution.

Third, Raymond W. Goldsmith began putting together national balance sheets for the United States. Over a period of many years this work led to balance sheets with sector accounts for business, government, and households. The household sector in the national balance sheets is a residual sector, absorbing all the errors made in allocating assets to the other sectors. Nevertheless, as Goldsmith continually refined the balance sheets, the maximum value of the assets of households emerged. He thus set the stage for estimating the concentration of wealth in the hands of subpopulations. These three events set the stage for an intensive field survey and numerous estate multiplier applications to estimate the distribution of personal wealth in the 1960s and '70s.

In 1962 Lampman published *The Share of Top Wealth-Holders in National Wealth, 1922–1954*. He obtained from the Internal Revenue Service a large set of detailed tabulations of estate tax returns filed in 1954. The data were organized by age, sex, marital status, asset type, and a few other variables. Each of the cells was then weighted by the appropriate death probability reciprocal to obtain estimates of the size of the living population with wealth great enough to have required the filing of an estate tax return were they to have died in 1953.[6] Using published data from estate tax returns filed in previous years, he also made estimates of the wealth held by top wealthholders for as early as 1922. Then, comparing his estimates with Goldsmith's national balance sheets, he determined the share of the nation's personal wealth held by individuals with gross assets of $60,000 or more.

At the time Lampman published *The Share of Top Wealth-Holders,* the Survey of Financial Characteristics of Consumers, funded by the

Board of Governors of the Federal Reserve System, was organized by Dorothy Projector, with field work carried out by the Bureau of the Census. The Survey, built on the earlier work of the Survey Research Center, was intended to measure the distribution of wealth across the entire population. By a second interview a year later, saving was also to be measured. The Survey was preceded by more methodological work than had been undertaken before or since in preparation for a U.S. economic survey. Furthermore, in a parallel effort, an external research group was organized to carry out validation work for the express purpose of determining where measurement errors were occurring and their magnitude. The Survey of Financial Characteristics of Consumers was significant for scientific inquiry in another important way: for the first time government-collected microdata from an economic field survey were made generally available to the research community.

By the mid-sixties, Smith, using a special Internal Revenue Service tabulation, had made an estate multiplier estimate for 1958. Then, after pushing the Internal Revenue Service to release microdata from estate tax returns, he obtained computer tapes for federal estate tax returns filed in 1963, 1966, 1970, and 1973. These provided the basis for a detailed examination of the sensitivity of estate multiplier estimates to various assumptions inherent in the method. It also permitted detailed estimates of the concentration of wealth in the years 1962, 1965, 1969, and 1972.

Thus in a span of a few years substantial microdata on personal wealth distributions became available from their two major sources: field interviews and estate tax returns. For researchers interested in analyzing the distribution of wealth, this was an embarrassment of riches. The microdata permitted the detection of weaknesses in both methods and suggested avenues for improvement.

Unfortunately, just as sufficient knowledge had been accumulated to suggest research that would overcome the problems of field surveys, funding agencies began losing interest in supporting them. We have never satisfactorily measured personal wealth distribution with a field survey. Although the Survey of Financial Characteristics of Consumers was a great leap forward, it fell short of the expectations held for it, and there has been no subsequent effort.[7] Rather, there appears to be a prejudice among many survey practitioners that one cannot ask survey respondents about their assets without offending them. Unlike analysts, who may have only a short-run professional interest in survey data, survey practitioners have a long-term commitment to field measurement and are understandably cautious not to sour their future relations with respondents.

This conservative bias of field measurement specialists can be overcome if it is shown to be methodologically unfounded, but unfortunately there has been little inclination on the part of agencies of the federal government or foundations to support such methodological work. And since the estate multiplier method can be used for estimating only the upper tail of U.S. wealth distribution, because returns are not required for estates of decedents of modest wealth (until recently, less than $60,-000 gross assets),[8] the momentum which built up in the early sixties and produced exciting breakthroughs fizzled out by the end of the seventies. That first good estimate of the distribution of wealth seems a long way down the road.

Thus the obstacles to obtaining a good estimate of the distribution of wealth are formidable. Field surveys cannot reach the upper tail, and data which would permit the estate multiplier method to reach the bottom are scarce. Some combination of field interviews, estate tax returns, and other administrative records probably will be required. Obtaining information from administrative records is cheap, but severe organizational and bureaucratic impediments exist. A field survey adequately prepared for and carried out would now appear to cost at least $20 to $30 million.

Fortunately, the need for measured cross-sectional wealth distributions is lessening. One or two very good estimates are desperately needed, but once they have been made, it would be a misuse of resources to engage in repetitive annual or biennial measurements as we do with income. A cross-section measurement every ten years or so would appear adequate.

One of the messages of the conference is that the important things to be measured are the process and behavior by which individuals accumulate and disaccumulate wealth. Answers are needed to questions about the factors which influence individuals to save out of current income, the role of assortative mating, the wealth ownership arrangements of married couples, the division of wealth between parties at the time of divorce, the pattern of gifts among family and nonfamily members, and the bequeathing patterns of decedents. Once these and related questions are answered, simulation and analytical models can be used to generate the cross-sectional distributions and to address public policy issues which affect citizens' economic activity and status. In fact, as demonstrated by Wolff and by Smith and Orcutt in this volume, for many questions synthetic cross-sections are adequate.

In the first chapter of this volume, Jeffrey Williamson and Peter Lindert do three important things. They give us a rapid review of much of the wealth distribution work which has been done, primarily in the U.S.; they provide a process for decomposing measured wealth distributions and the forces which determine them; and they bring to bear demographic and economic history to test their own and others' interpretations of U.S. wealth distribution dynamics. Based on their analysis of others' data, three points in U.S. history contend for the pinnacle of wealth concentration: 1860, 1914, and 1929.

In the second chapter, William Newell does what Williamson and Lindert urge researchers who would understand the distribution of wealth to do. He assembles a data base out of wills and an assortment of administrative records, and analyzes it taking into account both macro and micro variables.

Newell examined the wills of testate decedents in Butler County, Ohio, from 1803 to the Civil War and combined their information with a variety of administrative records to construct a sixty-two-year time series of testators' wealth. After adjusting the value of these decedents' estates to constant dollars, Newell examined the concentration of wealth among testate decedents over the sixty-two-year period. He found an increasing concentration of wealth up to 1825, followed by a decade of increasing equality and then by a steady increase in concentration up to the Civil War.

He finds the explanation for the changing concentration of wealth in national economic conditions and local demographic change. The importance of Newell's work is not that it explicates the relative economic status of the citizens of Butler County, Ohio, but that it contributes to our understanding of the forces which shape the distribution of wealth.

In chapter 3, Michael Allen presents a simulation model of the intra-generational and intergenerational transmission of wealth which he considers the basis for more elaborate models. He takes into account the amount of wealth left by a decedent, the diminution of the decedent's wealth by death taxes, the distribution of the remaining estate among heirs, and the accumulation of wealth by the heirs over their lifetime before the cycle is repeated.

In the next chapter, Paul Menchik analyzes the importance of inheritance and saving for the wealth position of children of wealthy parents. To do this, he both assembles a data base and estimates two models. As in Newell's work, his data base is local—in this case, Connecticut—but his analysis leads to generalizations about the processes of wealth accumulation and transmission.

Menchik started with a set of about a thousand Connecticut residents who died in the 1930s and '40s and left estates of $40,000 or more. Examining death records, he found that sixty percent of the decedents had children who survived them. He then searched for the probate records of the surviving children for all years up to and including 1976. He estimates two models of the relationship of inherited wealth to the sum of inherited and potential earnings.

In chapter 5, Michael Wolfson presents a simulation model whose basic building blocks are density functions representing wealth distributions for families with specific, but limited, age-family-size characteristics. The density functions are derived from data from the 1970 Statistics Canada Survey of Consumer Finance, but the model yields results not dependent upon precise population measurements. The main parameters of the Wolfson model relate to how the wealth of decedents is parceled out to heirs, the age interval, or the devolution gap, between heirs and their benefactors, and finally the relationship between the wealth class of inheritors and the size of inheritances they receive.

In chapter 6, Edward Wolff presents estimates of the 1969 distribution of U.S. wealth based on a synthetic data base developed at the National Bureau of Economic Research. The data base was created by applying statistical matching techniques to the Public Use Sample of the 1970 Census of Housing and Population and federal income tax returns. Some asset values were derived by capitalizing income flows. Others were imputed to the file using information from still other data bases such as the Survey of Consumer Expenditures. The assets and income flows in the synthetic data base were aligned to totals available from the National Income Accounts and from national balance sheets developed by Goldsmith.

In chapter 7, James Smith and Guy Orcutt use a large simulation model to derive a synthetic representation of the 1960 U.S. population over a period of thirteen years, in order to explore the importance of the number of siblings on the value of inherited wealth. The results of the simulation are less important than the implications of their large, functioning model for future research. As evidenced by other papers in the conference, the identification of variables which predict the value of individual inheritances is of critical importance for modeling the intergenerational transmission of wealth. Attempts by Smith and Orcutt and by others to explain the variation in inheritance using personal characteristics of inheritors have been unsuccessful, because the observable characteristics of children of the rich, before they inherit, differ insufficiently from those of children with middle or lower class economic parentage. Using a population "grown" by simulation from 1960, in which they preserved the identity of each person's children and parents, they were able to transmit wealth to decedents' surviving relatives, circumventing the presently intractable problem of estimating inheritance from personal characteristics.

As the reader eases into Nelson McClung's essay in chapter 8, he may sense he is about to be dragged through a rehash of the old conflict between scholars, who desire data to test the propositions of pure science, and producers of data, who see the data needs of society as being met by repetitious measurement of rather obvious behavior and status. The reader is quickly disabused of any such notions, however. McClung is critical of both data producers and data users. The former he accuses of being too presumptuous about how a body of data will or should ultimately be used, and the latter he chides for clinging to old conceptual structures beyond their useful lives. He points out, for instance, that wage income and transfers cannot always be easily distinguished. Gifts and inheritances may be payments to alter the behavior of the recipient in the same spirit that wages are paid to alter the recipient's behavior.

McClung would place a substantial burden on the two largest data producers: the Bureau of the Census and the Internal Revenue Service. These agencies are producing more statistical information of higher quality and getting it into the hands of users faster than ever before. McClung argues, however, that this flood of information is less relevant than ever before for addressing fundamental scientific questions and public policy issues.

## Notes

1. An early interest in the dynamics of wealth ownership can be found in Lansing and Sonquist 1969, pp. 30–70.

2. Lampman notes that only ten scholars had attempted to estimate nation-wide size distributions prior to World War II. See Lampman 1962, p. 9.

3. Lee Soltow draw samples from the old census manuscripts and used them to make estimates of wealth distribution for the second half of the Nineteenth Century.

See Soltow, *1971, 1975*.

Also see the comments on Soltow's work by Williamson and Lindert in the first chapter of this volume.

4. For a discussion of the early efforts of the Survey Research Center and its subsequent development see Strumpel et al. 1972, pp. 1–34.

5. For a detailed explanation of the procedure see Smith, 1974.

6. There is a lag between the time of death and the date an estate tax return is filed. The assumption in early estate multiplier estimates was that an estate tax return represented a death in the preceding year.

7. One can hardly call the passing nod to assets in the Survey of Economic Opportunity an attempt to measure wealth distribution. Similarly there have been limited questions asked in other field surveys, for instance, the Retirement History Survey and the Survey of Income and Education. There is also an effort to include asset questions in the Survey of Income and Program Participation. The questions on specific assets in these surveys are not intended, however, to sum to net or gross wealth.

8. The method, of course, can be applied to estates of any size. Estate multiplier estimates for Washington, D.C., Oklahoma, and Tennessee have used local death tax returns required of decedents with as little as $1,000 in gross assets.

# References

Gallman, Robert E. 1969. "Trends in the Size Distribution of Wealth and Income." In Lee Soltow, ed., *Six Papers on the Size Distribution of Wealth and Income. Studies in Income and Wealth,* vol. 33. New York: Columbia University Press.

Jones, Alice H. 1970. "Wealth Estimates for the Middle Colonies, 1774." *Economic Development and Cultural Change* 18, no. 4, pt. 2.

King, W. I. 1927. "Wealth Distribution in the Continental United States at the Close of 1921." *Journal of the American Statistical Association,* n.s. 22, no. 158, pp. 135–53.

Lampman, Robert A. 1962. *The Share of Top Wealth-Holders in National Wealth.* Princeton: National Bureau of Economic Research.

Lansing, John B., and John Sonquist. 1969. "A Cohort Analysis of Changes in the Distribution of Wealth." In Lee Soltow, ed., *Six Papers on the Size Distribution of Wealth and Income. Studies in Income and Wealth,* vol. 33. New York: Columbia University Press.

Smith, James D. 1974. "The Concentration of Personal Wealth in America: 1969." *Review of Income and Wealth,* series 20, no. 2, pp. 143–80.

Soltow, Lee. 1971. "Economic Inequality in the United States in the Period from 1790 to 1860." *Journal of Economic History* 31, pp. 822–39.

———. 1975. *Men and Wealth in the United States, 1850–1870.* New Haven: Yale University Press.

Strumpel, Burkhard; James N. Morgan; and Ernst Zahn eds. 1972. *Human Behavior in Economic Affairs: Essays in Honor of George Katona.* Amsterdam: Elsevier.

# 1     Long-Term Trends in American Wealth Inequality

Jeffrey G. Williamson and Peter H. Lindert

## 1.1   The Inequality Issue

Public opinion and policy have always been influenced by perceptions about inequality, and recent research makes it possible to say much more about trends in wealth distribution than was the case a decade ago. The pioneering work of Lampman (1962) and others on twentieth-century estate tax returns has been revised and updated by James D. Smith and Stephen D. Franklin (1974), as well as by the U.S. Internal Revenue Service (1967, 1973, 1976). Robert Gallman (1969) and Lee Soltow (1975) have drawn large samples from the manuscript censuses of 1850, 1860, and 1870, which contained questions on wealth. Alice Hanson Jones (1977a, b) has put together a composite picture of the distribution of wealth on the eve of the American Revolution, drawing on a sample of probate inventories. A host of other scholars, most of them cited in sections 1.2 through 1.4 below, have drawn on probate and property tax records to sketch local trends in wealth inequality across the seventeenth, eighteenth, and nineteenth centuries.

Some striking patterns have begun to emerge from these studies. The inequality of American wealthholding is not an eternal constant. While

Jeffrey G. Williamson is professor of economics at the University of Wisconsin, Madison. Peter H. Lindert is professor of economics at the University of California, Davis.

We have benefited greatly from comments and suggestions by Richard Burkhauser, Sheldon Danziger, Robert Gallman, Victor Goldberg, James Henretta, Alice Hanson Jones, Robert Lampman, Gloria L. Main, Jackson T. Main, Paul Menchik, Gary B. Nash, and Gerard Warden. We are also grateful for research assistance provided by Celeste Gaspari and Roger C. Lister. The responsibility for any remaining errors is ours.

the colonial era was one of relative egalitarianism and stable wealth distribution, it was followed by an episode of steeply rising wealth concentration lasting for more than a century. By the early twentieth century, wealth concentration had become as great in the United States as in France or Prussia, though still less pronounced than in the United Kingdom, to judge from some tentative comparisons of probate returns. This episodic rise in wealth concentration seems to have occurred primarily in the antebellum period, with the most dramatic shift towards concentration apparently centered on the second quarter of the nineteenth century, a period when wage gaps and skill premia were rising, and profit shares increasing.

Wealth inequality declined in three periods. First, during the Civil War decade, while Northern wealth inequality remained almost unchanged, Southern inequality was reduced dramatically by slave emancipation. This revolutionary leveling in Southern wealth contrasted with and outweighed the opening of new inequalities in wealth (as well as income) between North and South. Second, both wealth and earnings leveled during the brief World War I episode. The third and last period of declining wealth inequality coincided with the "incomes revolution" documented by Kuznets (1953) and proclaimed by Arthur Burns. That is, wealth incquality declined between the late 1920s and the mid-twentieth century. In contrast with the previous periods of wealth leveling, the twentieth-century leveling has not been reversed.

American experience thus suggests confirmation of Simon Kuznets's hypothesis of an early rise and later decline in inequality during long term modern economic growth. There is even a close correspondence in the timing of income and wealth inequality turning points. We do not yet know whether the rise and fall of wealth and income inequality were of the same magnitude. It is apparent, however, that the inequality of wealthholding today resembles what it was on the eve of the Declaration of Independence.

Any effective theory of wealth distribution must deal with these long-term changes in concentration over time. The greatest challenge to existing theory, of course, will be the apparently episodic shifts in wealth concentration at two points in American history: (1) the marked rise in wealth concentration in the first half of the nineteenth century following what appears to have been two centuries of long-term stability; (2) the pronounced decline in wealth concentration in the second quarter of the twentieth century following what appears to have been six decades of persistent and extensive inequality with no evidence of trend. Furthermore and contrary to the popular view, these episodic shifts in American wealth inequality were not merely the product of changes in the demographic mix. Changes in age composition, for example, fail to account for either revolutionary shift in aggregate wealth inequality. Thus, while life cycle may help to account for inequality levels at points in time it fails to offer an explanation for inequality trends over time. Nor have American inequality trends been influenced in any important way by changes in the size of the immigrant population stock.

These are the tentative findings of this paper. Before going further, however, two issues must be confronted: motivation and measurement. While some observers care about income and wealth inequality itself, others appear to be more concerned about justice, opportunity, and social mobility. Injustice, not inequality, is central to debate over institutions which foster discrimination by race or sex. Immobility, not unequal outcomes, is the central issue to those concerned with the impact of genes, inheritance, and other dimensions of family background. Yet information on wealth inequality is central even to debates on economic justice, mobility, and opportunity. To judge the importance of discrim inatory rules or other barriers to mobility in producing economic inequality, it is important to measure wealth gaps between rich and poor. If the richest one percent of households has always held only twenty percent more wealth than the poorest one percent, then being born male to rich parents can buy only a twenty percent ticket at most. By contrast, if the richest one percent has always held a thousand times more wealth than the poorest one percent, then investigating the extent and sources of injustice and immobility would have far more to recommend it. Furthermore, inequality may itself help foster attitudes of contempt that exacerbate discrimination and socioeconomic immobility.

The problems of measurement are well known and they involve choice of time span, income or wealth concept, recipient unit, and the summary statistic for computing inequality. As for time span, it seems clear that the greatest welfare meaning can be attached to lifetime income from all sources, or its capitalized counterpart—total personal wealth—viewed from a given age. Such measures better capture material well-being than any one of those usually available: annual income, annual earnings, or the stock of nonhuman wealth. Like other researchers, however, we have been forced to retreat to less perfect measures. We have analyzed the available data on the distribution of nonhuman net worth alone (including the ownership of slaves). These data shed light on trends in lifetime inequality in two ways. First, movements in nonhuman wealth inequality are likely to reflect movements in current property income if the slope relating the average rate of return to the size of household wealth does not change significantly over time. Second, wealth inequality trends are likely to correspond with earlier movements in overall income inequality if the marginal propensities to save and rates of return maintain stable relationships with levels of income and wealth, respectively. Time series on wealth inequality are valuable mainly because they relate to the inequality of lifetime income in these indirect ways, and also because wealth distribution data exist from earlier time periods, well before household surveys and income tax returns supplied estimates for the distribution of current income.[1]

Ambiguity relating to the population unit selected and the summary inequality statistic employed also blurs, though it does not totally obscure, the meaning of trends and levels in wealth inequality. Wealth is shared to varying degrees among relatives and coresidents, complicating the definition of just who it is that has access to that wealth. The "household" offers a unit of observation which is probably as satisfactory a resolution as can be had for the question, Whose wealth is it? In addition, recent work has shown that the summary inequality statistic selected can influence the ranking of different distributions by inequality. One distribution may look more unequal than another by a Gini coefficient measure, just as equal by an entropy measure, and more equal by top shareholder percentages (Atkinson 1970). Behind this diversity in rankings of given distributions lie more basic differences in what aspects of inequality we care about most: some observers care most about the gap between the richest and the median, which is featured by some statistics, and others care most about the gap between the median and the poorest, which is featured by competing statistics. We cannot treat this issue at any length here. In order to compare studies of wealth distribution in different time periods, we shall concentrate on the three measures most commonly provided by these studies—the share of wealth held by the richest one percent of households, the share held by the richest ten percent, and the Gini coefficient—with attention to variance measures where decomposition identities are useful. Our conclusions imply a belief that the major changes in wealth inequality revealed by American history would be evident regardless of the inequality statistic employed.

These comments set the stage. Measurement of inequality through historical time is fraught with problems and thus our paper is long. But the exercise is an essential prerequisite to any serious modeling of long-term inequality dynamics in America.

## 1.2   In the Beginning: The Distribution of Wealth in Colonial America

### 1.2.1   The American Dream and the Revisionists

Visiting contemporary observers were unanimous in describing colonial America as a utopian middle class democracy, where economic opportunities were abundant and egalitarian distributions the rule. After his 1764 visit to Boston, Lord Adam Gordon remarked: "The levelling principle here, everywhere operates strongly and takes the lead, and everybody has property here, and everybody knows it" (Mereness 1916, pp.449–52). A French visitor, Brissot de Warville, viewed Boston in 1788 and "saw none of those livid, wragged wretches that one sees in Europe, who, soliciting our compassion at the foot of the altar, seem to bear witness . . . against our inhumanity" (Kulikoff 1971, p. 383). Of colonial Philadelphia, visitors pronounced that "this is the best poor man's country in the world" (Nash 1976a, p. 545). According to early America's most famous foreign observer, Alexis de Tocqueville, things were pretty much the same by the 1830s. Indeed Tocqueville's hope coincided with the American dream that the New World could some- how continue to avoid the classic conflict between growth and inequality, a conflict so painfully obvious in England and on the European conti- nent when Tocqueville and his predecessors made their visits to America.

These early observers thought America was egalitarian by European standards, and modern social historians have done nothing to upset these early impressionistic judgments. The modern quantitative evidence is effectively summarized by Allan Kulikoff's (1971, p. 380) statement that "in the seventeenth century wealth in American towns was typically less concentrated than in sixteenth-century English towns, where . . . the richest tenth owned between half and seven-tenths."

While comparative *levels* of European and American inequality have never been seriously debated, there has been lively debate regarding co- lonial *trends* in America. Three competing hypotheses have emerged in the literature. Following Jackson T. Main (1976, p. 54), the first thesis holds that a European class structure and highly concentrated wealth distribution were exported to seventeenth-century America. The frontier made short work of the European model, however, and the Revolution eventually ensured its demise. While the first thesis predicts an egalitar- ian trend economy-wide in the colonial era, that it predicts as well an egalitarian trend in the older Eastern settlements where the English model was first imported is not clear.

In contrast, the second thesis argues that the presence of the frontier made it possible right at the start to achieve a very equal distribution of land and thus wealth. But as the readily accessible colonial frontier be- came exhausted, a trend toward inequality and wealth concentration emerged, which the Revolution served only temporarily to halt. This second thesis has many proponents; for simplicity, we shall label them "the revisionists." Kenneth Lockridge (1970, 1972), for example, uses his colonial economic stress theory to describe increasing wealth con centration and diminished opportunities for accumulation in settled agrarian coastal regions. Man/land ratios rose, land values shot up rela- tive to wages making it increasingly difficult for the landless to purchase an acre of farmland and earn rent, and increased wealth and income in- equality resulted. Lockridge makes two assumptions in reaching his conclusions: that nonagricultural opportunities can be ignored, and that young men were reluctant to leave for the frontier. Lockridge is asking us to view Eastern settled colonial townships as closed agrarian systems. His "crowding" thesis quite naturally predicts inequality as the European classic steady state emerged. There is another band of revisionists who share the rising inequality view, but the city is their window on colonial America. Bridenbaugh (1955), J. Main (1965, 1971), Henretta (1965), Kulikoff (1971), and Nash (1976a, 1976b) have argued that poverty was on the rise in American cities, and that urban trends were toward propertylessness, swollen relief rolls, increasing stratification, declining opportunity and general inequality. For these scholars, inequality trends in Boston, Philadelphia, and New York City are far more important than colony-wide performance or even settled coastal agrarian township performance, because in their view these cities were the flash points for revolution, political change, and social reform. It matters little to the urban revisionists that these towns were a small and sharply declining share of total colonial population.

The third thesis is the romantic one, and it is the one we adopt here: trends were mixed, but *in the aggregate* colonial inequality was stable at low levels.[2] In some cities, inequality was on the rise. These were the fast growers who attracted the young adult or the propertyless. In others, no rise in inequality can be observed. These were typically slow growers who failed to attract the young and propertyless. Some settled agrarian regions exhibited inequality trends, others not. Even frontier settlements exhibited some evidence of rising inequality. The colonial era exhibits a lack of consistent local behavior, in contrast to the century following the second or third decade of the nineteenth century. Indeed, when the New England or Middle colonies are examined as a whole we believe there is no evidence which supports the view of drifting colonial inequality.

It appears to us that participants in the "great colonial wealth debate" have fallen victims of the fallacy of composition. Were there evidence of rising inequality in *all* town and rural communities, the case for aggregate colonial inequality trends would still not be established, for as we shall see, populations may shift toward regions with both lower inequality and more rapid wealth accumulation per capita. These were in fact the ingredients of colonial extensive and intensive frontier development, ingredients absent in the nineteenth-century economy, so that it thus was not spared from the inequality produced by modern economic growth.

### 1.2.2   Wealth Inequality in the Colonies

*A Word about Data*

Colonial social historians have made great strides in establishing a broad data base documenting wealth inequality trends in the Northern colonies. Whether based on tax assessments or probate inventories, these wealth distributions can be used as indicators of income inequality only with a solid understanding of their limitations. Since probate records are by far the best source of colonial inequality information, what follows is primarily directed toward this type of information.

Historians can get valuable clues as to the inequality of property and total income distributions among the living by observing the inequalities in the wealth that individuals left upon death. Research into colonial probate records has shown clearly that wealth inequality at death exhibits much the same trends (but different levels) as wealth inequality among the living where both kinds of documentation are available. This is apparent in the studies by Jackson T. Main (1976), Gloria Main (1976), Gary Nash (1976a), Alice Jones (1970, 1971, 1972, 1977a, 1977b) and others, all of whom have been able to classify numerous extant colonial wealth distributions for decedents by age so as to reweight them to conform to the age distributions of the living (following the estate multiplier method, e.g., Mendershausen 1956 and Lampman 1962). In no case do the resulting trends in wealth inequality among the living depart from those based on the deceased. In short, while the first limitation of colonial wealth probate data is that they fail in theory to describe the living, past studies have established unambiguously that adjusting for age distribution affects only the levels and not the trends in wealth inequality.

Some critics argue that extant colonial wealth distributions fail to gauge *income* inequality, and that it is this which should be the relevant focus. The critics can be answered in the following way: Wealth inequality measures will be monotonically related to income inequality measures when a few innocuous assumptions are satisfied. Wealth inequality *levels* are monotonically related to inequality in current property (human and conventional) incomes if rates of return on assets (including consumer durables) vary little across wealth classes. Even if rates of return rise with size of wealth holdings, the correlation still holds; parallel inequality trends in property income and property values would still be assured in this case, although income inequality levels and trends would be magnified. Indeed, while twentieth-century evidence shows that property income is more highly concentrated than wealth, implying higher rates of return among the more wealthy, the temporal correlation between the two after 1929 can be established with ease. Compared with those of the twentieth century, colonial wealth distributions are likely to exhibit an even closer parallel to *total,* as opposed to only property, income distributions. After all, conventional property income is a far larger share of total income in early stages of growth when human capital, and thus labor earnings above "subsistence," is less important. On these grounds alone, the distribution of real estate and mercantile wealth was more important in determining total wealth and income distribution early in America's growth experience than late. Finally, wealth inequality trends will accurately reflect *prior* income inquality trends if average propensities to save do not decline with income and if the income slope of the average-propensity-to-save function is relatively stable over time. Neither of these assumptions can be rejected on the basis of colonial and early national data.

We now turn to another problem in dealing with colonial wealth data. Owing to small sample size, probate wealth distributions, appropriately deflated, must be averaged over several years in order to shed light on long-term trends in wealth distributions. Wealth inequality statistics drawn from only a year or two are much too sensitive to the timing of death among the very rich. In response to this problem, some researchers report the full distribution from which has been subtracted the effect of the richest few. Although this procedure has been favored by some (e.g., J. Main's [1976] use of the "trimmed mean" in Connecticut colonial probates), we shall rely instead on multiyear averages.

Two remaining limitations on the probated wealth distributions are more important than those just mentioned. First, many decedents failed to leave wills or to have their estates administered at death. The records that survive thus supply only a sample of all decedents. Fortunately, these samples are usually large enough to predict population wealth distributions. While the samples are not free of coverage bias, colonial historians have been impressed at how well represented are both the very poor and the very rich in probate records. To be sure, samples may exhibit better coverage among estates of middle and high value, and those too poor to leave any wealth are often seriously underrepresented. Yet these problems are hardly intractable, and consistent rules for augmenting colonial probate records have been well established (Jones 1977a, 1977b; J. Main 1976; G. Main 1976; D. Smith 1975) to correct for the coverage bias. The essential point is that probate samples will accurately reflect *trends* in wealth inequality unless there were changes in coverage.

Second, probate records are limited in their asset and liability coverage. As a rule, the Middle colonies did not include real estate (land, improvements, and buildings), but covered only personal estate. The New England colonies were more complete in asset coverage. In both cases, financial liabilities were rarely included. As we shall see, this variety in asset coverage is a serious defect only if comparative judgments across colonies or short-term instability is the focus. The problem of limited coverage appears not to be quantitatively significant when evaluating long-run trends, since colonial wealth inequality measures normally trace the same secular pattern regardless of probate asset coverage.

What, then, do these sources tell us about the distribution of colonial wealth and opportunity?

*Colonial Wealth Inequality Trends*

Appendix 1 collects estate and tax list distributions from New England and the Middle colonies, producing twenty-nine series in all. Connecticut and Massachusetts are both very well represented from the mid–late seventeenth century to the Revolutionary War. We have long time series on urban and rural areas, and the series yield a wide geographic representation. The Middle colonies are less extensively documented, but even in this case we have time series on Philadelphia and New York City as well as Maryland and rural Pennsylvania. The data have two limitations. First, they fail to supply summary descriptions of trends in aggregate performance for any colony or region, with the possible exception of Maryland. While manuscript censuses for 1860 and 1870 yield returns on total personal wealth for America as a whole and the major regions, no such aggregates are available for the colonial era, with the exception of Alice Jones's benchmark for 1774 (Jones 1970, 1972, 1977a, 1977b). This attribute of colonial wealth concentration trends has the effect of producing an inherent upward bias and, as we shall see in section 1.2.3, has produced erroneous inferences in the recent literature. Second, wealth distributions derived from tax lists must be treated with great caution. Since so much of the revisionist literature (Henretta 1965; Lemon and Nash 1968) was initially based on tax lists, it might be useful to discuss its limitations before proceeding further.

Some ten years ago, Henretta (1965) reported steep wealth inequality trends for colonial Boston. His pioneering work was based on very imperfect tax list data. He thought he observed a striking trend toward wealth concentration, since the top ten percent increased their share from 46.6 percent in 1687 to 63.6 and 64.7 percent in 1771 and 1790 (table 1.A.4, col. 12). Apart from the fact that Gloria Main and Gary Nash's Boston probate data (table 1.A.3, cols. 8 and 9) now make it apparent that the 1680s and '90s were decades of atypical low concentration ratios, the tax data have now been shown to be seriously flawed. Gerard Warden's adjustments (table 1.A.4, col. 13) suggest a much more modest rise from the atypical trough of the 1680s, from 42.3 to 47.5 percent between 1681 and 1771. Warden's "adjustments" deal with problems of undervaluation. Undervaluation ratios varied greatly across assets and over time, many assets escaped assessment altogether, and asset mixes varied over time and across wealth classes. Apparently, these valuation problems tend to yield a spuriously steep inequality trend for Boston. Although no one to our knowledge has yet attempted similar adjustments to the Philadelphia, Chester County (Pennsylvania), Hingham (Massachusetts), and New York City tax list wealth distributions, they must by inference be treated with equal caution. It is for this reason that figures 1.1–1.4 rely almost exclusively on probate data.

What do the probate wealth inequality trends tell us? Was the colonial era one of drifting inequality? If one were to take 1690 or 1700 as a base, the wealth inequality series reported in figures 1.1–1.4 would suggest mixed trends but, on average, a drift toward greater wealth concentration for the seven or eight decades prior to the Revolution. This characterization holds for rural Connecticut (but not for Hartford County),

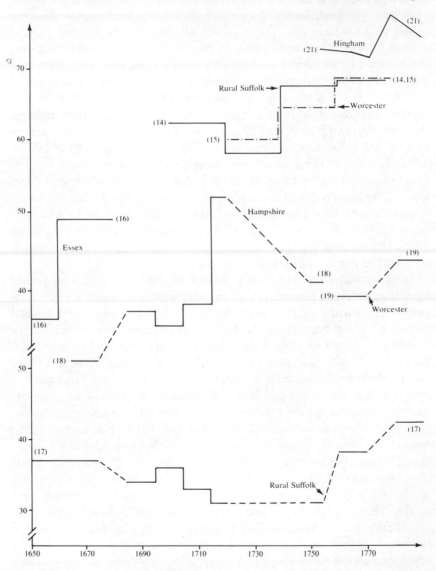

**Fig. 1.1**        Colonial Wealth Inequality Trends: Rural Massachusetts (percent held by top wealthholders). Source: tables 1.A.5 and 1.A.6, cols. 14–19 and 21.

for rural Massachusetts (but not for rural Suffolk County), for Boston as well as Portsmouth (New Hampshire), and for Philadelphia as well as nearby Chester County. It does not hold for Maryland, however, which exhibits stability from the 1690s onward. New York City is an-

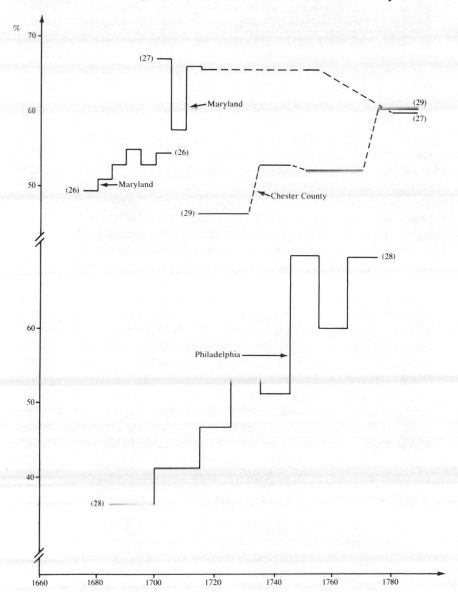

**Fig. 1.2**     Colonial Wealth Inequality Trends: Middle Colonies (percent held by top wealthholders). Source: table 1.A.8, cols. 26–29.

other exception since it had a stable wealth distribution between 1695 and 1789 (table 1.A.7, col. 25), but it is based on tax list data.

Selection of benchmark dates is critical in evaluating colonial inequality trends. Boston traces out inequality trends only if the 1690s are taken as a starting point, while no perceptible trend can be identified when the 1770s are compared with the 1670s or 1730s instead. "Cycles" in wealth inequality are also reported by Gloria Main for both Boston and Suffolk County probates (table 1.A.3, cols. 8–10). Wealth concentration rose after a trough in the 1680s and '90s, but far higher inequality was recorded in the colonial era beginning in 1650. If the 1690s were years of atypical economic conditions accounting for unusually low concentration levels, then the case for stability in Boston colonial inequality trends would be reinforced. It hardly seems coincidental that New England imports were low and declining from 1697 to 1706, high and rising from 1707 to 1730, declining again from 1731 to 1746, and rising thereafter to 1771.[3] These episodes of "bust" correspond very well with periods of low inequality in Boston and Suffolk County (figure 1.3), a predictable result since extended depression must have produced capital losses at the top of the distribution and thus a leveling in wealth concentration. Subsequently, the improvement in Boston trade (and associated capital gains) produced increased wealth concentration following ca. 1705 and again following ca. 1750. What we may be observing between 1700 and 1730 is not a pervasive secular shift in *physical* asset accumulation at the top of the wealth pyramid, but an uneven rise in average asset values among the very rich who held mercantile capital in relatively high proportion. After all, real estate was far more equally distributed in mercantile Boston than was "portable" personal property (Nash 1976a, pp. 552–53), and the latter included slaves, servants, currency, bonds, mortgages, book debt, stock in trade, and ships. Short-term capital gains and losses must have been more typical for these types of assets than for real estate, at least for a trading center like Boston which was subjected to the whims of exogenous world commercial conditions. Since the very wealthy held non-land-type assets in relatively high proportions, their relative fortunes were far more sensitive to the vagaries of mercantile conditions. (For a twentieth century example, see Robert Lampman's [1962, pp. 220–29] discussion of asset price changes and wealth inequality during the 1920s and '30s.) Thus the "cycles" in wealth concentration can be readily associated with Boston's trade conditions, and since the 1680s and '90s were years of atypically poor trade conditions, while the 1670s or 1710s were not, long-term stability (or decline) seems the best characterization of Boston's wealth concentration for the whole colonial era.

Mercantile centers were not the only colonial areas to exhibit wide instability in wealth concentration. Maryland supplies another example, and thus the choice of benchmark dates plays a crucial role here too. While wealth concentration was remarkably stable after 1710 (table 1.A.8, col. 27), the social historian beginning his analysis with 1675 would have cited instead evidence of a slight drift in Maryland inequality throughout the colonial era. While Gloria Main's estimates (table 1.A.8,

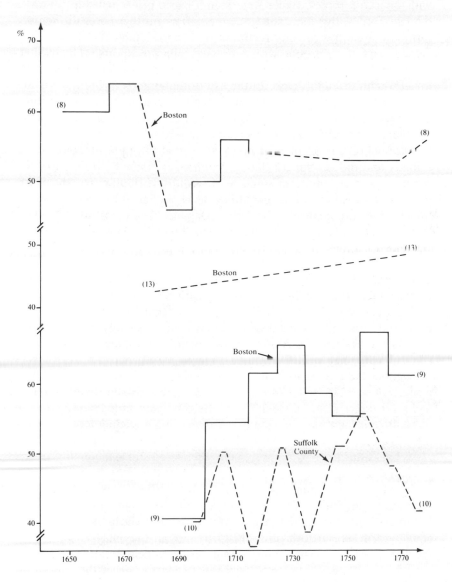

**Fig. 1.3**    Colonial Wealth Inequality Trends: Boston and Suffolk County (percent held by top wealthholders). Source: tables 1.A.3 and 1.A.4, cols. 8–10 and 13.

col. 26) show a modest rise in Maryland wealth inequality from 1675 to 1690, Menard, Harris, and Carr (1974, p. 174) have shown that the 1670s were unusual since a leveling in the wealth distribution had been at work for the quarter-century following 1640, at least along the lower western Chesapeake shore. This pattern seems to correspond fairly well with tobacco fortunes. While American tobacco prices fell sharply up to the late 1660's, they bottomed out thereafter. Furthermore, the temporarily low wealth inequality recorded in 1705–9 (table 1.A.8, col. 27) also appears to correspond with depressed tobacco exports.[4] The capital-gains-and-losses-export-staple thesis seems to account for Maryland colonial wealth instability, too. In the 1690s, conditions facing Maryland's key export staple, tobacco, were more typical; therefore, the stable long-term wealth inequality levels from that benchmark seem to describe Maryland's colonial inequality experience best.

Hartford, Connecticut, will serve as a final example of colonial instability and the benchmark dating problem. Jackson T. Main's (1976) recent finding of long-term stability of wealth distribution for the Hartford probate district can be seen quite clearly in figure 1.4. Main's trends for Hartford are confirmed by Bruce Daniels (1973–74, pp. 129–31). Daniels also finds, however, that wealth inequality was on the rise in small and medium-sized Connecticut towns after the early 1700s. Daniels reports a steep trend in wealth concentration in Danbury, Waterbury, and Windham after 1700, and in the smaller frontier towns in Litchfield County after 1740 (table 1.A.2, cols. 5 and 6). But a comparison with Main's data reproduced in figure 1.4 shows that the contrast between rural and "urban" Connecticut experience may be only apparent, not real. While Hartford personal wealth inequality (figure 1.4, series 1a and 2a) and total wealth inequality (table 1.A.2, col. 4) were stable throughout the eighteenth century, *real* wealth inequality was not, for it rose between 1710 and 1740 or 1750. Since the smaller frontier towns had a far larger share of wealth in real estate (and thus land),[5] the rise in wealth concentration outside of the Connecticut trading towns following 1710 seems less anomolous. Indeed, had Daniels extended his analysis backward to 1680, he may have discovered stable inequality trends in rural Connecticut too. J. Main's real estate concentration figures for Hartford County (figure 1.4, series 3) show a very striking leveling in real wealth distributions from the 1680s to 1710. Had we, like Daniels, begun our analysis in 1700 we would have observed a real wealth inequality drift in Hartford up to 1774. If instead the analysis starts with the 1680s or earlier, no trend in real wealth concentration can be observed. By inference, it seems likely that at least some of the wealth inequality trends following 1700 noted by Daniels in rural Connecticut are spurious.[6]

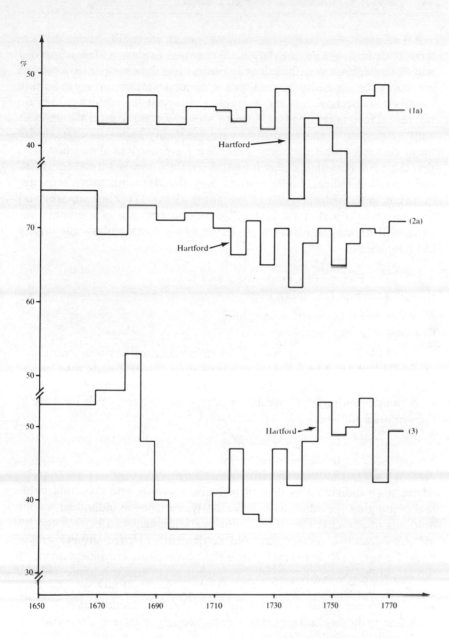

**Fig. 1.4**  Colonial Wealth Inequality Trends: Hartford, Connecticut (percent held by top wealthholders). Source: table 1.A.1, cols. 1–3.

To summarize, among those probate wealth inequality series that extend backward before the 1690s, Worcester County (Massachusetts) and Philadelphia reveal the minority position: a clear secular drift toward inequality for the entire colonial era. Connecticut, Boston, rural Suffolk County (Massachusetts), and Maryland represent the majority: they do not reveal inequality trends. If instead one is content to start the analysis with 1700, then a modest drift toward inequality seems to characterize these colonial "local histories" best. We have tried to show, however, that the 1700 benchmark may impart a spurious upward trend to wealth concentration indices. Some readers may disagree with this interpretation, but those historians who have adopted the 1700 benchmark, and thus view the mixed "local history" trends as evidence of a colonial inequality drift, may be inadvertent victims of yet another bias—the fallacy of composition.

### 1.2.3    The Fallacy of Composition and the Trending Inequality Bias

*New Frontiers, Old Settlements, and*
*Colonial Wealth Inequality*

As we have seen, the probate or tax data necessary to document trends in colony-wide wealth inequality do not exist. These trends may be inferred, however, with the help of some variance properties. Our interest is in the concentration of wealth colony-wide and one such measure is the *variance statistic*:[7]

$$\sigma^2 = \frac{\sum_i (W_i - \overline{W})^2}{P}$$

where $W_i$ is individual wealth, $\overline{W}$ is average wealth, and $P$ is total colonial population (or adult males). Similarly, variance in individual wealth holdings in any city, township, county or settlement can be denoted by $\sigma_j^2$. Consider two regions, an "old settlement" ($U$, for urban) and a "new frontier" ($R$, for rural). Since the two regions are independent in the statistical sense (but hardly independent in the economic sense), colony-wide wealth concentration can be decomposed into the weighted sum of variance within and between the two regions. Since *relative* mean deviation is the key to inequality trends, we might instead deal with the coefficient of variation (or its square):

$$\left(\frac{\sigma}{\overline{W}}\right)^2 = \frac{U\sigma_U^2 + R\sigma_R^2 + U(\overline{W}_U - \overline{W})^2 + R(\overline{W}_R - \overline{W})^2}{P \cdot \overline{W}^2}$$

Let $I$ be this wealth inequality statistic, and call the population share in settled regions $u$. Then at any point of time between 1620 and 1776

$$I = u\left(\frac{\overline{W}_U}{\overline{W}}\right)^2 I_U + (1-u)\left(\frac{\overline{W}_R}{\overline{W}}\right)^2 I_R$$

$$+ \frac{u}{1-u}\left(\frac{\overline{W}_U}{\overline{W}} - 1\right)^2$$

Colonial wealth inequality *levels* were determined by four forces: (1) inequality in settled regions; (2) inequality at the frontier; (3) the relative average wealth differential between frontier and settled regions; and (4) the relative size of the settled region.[8] Our interest is in colonial wealth inequality *trends,* not levels, so:

$$dI = dI_u\left\{u\left[\frac{\overline{W}_U}{\overline{W}}\right]^2\right\} + dI_R\left\{(1-u)\left[\frac{\overline{W}_R}{\overline{W}}\right]^2\right\}$$

$$+ du\left\{\left[\frac{\overline{W}_U}{\overline{W}}\right]^2 I_u - \left[\frac{\overline{W}_R}{\overline{W}}\right]^2 I_R + \left[\frac{\overline{W}_U - \overline{W}}{\overline{W}(1-u)}\right]^2\right.$$

$$+ 2I_R\left[\frac{\overline{W}_R}{\overline{W}}\right]\left[\frac{\overline{W} - \overline{W}_U}{\overline{W}(1-u)}\right]\right\}$$

$$+ d\left(\frac{\overline{W}_U}{\overline{W}}\right)\left\{2u\left[I_U\left(\frac{\overline{W}_U}{\overline{W}}\right) - I_R\left(\frac{\overline{W}_R}{\overline{W}}\right)\right.\right.$$

$$+ \left.\left.\left(\frac{\overline{W}_U}{\overline{W}} - 1\right)\left(\frac{1}{1-u}\right)\right]\right\}$$

Four forces were driving trends in colonial wealth concentration: (1) trending concentration in settled regions; (2) trending concentration at the frontier; (3) the changing relative size of the older settlements; and (4) the ratio of per capita wealth in settled regions to that of the colonies as a whole.

There is little conflict among colonial social historians regarding the following two assertions: (1) wealth was more concentrated in older seacoast settlements; and (2) per capita wealth was higher in the older seacoast settlements. Although we shall provide empirical support for these innocuous assumptions below, for the moment consider their implications.

Colonial historians almost always draw their data from either settled urban areas (Boston, Philadelphia, Hartford, New York City) or from older eastern townships or counties (Hingham, Chester). Yet our inequality formula reminds us that an upward drift in Philadelphia inequality hardly implies an inequality trend for eastern Pennsylvania. Nor does an upward drift in eighteenth century wealth concentration in Boston or Suffolk County necessarily imply an increase for Massachusetts Commonwealth as a whole. A shift in population away from the older settlements would have a leveling influence, and so too would any trend which diminished the average wealth differential between frontier and seacoast regions. Even if we were to agree (and we do not) that rising inequality was characteristic of both settled and frontier regions in the colonial era, this evidence would hardly establish the case for drifting inequality in the eighteenth century. On the contrary, if *extensive* or *intensive* development in colonial areas away from the seaboard was sufficiently rapid, the opposite could have been the case.

The foregoing section serves to identify the component sources of colonial inequality trends, but it also offers a tool for estimating otherwise unobservable colony-wide trends. All we require are benchmark estimates for the percent of population residing in settled regions, estimates of average wealth in both settled and rural regions, and surrogates for wealth inequality in both regions.

### Interior Development and the Irrelevance of Boston

Let us now apply the decomposition formula to New England colonial performance. Four forces were driving trends in New England wealth concentration: (1) trending inequality in the seaports generally, and Boston in particular $(dI_B)$; (2) changing patterns of wealth concentration in newly settled interior counties and townships $(dI_{NB})$; (3) the changing relative size of older seaport settlements like Boston $(du)$; and (4) the ratio of per capita wealth in Boston $(\overline{W}_B)$ to that of New England as a whole $(\overline{W}_{NE})$.[9] The first two terms in the decomposition formula are simply a weighted average of inequality trends in Boston and in the remainder of New England. Table 1.1 and appendix 2 supply the necessary information to estimate these weights. In 1774, for example, the weight attached to Boston inequality trends is .05, while that attached to the remainder of New England is .95. It looks very much as if Boston's wealth inequality trends were irrelevant to New England's experience. Then why all the fuss about Boston? While some may argue that Boston was the focus of political change, Boston's experience with trending wealth inequality—falling after the 1670s, rising after the 1680s, stable after the 1710s—tells us almost nothing about New England experience. In short, even if we were to adopt the atypical 1680s as a benchmark, Boston's trends would grossly exaggerate any alleged inequality drift in New England as a whole.

Turn now to the third term in the decomposition expression. According to Gary Nash and Allan Kulikoff, Boston's population share must have undergone a consistent and extended decline between 1687 and 1774; in contrast with nineteenth-century city growth, the colonial era is hardly one of dynamic urbanization. Indeed, while Boston contained 7.5 percent of New England's population in 1710, the figure had fallen to 4.4 percent in 1750 and 2.7 percent in 1771 (table 1.1). We have al-

**Table 1.1          Colonial Population Trends**

*New England Colonies*

| Year | (1) Boston | (2) New England | (3) (1) ÷ (2) $u$ |
|------|-----------|-----------------|-------------------|
| 1680 |          | 68,400  |      |
| 1690 |          | 86,900  |      |
| 1700 |          | 92,800  |      |
| 1710 | (8665)   | 115,200 | .075 |
| 1720 |          | 170,900 |      |
| 1730 | 13,875   | 217,400 | .064 |
| 1740 | 16,800   | 289,800 | .058 |
| 1750 | 15,800   | 360,000 | .044 |
| 1760 | 15,631   | 449,700 | .035 |
| 1770 | 15,500   | 581,100 | .027 |
| 1780 | 10,000   | 712,600 | .014 |

*Middle Colonies*

| Year | (1) Middle Colonies | Period | (2) Phila-delphia | (3) New York City | (4) (2) + (3) ÷ (1) $u$ |
|------|--------------------|--------|-------------------|-------------------|--------------------------|
| 1700 | 83,200  | 1700–10 | 2,450  | 4,500  | .083 |
| 1710 | 112,300 | 1711–20 | 3,800  | 5,900  | .087 |
| 1720 | 169,200 | 1721–30 | 6,600  | 7,600  | .084 |
| 1730 | 238,100 | 1731–40 | 8,800  | 10,100 | .079 |
| 1740 | 336,700 | 1741–50 | 12,000 | 12,900 | .074 |
| 1750 | 437,600 | 1751–60 | 15,700 | 13,200 | .066 |
| 1760 | 590,200 | 1761–70 | 22,100 | 18,100 | .068 |
| 1770 | 758,500 | 1771–75 | 27,900 | 22,600 | .067 |
| 1780 | 968,300 |         |        |        |      |

*Sources*: New England and Middle colonies totals are from U.S. Bureau of the Census (1976, Part 2, p. 1168). The New York City and Philadelphia figures are from Nash (1976, table 4, p. 13). The Boston figures are from Nash (1976, table 4, p. 13), and Kulikoff (1971, table V, p. 393).

ready seen that the distribution of wealth in the interior was of far greater significance (by a factor of 20 to 1) to mid-eighteenth-century New England wealth inequality trends than was Boston itself. In addition, we now learn that Boston's relative decline must have produced a leveling influence in New England as a whole. After all, colonial Boston *always* exhibited higher wealth concentration than the interior. In the 1760s, for example, the top 10 percent of probated wealth holders had 53 percent of the wealth in Boston, while the figure was 38 percent for rural Suffolk County, 39 percent for Worcester County, and 40 percent for Hingham. The top 30 percent controlled 88 percent of the (probated) wealth between 1740 and 1760, a figure far in excess of Worcester's 64 percent, rural Suffolk's 68 percent, and Hingham's 73 percent. Indeed, the top 30 percent in Connecticut's small and medium-sized towns held from 61 to 69 percent of total wealth during the same period.

How important was Boston's decline in contributing to an overall egalitarian leveling in New England? Or to put it another way, how important was the *extensive* development in rural New England to wealth leveling during the colonial period? The third term in the decomposition expression can be estimated,[10] and it implies the following: between 1710 and 1774, the decline of Boston (*u* fell from .075 to .027) contributed to a wealth leveling in New England of about $dI_{NE} = -.07$ using weights from the 1770s, or $dI_{NE} = -.13$ using weights from the 1680s. This leveling influence is not insignificant when compared with Alice Jones's 1774 benchmark $I_{NE} = 1.88$ since it implies a 4 to 7 percent reduction in aggregate inequality. It seems unlikely that this conclusion would be changed if the seacost urban settlement was expanded to include far smaller centers like Portsmouth, Hartford, or New Haven, but it is true that none of these underwent anything like Boston's decline.

While Boston's share of New England's population declined, the rest of New England slowly made good an initial disparity in per capita wealth levels. Indeed, appendix 2 reveals that Boston's per capita taxable wealth (adjusted by Gerard Warden) as a ratio of New England's per capita physical wealth *fell* from 1.608 to 1.339 between 1687 and 1774. These two wealth concepts are, of course, somewhat different, but if the ratio of taxable to physical wealth was fairly stable over the eighteenth century, we can safely conclude that rural New England achieved more impressive wealth accumulation than did Boston and other seacoast settlements. This tended to equalize wealth in the region at large.

By how much did interior intensive development contribute to an overall colonial leveling? Although the calculation is based on slim evidence, it would take an enormous error to change our results. The narrowing of the wealth per capita gap between Boston and the remainder of New England over the century 1687–1774 served to lower the New England wealth inequality statistic by .025 (1.3%) if 1771 weights are used and .064 (3.4%) if 1687 weights are used. The relatively rapid *intensive* development in Boston's hinterlands must have contributed significantly to a leveling of wealth in New England.

Even the most skeptical reader must agree that wealth inequality trends in Boston and other settled coastal regions mask New England trends. Our experiments show the following: (1) inequality trends outside Boston were far more important to New England colonial inequality experience by a factor of 20 to 1; (2) the relative decline of Boston, as rural New England underwent *extensive* settlement, contributed significantly to a leveling of wealth distribution in the region as a whole; (3) the relative decline of Boston, as rural New England underwent *intensive* wealth accumulation and relatively rapid economic development, also contributed to a leveling of wealth distribution in the region as a whole. The present colonial data base makes it impossible to pursue these components of wealth inequality in much greater detail. What we need, of course, is a far more extensive sampling of wealth records from the early eighteenth century to serve as a benchmark with which Alice Jones's 1774 observations may be compared. Then our "analysis of variance" experiment would have far greater legitimacy. Until that time, however, the hypothesis must be that rising New England wealth inequality cannot be inferred from mixed "local" trends, but rather that stability or leveling was the case for New England as a whole prior to the Revolution.

### Interior Development and the Doubtful Relevance of Philadelphia

In contrast with Boston, the main seaports in the Middle colonies, Philadelphia and New York City, both underwent consistent and rapid growth between 1710 and 1774. Nevertheless, even Philadelphia—the faster growing of the two—failed to match the rate of interior settlement after 1720 (table 1.1). From the 1720s to the Revolutionary War, Philadelphia's population share in the Middle colonies fell from 3.9 to 3.7 percent. The population of New York City and Philadelphia combined fell from 8.4 to 6.7 percent of the regional total over the same period. As in New England, wealth was far more heavily concentrated in the settled coastal areas than in the interior,[11] so that the relative decline of these two seaports served to lower wealth inequality in the region as a whole. How important was the *extensive* development in the interior of the Middle colonies as a wealth leveling influence during the colonial period? Since New York City and Philadelphia population shares declined by only 1.7 percent in the half-century following 1720, the leveling influence, though positive, could not have been very great.

Did inequality trends in Philadelphia contribute significantly to Middle colony trends? Could trending inequality in Philadelphia have taken place simultaneously with leveling in the Middle colonies as a whole? Since Philadelphia is the prime example of trending probate wealth inequality cited by Gary Nash, the bifurcation has special relevance, and once again the decomposition formula will prove helpful. If we use the 1770s as a benchmark, each parameter in the decomposition formula can be estimated.[12] Thus, we can decompose the (unobserved) eighteenth-century wealth inequality trends of the Middle colonies into the following component parts:

$$dI_{MC} = (.071)dI_P + (.933)dI_{NP} + (2.770)du$$
$$+ (.193)d(\overline{W}_P/\overline{W}_{MC}),$$

where *MC, P,* and *NP* denote, respectively, Middle colonies, Philadelphia, and non-Philadelphia.

In terms of *potential* impact on Middle colony wealth concentration trends, the rate of extensive development ($du$) and inequality trends in rural inland settlements ($dI_{NP}$) were clearly most important, while inequality trends in Philadelphia were least important. The *actual* impact, of course, can be determined only by documentation of the four trending variables on the right-hand side of the decomposition expression. Since interior extensive development was a minor force from the 1720s to 1775 ($du = -.002$), the actual impact of extensive development on Middle colony inequality trends must have been minor. How relevant was Philadelphia's trending wealth inequality to Middle colony performance? Between 1700–1715 and 1766–75, probate inequality data imply a sharp rise in Philadelphia wealth concentration. Judged by Gary Nash's trends and using Alice Jones's 1774 Philadelphia county estimates as a base (appendix 2), $dI_P \cong .557$. Philadelphia trends by themselves would have raised Middle colony wealth inequality by .040 (3%). Once again, the debate over inequality trends has been based on a city whose contribution to overall Middle colony inequality trends was quite small. Only if Philadelphia was representative of all regions would the attention lavished on her be warranted. The truth of the matter is that Philadelphia was not typical even of all seaports in the Middle colonies. New York City and Philadelphia had very similar wealth concentration in the 1690s. The top 10 percent of taxpayers claimed 44.5 percent of New York's taxable wealth in 1695, while they held 46 percent of Philadelphia's taxable wealth in 1693. By 1789, New York City had hardly changed at all (the top 10 percent of taxpayers claiming 45 percent of taxable wealth), while Philadelphia had undergone the extraordinary inequality trends analyzed so well by Gary Nash (reaching 72.3 percent by 1774). In short, if we believe Philadelphia to be representative of seacoast cities, it contributed very little to Middle colony wealth concentration trends. Since there is evidence that Philadelphia was an extreme case of trending urban inequality, "very little" seems more likely to have been "trivial." Philadelphia inequality experience was indeed of doubtful relevance.

What about the remaining two forces: (1) trending wealth concentration in the interior; and (2) intensive development in the interior? The only probate wealth data for the Middle colonies outside of Philadelphia that would supply $dI_{NP}$ are Gloria Main's estimates for Maryland. From 1700 to 1754 there appears to be a slight decline in Maryland's wealth concentration. Lemon and Nash (using taxable wealth) and Duane Ball (using a very small probate sample) find the opposite trends in Chester County between 1693 and 1770. Interior trends are mixed. But note the following: those vast Middle colony frontier regions, whose trends are left undocumented, must have been regions of relatively equal distributions of wealth. Evidence of "frontier equality" is repeated for every

New England and Middle colony wealth study cited in table 1.A.1, so it seems quite legitimate to make use of it here. Furthermore, we know that over time and with settlement, these frontier New York and Pennsylvania counties increased in importance. The process must have had an important leveling influence in the interior. To judge interior inequality trends by examining the experience of a single county, say Chester County, is to commit the fallacy of composition once again. All of this suggests to us that to presume anything about interior wealth inequality trends would be folly.

We are left with only one final potential source of alleged increased wealth concentration in the Middle colonies. Did Philadelphia increase in per capita wealth more rapidly than the Middle colonies in general? If so, then the recent attention devoted to Philadelphia's pre-Revolutionary inequality trends might be justified. If, like Boston, it did not, then Philadelphia's performance tells us little about Middle colonial inequality. Until such evidence on interior intensive development is made available, colonial Philadelphia inequality trends remain of doubtful relevance.

*Age, Wealth, and Selective Migration*

Demographic forces may also have acted to produce a spurious drift in colonial wealth inequality. To judge what truly happened to life cycle wealth inequality, an effort must be made to hold age distribution constant. After all, young adults have far smaller average wealth holdings (table 1.2 and figures 1.5–1.6). On these grounds alone, if young adults are added to a static adult population through immigration or natural increase, wealth inequality may rise even though life cycle inequalities change not at all. The larger the differential in average wealth levels by age, the more potent the effect. In addition, we must consider wealth inequality within age classes. Using 1870 total estate and 1850 real estate census data, Lee Soltow (1975, p. 107) has shown that inequality was high in the age group 20–29, much lower in the age group 30–39, and fairly stable in subsequent age groups. It is possible that as the share of adult males in their twenties rose over time, inequality would also appear to rise when no true inequality trend was present.[13]

What is the colonial evidence on wealth and age? We would be satisfied with either of two kinds of wealth concentration data: (1) measures of wealth concentration over time *within* fairly narrow age classes; (2) detailed information on changing age distributions which could be combined with our knowledge of age profiles on wealth means and variances. Since the colonial data base does not yet fulfill these rigorous demands, we must be content with Soltow's 1850 estimates of wealth dispersion within age classes.[14] What about wealth by age class? Does the colonial age-wealth life cycle trace out a profile much like mid-nineteenth and twentieth-century patterns? Table 1.2, figure 1.5, and figure 1.6 exhibit an age-wealth profile that is consistent over time and across regions. Whether late-seventeenth-century Maryland, mid-eighteenth-century Hartford, or Revolutionary New England, the patterns are very similar to twentieth-century age-wealth profiles. It is a simple matter, therefore, to establish a *potential* role for demographic forces as a source of measured wealth inequality change in pre-Revolutionary decades.

The actual role of demographic forces is far more difficult to isolate. Demographic data for the colonial era are very skimpy, and the time series that are available rarely supply more than three age classes (most

**Table 1.2**     **Age and Wealth in the Colonies, 1658–1774: Average Wealth by Age Class Relative to Total**

| Age Class | (1) Maryland 1658–1705 |
|---|---|
| 25 and under | .246 |
| 26–45 | .940 |
| 46–60 | 1.334 |
| 61 and over | 1.021 |
| All adult males | 1.000 |

| Age Class | (2) Hartford 1710–14 | (3) Hartford 1750–54 | (4) Connecticut 1700–1753 |
|---|---|---|---|
| 21–29 | .340 | .383 | .264 |
| 30–39 | .744 | .767 | .607 |
| 40–49 | 1.545 | 1.208 | 1.014 |
| 50–59 | 1.330 | 1.342 | 1.383 |
| 60 and over | .898 | 1.192 | 1.283 |
| All adult males | 1.000 | 1.000 | 1.000 |

| Age Class | (5) Middle Colonies 1774 Net Worth | (6) Middle Colonies 1774 Physical Wealth | (7) New England 1774 Total Wealth | (8) New England 1774 Physical Wealth |
|---|---|---|---|---|
| 25 and under | .121 | .881 | .184 | .197 |
| 26–45 | .770 | .891 | .731 | .732 |
| 46 and over | 1.338 | 1.295 | 1.270 | 1.269 |
| All adult males | 1.000 | 1.000 | 1.000 | 1.000 |

*Sources*: (1): Value of total estate (excluding land and improvements), inventoried at death, lower western shore of Maryland. Menard, Harris, and Carr (1974, table II, p. 178). (2) and (3): Hartford probate district, personal wealth only. J. Main (1976, table XI, p. 84). These are periods for which Main's samples are relatively large. (4): All Connecticut inventoried wealth, including land. J. Main (1976, table XIX, p. 95). (5) and (6): Middle Colonies, decedent wealth. A. H. Jones (1971, table 5). (7) and (8): New England, decedent wealth. A. H. Jones (1972, table 4, p. 114).

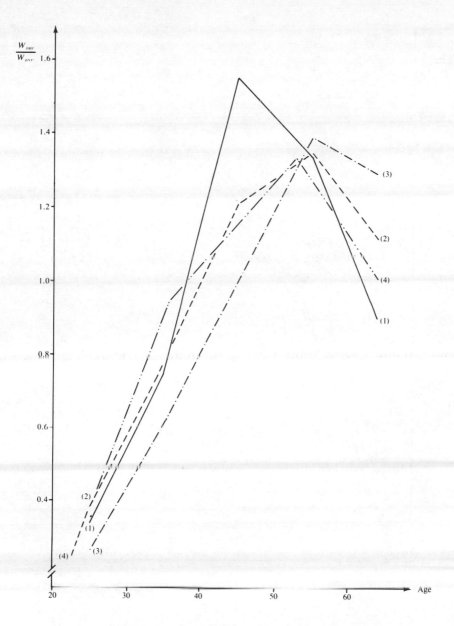

**Fig. 1.5**     Age and Wealth in the Colonies, 1658–1753. Key: (1) Hartford, Connecticut, 1710–14; (2) Hartford, Connecticut,
1750–54; (3) Connecticut, 1700–1753; (4) Maryland, 1658–
1705. Source: table 1.2.

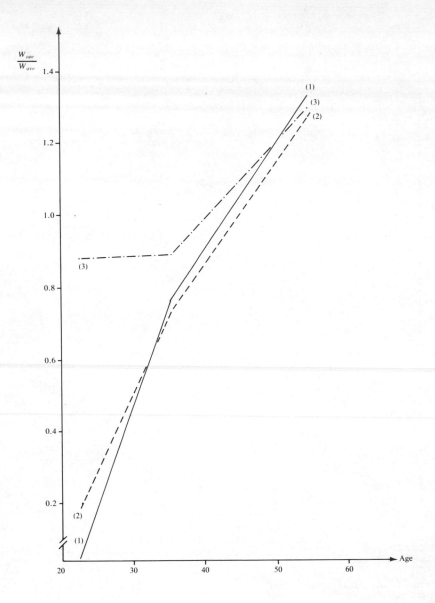

**Fig. 1.6**      Age and Wealth in the Colonies, 1774. Key: (1) Middle colonies, 1774 (net worth); (2) New England, 1774 (total and physical wealth); (3) Middle colonies, 1774 (physical wealth). Source: table 1.2.

commonly, under 16, 16–60, and over 60). What we have suggests stability in colonial age distributions. If we ignore the Revolutionary War years, when (young) men in the army were undercounted or missed entirely, the evidence suggests very little change in age distributions in New Hampshire between 1767 and 1773, in New York between 1712–1714 and 1786, or in New Jersey between 1726 and 1745 (U.S. Bureau of the Census 1976, part 2, p. 1170). Indeed, the age distribution of adult males (free *and* slave) was not much older or more dispersed even in 1860 compared with colonial times.[15]

While age distributions appear to have been stable colony-wide in the eighteenth century, and thus would impart no bias in an aggregate inequality index, the same cannot be said for colonial cities and more urbanized eastern settlements. A widening of inequality may have resulted if urban populations got younger. Rapid growth in Philadelphia, for example, could not have been achieved in the absence of native emigration from the countryside as well as a foreign influx. These tended to consist of younger and, more frequently, single males. Thus, those cities enjoying the most rapid growth were likely to have the steepest inequality trends, not necessarily because average ages were lower but rather because ages were far more widely dispersed. This prediction of an upward inequality trend bias in the cities is confirmed by Philadelphia's colonial performance, on the one hand, and Boston's and New York's, on the other. One cannot help but wonder to what extent the rise in Philadelphia's "poor," documented by Gary Nash, could be explained simply by the increased preponderance of youth in the city's population.[16]

There is yet another upward bias in the urban wealth concentration trends. Migration is, by definition, selective. The vast majority of young in-migrants to Boston, New York, and Philadelphia chose to leave the settled countryside or Europe because they had better "opportunities" in the eastern seaports. Since they had no land to keep them at home, some (the majority) joined frontier settlements and became part of intensive and extensive colonial interior development. A smaller number migrated to the towns. The point is obvious: while young adults have, on average, low wealth holdings, the young urban immigrant has even lower wealth holdings. This selective aspect of urban immigration imparts an upward bias to urban inequality trends beyond the bias imparted by age itself.[17]

One can only speculate but it seems likely that changing urban age distributions imparted an upward bias to eighteenth-century wealth inequality trends in Boston and Philadelphia. While the same cannot be said for colony-wide trends, the fact remains that it is the experience of these two cities that has attracted much of the social historian's attention.

This section has suggested yet another reason for rejecting trending inequality as a description of the colonial era.

### 1.2.4 Colonial Quiescence

It could be argued that all the protagonists in the colonial wealth debate are correct, but none of them has articulated how local trends relate to trends for the thirteen colonies combined. Urban inequality did rise in some cities, perhaps supplying fuel for revolution and social change. Inequality and social stratification did rise to high levels in some settled agrarian regions along the Atlantic coast, especially those from which young men were slow to emigrate. Inequality even rose over time in some frontier settlements. The important point, however, is that new frontiers were being added at a very rapid rate. The opportunities for wealth accumulation were there in the interior, and they were exploited assiduously. The result was both extensive and intensive development in the interior of the Northern colonies. Wealth per capita grew there relative to the seacoast settlements, thus producing a leveling influence since the new settlements were comparatively poor to start with. Total wealth and population shifted to the interior as well, and this too had a leveling influence since equality was more a frontier attribute.

The net effect was to produce quiescence in colonial inequality. A comfortable result, indeed, since per capita wealth and income growth was fairly quiescent during the pre-Revolutionary years too.

## 1.3   Wealth Concentration in the First Century of Independence

### 1.3.1   The 1774, 1860, and 1870 Benchmarks

For the century inaugurated by the Declaration of Independence, we now have benchmarks for nation-wide wealth distributions. Alice Hanson Jones (1977a) has constructed one set of estimates for 1774 using probate inventories and the estate multiplier method by which the wealth distribution of the living is reconstructed from that of decedents. Lee Soltow (1975) has used large manuscript census samples to derive size distributions of total assets for 1860 and 1870.

Table 1.3 reports these benchmark size distributions. Around 1774, the top one percent of free wealthholders in the thirteen colonies held 12.6 percent of total assets, while the richest ten percent held a little less than half of total assets. In 1860, the richest percentile held 29 percent of total America assets, and the richest decile held 73 percent.[18] Thus, the top percentile share more than doubled and the top decile increased its share by half again of its previous level. Among free adult males, the Gini coefficient on total assets rises from .632 to .832. Equally dramatic surges are implied for the South and non-South separately.

**Table 1.3**    **Selected Measures of Wealth Inequality, 1774, 1860, 1870, and 1962**

| | Net Worth | | | Total Assets | | |
|---|---|---|---|---|---|---|
| | Percent Share Held by Top 1% | Percent Share Held by Top 10% | Gini | Percent Share Held by Top 1% | Percent Share Held by Top 10% | Gini |
| *1774 (13 colonies)* | | | | | | |
| Free households | 14.3% | 53.2% | .694 | 12.6% | 49.6% | .642 |
| Free and slave households | 16.5 | 59.0 | | 14.8 | 55.1 | |
| Free adult males | 14.2 | 52.5 | .688 | 12.4 | 48.7 | .632 |
| All adult males | 16.5 | 58.4 | | 13.2 | 54.3 | |
| Southern free households | 10.7 | 47.3 | .664 | 9.9 | 46.3 | .649 |
| Non-South, free households | 17.1 | 49.5 | .678 | 14.1 | 43.8 | .594 |
| *1860* | | | | | | |
| Free adult males | | | | 29.0 | 73.0 | .832 |
| | | | | 30.3– | 74.6– | |
| Adult males | | | | 35.0 | 79.0 | |
| Southern free adult males | | | | 27.0 | 75.0 | .845 |
| Non-South, free adult males | | | | 27.0 | 68.0 | .813 |
| *1870* | | | | | | |
| Adult males | | | | 27.0 | 70.0 | .833 |
| Southern adult males | | | | 33.0 | 77.0 | .866 |
| Southern adult white males | | | | 29.0 | 73.0 | .818 |
| Non-South, adult males | | | | 24.0 | 67.0 | .816 |
| *1962* | | | | | | |
| All consumer units ranked by total assets, unadjusted | 36.9 | 69.1– 82.6 | | 26.0 | 61.6 | .76 |
| All consumer units ranked by total assets, revised (see section 1.5.2 below) | 20.6 | 38.5– 46.1 | | 15.1 | 35.7 | |

*Sources and notes*: The 1774 wealth distributions are from Alice Hanson Jones (1977, vol. 3, table 8.1). We are grateful to Professor Jones for advice and access to unpublished calculations that were useful as cross-checks to our own computations. We also wish to thank Roger C. Lister for performing the 1774 computer calculations for this and the next table. The 1860 and 1870 figures are from Lee Soltow (1975, pp. 99, 103). The 1962 figures are derived from Projector and Weiss (1966, tables 8, A2, A8, A14, and A36).

The sample sizes on which these calculations are based follow: *1774*, 919 decedents, of whom 839 were males and 298 were from the South; *1860*, spin sample

The antebellum rise in wealth inequality is evident even if one includes slaves as part of the population. Counting slaves both as potential wealthholders and as wealth has the effect of raising estimated inequality before the Civil War. This follows from the reasonable assumption that slaves had zero assets and net worth. Adding extra "wealthholders" with zero wealth is equivalent to scaling down the share of the population represented by the same number of top wealthholders. This adjustment should be greater for 1774 than for 1860, since the slave share of the population peaked at about 21.4 percent in 1770 and declined to about 11 percent by 1860. Thus counting slaves as both people and property, a defensible procedure, should have raised the inequality measure more for 1774 than for 1860. Nevertheless, table 1.3 suggests that this adjustment has little or no effect on the net rise in inequality between these two dates.

---

Table 1.3  Sources and notes (*cont.*)

of 13,696 males, of whom 27.6 percent were from the South; *1870*, spin sample of 9,823 males; *1962*, 2,557 consumer units.

For definitions of net worth, total assets, and the population unit, see the sources cited above. It should be remembered that the 1774 and 1860 calculations include the asset values of slaves in the total assets and net worth of their owners.

The calculations referring to the total population, free plus slave, include slaves as households with zero assets and net worth as part of the population. In these calculations, slaves are thus both people and property. Their share of the 1770 population of households was estimated by multiplying both the total free and slave populations by a proxy for the ratio of households to population. This proxy was the share of negroes and mulattoes over sixteen years of age in Maryland in 1755 in the case of slaves (U.S. Bureau of the Census, 1976, chapter Z), and the share of white males over sixteen in 1790 (ibid., series A119–34) for the free population. Assuming the same ratio of household heads to adults among slaves as among the free, and applying the adult-to-population ratios to the slave and free populations, yield the estimate that slave households were 20.2 percent of all households in 1770, which is applied to 1774.

Point estimates (single values) are reported for cases in which we judged the range between high and low estimates based on different interpolations within wealth classes to be sufficiently narrow. Where the range implied by alternative methods of interpolation was wide, we have reported a range of values. The latter is not to be interpreted as indicating true lower and upper bounds, since errors could arise from factors other than just interpolating shares within the wealth classes supplied by the underlying data.

Our results show lower inequality for 1774 than was reported by Alice Hanson Jones (1977a) for two reasons. The first is that Professor Jones has concluded that her regional weights within the South require revision so as to reduce the weight of prosperous Charleston to 1 percent of the South, as she will report in her forthcoming volume (1977b). We have used her revised regional weights here, and wish to thank her for informing us of the revision. The second reason relates to an apparent slight deviation in our procedures in constructing the "w*B" weights used to convert the sample of decedents to the estimated population of living wealthholders. We are checking the computer programs used by Professor Jones and ourselves to pinpoint the discrepancy. The differences are slight in any case, with Professor Jones's revised size distributions (1977b) resembling ours much more than they resemble those of her earlier volume (1977a).

The 1774 wealth distribution bears some resemblance to the (revised) distribution implied by the Federal Reserve survey for 1962. The share held by the richest one percent was apparently a little lower in 1774, both among the free and among the free plus slaves. On the other hand, the top decile share appears to have been somewhat higher on the eve of the Revolution than it was nearly two centuries later.

If the figures in table 1.3 are allowed to stand without adjustment, they reveal an epochal rise in wealth concentration between 1774 and 1860. Tocqueville anticipated this trend toward concentration, pointing to the rise of an industrial elite which he feared would destroy the economic foundation of American egalitarianism:

> I am of the opinion . . . that the manufacturing aristocracy which is growing up under our eyes is one of the harshest that ever existed. . . . The friends of democracy should keep their eyes anxiously fixed in this direction; for if a permanent inequality of conditions and aristocracy . . . penetrates into [America], it may be predicted that this is the gate by which they will enter. [Tocqueville 1963 ed., p. 161.]

Jackson T. Main suspected that Tocqueville's fear was borne out by subsequent events, at least based on his early rough estimates of wealth inequality on the eve of the Revolution and Gallman's (1969) findings for 1860 (J. Main, 1971). Gallman suspected a rise in wealth inequality after 1810, though for different reasons. Edward Pessen took a similar position, debunking "the era of the common man" with evidence of rising wealth inequality and social stratification (1973). Lee Soltow (1971b, 1975) has opposed this view, arguing instead that wealth inequality remained unchanged across the nineteenth century.

Did a marked shift toward wealth concentration really take place?

## 1.3.2    Possible Benchmark Biases and Weight Shifts

There are several ways that the figures in table 1.3 might be judged misleading. The obvious frontal assault is to claim that the underlying data are simply unreliable.

Since her 1774 sample consisted of only 919 observations, as against the 13,696 observations used by Lee Soltow for 1860, it is natural to point the finger of suspicion at Alice Hanson Jones's estimates. As far as the asset coverage and population unit are concerned, however, we see no clear bias. While the probate inventories she used may well exclude some financial assets or liabilities, no clear effect on the size distribution of net worth or total assets is obvious. Unleased real estate was excluded from the inventories outside of the New England colonies, yet Professor Jones supplied the missing real estate values from predictions implied by regressions estimated on the New England observations. As for the population unit, Professor Jones tried to make the basic population that of all households in the thirteen colonies by assuming that a large majority of adult females were not household heads. Should one wish to compare an all male wealth distribution in 1774 with that for 1860 or 1870, that comparison is also reported in table 1.3, with little difference in the implied trend toward concentration.

The most serious criticism of the underlying probate data is that they cover a biased sample of the population of potential wealthholders. We know that only a minority of decedent household heads left wills and inventories. We know that the set of decedents for whom no inventory survives includes people from all wealth classes. We also know that the main excluded group is the very poor, who left no inventory because they left no wealth to appraise. The net effect is likely to be an undersampling that is more serious for the poorest classes, producing a probate sampling bias that could make wealth inequality look misleadingly low. Given the extent to which probate records will remain a critical data base in future historical research, it is important that more detailed studies be devoted to cross-checking the probate inventory samples against other primary data identifying the wealth, occupation, and other attributes of the population from which the probates survive. It is especially important to identify the wealthiest and most prominent citizens in earlier centuries, in order to quantify the sampling ratio for the rich. Such research into probate bias has already begun (G. Main 1976; D. Smith 1975), but much remains to be done.

Professor Jones has already performed sensitivity analyses to determine the importance of the probate sampling bias. Her estimates reported in table 1.3 are based on the assumption that the probate inventories undersampled the poorer wealth classes. In the net worth size distribution, for example, these "w*B - weighted" results are based on an underlying assumption that the bottom net worth decile includes from five to eighty times more nonprobated decedents than the top decile, the relative ratio varying from region to region. These multipliers are based in part on Professor Jones's own limited cross-checks between the probate samples and other source materials, such as local tax lists. The multipliers must, however, be characterized as guesses, and guesses which lack the guidance of any colonial contemporary judgments regarding which people were eluding probate.

Let us consider what kinds of errors in these probate sampling multipliers might have led to a serious underestimation of wealth inequality in 1774. Perhaps the poor have still been relatively undersampled, despite Professor Jones's attempt to scale up their numbers. While this is possible, the missing extra poor would have to be at the very bottom of the wealth spectrum. An alternative set of weights that uniformly expanded the numbers with wealth low enough to be in the bottom quarter of those probated, Professor Jones's "w*A" weights, showed no greater inequality than the preferred "w*B" weights used here. Suppose, however, that the undersampled groups are the very rich as well as the very poor. While this is also possible, it must be remembered that in this era the very wealthy would have had little incentive to hide their wealth from probate. There were no estate taxes to avoid, and even the local property taxes on the living were light enough to offer little incentive to keeping property hidden from the probate appraiser, or to transfers *inter vivos*.

One can also question the reliability of the 1860 census returns underlying Lee Soltow's recent book. Perhaps people gave very casual answers to the census takers. In particular, a large number of them may have reported zero wealth in order to avoid the bother of estimating asset value. Fully 38 percent of free adult males reported property less than $100 in the 1860 census sample, but it is hard to tell what share of these actually reported zero wealth. At the other end of the wealth spectrum, one might speculate that the very rich overstated their wealth in the 1860 and 1870 censuses, but this is a hard conjecture to sustain. Again, we know of no clear bias in the estimates, either for 1774 or for 1860.

Another common suspicion relates not to the quality of the data but to the potentially distorting effect of shifts in demographic weights, such as changes in the age distribution or changes in nativity. Reflecting the sophistication with which economists approach measures of income or wealth inequality in the 1970s, many have expressed the view that the antebellum rise in wealth inequality may be a mirage caused by shifts toward an older population or by shifts in the share of foreign-born or the share living in cities. To address such skepticism, we need to ascertain whether there was a rise in wealth inequality among people of given age, place of birth, and area of residence.

To sort out the contributions of such population group shifts to the apparent rise in wealth inequality between 1774 and 1860, we first perform a set of reweighting experiments using Professor Jones's 1774 data.[19] This involves transforming the weights on the 919 individual observations in her sample so as to reflect the age distribution or the rural-urban mix of 1860, and recalculating top quantile shares and Gini coefficients to see how much shift in wealth inequality is implied by combining different demographic distributions with the same within-group wealth data. These experiments are summarized in table 1.4.

Before concluding that wealth concentration rose dramatically in the antebellum era, one must first establish that the rise was not the sole result of a change in the age mix of the adult population. From section 1.2 and table 1.7, we know that average wealth rose steeply with age both in the colonial era and in the mid–nineteenth century. We also know that the age distribution of adults became more dispersed over the century following 1774. This evidence encourages the intuition that wealth inequality may have remained the same within age groups, and that the rise in aggregate inequality was the result of population aging alone. Table 1.4 appears to reject this intuition. Application of the 1860 age distribution to the 1774 wealth data serves only to raise the top percentile share of total assets held by males from 12.4 percent to 12.9 percent, and the top decile share from 48.7 percent to 50.1 percent. These age effects account for less than 6 percent of the aggregate trend toward wealth concentration. Similarly, the shift from the 1774 age distribution[20] to the 1962 age distribution explains only a small share of the apparent rise in top quantile shares over the intervening two centuries. It appears that shifts in age distribution were not sufficiently dramatic to

| Table 1.4 | **Effects of Changing Group Weights on Measures of Wealth Inequality among Nonslaves, 1774 Versus 1860 and 1962** | | | | | |
|---|---|---|---|---|---|---|
| | Net Worth | | | Total Assets | | |
| | Percent Share Held by Top 1% | Percent Share Held by Top 10% | Gini | Percent Share Held by Top 1% | Percent Share Held by Top 10% | Gini |
| *1774* | | | | | | |
| Original weights | 14.3% | 53.2% | .694 | 12.6% | 49.6% | .642 |
| Males only | 14.2 | 52.5 | .688 | 12.4 | 48.7 | .632 |
| Males only, 1860 age distribution | 15.6 | 55.0 | .715 | 12.9 | 50.1 | .644 |
| 1962 age distribution | 14.2 | 54.3 | .706 | 12.7 | 50.5 | .656 |
| Rural only | 12.0 | 50.8 | .675 | 11.4 | 48.8 | .629 |
| Urban only | 29.4 | 70.8 | .817 | 24.8 | 61.4 | .736 |
| *1860* | | | | | | |
| All (free) males | | | | 29.0 | 73.0 | .832 |
| *1962* | | | | | | |
| All consumer units, unadjusted | 36.9 | 69.1– 82.6 | | 26.0 | 61.6 | .760 |
| All consumer units, revised (see section 1.5.2 below) | 20.6 | 38.5– 46.1 | | 15.1 | 35.7 | |

*Sources and notes*: The sources are the same as for table 1.3.
In adjusting the 1774 wealth distribution to reflect the 1860 and 1962 age distributions, we use the age group division offered by Professor Jones: 25 and under, 26–44, and 45 and over. The 1860 and 1962 distributions were calculated from U.S. Bureau of the Census (1976, chapter A), with age group interpolations for 1860. The rural sample population for 1774 consisted of those scoring 9 (most rural) on Professor Jones's regional code. The urban sample consisted of codes 1 through 3, or essentially Boston, Philadelphia, Charleston, and New York City.

explain much of the aggregate wealth inequality trends for the first century of independence.

Urbanization appears to offer more explanatory power than age distribution changes. On the eve of the Revolution, as elsewhere in U.S. history, wealth inequality was consistently higher in the cities than in the countryside. To judge the contribution of urbanization to the 1774–1860 trend in concentration, one must quantify the amount of urbanization that occurred. This cannot be done in a satisfactory way since Professor Jones used a rural-urban code that does not conform to the rural-urban census definitions for 1860. Within the context of the present 1774 reweighting experiment, we can offer only clues to the importance of the rural-urban shift. One clue is that while the urban top quantile shares in 1774 were much higher than similar colony-wide shares, they were not so high as the top quantile shares for the total male population in 1860. This suggests that even if cities had engulfed the entire U.S. population by 1860, this movement could not have explained all of the observed rise in wealth inequality. Another comparison points to the same conclusion. Professor Soltow's 1860 results imply that if the entire colonial free male population had lived on farms in 1774, the Gini coefficients and top quantile shares for the total assets would have been much lower, but still not so low as those observed in 1774. The actual shift from rural to urban residence, or from farm to nonfarm, was much less over the century than these comparisons presume, of course. This, and evidence offered in section 1.3.5, suggest that the true shift in population toward the cities is unlikely to have accounted for the observed rise in aggregate inequality.

It appears that the trend toward wealth concentration in the early nineteenth century was no mirage. Mere shifts in age and residence cannot account for the massive change in the structure of American wealthholding. This conclusion is too important to rest solely on the evidence presented thus far. We need to perform further tests on the relevance of age, residence, and nativity shifts across the nineteenth century.

### 1.3.3  Aging in the Nineteenth Century

We have argued that shifts in the age distribution had little effect on wealth inequality trends in either the colonial period or the first century of independence. Is the same conclusion warranted for the shorter term antebellum period or for the nineteenth century as a whole?

Tables 1.5 and 1.6 report changes in the U.S. adult age distribution between 1830 and 1900. The age distribution among American white adult males did change markedly between 1830 and 1870, the most dramatic shift occurring in the last two decades. The percent of white males in their twenties declined from 40.6 in 1830 to 36.1 in 1860 and to 34.4 percent in 1880. The decline appears to have been even more pro-

Table 1.5          Percent Distribution of White Adult Males by Age, 1830–1900

| Census Year | Age Class | | | | | |
|---|---|---|---|---|---|---|
| | 20–29 | 30–39 | 40–49 | 50–59 | 60+ | Total |
| 1830 | 40.58 | 25.14 | 15.61 | 9.73 | 8.95 | 100.01 |
| 1840 | 39.87 | 26.12 | 16.16 | 9.47 | 8.38 | 100.00 |
| 1850 | 38.10 | 26.25 | 17.12 | 10.15 | 8.38 | 100.00 |
| 1860 | 36.06 | 26.96 | 17.68 | 10.69 | 8.62 | 100.01 |
| 1870 | 33.61 | 25.09 | 18.79 | 12.41 | 10.09 | 99.99 |
| 1880 | 34.41 | 24.61 | 17.58 | 12.43 | 10.97 | 100.00 |
| 1890 | 32.93 | 25.79 | 17.70 | 12.00 | 11.58 | 100.00 |
| 1900 | 31.30 | 25.60 | 19.06 | 12.53 | 11.52 | 100.01 |

*Source*: U.S. Bureau of the Census (1976, pp. 16, 23).

Table 1.6          Percent Distribution of White Adults by Age: U.S. and
               Northeast, 1800–1870

| Age Class | U.S. Males & Females | | Northeast Males | |
|---|---|---|---|---|
| | 1800 | 1820 | 1830 | 1870 |
| 15–24 | | | 50.99 | 29.91 |
| 25–44 | | | 40.75 | 42.12 |
| 45–64 | | | 7.47 | 21.61 |
| 65+ | | | .80 | 6.36 |
| 16–25 | 36.2 | 38.0 | | |
| 26–44 | 39.7 | 37.6 | | |
| 45+ | 24.1 | 24.3 | | |

*Source*: U.S. Bureau of the Census (1976, pp. 16, 23).

nounced in Northeastern states; the share of adults (male and female) in the 15–24 age group falls from 51 percent in 1830 to 30 percent in 1870, a steep decline indeed. The era of great inequality surge was therefore also one of pronounced aging in the American adult population.

Such shifts in the age distribution could have raised or lowered aggregate inequality. The outcome would depend in part on whether the aging of the adult population raised age dispersion, as in the earlier stages of mortality improvement, or lowered it, as in the present stage of low and declining fertility, when the adult population pushes against the modern limits of life expectancy. Life cycle wealth patterns imply that greater wealth dispersion would be associated with greater age dispersion. In addition, wealth inequality is highest among the youngest adults, and an aging of the adult population would on these grounds tend to reduce wealth inequality.[21] Which effects prevailed? Let us turn first to a crude national calculation and then to a firmer one based on Wisconsin data.

We can use Soltow's data on the relationship of age to real estate wealth in 1850 to calculate one component of the age effect. Table 1.7 shows mean wealth and Gini coefficients for different age groups in 1850. Ignoring the Ginis within age groups for the moment, let us calculate what would have happened to the top decile share of real estate wealth if all age groups held their mean values and the age distribution shifted as it actually did between 1830 and 1860. If the age distribution alone had changed, the top 10 percent (the oldest) would have claimed 23.6 percent, 22.3 percent, and 21.5 percent of all real estate in 1830, 1860, and 1880 respectively. Of course, aging would also affect aggregate real estate inequality by shifting the adult population to older age groups having lower within-group Gini coefficients. This second impact would reinforce the presumption that aging after 1830 served to *reduce* wealth inequality. What we know about age effects thus far serves to magnify the aggregate wealth inequality trend that requires explanation.[22]

Wealth data currently exist which would allow a more explicit accounting of these age and life-cycle effects, since the sample underlying Soltow's 1975 book yields total estate values by age, sex, nativity, and region. Unfortunately, Professor Soltow was unable to make his 1860 or 1870 samples available to us, so we settled on a second best strategy. Soltow's 1971 book on Wisconsin wealthholding reports the 1860 distributions for adult males reproduced in table 1.8. If we hold the variance within age classes constant, how would American aggregate wealth inequality have behaved between 1830 and 1900 if the observed changes in the age distribution of the adult male population (table 1.5) had been the only changes taking place? How important was population aging in producing a downward bias in aggregate wealth inequality trends? The answers are supplied in table 1.9. The Gini coefficient would have drifted downward until 1870 while remaining stable thereafter.

In short, attention to age distribution trends in the antebellum era

| Table 1.7 | Age and Real Estate Wealth in 1850 | | | | | |
|---|---|---|---|---|---|---|
| Age Class | Mean Wealth | Gini Coefficient | | Age Class | Mean Wealth | Gini Coefficient |
| 20–29 | $253 | .92 | | 50–59 | 1950 | .77 |
| 30–39 | 835 | .82 | | 60–69 | 2253 | .77 |
| 40–49 | 1639 | .81 | | 70+ | 2439 | .81 |

*Source*: Soltow (1975, pp. 70 and 107) based on census samples, free males, aged 20 and older.

Table 1.8    Percent Distribution of Wealth by Class, Males Classified by Age: Wisconsin, 1860

| Wealth Class, $j$ ($) | Mean Wealth $W_j$ ($) | Total Distribution 20+ ($a_j$) | Percent Distribution by Age ($a_{ij}$) | | | | |
|---|---|---|---|---|---|---|---|
| | | | 20–29 | 30–39 | 40–49 | 50–59 | 60+ |
| 0–1 | .5 | .288 | .166 | .058 | .025 | .015 | .024 |
| 1–100 | 50.5 | .041 | .015 | .013 | .006 | .003 | .004 |
| 100–200 | 150.0 | .062 | .020 | .023 | .010 | .005 | .004 |
| 200–300 | 250.0 | .049 | .016 | .017 | .009 | .005 | .002 |
| 300–400 | 350.0 | .037 | .011 | .013 | .007 | .003 | .003 |
| 400–500 | 450.0 | .032 | .008 | .013 | .007 | .003 | .001 |
| 500–600 | 550.0 | .034 | .008 | .013 | .007 | .003 | .003 |
| 600–700 | 650.0 | .029 | .007 | .010 | .007 | .003 | .002 |
| 700–800 | 750.0 | .025 | .005 | .009 | .006 | .002 | .003 |
| 800–900 | 850.0 | .024 | .004 | .009 | .005 | .004 | .002 |
| 900–1,000 | 950.0 | .021 | .005 | .006 | .005 | .003 | .002 |
| 1,000–1,100 | 1,050.0 | .027 | .005 | .009 | .006 | .005 | .002 |
| 1,100–1,200 | 1,150.0 | .019 | .003 | .008 | .006 | .002 | 0 |
| 1,200–1,300 | 1,250.0 | .023 | .005 | .006 | .006 | .004 | .002 |
| 1,300–1,500 | 1,400.0 | .032 | .006 | .011 | .007 | .005 | .003 |
| 1,500–2,000 | 1,750.0 | .058 | .010 | .019 | .017 | .007 | .005 |
| 2,000–2,500 | 2,250.0 | .046 | .006 | .016 | .013 | .008 | .003 |
| 2,500–3,000 | 2,750.0 | .027 | .002 | .008 | .010 | .005 | .002 |
| 3,000–4,000 | 3,500.0 | .041 | .004 | .013 | .014 | .006 | .004 |
| 4,000–5,000 | 4,500.0 | .023 | .002 | .007 | .007 | .005 | .002 |
| 5,000–10,000 | 7,500.0 | .042 | .003 | .011 | .016 | .008 | .004 |
| 10,000+ | 19,642.1 | .019 | .002 | .006 | .006 | .004 | .001 |
| Total | 1,486.0 | .999 | .313 | .298 | .202 | .108 | .078 |

*Sources and notes*: The underlying data taken from Soltow (1971b, table 6, p. 45). The $a_{ij}$ are calculated as a percent of all adult males. Soltow does not report mean wealth or total wealth by class, nor has he been able to supply us with the underlying data. Thus, we have assumed the mean wealth by class to be the midpoint in each size class, with the exception of $10,000 and above. The latter is computed as a residual, since Soltow does report the total mean of $1,486. In the absence of the underlying data, we have also assumed that these class means apply to each age group within the given class. Our imperfect data imply a Gini coefficient of 0.735, while Soltow reports a figure of 0.752.

hardly suggests that our aggregate inequality indices are mirages. On the contrary, they understate the true inequality trends.

## 1.3.4 The Foreign-Born Myth

Perhaps the surge toward wealth inequality was the result of a rising share of impecunious immigrants in the total population. A rise in the foreign-born share could have increased aggregate wealth inequality without any change in inequality among persons classified by nativity.

Indeed, since immigrants were normally skewed toward the young male categories, one might have thought that immigration would have produced an inequality trend on these age considerations alone. We have already seen this to be false for the Northeast and for the United States as a whole.

An increasing foreign-born share could play a role in two ways. First, given a gap in average wealth between native and foreign born, a rise in the foreign-born share would serve to increase total inequality without any increased wealth inequality within either group. Such evidence could be grounds for dismissing the study of American inequality experience. If the antebellum inequality surge was simply the result of poverty influx from Europe, it would hardly warrant detailed analysis. And these wealth gaps were large. After standardizing for age, Soltow shows that in 1860 in the Northeast, those native Americans born in southern New England or the Middle Atlantic had average wealthholdings more than two times those of male heads born in Germany, almost three times the Irish male head, and a little less than double the British male head (Soltow 1975, table 6.2, p. 152). Whether due to discrimination, inability to speak English, a relatively poor European environment, or length of time in America, the gaps were a fact of life. To be more precise, for free men in their thirties, those native born had average total estates of $2,444 in 1860, while those foreign born had only $1,051; native born had wealthholding on an average 2.3 times that of foreign born (Soltow 1975, table 3.4, p. 77). Second, if the distribution of wealth was more unequal among the foreign born, their increased relative importance would also produce rising total inequality. In fact, wealth was indeed more heavily concentrated among the foreign born in midcentury.[23]

It seems to us, however, that these two forces could not have had an important quantitative impact on the measured aggregate trends. Even if the entire population of adult males had been native born in 1820, the

**Table 1.9**    **Impact of Changing Age Distributions on Trends in American Wealth Concentration, 1830–1900: Wisconsin 1860 Weights**

| Census Year | Gini Coefficient | | Census Year | Gini Coefficient | |
|---|---|---|---|---|---|
| | U.S. | Wisconsin | | U.S. | Wisconsin |
| 1830 | .716 | | 1870 | .702 | |
| 1840 | .714 | | 1880 | .705 | |
| 1850 | .710 | | 1890 | .703 | |
| 1860 | .707 | .735 | 1900 | .698 | |

*Sources and notes*: Underlying age data used in the calculation are taken from tables 1.5 and 1.6. The U.S. age distributions are applied using Wisconsin 1860 "wealth distribution weights." The procedure assumes the distribution across wealth classes within age groups to be constant.

rise in the foreign-born share to its actual values in 1860 or 1870 could not account for much of the observed surge toward inequality. The truth of this assertion can be made most apparent with the help of the inequality algebra introduced in section 1.2:

$$
dI = dI_N \left[ n \left( \frac{\overline{W}_N}{\overline{W}} \right)^2 \right] + dI_F \left[ (1 - n) \left( \frac{\overline{W}_F}{\overline{W}} \right)^2 \right]
$$

$$
+ dn \left[ \left( \frac{\overline{W}_N}{\overline{W}} \right)^2 I_N - \left( \frac{\overline{W}_F}{\overline{W}} \right)^2 I_F + \left( \frac{\overline{W}_N - \overline{W}}{\overline{W}(1 - n)} \right)^2 \right.
$$

$$
\left. + 2I_F \left( \frac{\overline{W}_F}{\overline{W}} \right) \left( \frac{\overline{W} - \overline{W}_N}{\overline{W}(1 - n)} \right) \right]
$$

$$
+ d \left( \frac{\overline{W}_N}{\overline{W}} \right) \left\{ 2n \left[ I_N \left( \frac{\overline{W}_N}{\overline{W}} \right) - I_F \left( \frac{\overline{W}_F}{\overline{W}} \right) \right. \right.
$$

$$
\left. \left. + \left( \frac{\overline{W}_N - \overline{W}}{\overline{W}(1 - n)} \right) \right] \right\}
$$

where $N$ and $F$ refer to native-born and foreign-born males, respectively, and $n$ is the native-born share in the total male population. The remaining notation follows that of section 1.2, where $\overline{W}$ refers to mean wealth and $I$ is the squared coefficient of variation. The first two terms in this expression measure the contribution to the aggregate inequality surge of changing inequality *within* native-born and foreign-born groups. We view these two sources to be far and away the most important, but our position can be substantiated only if the remaining two sources can be shown to have been minor.

Consider the contribution of the changing variance in between-group means, the fourth term in the changing inequality expression. While $I_F$ was slightly larger than $I_N$ in midcentury, $\overline{W}_N$ exceeded both $\overline{W}_F$ and $\overline{W}$ by a much larger proportion. It follows that if the relative mean wealth position of the native born rose over time—if $d(\overline{W}_N/\overline{W})$ were positive—then aggregate inequality would have been fostered as the poorer immigrant groups fell behind the average accumulation performance of native American. The evidence, however, fails to support this view. On the contrary, the ratio of the mean value of real estate belonging to native and foreign-born white males (nonfarm) was 2.12 in 1850, 1.99 in 1860, and 2.02 in 1870 (Soltow 1975, table 3.3, p. 76). The surge in aggregate antebellum wealth inequality cannot be explained by a rising "wealth gap" between native and foreign born, at least not after 1850, the first year for which we have data.

Consider the third term in the changing inequality expression. What was the impact of the fact that the native-born share was falling and the foreign-born share was rising? We have already indicated the primary way that rising foreign-born shares might have served to increase aggregate inequality: by increasing the relative importance of the impecunious, thus augmenting inequality. While $I_N$ and $I_F$ were roughly the same in the mid–nineteenth century, and while $\overline{W}_N$ exceeded $\overline{W}_F$, it is also true that $(\overline{W} - \overline{W}_N)$ was negative. Thus, the long expression in brackets following $dn$ does not have an unambiguous sign. The fall (rise) in the native (foreign) born share could have raised or lowered aggregate inequality trends, depending on the initial magnitudes of mean wealth by nativity, within variance by nativity, and the distribution of adult males by nativity.

The issue is an empirical one which will be resolved only when further samples from the U.S. 1850, 1860, and 1870 censuses are drawn, or when Professor Soltow's data are made available. We can speculate on the outcome, however, by appeal to a simple experiment. Was wealth inequality among all Americans in midcentury larger than that among native Americans? It was, but the differences are trivial. In 1860, the Gini coefficient for native born was .816, while for all free adult males the figure was .832. The presence of foreign born in the American wealth distribution served to raise the Gini coefficient by 2 percent, hardly the magnitude necessary to account for a significant portion of the antebellum inequality surge, especially given that the foreign born were hardly absent from America earlier, in 1820, for example. In 1870, the differences are even smaller. The Gini coefficient for total estate values was .831 for native born and .833 for all adult males. The presence of immigrants in 1870 served to raise the Gini measure of wealth inequality by two-tenths of one percent (Soltow 1975, pp. 107, 149)!

In summary, the source of wealth inequality trends lay *within* the native-born and the foreign-born groups. It was not merely a statistical mirage resulting from the increased preponderence of foreign born in America, or from an increased wealth gap between native and foreign born.

### 1.3.5   The Impact of Urbanization

The antebellum wealth inequality trend is not a mirage induced by age and nativity forces, but perhaps urbanization accounts for the aggregate trend. Its importance would not be diminished in this case, unlike the cases of age and nativity; after all, while nativity and age distribution changes may be viewed in large part as exogenous variables in American antebellum development, urbanization surely may not. In any case, it would be of some value to sort out the key sources of the antebellum inequality trend along urban-rural lines, especially given the conventional wisdom that urbanization can "account for" the vast majority of inequality trends during early modern growth.

This line of inquiry follows in the intellectual tradition stretching from Simon Kuznets (1955) to, most recently, Sherman Robinson (1976).

Once again, we can decompose aggregate inequality trends into four component parts:

$$dI = dI_U \left[ u \left( \frac{\overline{W}_U}{\overline{W}} \right)^2 \right] + dI_R \left[ (1-u) \left( \frac{\overline{W}_R}{\overline{W}} \right)^2 \right]$$

$$+ du \left[ \left( \frac{\overline{W}_U}{\overline{W}} \right)^2 I_U - \left( \frac{\overline{W}_R}{\overline{W}} \right)^2 I_R + \left( \frac{\overline{W}_U - \overline{W}}{\overline{W}(1-u)} \right)^2 \right.$$

$$\left. + 2I_R \left( \frac{\overline{W}_R}{\overline{W}} \right) \left( \frac{\overline{W} - \overline{W}_U}{\overline{W}(1-u)} \right) \right]$$

$$+ d \left( \frac{\overline{W}_U}{\overline{W}} \right) \left\{ 2u \left[ I_U \left( \frac{\overline{W}_U}{\overline{W}} \right) - I_R \left( \frac{\overline{W}_R}{\overline{W}} \right) \right.\right.$$

$$\left.\left. + \left( \frac{\overline{W}_U - \overline{W}}{\overline{W}(1-u)} \right) \right] \right\}$$

where the notation follows that of section 1.2 above. Let us take the last term first, the rural-urban (here, farm-nonfarm) wealth gap. Average wealth was *higher* among farmers than among other Americans. For example, among free adult males in 1860, farmers had total estates which averaged $3,166 while nonfarmers averaged only $2,006 (Soltow 1975, table 3.4, p. 77). Furthermore, the farmer's wealth advantage cannot be attributed to his older average age, since the same wealth differential appears in all age classes. In addition, the differential did not increase over time; the ratio of farm to total average wealth among free males actually fell from 1.38 in 1850 to 1.27 in 1860, and the trend continues until 1870 (Soltow 1975, p. 76). The declining "wealth gap" should have generated an egalitarian drift in America as a whole. Obviously, we must look elsewhere for the source of the antebellum surge.

How about off-farm migration and the rise of nonfarm employment $(du)$? It is true that wealth was far more equally distributed among farm families than among nonfarm families in the 1870 census sample drawn by Lee Soltow. Indeed, while the top 10 percent of farmers owned 59 percent of farm wealth, the top 10 percent of nonfarmers owned 81 percent of nonfarm wealth (Soltow 1975, p. 108). Gallman (1969, table A-1, p. 22) found similar results in the 1860 census. While Baltimore's top decile claimed 86.8 percent of gross wealth, in the remainder of Maryland the figure was 64.5 percent. Similarly, New Orleans's top decile claimed 82.6 percent while the rural "cotton counties" claimed 58.6 percent. It follows that urbanization did serve to raise inequality in America. In 1820, about 28 percent of the work force was nonfarm while the figure was 41 percent in 1860 (U.S. Bureau of the Census 1976, part 1, p. 134). The share of total Northern population in urban areas rose from 9.4 to 25.6 percent over the same period (table 1.10).

**Table 1.10**          **Distribution of Northern Population by Urban and Rural Residence, 1790–1900**

| Year | Population (000) Urban | Rural | Urban Share | Year | Population (000) Urban | Rural | Urban Share |
|------|------|------|------|------|------|------|------|
| 1790 | 160 | 1,809 | .081 | 1850 | 2,788 | 11,242 | .199 |
| 1800 | 245 | 2,442 | .091 | 1860 | 5,050 | 14,640 | .256 |
| 1810 | 383 | 3,397 | .101 | 1870 | 8,150 | 17,130 | .322 |
| 1820 | 490 | 4,730 | .094 | 1880 | 11,568 | 20,303 | .363 |
| 1830 | 827 | 6,327 | .116 | 1890 | 17,684 | 22,133 | .444 |
| 1840 | 1,382 | 8,730 | .137 | 1900 | 24,076 | 23,304 | .508 |

*Source*: U.S. Bureau of the Census 1976, p. 22.

These arguments could be quantified if Soltow's (1975) underlying urban-rural or farm-nonfarm wealth distributions for 1860 or 1870 were made available. In their absence, the Wisconsin 1860 urban and rural wealth distributions reported in table 1.11 will have to serve. If we hold the variance *within* urban and rural areas constant, how would Northern aggregate wealth inequality have behaved over the nineteenth century if the observed changes in the urban population share were the only ones that had taken place? What was the quantitative impact of urbanization on Northern wealth concentration trends? The results are summarized in table 1.12. There we see that the Gini coefficient would have drifted upward hardly at all between 1790 and 1840, from .740 to .748. Even after 1840, the impact of rapid urbanization in the Northeast served to raise aggregate inequality only modestly, from .748 in 1840 to .771 in 1870, a rise of some 3 percent. In short, while urbanization served to raise inequality in the first three-quarters of the nineteenth century, its contribution to the aggregate inequality surge appears to have been relatively minor. This again implies that the vast majority of the antebellum wealth inequality surge in America had its source *within* sectors and regions. To judge from figure 1.7 below, however, much of the inequality drama must have centered on the cities.

### 3.6   When and Where Did Wealth Become More Concentrated?

Other independent measures of wealth inequality trends between these 1774 and 1860 benchmarks are essential to test the implications of the Jones and Soltow-Gallman research.

Gathering data on the estates of the very richest .031 percent of U.S. families and comparing their aggregate value with rough estimates of the wealth of the entire nation, Robert Gallman (1969, table 2) found that the share held by this superrich group rose from 6.9 percent in 1840 to 7.2–7.6 percent in 1850, and then to 14.3–19.1 percent in 1890. The

Table 1.11          Distribution of Wealth by Class, Males 20 and Older, Urban
                    and Rural: Wisconsin, 1860

| Wealth Class | Mean Wealth ($) | | Adult Male Population | |
|---|---|---|---|---|
| ($) | Rural | Urban | Rural | Urban |
| 0–1 | .5 | .5 | 55,134 | 5,707 |
| 1–100 | 50.5 | 50.5 | 6,897 | 1,320 |
| 100–200 | 150.0 | 150.0 | 9,859 | 1,520 |
| 200–300 | 250.0 | 250.0 | 8,878 | 840 |
| 300–400 | 350.0 | 350.0 | 7,191 | 420 |
| 400–500 | 450.0 | 450.0 | 6,006 | 400 |
| 500–600 | 550.0 | 550.0 | 6,839 | 780 |
| 600–700 | 650.0 | 650.0 | 5,784 | 520 |
| 700–800 | 750.0 | 750.0 | 4,951 | 240 |
| 800–900 | 850.0 | 850.0 | 4,690 | 100 |
| 900–1,000 | 950.0 | 950.0 | 3,766 | 220 |
| 1,000–1,200 | 1,100.0 | 1,100.0 | 8,684 | 580 |
| 1,200–1,400 | 1,300.0 | 1,300.0 | 7,213 | 320 |
| 1,400–1,600 | 1,500.0 | 1,500.0 | 5,599 | 140 |
| 1,600–1,800 | 1,700.0 | 1,700.0 | 4,170 | 280 |
| 1,800–2,000 | 1,900.0 | 1,900.0 | 3,598 | 120 |
| 2,000–2,500 | 2,250.0 | 2,250.0 | 7,938 | 360 |
| 2,500–3,000 | 2,750.0 | 2,750.0 | 5,191 | 120 |
| 3,000–4,000 | 3,500.0 | 3,500.0 | 7,401 | 340 |
| 4,000–5,000 | 4,500.0 | 4,500.0 | 4,188 | 240 |
| 5,000–10,000 | 7,500.0 | 7,500.0 | 6,747 | 680 |
| 10,000+ | 19,315.0 | 38,582.0 | 2,851 | 642 |

*Sources and notes*: The underlying data are taken from Soltow (1971b, pp. 52–
53). Soltow does not report mean wealth or total wealth by class. Thus, we have
assumed the mean wealth by class to be the midpoint in each size class with the
exception of $10,000 and above. The latter is computed as a residual since Soltow
does report urban and state total means, $1,450 and $1,370 respectively. In the
absence of the underlying data, calculated Ginis from the above data need not
necessarily coincide with those reported by Soltow. Soltow reports a statewide Gini
of .757, while we computed a value of .750. *Urban* refers to Milwaukee County
and *rural* to the remainder of the state.

suggestion that inequality between the superrich and the rest of the nation rose across the 1840s supplies a valuable clue, even though Gallman's data do not allow a comparison between middle and low wealth
shares.

Lee Soltow reaches the opposite conclusion based on real estate distributions in 1850 and 1860. For both these years, and for 1870, the
U.S. census asked respondents to state the value of their land and buildings gross of lein. Sampling these returns, Soltow (1975, ch. 4) has found
no net change in real estate inequality across the 1850s, the top quantile
shares almost exactly matching the same shares of total estate in 1860.
Stability in the inequality of real estate would surely limit inequality
trends for the 1850s, given that real estate was nearly 60 percent of the

**Table 1.12**       **Impact of Urbanization on Trends in Northern Wealth Concentration, 1790–1900: Wisconsin 1860 Weights**

| | Gini Coefficient | | | Gini Coefficient | |
|---|---|---|---|---|---|
| Census Year | Northern States | Wis- consin | Census Year | Northern States | Wis- consin |
| 1790 | .740 | | 1850 | .756 | |
| 1800 | .742 | | 1860 | .763 | .750 |
| 1810 | .743 | | 1870 | .771 | |
| 1820 | .742 | | 1880 | .776 | |
| 1830 | .745 | | 1890 | .785 | |
| 1840 | .748 | | 1900 | .792 | |

*Sources*: Underlying data used in the calculation are taken from the sources to tables 1.5 and 1.11. The urban-rural population distribution in Northern states is applied using Wisconsin 1860 "wealth distribution weights." The procedure assumes the distribution *within* urban and rural areas to be constant. It also assumes the urban-rural mean wealth differentials to be constant. Thus, only the relative weights, or the share urbanized, is allowed to change over time.

total value of wealth in 1860. Still, firm conclusions about inequality in total estate cannot be reached from the distribution of real estate alone.

The remaining time series evidence comes from regions and cities. For the late antebellum South, Gavin Wright (1970) has presented data on the inequality of improved acreage, farm real estate values, farm physical wealth (land, buildings, slaves, implements), and cotton output from the Parker-Gallman farm sample in cotton counties. Wright found no net inequality trend for the 1850s, though the second and third deciles from the top gained noticeably at the expense of the top decile and the lower seventy percent. This result seems to reinforce Soltow's finding of no net change in real estate concentration for the South (as well as for the nation) across the 1850s.

Enough data do exist to construct size distributions for slaveholding over a much longer antebellum period. Soltow's work with the slave-owning data has led to the summary figures shown in table 1.13. Soltow himself (1971a) concluded that there was no change in slaveholding inequality among slaveholders. Yet the more relevant measure is one that examines inequality among *all* families, not just slaveholders. As Soltow notes, slaveholders were a declining share of all families. Therefore what is at most a modest rise in inequality of slaveholding among slaveholders after 1830 becomes a pronounced rise in slaveholding inequality among all families (table 1.13). Contrary to the findings of Gavin Wright for the cotton South, the entire South shows a rise in the 1850s in slaveholding inequality, apparently part of a longer term trend. The years after 1830, and perhaps even after 1790, exhibit rising inequality in Southern slaveholding.

Table 1.13          Unequal Slaveholding in the South, 1790–1860

| Region | 1790 | 1830 | 1850 | 1860 |
|---|---|---|---|---|
| *Five regions on the Eastern seaboard* | | | | |
| Slaves per slaveholder | 8.3 | 9.6 | 9.8 | 10.2 |
| Slaveholders/family | .35 | .36 | .30 | .25 |
| Slaves/family | 2.9 | 3.5 | 2.9 | 2.6 |
| Gini coefficient, among slaveholders | .572 | .573 | .582 | .597 |
| Share held by top 1% | | | | |
| of slaveholders | 13.4% | 13.0% | 14.2% | 13.7% |
| of families | 22.5% | 26.7% | 27.9% | 30.5% |
| *Four regions on the Eastern seaboard* | | | | |
| Share held by top 10% | | | | |
| of families | 74.0% | 75.2% | | |
| *Entire South* | | | | |
| Share held by top 10% | | | | |
| of families | | | 71.5% | 82.3% |

*Source and notes*: Soltow (1971a, tables 1 and 2) draws on both official census publications and his own sample of families and slaveholders from the manuscript censuses.

The regions consisted of most of Maryland, the District of Columbia, and North Carolina, plus parts of South Carolina. The fifth region added to these was most of Virginia, with some property tax returns for 1780 educating the underlying estimates for Virginia.

Professor Soltow reported some of the assumed class means for classes defined by number of slaves held. We have assumed others using what seem to be comparable procedures.

The remaining antebellum observations on wealth distributions are mainly from Northeastern cities.[24] The tax and probate data for these areas have yielded the top quantile shares displayed in figure 1.7. These are a valuable cross-check on the 1774 and 1860 benchmarks, since they are derived by different scholars, with possibly different sampling techniques, and in some cases with different kinds of data (e.g., tax returns).

Two striking patterns emerge from figure 1.7. First, it suggests when the steepest trend toward concentration set in. The local tax returns from Boston and neighboring Hingham show trough observations in the 1810s and '20s. The two top quantile shares from this period for New York City and Brooklyn are also much lower than that for the 1840s. Each series shows steep increases after 1830, as did the Southern slaveholding returns (but not the already cited Soltow and Wright results confined to the 1850s). Second, rates of increase in the top decile shares per decade seem to average about the same as that derived for total assets among all free households in the U.S. between 1774 and 1860 (about 4.6 percent per decade as a percent of the share itself, according to table 1.3 above). It appears, therefore, that the movement toward wealth concentration occurred *within* regions, just as it seems to have occurred within given age groups, among native or foreign born, and within rural and urban populations.[25]

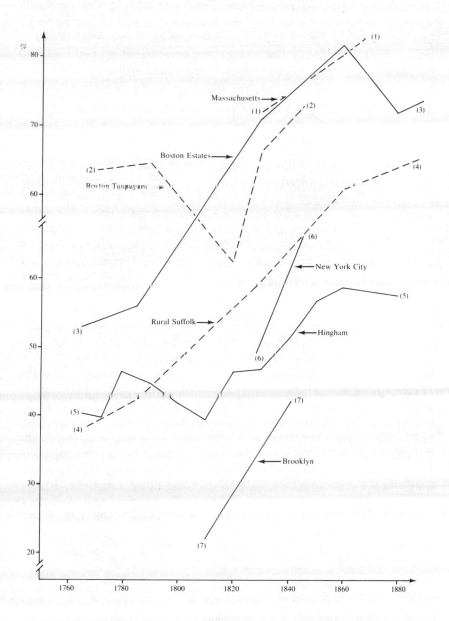

**Fig. 1.7**    Dating the Rise in Antebellum Wealth Concentration (percent held by top wealthholders): Northeast. Source: appendix 3.

While no rich empirical feast can be prepared from such scraps, the appetizer should certainly stimulate further interest in early-nineteenth-century archives. The working hypothesis seems now to be that wealth concentration rose over most of the period 1774–1860, with especially steep increases from the 1820s to the late 1840s. It should also be noted that these two or three decades coincide with early industrial acceleration, and with a period in which wage gaps between skilled and unskilled occupational groups seemed to widen (Lindert and Williamson 1976).

### 1.4    The Uneven High Plateau: Civil War to Great Depression

#### 1.4.1    Time Series Clues

The seven decades following the Civil War mark a period for which wealth inequality remained very high and exhibited no significant long-term trend. This judgment is based on slim evidence, since the period is illuminated statistically only near its start and finish. The half-century between the 1870 census and the onset of modern estate tax returns—begun in 1919 and reported after 1922—is an empirical Dark Age for wealth distributions. It need not remain this way. Probate records are rich for most of this pretax era. For the moment, however, we must rely on a data base which is less extensive for this half-century than for 1860 or even 1774.

The manuscript censuses have allowed Soltow to compare the distribution of total assets in 1860 and 1870. The dominant intervening event during the decade was slave emancipation, a massive confiscation from the richest strata of Southern society. Thus, the net change across the 1860s was a shift toward more equal wealthholding for the United States as a whole, whether we count slaves as part of the wealthholding population or not. The movement of top decile shares is shown in table 1.14. The leveling within the South was apparently sufficient to outweigh the contribution to total U.S. wealth inequality implied by the opening up of a new wealth gap between North and South. Within the North, meanwhile, there was either no change or a slight leveling across the 1860s.

Table 1.14    Top Decile Shares of Total Wealth among Adult Males, 1860 and 1870 (%)

| Region | 1860 | | 1870 | |
|--------|------|------|------|-----|
| | Free | All | White | All |
| U.S. | 73 | 74.6–79.0 | 68 | 70 |
| South | 75 | (very high) | 70 | 77 |
| North | 68 | 68 | 67 | 67 |

*Sources*: Table 1.13 and Soltow (1975, p. 99).

The next set of clues is offered by the census year 1890. As we noted above, the share of wealth held by Gallman's richest .031 percent of wealthholders rose to 14.3–19.1 percent in 1890, from 7.2–7.6 percent at midcentury. The rest of the Lorenz curve for 1890 has been estimated by George K. Holmes (1893). The 1890 census supplied data on farm and home ownership in twenty-two states, and Holmes extrapolated this sample to the national distribution. Furthermore, using mortgage debt reported in the census, Holmes was able to approximate net worth as opposed to gross wealth, thus making the distributions more comparable to Lampman's 1922 net estate benchmark. Holmes guesstimated full distribution of wealth from this data base and, by the imaginative use of other information, generated the distribution for 1890 reproduced in table 1.15.

Holmes's guesses imply that the top one and ten percent of American families held, respectively, 25.76 and 72.17 percent of wealth. Interpolation suggests that the top 1.4 percent claimed 28.13 percent of total wealth. By comparison, Lampman (1959, table 6, p. 388) calculated that the top 1.4 percent of families held 29.2 percent of the total wealth in 1922.[26] To the extent that comparability holds, wealth concentration increased only slightly between 1890 and 1922.[27]

Better estimates of national wealth distributions around World War I are offered by the Federal Trade Commission's early research. In 1926 the FTC published the results of a special survey in which they collected 43,512 probate estate valuations from twenty-three counties in thirteen states plus the District of Columbia. The survey covered the years 1912–23.[28] While table 1.16 exploits the FTC data, it should be emphasized that these distributions relate to those dying in the sampled counties, and the sample contains only one major city, Washington, D.C. If the sample had contained a more accurate representation of the urban East-

| Table 1.15 | Holmes's Estimated Wealth Distribution for American Families in 1890 | |
|---|---|---|
| Wealth Class | Number of Families (000) | Net Worth ($000,000) |
| Lowest to | 1,440.0 | 216.0 |
| | 752.8 | 1,359.7 |
| | 1,756.4 | 5,309.6 |
| | 5,159.8 | 2,579.9 |
| | 720.6 | 1,142.5 |
| | 1,764.3 | 6,749.1 |
| | 1,092.2 | 30,643.2 |
| Highest | 4.0 | 12,000.0 |
| Total | 12,690.2 | 60,000.0 |

Source: Holmes (1893, pp. 591–92).

Table 1.16  Distribution of Wealth from FTC Sampled Estates, 1912 and 1923

| | 1912 | | | | 1923 | | | |
| | King | | Williamson-Lindert | | King | | Williamson-Lindert | |
| Wealth Class | No. | Value ($) | No. | Value ($) | No. | Value ($) | No. | Value ($) |
|---|---|---|---|---|---|---|---|---|
| Not probated | 4,624 | 448,528 | 5,914 | 573,658 | 4,805 | 494,915 | 6,146 | 633,038 |
| <$500 | 469 | 119,353 | 469 | 119,353 | 462 | 124,775 | 462 | 124,775 |
| 500–1,000 | 360 | 255,070 | 360 | 255,070 | 406 | 287,638 | 406 | 287,638 |
| 1,000–2,500 | 599 | 983,480 | 599 | 983,480 | 817 | 1,334,301 | 817 | 1,334,301 |
| 2,500–5,000 | 486 | 1,715,689 | 486 | 1,715,689 | 731 | 2,607,015 | 731 | 2,607,015 |
| 5,000–10,000 | 370 | 2,613,262 | 370 | 2,613,262 | 643 | 4,585,009 | 643 | 4,585,009 |
| 10,000–25,000 | 316 | 4,822,552 | 316 | 4,822,552 | 623 | 9,411,982 | 623 | 9,411,982 |
| 25,000–50,000 | 140 | 4,966,955 | 140 | 4,966,955 | 242 | 8,464,878 | 242 | 8,464,878 |
| 50,000–100,000 | 54 | 3,699,454 | 54 | 3,699,454 | 136 | 9,064,680 | 136 | 9,064,680 |
| 100,000–250,000 | 42 | 6,464,171 | 42 | 6,464,171 | 62 | 9,824,211 | 62 | 9,824,211 |
| 250,000–500,000 | 12 | 4,135,571 | 12 | 4,135,571 | 27 | 8,718,762 | 27 | 8,718,762 |
| 500,000–1,000,000 | 4 | 2,521,647 | 4 | 2,521,647 | 9 | 6,198,199 | 9 | 6,198,199 |
| 1,000,000< | 2 | 8,165,326 | 2 | 8,165,326 | 2 | 5,599,535 | 2 | 5,599,535 |
| Total | 7,478 | 40,911,058 | 8,768 | 41,036,188 | 8,965 | 66,715,900 | 10,306 | 66,854,023 |

*Sources and notes:* The FTC data is reported in 69th Cong., 1st Session, Senate Doc. No. 126, *National Wealth and Income* (1926), pp. 58–59. The King estimates are derived from his assumption that those not probated had, on average, $100 at death. The Williamson-Lindert estimates allow for the same average among those not probated, but for a rise from $97 in 1912 to $103 in 1923, the observed rate of increase in the less-than-$500 class. In addition, numbers not probated are estimated as a residual from mortality data. The mortality statistics are for registered states reported in the 19th and 24th Annual Reports, Department of Commerce,

Bureau of the Census, *Mortality Statistics* (1918 and 1923). These supply a trend in crude death rates which is then applied to the FTC aggregate estimate of 184,958 for the whole 1912–23 period to yield annual estimates for 1912 and 1923. This figure is distributed by sex using 1921 *Mortality Statistics* proportions. Total potential wealthholders at death are then estimated assuming 25.3 percent of deceased females were potential wealthholders. The 25.3 percent figure is derived from FTC 1944 estate tax returns (Mendershausen 1956).

ern seaboard, inequalities at death would look even greater for these years. On the other hand, both King's and our procedures for including the nonprobated decedents may tend to overstate the wealth inequality of decedents. These potential biases make it hazardous to compare these size distributions with ones that attempt to estimate wealth inequality among the living.

The FTC results for 1912 and 1923 can, however, be used to reveal the likely net change in net worth inequality between these dates. Table 1.17 reveals a sharp drop in wealth inequality across World War I, either in terms of the top quantile share or in terms of the Gini coefficient. The wealth leveling replicates findings emerging from two other strands of research. First, it appears that World War I was a pronounced leveler of incomes and wage ratios (Lindert and Williamson 1976). Second, Stanley Lebergott's (1976) evidence suggests that mobility into and out of the ranks of top wealthholders was great across the same era. World War I was a sharp but brief leveler, perhaps because of its sudden inflation, perhaps because of its effects on labor supply and product demand.

Wealth inequality trends across the 1920s can be gauged by the application of estate multiplier methods to the returns of the estate tax initiated in 1916. Robert Lampman (1962) performed that task some time ago and his figures (examined in more detail below) show an unmistakable rise in the share held by the richest between 1922 and 1929. The top percentile share among all adults rose from 31.6 percent of total equity in 1922 to 36.3 percent in 1929. Here again the top quantile measures of wealth inequality display positive correlation with movements in income inequality. The 1920s were years in which the top percentile share of income, the ratios of skilled to unskilled wage rates, and the inverse Pareto slope of income inequality among top income groups also rose (Lindert and Williamson 1976).

The period from 1860 to 1929 is thus best described as a high uneven plateau of wealth inequality. When did wealth inequality hit its historic peak? We do not yet know. We do know that there was a leveling across the 1860s. We also know that there was a leveling across the World War

**Table 1.17     Percent Share of Wealth, 1912–23**

| Wealth Class | 1912 | | 1923 | |
| --- | --- | --- | --- | --- |
| | King | Williamson-Lindert | King | Williamson-Lindert |
| Top  1% | 54.38 | 56.38 | 43.10 | 45.68 |
| Top  5% | 77.69 | 79.83 | 70.18 | 72.44 |
| Top 10% | 88.08 | 90.03 | 81.24 | 84.10 |
| Gini coefficient | .9186 | .9252 | .8878 | .8988 |

*Source*: Table 1.16.

I decade (1912–22), which was reversed largely or entirely by 1929. This leaves three likely candidates for the dubious distinction of being the era of greatest inequality in American personal wealth: ca. 1860, ca. 1914, and 1929. That each of these pinnacles was followed by a major upheaval—civil war and slave emancipation, world war, or unparalleled depression—suggests interesting hypotheses regarding the effects of these episodic events on wealth inequality (or perhaps even the impact of inequality on these episodic events). These cannot be explored here. We shall note only that the existence of a trend in wealth inequality within this period cannot be established, primarily because we lack good time series spanning the four decades from 1870 to the early 1910s.[29]

## 1.4.2    International Comparisons

The shaky quality of the available wealth distribution data around the turn of the century makes comparisons between the U.S. and other countries hazardous. Yet a rough comparison can at least be suggested, since the early years of this century were ones for which several countries reported information on one particular kind of wealth distribution, the distribution of wealth among probated decedents.

The comparison in table 1.18 pivots on the FTC probate distribution of 1912, which shows more inequality than any other measurement of wealth dispersion from the entire history of the U.S. It may be a biased indicator but, as we have argued, it is not clear which way the bias runs. The FTC probates understate inequality with their underrepresentation of large cities, yet the assumptions used by King and ourselves to include nonprobated estates may overstate inequality. With all of these qualifications, it appears that America had joined industrialized Europe in terms of its degree of reported wealth inequality. Whatever leveling effect the American "frontier" and more rural orientation may have imparted, they did not show up in the form of a clearly lower degree of wealth inequality. By the eve of World War I, wealth—or at least decedents' wealth—was as unequally distributed here as in Western Europe. Tocqueville was right; less than a century after his visit, the American egalitarian dream had been completely lost.

If further studies confirm this tentative comparison, several corollaries demand attention. First, it is important to establish whether differences in age distribution and urbanization affect the international comparison. Second, was there a stable and high degree of wealth inequality in Western Europe that the post-1774 rise in American wealth inequality was approaching? Or was the trend toward wealth concentration as strong in Europe as in the United States across the nineteenth century? Third, who migrated, and did their departure from Europe and arrival in America serve to raise wealth inequality on both sides of the Atlantic? Finally,

**Table 1.18**    **Wealth Shares Held by Top One and Ten Percent of Decedents and the Living: Four Nations, 1907–13**

| | Wealth Share of | |
| --- | --- | --- |
| Country | Top 1% | Top 10% |
| *Among decedents* | | |
| U.S., 1912: FTC probate sample | 56.4% | 90.0% |
| U.K., 1907–11: succession | 57.8– | |
|    duty returns for males over 25 | 64.3 | 91.9 |
| France, 1909: all probated estates | 50.4 | 81.0 |
| *Among the living* | | |
| England and Wales, 1911–13: persons | | |
|    over 25 (estate multiplier method) | 70.0 | |
| Prussia, 1908: family wealth | | |
|    (based on tax assessments) | 49.1 | 82.3 |

*Sources and notes*: The sources are table 1.17, Willford King (1915, pp. 86–95), and Robert Lampman (1962, pp. 210–15) citing an earlier study by Kathleen Langley. In constructing the probate size distribution for the United Kingdom, King assumed that the estates in the poorest class of men averaged 60 pounds ($292) each, and that women owned the same fraction of the number and value of estates as in Massachusetts in 1890. It should also be noted that the British estate duty returns are likely to be distorted by a peculiar cause for tax avoidance. The British succession duties were a step function of total estate, so that the duty jumped by large numbers of pounds as one's estate gained the extra few pennies that put it into a higher tax bracket. Our preliminary inspection of the summary returns published in the *Statistical Abstract of the United Kingdom* suggests that in high wealth brackets the average declared wealth was noticeably above the midpoint, while this was not true of lower tax brackets. This is not the pattern one would expect of a distribution that rises and then falls with size. We suspect that rich heirs prevailed on themselves and their assessors to pull down their taxable estate into lower wealth brackets, thus understating British wealth inequality.

King felt that the French returns appeared to list all estates, and left the probate tax return distribution unadjusted. He estimated the lower 86 percent of the Prussian distribution assuming "that the curve for small properties would resemble in form that known to exist for France" (p. 91).

what became of the European-American comparison following World War I? This last question has already been explored by Harold Lydall and J. B. Lansing (1959), as well as by Robert Lampman (1962, pp. 210–15). They find that the top quantile shares among living wealthholders in England and Wales dropped with each decade from 1911–13 to midcentury, yet that wealth inequality always remained more pronounced there than in the United States from the 1920s on. Either the prewar comparison is misleading, or the age adjustment from the deceased to the living serves to raise American inequality more markedly, or there was an even more dramatic leveling of wealth in the United States across World War I than the available figures have revealed. This issue has yet to be resolved.

## 1.5    The Twentieth-Century Leveling

### 1.5.1    The Post–World War I Estimates

Our understanding of levels and trends in wealth inequality since World War I rests on two kinds of data. One source relies on estimates of top wealthholder shares using estate tax returns and estate multiplier methods (Lampman 1962; Smith and Franklin 1974). The other main source is the Federal Reserve Board's oft-cited Survey of Financial Characteristics of Consumers taken on 31 December 1962 (Projector and Weiss 1966).

The top quantile shares reported in table 1.19 reveal unambiguous and well-known trends. Top wealthholders increased their share markedly between 1922 and 1929, apparently recovering their pre–World War I shares. Their share then dropped secularly over the next twenty years, hitting a trough around 1949. Thus, the leveling in wealth distributions after 1929 parallels the "revolutionary" income leveling over the same period. Furthermore, as with incomes the wealth leveling is not solely a wartime phenomenon, since an equally dramatic leveling took place early in the Great Depression. While this revolutionary change in the distribution of wealth has become a permanent feature of the mid–twentieth century, the postwar period has not recorded any further trend toward wealth leveling.

**Table 1.19**    **Share of U.S. Personal Wealth Held by Top Wealthholders, 1922–72**

| Year | Percent Share of Equity (or Net Worth) Held by Richest | | | |
| | 1.0 Percent of Adults (1) | 0.5 Percent of Population (2) | (3) | 1.0 Percent of Population (4) |
|---|---|---|---|---|
| 1922 | 31.6 | 29.8 | | |
| 1929 | 36.3 | 32.4 | | |
| 1933 | 28.3 | 25.2 | | |
| 1939 | 30.6 | 28.0 | | |
| 1945 | 23.3 | 20.9 | | |
| 1949 | 20.8 | 19.3 | | |
| 1953 | 24.3 | 22.7 | 22.0 | 27.5 |
| 1954 | 24.0 | 22.5 | | |
| 1956 | 26.0 | 25.0 | | |
| 1958 | | | 21.7 | 26.9 |
| 1962 | | | 21.6 | 27.4 |
| 1965 | | | 23.7 | 29.2 |
| 1969 | | | 20.4 | 25.6 |
| 1972 | | | 20.9 | 26.6 |

*Sources*: Columns 1 and 2: Lampman (1962, pp. 202, 204). Columns 3 and 4: Smith and Franklin (1974, and unpublished estimates).

## 1.5.2    Adjustments and Anomalies

So say the unadjusted estate tax series. But when these are compared with the 1962 Federal Reserve Board survey, the estimates begin to reveal serious gaps. The Fed survey implies that the top 1 percent of all consumer units held 36.9 percent of net worth at the end of 1962. In contrast, the top 1 percent of total population held only 27.4 percent in the same year, according to Smith and Franklin. This significant gap must be explained.

Elimination of the gap between these inequality estimates might well begin with standardization of population units. The Fed survey dealt with households or, more accurately, "consumer units." The estate tax studies could not easily follow the same convention, however. Given data on top individual wealthholders, they projected these top wealthholders onto the total population or the total adult population. Converting the estate tax results into a size distribution among households is of course impossible in the absence of data on the wealth of other family members. It is crucial to know, for example, the frequency with which male and female millionaires estimated from the decedent returns are married to each other. If it is high, then wealth inequality among households is greater than that implied by calculations which treat male and female millionaires as living in separate households.

While point estimates of wealth inequality among households are elusive, we can establish ranges. Table 1.20 performs an exercise of this sort, accepting the underlying wealth data and converting the top wealthholder aggregates from an individual to a household basis. These estimates cannot be proved to bound the true top percentile shares, but it is our judgment that the truth lies within the range given here. In any case, table 1.20 suggests that twentieth-century inequality trends are not much affected by converting the top share estimates to a household basis. The rise in wealth concentration between 1922 and 1929 persists, a somewhat larger decline from 1929 to midcentury emerges, but the stability since the early 1950s remains.

While the revisions fail to change trends by much, they do add to the anomalous discrepancy between the estate tax and the Federal Reserve Board survey estimates. It now appears that the top 1 percent of households held only 19.2–21.1 percent of 1962 net worth according to the estate tax estimates, while the 1962 Fed survey reports 36.9 percent. The anomaly grows.

Perhaps the discrepancy lies in different definitions or measurements of wealth. Yet the two studies seem to have used similar definitions, although Lampman's economic estate and Smith and Franklin's net worth are not exactly the same as the Federal Reserve Board's definition of net worth.

Our suspicion turns quite naturally to the way of reporting wealth to the estate tax authorities. Tax avoidance certainly must be considered, since top wealthholders face estate taxes now rising to marginal rates as high as 74 percent. Perhaps the richest have simply been much more adept at hiding their wealth from fiscal authorities, and increasingly so as the marginal tax rates rose with time. Perhaps the Federal Reserve

**Table 1.20    Top Percentile Shares of Estimated Net Worth among Households, 1922–72**

| | | High Estimates | |
| Year | Low Estimates | Lampman Procedure | Alternative Procedure |
|---|---|---|---|
| 1922 | 22.8% | 26.0% | |
| 1929 | 27.7 | | |
| 1953 | 17.65 | 22.4 | |
| 1962 | 19.2 | 21.1 | |
| 1969 | 17.9 | 20.4 | 26.2% |
| 1972 | 18.9 | | |

*Sources and notes*: The sources are those cited in table 1.19 plus, for the total number of households, the U.S. Bureau of the Census (1976) and *Statistical Abstract of the United States.*

The *low estimates* were based on the following definitions:

$$\text{Percent of top wealth-holding households (wealth above } \$x) = \frac{\text{No. of individual estates above } \$x \text{ (among estimated living population)}}{\text{No. of households in the U.S.}} \times 100$$

$$\text{Their percent share of wealth} = \frac{\text{Total value of estates individually above } \$x}{\text{Wealth of the entire household sector}} \times 100$$

Note that this *low estimate* intentionally ignores the fact that more than one personal estate can exist in the same household.

The *Lampman procedure* (1962, pp. 204–7) generates what is probably a *high estimate* of the top wealthholders' share by subtracting the number of married women among individual top wealthholders from the top wealthholder ranks, with no other adjustments. This amounts to dividing the husbands with individual estates above the top wealthholders' threshold into two groups. The first group is married to wives also having more than the threshold individual wealth. The second group has wives and children with zero personal wealth.

The *alternative procedure* for developing a *high estimate* marries all the top wealthholding husbands off to the richest possible wives and gives them all the children with individual estates. That is, this procedure uses the definitions:

$$\text{Percent of top wealth-holding households (wealth above } \$x) = \frac{\text{No. of individual estates above } \$x, \text{ excluding all wealthholders under age 20 and all married women with wealth above } \$x}{\text{No. of households in the U.S.}} \times 100$$

$$\text{Their percent share of wealth} = \frac{\text{Total value of estates over } \$x \text{ among adult males, adult females not currently married, all minors, richest married women equal in number to the married males with estates over } \$x}{\text{No. of households in the U.S.}} \times 100$$

Board survey of 1962 is correct, and there is much less to the wealth leveling since World War I than meets the eye.

The difficulty with this obvious possibility is that it does not offer a clear explanation of why the Fed survey got such different results. Inheritance tax avoidance by the rich implies large transfers to heirs *inter vivos* and through trusts, some of which go unreported altogether (Lampman 1962; Smith and Franklin 1974; Mendershausen 1956). But in that case, why did they have such a larger share of total wealth still in hand to report to the interviewers in the Fed survey? Alternatively, if we think they are *not* taking these legal means of transfering their bequests before death, but rather are hiding vast sums from the assessors, why would they be so much more candid when interviewed by the Federal Reserve in 1962? We can well believe that people might lie to avoid a 74 percent marginal tax rate, but it is not yet clear how or why their lying was so inconsistent. There must be another explanation for the discrepancy.

There are only small gaps between the amounts of wealth reported for top wealthholders to the Fed survey, the Internal Revenue Service, and the Smith-Franklin modification of the IRS data. For either the top million wealthholders or the top two million, the estimated amounts of wealth in the Fed survey run something like 10 percent above the amounts implied by the Smith-Franklin estimates. The discrepancy is not large enough to explain the top share gap already noted. Furthermore, the same top million or two reported even more to the IRS itself, according to its own estimates (U.S. Internal Revenue Service 1967). Differences in the amounts of wealth attributed to top wealthholders apparently do not account for the differences in the 1962 share estimates.

The key to the 1962 puzzle must lie with competing estimates of the total net worth of the entire personal sector. The Fed survey never reported its estimate of total personal wealth, but the mean net worth and and the estimated population size imply an aggregate net worth of $1,198 billion. This is very close to John Kendrick's (1976, p. 70) recent estimate of the personal sector's gross assets of $1,175 billion for the same date. Unfortunately, both figures are well below the $1,779.9 billion total net worth used by Smith and Franklin—and supplied to them by Helen Stone Tice of the Federal Reserve Board. It appears that the Fed survey somehow erred by using a total net worth estimate which which is only 56 percent of the figure later disseminated by the Fed itself. A look at Projector and Weiss's (1966, pp. 61, 62) technical notes to the survey reveals that they were already aware of a serious underestimation of total assets and net worth. If we conclude that the better estimate of total net worth was that later supplied by the Fed to Smith and Franklin, then the Fed survey itself implies a top percentile share of only 20.6 percent of net worth, well within the range estimated in table 1.20 above.

If the estimates are now consistent with each other, they still do not reveal what made wealth inequality decline between 1929 and midcentury. We must take care to subject this aggregate leveling to the same kind of scrutiny applied to the nineteenth-century wealth concentration trends. In particular, could the leveling be just an artifact of changes in the age distribution? Pursuing this point, table 1.21 displays the percent distribution of male-headed households by age of head. Between 1930 and 1940 or between 1930 and 1960, there was indeed an aging in the population of male household heads, but it takes a different form from that of the antebellum aging discussed above in section 1.3. Over the nineteenth century, young adult males declined in importance, thus imparting a downward drift to aggregate inequality indicators as the age distribution compressed. The twentieth-century experience appears to be somewhat different. While young adults (under 35) decline in relative numbers from the 1920s to the 1960s, adults at the other end of the age distribution increase in relative importance (aged 55 and above). The net life cycle impact on aggregate wealth concentration trends is unclear. The issue can be resolved only by applying wealth distributions by age to this trending demographic data. The only distribution data suitable for this purpose are those for 1962 reproduced in table 1.22.

If we hold both the variance within and the mean values between age classes constant at their 1962 magnitudes, what would have been the impact of the changing age distribution of male household heads on aggregate inequality trends following 1930? The answers appear in table 1.23. First, and in sharp contrast with the implications of the "Paglin debate" (Paglin 1975, and the subsequent exchange in later issues), age–life cycle effects appear to be a trivial component of aggregate wealth concentration trends in the mid–twentieth century. Regardless of the time span selected, Gini coefficients vary hardly at all in response to these demographic forces. Second, the impact—although very small—is to produce *increased* wealth concentration over time. Thus, it appears that

**Table 1.21    Percent Distribution of Male-Headed Households by Age of Head, 1930–70**

| Year | Under 35 | 35–44 | 45–54 | 55–64 | 65 and Over | Total |
|------|------|-------|-------|-------|-------------|-------|
| 1930 | 27.3 | 27.1 | 22.0 | 14.1 | 9.3  | 99.8  |
| 1940 | 26.3 | 24.5 | 22.6 | 15.3 | 11.2 | 99.9  |
| 1950 | 27.9 | 24.2 | 20.3 | 15.5 | 12.2 | 100.1 |
| 1960 | 25.8 | 23.9 | 20.9 | 15.5 | 13.8 | 99.9  |
| 1962 | 25.3 | 23.6 | 20.7 | 15.6 | 14.8 | 100.0 |
| 1970 | 27.9 | 20.5 | 20.7 | 16.4 | 14.6 | 100.1 |

*Source*: Underlying data taken from various census publications.

**Table 1.22**   Mean Wealth and Percent Wealth Distribution by Wealth Class, Consumer Unit Heads Classified by Age, 1962

| Age | Neg. or 0 | $1–999 | $1,000–4,999 | $5,000–9,999 | $10,000–24,999 | $25,000–49,999 | $50,000–99,999 | $100,000–199,999 | $200,000–499,999 | $500,000 and over |
|---|---|---|---|---|---|---|---|---|---|---|
| | | | | *Mean Wealth ($)* | | | | | | |
| All units | 0 | 396 | 2721 | 7257 | 16,047 | 35,191 | 68,950 | 132,790 | 300,355 | 1,260,667 |
| Under 35 | 0 | 411 | 2552 | 7116 | 15,493 | 30,911 | 75,861 | 117,437 | 281,433 | 4,972,437 |
| 35–44 | 0 | 392 | 2801 | 7410 | 15,897 | 35,068 | 68,026 | 130,385 | 294,846 | 1,194,630 |
| 45–54 | 0 | 392 | 2801 | 7410 | 15,897 | 35,068 | 68,026 | 130,385 | 294,846 | 1,194,630 |
| 55–64 | 0 | 358 | 2804 | 7216 | 17,056 | 36,067 | 68,513 | 141,236 | 309,196 | 1,353,921 |
| 65 and over | 0 | 365 | 2775 | 6988 | 15,572 | 35,131 | 70,645 | 122,569 | 298,141 | 1,034,548 |
| | | | | *Percent Wealth Distribution* | | | | | | |
| All units | 10 | 15 | 19 | 6 | 23 | 11 | 4 | 1 | 1 | |
| Under 35 | 14 | 36 | 26 | 24 | 8 | 2 | | 1 | 1 | |
| 35–44 | 9 | 14 | 20 | 21 | 25 | 8 | 4 | 1 | 1 | |
| 45–54 | 8 | 10 | 20 | 20 | 31 | 14 | 5 | 1 | 1 | |
| 55–64 | 9 | 7 | 12 | 26 | 28 | 16 | 3 | 3 | 2 | |
| 65 and over | 11 | 8 | 13 | 25 | 25 | 15 | 5 | 1 | 2 | 1 |

*Sources and notes*: Underlying data taken from Projector and Weiss (1966, tables A2 and A8, pp. 98–99 and 110–111). Mean wealth is not reported separately by size for age groups 35–44 and 45–54, but rather for 35–54. We have, therefore, assumed the 35–54 mean values to apply to both age groups. Furthermore, we set negative wealth values at zero, since no alternative was possible.

Table 1.23    Impact of Changing Age Distribution on Trends in American Wealth Concentration, 1930–70: Projector and Weiss 1962 Weights

| | U.S. Gini Coefficient | | | U.S. Gini Coefficient | |
|---|---|---|---|---|---|
| Year | Male-Headed Households | Consumer Units | Year | Male-Headed Households | Consumer Units |
| 1930 | .718 | | 1960 | .720 | |
| 1940 | .719 | | 1962 | .719 | .76 |
| 1950 | .722 | | 1970 | .725 | |

*Sources and notes*: Underlying data are taken from tables 1.21 and 1.22. U.S. male-headed household age distributions are applied using Projector and Weiss 1962 "wealth distribution weights" for consumer units, applying constant (1962) conversion factors to get from male-headed households to consumer units. The procedure assumes the distribution across wealth classes *within* age groups to be constant. We fail to replicate the Projector and Weiss reported Gini (1966, table 8, p. 30) of .76 since we were forced to set the mean negative wealth class at zero and the mean wealth detail in the 35–54 age group is different from Projector and Weiss (see note to table 1.21). Thus, our 1962 Gini of .72 reflects greater equality. Presumably, the trends reported above are unaffected by these assumptions.

the post-1929 leveling in wealth distribution is *understated*, and proper adjustment for life cycle effects would serve to make the trend toward greater wealth equality even steeper.[30]

### 1.5.3   Toward Size Distributions of Total Wealth

Thus far we have addressed only the size distribution of nonhuman wealth (inclusive of slaveholding), and have ignored total wealth. The latter augments "conventional" wealth by the capitalization of all expected future income streams accruing from human capital as well as claims on retirement income. So basic an omission is easily justified for the nineteenth century and earlier, when human capital was a far less important mode of accumulation and pensions were uncommon. For this century, however, we should at least begin the task of discerning what better measures of total wealth would show, since better measures should soon be available.

### Human Capital

It is well known that earnings are far more equally distributed than conventional property income or total income. The implication for wealth distributions is straightforward: *total* personal wealth must be far less concentrated than conventional wealth, and intangible human capital must, by inference, be more equally distributed. Frequency distributions of adults by formal schooling are certainly consistent with that inference, and a recent publication by Lee Lillard (1977, p. 49) supplies more specific support. Lillard reports an explicit calculation of the distribution of human capital for a male cohort born between 1917 and 1925. Gini coefficients are calculated for the cohort between ages 35 and 44 (e.g., over the years 1943 to 1970), taking on an average value of .45 and ranging between .39 and .53. By comparison, Projector and Weiss (1966, table 8, p. 30) report a Gini coefficient of .71 for "conventional" 1962 wealth in the same age class. What is true for the age class 35–44 is likely to be even more true of all adult potential wealthholders.

From the properties of variance, we also know that the coefficient of variation describing the concentration of *total* wealth ($W$) can be decomposed into three parts:

$$\left(\frac{\sigma_W}{\overline{W}}\right)^2 = \left(\frac{H}{\overline{W}}\right)^2 \left(\frac{\sigma_H}{\overline{H}}\right)^2 + \left(\frac{C}{\overline{W}}\right)^2 \left(\frac{\sigma_C}{\overline{C}}\right)^2 + \frac{2\sigma_{HC}}{\overline{W}^2}$$

i.e., (1) the coefficient of variation describing human capital ($H$) concentration weighted by the share of human capital in total wealth economy-wide;[31] (2) the coefficient of variation describing conventional capital ($C$) concentration, weighted by the share of conventional capital in total wealth economy-wide; and (3) a covariance term. It follows that total wealth will become more equally distributed over time for any of four reasons, singly or in concert: (1) a leveling in human capital distribution; (2) a leveling in conventional capital distribution; (3) an economy-wide rise in the importance of human capital in total wealth; and (4) a diminution in the (presumably positive) correlation between conventional and human wealthholdings.

Table 1.24 explores the potential impact of the third item, namely the shift in the economy-wide portfolio mix toward human capital following 1929. For net national wealth held by *persons,* John Kendrick estimates that the intangible human capital share in total wealth rose from 50.3 percent in 1929 to 58.7 percent in 1969. Based on the tentative estimates supplied by Theodore Schultz and Edward Denison, 1929 was a watershed since there is very little evidence supporting a shift in portfolio mix prior to that data. Indeed, it appears that conventional wealth was a *higher* share of total wealth in 1929 than in 1896. The implication would appear to be that the trend toward less concentrated wealth holdings following 1929 is significantly understated by our inattention to this fundamental shift in the wealth portfolio mix during the middle third of the twentieth century.[32]

The first-order causes of the portfolio mix shift following 1929 are not hard to find. John Kendrick's estimates[33] show that net rates of return for human capital have exceeded those for nonhuman capital over the past four decades. Furthermore, there appears to be considerable evi-

**Table 1.24**     Composition of Wealth: Three U.S. Estimates, 1896–1973 (percent shares)

| Year | Schultz | | Denison-Schultz | | Kendrick | | |
|---|---|---|---|---|---|---|---|
| | Education Stock | Reproducible Nonhuman Stock | Intangible Human Capital Stock | Reproducible Nonhuman Stock | Education Stock | Intangible Human Capital Stock | Tangible Nonhuman Stock |
| 1896 | | | 32.1 | 67.9 | | | |
| 1899 | | | 33.3 | 66.7 | | | |
| 1900 | 18.3 | 81.7 | | | | | |
| 1909 | 18.9 | 81.1 | 33.4 | 66.6 | | | |
| 1910 | | | | | | | |
| 1914 | | | 32.5 | 67.5 | | | |
| 1919 | | | 31.9 | 68.1 | | | |
| 1920 | 19.4 | 80.6 | | | | | |
| 1929 | 19.2 | 80.8 | 29.8 | 70.2 | 42.9 | 50.3 | 49.7 |
| 1930 | 19.7 | 80.3 | | | | | |
| 1940 | 24.7 | 75.3 | | | | | |
| 1948 | | | 34.3 | 65.7 | 45.1 | 51.7 | 48.3 |
| 1950 | 27.0 | 73.0 | | | | | |
| 1957 | 29.6 | 70.4 | | | | | |
| 1969 | | | | | 50.5 | 58.7 | 41.3 |
| 1973 | | | | | | 60.7 | 39.3 |

*Sources: Schultz:* The education stock refers to members of the labor force with ages over 14. The reproducible nonhuman wealth stock is Raymond W. Goldsmith's estimates for the U.S. economy as a whole. Both series are in constant 1956 prices. Schultz (1961, table 14, p. 73; and 1963, table 4, p. 51).

*Denison-Schultz:* Denison's labor quality input index 1896–1948 is applied to Schultz's educational capital stock benchmark for 1929. Reproducible nonhuman stock is private domestic economy capital stock, Kendrick (1896–1909) and Denison (1909–48) linked. Denison (1962, tables 11 and 12, pp. 85 and 100). Kendrick (1961, tables A–XV and A–XXII, pp. 320–22 and 333). All series in 1929 prices.

*Kendrick:* Net national wealth held by persons, current dollars. Estimates exclude intangible nonhuman capital (e.g., R&D) and tangible human capital (e.g., rearing costs). Kendrick (1976, tables 2–9, 2–10, 2–11, and C–7, pp. 50–51 and 239).

dence that human capital has become less concentrated since 1929, at least based upon earnings distribution data (see Lindert and Williamson 1976, for a summary of the evidence).

This implies that low income and/or younger families have been more able to exploit the higher rates of return to human capital. This would constitute a mechanism inducing a greater concentration of capital since 1929, to the extent that the portfolio shift to human capital has been more pronounced among households with low holdings of conventional wealth.[34] We have, then, two reasons for believing that trends in conventional wealth distributions understate the true leveling in total wealth distributions.

*Social Security and Pensions*

Conventional wealth estimates exclude the present value of contingent claims to social security benefits. Since its introduction in 1937, the social security system has expanded dramatically. Since wealth in this form has markedly increased in relative importance, and given its more equal distribution, we have reason to expect that its exclusion from wealth concentration statistics tends to create an upward bias in total wealth inequality trends since the 1920s. Furthermore, if low and middle class groups have tended as a result to shift out of conventional accumulation much more dramatically than the rich, then the measured concentration of "conventional" wealth has an upward bias over time as well.

Martin Feldstein (1974) has estimated that in 1971 social security wealth increased wealth of the entire population by 37 percent net of the present value of social security taxes paid by those currently in the labor force. A similar calculation for 1962 yields an estimate of 31 percent, while for those households in which there is a man aged 35–64 the figure is 35 percent (Feldstein 1976). James Smith (1974) has estimated that pension fund reserves amounted to about 7 percent of individual net worth in 1962. Not all pension plans are fully funded, of course, so this figure might be viewed as an understatement. Who benefits from pensions and social security? On the face of it, wealth held in these contingent forms must be most important for middle and low income individuals with little conventional nonhuman wealth except for house equities and consumer durable stocks.

Feldstein (1976) has made an explicit calculation of the impact of social security wealth on the distribution of total 1962 wealth reported by Projector and Weiss. The calculation is based on the assumption that social security taxes reduce human wealth but not nonhuman wealth, so that his results are gross of taxes. Feldstein thus estimates (1976, table 2) that the share of the top 1 percent of wealthholders aged 35–64 falls from 28.4 percent of fungible wealth to 18.9 percent of total wealth when social security wealth is included. No doubt somewhat less striking results would be forthcoming if the calculation was expanded to include all adults, but what does this 9.5 percent difference suggest regarding "conventional" wealth concentration trends offered by Lampman and Smith and Franklin? As a share in adult population, the top 1 percent had their share in conventional wealth decline from 31.6 percent in 1922 to 26.0 percent in 1956 (table 1.19). If the Feldstein 1962 adjustment was roughly applicable to 1956 as well, the true decline would have been from 31.6 to 16.5 percent, a leveling in wealthholdings far more consistent with the observed leveling in incomes.[35]

There is, of course, an active debate (Feldstein 1974; Barro 1977; Munnell 1976) over the response of total private saving to the presence of pension and social security plans, a debate which extends to labor supply and the retirement decision. However, no one has challenged the view summarized above that these mid-twentieth-century plans have induced a pronounced shift in wealth portfolios in such a fashion that the wealth leveling as reflected in "conventional" wealth measures is significantly understated.

## 1.6   Overview

This survey suggests one obvious moral: more data can and should be gathered on the size distribution of wealth throughout American history. Unlike data on incomes, the extant wealth data do not improve in quantity and quality over time. The twentieth-century wealth distributions are based on numbers only a little more plentiful and probably more flawed than wealth data for earlier centuries. The most critical flaw results from the charge of tax distortion, an alleged distortion unique to the twentieth century. To the extent that tax distortions have escalated with the estate tax burden, we shall have understated recent wealth inequalities and overstated the post-1929 leveling. While the tax distortion problem may never be fully resolved, it seems likely that an extension of our wealth accounting to include contingent claims on retirement income and human wealth is on the way.

The available estimates yield more than just caveats, however. This paper has presented a tentative three-century accounting starting with the mid–seventeenth century. From that time until the eve of the American Revolution, colonial wealth inequality seems to exhibit stability despite some noteworthy increases in urban wealth inequality just before the Revolution. Between 1774 and the outbreak of the Civil War, a revolutionary change took place in the distribution of wealth. Our nationwide estimates point to a near tripling in the ratios of the average wealth of the top one or ten percent of wealthholders to the average wealth of all other groups. Estimates from local probates and tax return sources seem to confirm this dramatic trend toward concentration. Furthermore, regional estimates suggest that most of the antebellum shift to wealth concentration occurred from the 1820s to the late 1840s, although the supply of such shorter run data is still inadequate. In addition, our calculations show that the apparent rise in wealth inequality before the Civil War cannot be explained by mere shifts in the age distribution, by the increasing share of foreign born, or by urbanization, although this last item contributes noticeably to the rise of wealth concentration.

We still know little about wealth inequality trends within the long period from the Civil War to World War I. Slave emancipation unambiguously leveled wealth inequality within the South and for the nation as a whole across the 1860s. For the half-century after 1870 we are in the dark, so that we cannot with confidence identify peak wealth inequality with 1929, 1914, or 1860. Nevertheless, it is apparent that no significant long-term leveling took place during the period and that inequality persisted at very high levels.

The twentieth-century figures suggest a clear pattern. Wealth inequality, like income inequality, dipped across World War I and rose across the 1920s, although it is hard to say whether the 1929 distribution was more or less equal than that of 1912 or some nearby year. From 1929 until midcentury, wealth inequality seems to have dropped, again paralleling the movement in income inequality. After midcentury, neither wealth nor income inequality has shown a trend that can be judged significant on existing data. The American record thus documents a "Kuznets inverted $U$" for both wealth and income inequality. Significant inequality in either form apparently did not appear on the American scene until the onset of modern economic growth in the early nineteenth century.

Throughout the paper we have followed the usual convention of exploring the size distribution of *nominal* wealth. Yet rich and poor consume different items with their wealth. The size distribution of *real* wealth can thus be influenced by movements in the ratio of the cost-of-living index for the rich to the corresponding index for the poor. Elsewhere (Williamson 1977; Williamson and Lindert 1978) we have explored the class difference in cost-of-living movements, and have found these to have moved in a fashion which serves to reinforce the nominal distribution trends. In particular, what we know about class differences in the cost-of-living suggests no revision of the position that wealth inequality rose before the Civil War. A rise in the relative cost-of-living for poorer families between 1890 and 1914 adds force to the belief that real wealth inequality ascended to a historic peak just before World War I. Movements in class cost-of-living indices also reinforce the nominal distribution trends over the last half-century.

To the extent that further research upholds these findings, it will underscore the importance of identifying those forces driving the distribution of wealth in America. An essential first step is to decompose changes in aggregate wealth inequality (among persons of given age) into its four components: (1) changes in the prior inequalities of bequests inherited by the age group, (2) changes in the inequalities of prior earnings and public transfers received by the age group, (3) changes in the correlation between size of wealth and average propensities to save in nonhuman form, and (4) changes in the correlation between size of wealth and rates of return received on that wealth. This decomposition is pregnant with social implications, of course. Defenders of the American record may endeavor to find that shifts in savings propensities explain the nineteenth-century rise in wealth inequality, but not the twentieth-century leveling. Critics will feel some compulsion to show the opposite. We cannot enter such a debate here, although we feel that changes in the inequalities of prior incomes will be central to successful explanatory models, and that such models will have to deal with the full general equilibrium determinants of quasi-rents on assets of all sorts, human and nonhuman. It should suffice for the present to point out that American wealth inequality paints a fascinating picture, one awaiting explanation.

# Appendix 1   Colonial Wealth Inequality Trends

## New England Colonies

### Table 1.A.1    Connecticut: Probate Wealth

| Period | (1a)<br>Top 10%<br>Hartford<br>(personal) | (1b)<br>Top 10%<br>Hartford<br>(total) | (2a)<br>Top 30%<br>Hartford<br>(personal) | (2b)<br>Top 30%<br>Hartford<br>(total) | (3)<br>Top 10%<br>Hartford<br>(real) |
|---|---|---|---|---|---|
| 1650–69 | 45.5 | 47.8 | 75.0 | 76.2 | 53.0 |
| 1670–79 | 43.0 | 54.1 | 68.0 | 76.7 | 55.0 |
| 1680–84 | 47.0 | 56.4 | 73.0 | 81.6 | 60.0 |
| 1685–89 |  |  |  |  | 48.0 |
| 1690–94 | 43.0 | 52.1 | 71.0 | 74.9 | 40.0 |
| 1695–99 |  |  |  |  | 36.0 |
| 1700–09 | 46.0 | 40.3 | 72.0 | 69.4 | 36.0 |
| 1710–14 | 45.0 | 45.6 | 70.0 | 70.8 | 41.0 |
| 1715–19 | 43.5 | 45.0 | 66.5 | 71.4 | 47.0 |
| 1720–24 | 45.5 |  | 71.0 |  | 38.0 |
| 1725–29 | 42.5 |  | 65.0 |  | 37.0 |
| 1730–34 | 48.0 |  | 70.0 |  | 47.0 |
| 1735–39 | 33.0 |  | 62.0 |  | 42.0 |
| 1740–44 | 44.0 |  | 68.0 |  | 48.0 |
| 1745–49 | 43.0 |  | 70.0 |  | 53.5 |
| 1750–54 | 39.0 |  | 65.0 |  | 49.0 |
| 1755–59 | 34.0 |  | 68.0 |  | 50.0 |
| 1760–64 | 47.0 |  | 70.0 |  | 54.0 |
| 1765–69 | 48.5 |  | 69.5 |  | 42.5 |
| 1770–74 | 45.0 |  | 71.0 |  | 49.4 |

*Source*: Professor Jackson T. Main has kindly supplied us with these data underlying his 1976 article on Connecticut wealth. The estate inventory data, which cover the great majority of adult male decedents before the mid–18th century, have been age-adjusted to estimate the distribution of personal estate, real estate, and total estate among living adult males whose estates were likely to be inventoried at death.

### Table 1.A.2    Connecticut and New Hampshire: Unadjusted Probate Wealth, Top 30%

| Period | (4)<br>Hartford,<br>Conn. | (5)<br>Middle-Sized<br>Towns, Conn. | (6)<br>Small<br>Towns, Conn. | (7)<br>Portsmouth,<br>N.H. |
|---|---|---|---|---|
| 1700–20 | 74.03 | 50.12 |  | 65.5 |
| 1720–40 | 73.02 | 63.95 |  | 75.3 |
| 1740–60 | 77.27 | 69.05 | 60.83 | 79.7 |
| 1760–76 | 73.94 | 69.07 | 67.50 | 79.1 |

*Source and notes*: Unadjusted probate wealth, sampled counties, from Daniels (1973–74, tables 3 and 4, pp. 131–32). The middle-sized Connecticut towns are Danbury, Waterbury, and Windham. The small Connecticut towns are the "frontier settlements" Canaan, Kent, Salisbury, and Sharon, all of which are in Litchfield County.

Table 1.A.3    Massachusetts: Boston and Suffolk County, Probate Wealth, Top 10%

| Period | (8) Boston | Period | (9) Boston | Period | (10) Suffolk County | Period | (11) Top 30% Boston |
|--------|-----------|--------|-----------|--------|---------------------|--------|---------------------|
| 1650–64 | 60.0 | | | | | | |
| 1665–74 | 64.0 | | | | | | |
| 1685–94 | 46.0 | 1684–99 | 41.2 | | | | |
| 1695–04 | 50.0 | | | 1695–97 | 40.6 | | |
| 1705–14 | 56.0 | 1700–15 | 54.5 | 1705–06 | 50.2 | 1700–20 | 84.25 |
| 1715–19 | 54.0 | | | 1715–17 | 36.4 | | |
| | | 1716–25 | 61.7 | | | | |
| | | 1726–35 | 65.6 | 1726–27 | 50.8 | | |
| | | 1736–45 | 58.6 | 1735–37 | 38.7 | 1720–40 | 82.45 |
| 1750–54 | 53.0 | 1746–55 | 55.2 | 1746–47 | 50.9 | | |
| | | 1756–65 | 67.5 | 1755–57 | 55.7 | 1740–60 | 87.94 |
| 1760–69 | 53.0 | 1766–75 | 61.1 | 1766–67 | 48.6 | | |
| | | | | 1777–78 | 41.4 | 1760–76 | 85.30 |
| 1782–88 | 56.0 | | | | | | |

*Sources*: Col. 8: Wealth inventories of adult male decedents, total estate values. G. Main (1976, table IV).

Col. 9: Unadjusted inventoried personal wealth (excluding real estate). Nash (1976b, table 3, p. 9).

Col. 10: Suffolk County includes Boston. Inventoried total wealth, unadjusted. G. Warden (1976, table 2, p. 599).

Col. 11: Unadjusted probate wealth, total estate value. Daniels (1973–74, table 2, p. 129).

Table 1.A.4    Massachusetts: Boston, Tax Lists, Top 10%

| Year | (12) "Unadjusted" | (13) "Adjusted" | Year | (12) "Unadjusted" | (13) "Adjusted" |
|------|-------------------|-----------------|------|-------------------|-----------------|
| 1681 | | 42.30 | 1771 | 63.60 | 47.50 |
| 1687 | 46.60 | | 1790 | 64.70 | |

*Sources and notes*: Taxable wealth from Boston tax lists, augmented to include adult males without wealth. The 1687 and 1771 figures in col. 12 are from Henretta (1965, tables I and II, p. 185), while the 1790 entry is from Kulikoff (1971, table 2B, p. 381). Gerard Warden has warned that one takes great risks in trying to infer the level and trend of wealth inequality from Boston's tax assessments. Undervaluation ratios varied greatly over time and across assets, while many assets escaped assessment altogether. His adjustments for these valuation and coverage problems are presented in col. 13. G. Warden (1976, p. 595).

**Table 1.A.5**          **Massachusetts: Rural Areas, Probate Wealth**

| Period | (14) Top 30% Rural Suffolk | (15) Top 30% Worcester | (16) Top 10% Essex | Period | (17) Top 10% Rural Suffolk | (18) Top 10% Hampshire | (19) Top 10% Worcester |
|---|---|---|---|---|---|---|---|
| 1635–60 | | | 36.0 | 1650–64 | 37.0 | | |
| 1661–81 | | | 49.0 | 1665–74 | 37.0 | 30.0 | |
| | | | | 1685–94 | 34.0 | 37.0 | |
| | | | | 1695–04 | 36.0 | 35.0 | |
| 1700–20 | 62.52 | | | 1705–14 | 33.0 | 38.0 | |
| | | | | 1715–19 | 31.0 | 52.0 | |
| 1720–40 | 58.01 | 60.24 | | | | | |
| 1740–60 | 67.57 | 64.42 | | 1750–54 | 31.0 | 41.0 | |
| | | | | 1760–69 | 38.0 | | 39.0 |
| 1760–76 | 68.05 | 68.06 | | | | | |
| | | | | 1782–88 | 42.4 | | 43.0 |

*Sources and notes*: Cols. 14 and 15: Unadjusted probate wealth, total estate values. Daniels (1973–74, table 2, p. 129). Rural Suffolk refers to Suffolk County excluding Boston, while Worcester refers to the county.

Col. 16: Unadjusted total estate values from Koch (1969, pp. 57–59) as cited in G. Main (1976, table I).

Cols. 17, 18, and 19: County data where Suffolk excludes Boston. Total estate values among adult male decedents reported in G. Main (1976, table IV)

**Table 1.A.6**          **Massachusetts: Rural Areas, Hingham Tax Lists**

| Year | (20) Top 10% | (21) Top 30% | Year | (20) Top 10% | (21) Top 30% |
|---|---|---|---|---|---|
| 1754 | 37.44 | 72.90 | 1779 | 46.52 | 77.58 |
| 1765 | 40.09 | 72.40 | 1790 | 44.66 | 74.53 |
| 1772 | 39.93 | 71.43 | | | |

*Sources and notes*: Taxable wealth, adult males, from Hingham, Massachusetts, tax lists, adjusted to include males without property. D. Smith (1973, table III–1, p. 90). Smith also reports top wealth shares for 1647, 1680, and 1711, but these observations are unsuited for time series analysis. For justification of their exclusion see Smith (1973, Appendix tables III–1 and III–2) and Warden (1976, p. 595).

## Middle Colonies

**Table 1.A.7**        New York and Pennsylvania: Tax Lists

| Year | (22) Top 10% Chester, Pa. | (23) Top 10% Philadelphia | (24) Top 4% Philadelphia | (25) Top 10% New York City |
|---|---|---|---|---|
| 1693 | 23.8 | 46.0 | 32.8 | |
| 1695 | | | | 44.5 |
| 1715 | 25.9 | | | |
| 1730 | 28.6 | | | 43.7 |
| 1748 | 28.7 | | | |
| 1756 | | 46.6 | 34.0 | |
| 1760 | 29.9 | | | |
| 1767 | | 65.7 | 49.5 | |
| 1772 | | 71.2 | 54.7 | |
| 1774 | | 72.3 | 55.5 | |
| 1782 | 33.6 | | | |
| 1789 | | | | 45.0 |

*Sources and notes*:  Col. 22: Taxable wealth among taxpayers, unadjusted for propertyless, Lemon and Nash (1968, table I, p. 11). Lemon and Nash also report an observation for 1800–1802, but since it includes Delaware County as well, we exclude it from the time series.

Cols. 23 and 24: Taxable wealth among taxpayers, unadjusted for propertyless. Except for 1772, all observations from Nash (1976b, table 1, p. 6, and table 2, p. 7). The 1772 figure is from Nash (1976b, table 2, p. 11). Tax assessment data are beset with problems, and Philadelphia is no exception. For example, Nash (1976b, p. 8) notes that the 1756 records omitted all those in the lowest wealth class who, nevertheless, would have paid the head tax "ordinarily." It is not clear whether the same is true of 1693. Furthermore, since the minimum assessment was set at £8 in 1756, £2 in 1767, and £1 in 1774, there is an upward bias imparted to the inequality trends over time.

Col. 25: Taxable wealth among taxpayers, unadjusted for propertyless. The figure for 1730 is from Nash (1976b, table 1). The entries for 1695 and 1789 are from G. Main (1976, table I).

**Table 1.A.8**     **Maryland and Pennsylvania: Probate Wealth**

| Period | (26)<br><br>Top 10%<br>Maryland | (27)<br>Top 10%<br>Maryland<br>(adjusted) | Period | (28)<br>Top 10%<br>Phila-<br>delphia | Period | (29)<br><br>Top 20%<br>Chester |
|---|---|---|---|---|---|---|
| 1675–79 | 49.5 | | | | | |
| 1680–84 | 51.0 | | | | | |
| 1685–89 | 53.0 | | | | | |
| 1690–94 | 55.0 | | 1684–99 | 36.4 | | |
| 1695–99 | 53.0 | | | | | |
| 1700–04 | 54.7 | 67.2 | | | | |
| 1705–09 | 57.7 | 57.7 | 1700–15 | 41.3 | | |
| 1710–14 | | 66.2 | | | | |
| 1715–19 | | 65.5 | 1716–25 | 46.8 | 1714–31 | 46.41 |
| | | | 1726–35 | 53.6 | | |
| | | | 1736–45 | 51.3 | 1734–45 | 53.02 |
| 1750–54 | | 65.8 | 1746–55 | 70.1 | | |
| | | | 1756–65 | 60.3 | 1750–70 | 52.53 |
| | | | 1766–75 | 69.9 | | |
| 1782–88 | | (60.0) | | | 1775–90 | 60.49 |

*Sources and notes*: Cols. 26 and 27: "Maryland" is actually a pooling of six counties: Anne Arundel, Baltimore, Calvert, Charles, Kent, and Somerset. The 1675–1754 observations are based on inventoried adult male wealth, personal estate only. The 1782–88 observation is of questionable comparability since it is based on taxable wealth (real and personal) distribution among taxpayers. Both columns are taken from G. Main (1976, tables A–1 and IV). Col. 27 reports inventoried adult male personal estates, adjusted for underreporting. Main also reports the unadjusted top 10 percent for 1705 to 1754 but since the adjustments are so large, no purpose would be served in reporting the erroneous figures beyond 1704. She does not attempt to adjust the pre-1700 series.

Col. 28: Inventoried personal wealth. Nash (1976b, table 3, p. 9).

Col. 29: Chester County, Pennsylvania, inventoried wealth excluding land. Ball (1976, table 7, p. 637).

# Appendix 2    Underlying Data for Colonial Wealth Decomposition Analysis

**Table 1.A.9**    **Average Wealth Benchmarks: Colonial Boston and New England**

| Boston | 1687 | 1771 |
|---|---|---|
| Wealth | £   331,820 | £    815,136 |
| Population | 5,925 | 16,540 |
| Wealth per capita ($\overline{W}_B$) | £ 56.00 | £ 49.28 |

| New England | 1680–89 | 1774 |
|---|---|---|
| Wealth | £ 2,346,858 | £ 22,322,880 |
| Population | 67,376 | 606,596 |
| Wealth per capita ($\overline{W}_{NE}$) | £ 34.83 | £ 36.80 |

| Non-Boston | 1680–89 | 1774 |
|---|---|---|
| Wealth | £ 2,015,038 | £ 21,507,744 |
| Population | 61,451 | 590,056 |
| Wealth per capita ($\overline{W}_{NB}$) | £ 32.79 | £ 36.45 |

| | | |
|---|---|---|
| $\overline{W}_B/\overline{W}_{NE}$ | 1.608 | 1.339 |
| $\overline{W}_{NB}/\overline{W}_{NE}$ | .941 | .990 |
| $u$ | .088 | .027 |

*Sources*: Boston wealth estimates are based on taxable wealth adjusted by Gerard Warden (1976, pp. 588–89) for both undervaluation and incomplete lists. New England wealth estimates are based on probate samples. The 1680–89 figure is taken from Terry Anderson (1975, table 9, p. 169), while the 1774 figure is from Alice Jones (1972, table 1, p. 102). All population estimates are taken from the same sources except Boston's for 1687. Using Shattuck, Warden reports the following per annum Boston averages: 1692–99, 6600, and 1700–09, 7378. Applying the growth rate between 1692–99 and 1700–09 backward to 1687 yields a Boston population estimate of 5,925.

**Table 1.A.10**    **Wealth Held by All Living Potential Wealthholders: New England, 1774**

| Percentiles | Mean Wealth $\overline{W}_j$ | Population $\overline{P}_j$ |
|---|---|---|
| 0–10 | £   6.30 | 10 |
| 11–20 | 15.75 | 10 |
| 21–50 | 47.25 | 30 |
| 51–80 | 134.40 | 30 |
| 81–90 | 234.68 | 10 |
| 91–100 | 773.33 | 10 |
| All | £ 157.50 | 100 |

Gini = 0.62; $\sigma^2/\overline{W}^2 = I_{NE} = 1.88$

*Source*: Jones 1972, table 6, using assumption A for non-probates, "A– 1/4," p. 119.

Table 1.A.11    **Average Wealth Benchmarks: Philadelphia and the Middle Colonies, 1774**

|  | Wealth per Capita ($£$) | Inequality Measure ($I$) |
|---|---|---|
| Philadelphia | 525 | 2.432 |
| Middle colonies | 377 | 1.293 |
| Non-Philadelphia | 371 | 1.193 |

*Source*: Jones (1971, tables 13 and 17), based on net worth rather than physical wealth, and adjusted to all living potential wealthholdings.

# Appendix 3   Top Wealthholder Shares in the Northeast, 1760–1891

Table 1.A.12    **Top Decile Shares of Net Worth among All Decedents, Massachusetts, 1829–91**

| Year | Share (%) | Year | Share (%) |
|---|---|---|---|
| 1829–31 | 71.3–73.1 | 1879–81 | 87.2 |
| 1859–61 | 80.4 | 1889–91 | 82.5–83.4 |

*Sources and notes*: The shares of total estimated wealth held by the richest decile of the adult males dying in Massachusetts in the periods 1829–31, 1859–61, 1879–81, and 1889–91 show greater inequality than would the values held by living adult males at any point in time. The primary data on the values of probated estates are from Massachusetts Bureau of Statistics of Labor (1895). The figures for the latter three periods were adjusted for estimated deaths of males without wealth and for assumed distributions of wealth among uninventoried estates by King (1915, tables IX and X and accompanying text). A careful scrutiny of King's estimates revealed the specific assumptions he made. These assumptions were not given any careful justification but do not seem implausible. King's assumptions were also applied to the 1829–31 distribution of probated wealth. For 1829–31 it was assumed that the total number of adult male deaths was in the same ratio to the adult male population of Massachusetts as in 1859–61, an assumption based on a reading of Maris A. Vinovskis (1972, pp. 202–13).

Table 1.A.13    **Top Decile Shares of Taxable Wealth
among Taxpayers: Boston, 1771–1845**

| Year | Share (%) | Year | Share (%) |
|------|-----------|------|-----------|
| 1771 | 63.5 | 1830 | 66.2 |
| 1790 | 64.7 | 1845 | 72.9 |
| 1820 | 50.3 | | |

*Sources*: The eighteenth-century estimates are from Kulikoff (1971, table II) and Henretta (1965, tables I and
II, p. 185). The estimates for 1820, 1830, and 1845 were
taken from Gloria Main (1975, table II). She has re-
worked the data originally published in Pessen (1973,
pp. 38–40) and in Shattuck (1846, p. 95).

Table 1.A.14    **Top Decile Shares of Total Wealth
Inventoried at Death among Adult
Males: Boston, 1760–1891**

| Year | Share (%) | Year | Share (%) |
|------|-----------|------|-----------|
| 1760–69 | 53.0 | 1859–61 | 93.8 |
| 1782–88 | 56.0 | 1879–81 | 83.9 |
| 1829–31 | 83.0 | 1889–91 | 85.8 |

*Sources and note*: See Note to table 3.A.1, above. The
figures for 1760–88 are from G. Main (1975, table IV).
Those for 1829–91 are "adjusted" and taken from the
same source, table VI.

Table 1.A.15    **Top Decile Shares of Total Wealth
Inventoried at Death among Adult
Males: Rural Suffolk County,
Massachusetts, 1763–91**

| Year | Share (%) | Year | Share (%) |
|------|-----------|------|-----------|
| 1763–69 | 38.0 | 1859–61 | 72.9 |
| 1783–88 | 42.4 | 1889–91 | 80.8 |
| 1829–31 | 59.5 | | |

*Source*: G. Main (1975, table IX).

| Table 1.A.16 | Top Decile Shares of Total Taxable Wealth among Property Taxpayers Plus Adult Males with Zero Property: Hingham, Massachusetts, 1765–1880 | | |
|---|---|---|---|

| Year | Share (%) | Year | Share (%) |
|---|---|---|---|
| 1765 | 40.1 | 1820 | 46.2 |
| 1772 | 39.9 | 1830 | 47.0 |
| 1779 | 46.5 | 1840 | 51.4 |
| 1790 | 44.7 | 1850 | 56.7 |
| 1800 | 41.9 | 1860 | 58.8 |
| 1810 | 39.1 | 1880 | 57.5 |

*Source*: Daniel Scott Smith (1973, table III–1 and Appendix table III–2).

| Table 1.A.17 | Shares of Estimated Nonbusiness Wealth Held by Top 4 Percent of "Population": New York City, 1828–45 | | |
|---|---|---|---|

| Year | Share (%) | Year | Share (%) |
|---|---|---|---|
| 1828 | 49 | 1845 | 66 |

*Source*: Edward Pessen (1973, tables 3–1 to 3–4, pp. 33–37).

| Table 1.A.18 | Shares of Estimated Nonbusiness Wealth Held by Top 1 Percent of "Population": Brooklyn, 1810–41 | | |
|---|---|---|---|

| Year | Share (%) | Year | Share (%) |
|---|---|---|---|
| 1810 | 22 | 1841 | 42 |

*Source*: Edward Pessen (1973, tables 3–1 to 3–4, pp. 33–37).

# Notes

1. One should resist the meritocratic temptation to single out nonhuman wealth as that part of total lifetime income or wealth that is of special interest because it it is inherited and not based on individual productivity. The distribution of wealth is affected by much more than inheritance. Some people save a greater share of their earnings than others, giving rise to a component of wealth inequality that is less repugnant to most people than differences in inheritance. The present data do not allow us to separate the effects of differences in saving rates from those of differences in inheritance. The same mixing of inheritance with invidual accumulation also characterizes human capital and earnings, of course, since parental wealth and abilities are strong determinants of human investments. The case for studying the separate distribution of nonhuman wealth is not based on its having a separate welfare meaning, but on its greater accessibility.

2. Six years ago Lee Soltow (1971a) insisted that inequality and wealth concentration were high and stable during the nineteenth century, and that this had been a relatively permanent attribute of American experience before 1776 and after. That wealth inequality levels were high during the colonial era cannot be maintained on the basis of the enormous amount of data which has accumulated since 1971. (See Jackson Main [1976, p. 54] for a critical evaluation of Soltow's position.)

3. The import values in pounds sterling can be found in U.S. Bureau of the Census (1976, part 2, series Z–216, pp. 1176–77). Unfortunately, the series does not extend back to the mid–seventeenth century. For further discussion of Boston's cycles, see Gary Nash's (1976a, pp. 575–76) account of wartime boom, postwar recession and their "disfiguring effect on urban societies."

4. For tobacco prices and exports, see, for example, Paul Clemens (1974) and Russell Menard (1973).

5. For example, around 1700, "settled trading" towns in Connecticut had 52.2 percent of wealth in real estate, while for the "new frontier" towns the share was 62.1 percent (J. Main 1976, table IX, p. 78). Furthermore, land was the dominant asset in the real estate total—about 82 percent—if Hartford, Farmington, and Simsbury in the 1760s are typical (personal correspondence from Jackson T. Main dated 27 May, 1976).

6. Furthermore, concentration trends in real estate holdings closely follow rates of change in Connecticut relative land values. Taking the ratio of prices of an acre of meadow (J. Main 1976, pp. 101–2) to farm labor wages (U.S. Bureau of Labor Statistics 1929, pp. 9, 51, 53 and 124), we find the relative price of land stable from the 1680s to 1710. It rises sharply to 1759 and then stabilizes thereafter. The index is 16.67 for 1680–89, 36.30 for 1755–59, and 44.12 for 1774.

7. Log variance is a more commonly used inequality measure. The algebra, and the argument, which follow would be exactly the same if log means and log variance were used instead. See Sherman Robinson (1976).

8. The reader will note the obvious similarity between this discussion of colonial wealth and Simon Kuznets's (1955) decomposition of *income* inequality into urban and rural components. The same four forces were present in his analysis too: (1) urban inequality, (2) rural inequality, (3) urbanization, and (4) rural-urban income gaps. The framework has been used recently in a wide variety of circumstances. A general statement can be found in Lindert and Williamson (1976, p. 6) or Robinson (1976).

9. That is

$$
\begin{aligned}
dI_{NE} = {} & dI_B\left[ u\left(\frac{\overline{W}_B}{\overline{W}_{NE}}\right)^2 \right] + dI_{NB}\left[ (1-u)\left(\frac{\overline{W}_{NB}}{\overline{W}_{NE}}\right)^2 \right] \\
& + du\left[ \left(\frac{\overline{W}_B}{\overline{W}_{NE}}\right)^2 I_B - \left(\frac{\overline{W}_{NB}}{\overline{W}_{NE}}\right)^2 I_{NB} + \left(\frac{\overline{W}_B - \overline{W}_{NE}}{\overline{W}_{NE}(1-u)}\right)^2 \right. \\
& \left. + 2I_{NB}\left(\frac{\overline{W}_{NB}}{\overline{W}_{NE}}\right)\left(\frac{\overline{W}_{NE} - \overline{W}_B}{\overline{W}_{NE}(1-u)}\right) \right] \\
& + d\left(\frac{\overline{W}_B}{\overline{W}_{NE}}\right)\left\{ 2u\left[ I_B\left(\frac{\overline{W}_B}{\overline{W}_{NE}}\right) - I_{NB}\left(\frac{\overline{W}_{NB}}{\overline{W}_{NE}}\right) \right.\right. \\
& \left.\left. + \left(\frac{\overline{W}_B}{\overline{W}_{NE}} - 1\right)\left(\frac{1}{(1-u)}\right) \right] \right\} .
\end{aligned}
$$

10. Alice Jones's wealth estimates for 1774 (Jones 1972, table 6, p. 119) yield $I_{NE} = 1.88$. Using top wealthholder share data reported in table 1.A.1, we estimate $I_B = 2.2$ and $I_{NB} = 1.6$. Table 1.1 informs us that Boston's population was about 3.5 percent of New England's in 1760. Appendix 2 supplies the requisite per capita wealth ratios for both the early 1770s and the 1680s. This is all the data necessary to compute the third term in the expression given in note 9.

11. In terms of taxable wealth, by the middle of the eighteenth century the top 10 percent owned the following shares: 46.6 percent in Philadelphia (1756); 28.7 percent in Chester County, Pennsylvania (1748). In terms of inventoried wealth, the top 10 percent owned the following shares: 70.1 percent in Philadelphia, (1746–55); 65.8 percent in rural Maryland (1750–1754). These estimates can all be found in table 1.A.1. Furthermore, Alice Jones (1972, tables 13 and 17) has documented net worth shares for 1774; the top 10 percent in Philadelphia County claimed 54.7 percent, while in the Middle colonies as a whole they claimed only 40.6 percent.

12. The decomposition formula in note 9 can be rewritten where MC, P, and NP denote the Middle colonies, Philadelphia, and non-Philadelphia, respectively:

$$
\begin{aligned}
dI_{MC} = {} & dI_P\left[ u\left(\frac{\overline{W}_P}{\overline{W}_{MC}}\right)^2 \right] + dI_{NP}\left[ (1-u)\left(\frac{\overline{W}_{NP}}{\overline{W}_{MC}}\right)^2 \right] \\
& + du\left[ \left(\frac{\overline{W}_P}{\overline{W}_{MC}}\right)^2 I_P - \left(\frac{\overline{W}_{NP}}{\overline{W}_{MC}}\right)^2 I_{NP} + \left(\frac{\overline{W}_P - \overline{W}_{MC}}{\overline{W}_{MC}(1-u)}\right)^2 \right. \\
& \left. + 2I_{NP}\left(\frac{\overline{W}_{NP}}{\overline{W}_{MC}}\right)\left(\frac{\overline{W}_{MC} - \overline{W}_P}{\overline{W}_{MC}(1-u)}\right) \right] \\
& + d\left(\frac{\overline{W}_P}{\overline{W}_{MC}}\right)\left\{ 2u\left[ I_P\left(\frac{\overline{W}_P}{\overline{W}_{MC}}\right) - I_{NP}\left(\frac{\overline{W}_{NP}}{\overline{W}_{MC}}\right) \right.\right. \\
& \left.\left. + \left(\frac{\overline{W}_P - \overline{W}_{MC}}{\overline{W}_{MC}(1-u)}\right) \right] \right\} .
\end{aligned}
$$

where $u$ is Philadelphia's share in total Middle colony population. Table 1.1 and appendix 2 supply the wealth inequality estimates for 1774 ($I_P = 2.432$, $I_{MC} = 1.293$, and $I_{NP} = 1.193$), as well as those for per capita wealth ratios.

13. In contrast with Gallman's (1974) cautious speculations on the early national period, some historians write as if the impact of age distribution on aggregate wealth inequality trends was fully understood for the colonial era. On the

1714–90 period in Chester County, Duane Ball (1976, p. 637) states: "[The] distribution of wealth, though seemingly unequal, actually might be considered fairly egalitarian if we were to take the age of wealth holders into account. It is also possible that at least some of the increasing concentration . . . is attributable to a change in the age structure, . . . from relatively younger to relatively older." All things are possible, but as far as we know there is no adequate colonial data which would allow exploration of the influence of changing age distributions.

14. This is not entirely accurate. Jackson Main (1976, table VI, p. 93) reports the distribution of decedents by wealth and age class for all Connecticut towns. Unfortunately, he pools observations drawn from the century ending 1753, a sufficiently long period to make age-wealth analysis tenuous at best.

15. This sentence is based on an examination of the following age distributions: New England, white males, ca. 1690 (Thomas and Anderson 1973, p. 654); Westchester, Bedford, and New Rochelle, New York, adult males and both sexes, 1698 (Wells 1975, p. 117); U.S., white and total males, 1800 (U.S. Bureau of the Census 1976, part I, p. 16).

The discussion here is motivated by a different set of issues than that motivating Jackson T. Main's recent analysis of Connecticut eighteenth-century probates. He devotes considerable attention to the impact of age on wealth distribution from region to region and across occupations, but never across time. See J. Main (1976, pp. 77–97).

16. Jackson Main (1976, p. 61) thinks it could, at least based on Connecticut evidence: "Historians seem to have neglected this life-cycle. They have lamented a high proportion of nearly propertyless polls appearing on tax lists . . . without perceiving that most of these were just entering manhood."

17. Take the case of Boston. Rapid growth early in the eighteenth century would imply a rise in the share of young adults in the adult population, increased age dispersion and, given in addition migration selectivity, an inequality bias. We should count more poor, the percent on relief should have risen, and probate records along with tax lists should produce rising concentration ratios. The opposite should have been true following the 1730s when young people (without much wealth) must have fled Boston's stagnating economy. The Boston probate records document historical concentration trends which may be explained at least in part by these (alleged) age distribution changes. That is, some portion of the inequality trend from 1700 to 1730 (figure 1.3) must be accounted for by the presumed rise in the young adult share.

18. These dramatic trends can also be seen in shifts in the ratios of average wealth at the top to average wealth economy-wide. Between 1774 and 1860 the ratio of the average wealth of the top 1 percent of wealthholders to the average wealth of the lower 99 percent rose from 14.0 to 40.4. Over the same period, the ratio of the top decile's average wealth to that of the bottom 90 percent rose from 8.54 to 24.3. Both ratios nearly tripled.

19. We had hoped to perform the same experiments, including a test for nativity effects, on Professor Soltow's 1860 spin sample, but this sample was not available to us at the time of writing.

20. Actually, Professor Jones applies the 1800 age distribution to the 1774 wealth data.

21. The skimpy data on age distribution before 1830 suggest that this date may have been a watershed in the share of young adults in the adult population, as well as in the wealth distribution trends discussed in section 1.3.6 below. Table 1.6 shows a rise in the share of persons aged 16–25 in the total population aged 15 and over between 1800 and 1820. By itself, this shift would impart an *upward*

bias to aggregate inequality trends for the first two decades of the nineteenth century. This would reinforce the case for dating the rise of wealth concentration among fixed demographic groups from around the 1820s. It is after this date that we observe the aging referred to in the text.

22. Since this result is so striking, we performed another calculation using the adult (male and female) age distributions in the Northeast reported in table 1.6 and Soltow's 1870 income × age profile guesstimates (1975, table 3.7, p. 90). The results are similar. The top 10 percent of adult income earners would have found their share of total income declining from 16 percent in 1830 to 12.5 percent in 1870, were no other inequality forces at work. Robert Gallman (1974, p. 7) found similar results using a different age × income profile. He argued that the top 30 percent share in total income would have declined from 95.9 percent in 1830 to 92.0 percent in 1860, a result almost identical to ours. Gallman did not pursue the implication of this calculation for interpretations of nineteenth-century American inequality trends. His interest was primarily in the comparison between America and Europe.

23. For adult males in 1870, the U.S. Gini coefficients based on total estates were .831 for native born and .840 for foreign born. For free adult males in 1860, the U.S. Gini coefficients based on total estates were .816 for native born and .858 for foreign born. Soltow (1975, pp. 107 and 145). For adult males in 1850, the Wisconsin Gini coefficients based on real estates were .746 for native born and .786 for foreign born. Soltow (1971b, p. 81).

24. This state of affairs need not continue. For the 1850s, more can be done from the manuscript federal and state census returns on real estate value, farm acreage, and farm implements, either with the Bateman-Foust and Soltow samples, or with new samples. Local tax returns can also be exploited more fully. In addition, Gallman's procedure of tracking down the wealth of the richest individuals for comparison with rough wealth aggregates can be extended to other dates and to regions. Above all, as we shall mention in the text, the vast numbers of probate inventories, many of them collected and referenced in the Library of the Genealogical Society of the Church of Jesus Christ of Latter-Day Saints near Salt Lake City, promise better perspectives on wealth distributions from the colonial period until the onset of estate tax returns in the 1920s.

25. It would be interesting to explore the extent to which the rise in urban inequality was due to the influx of immigrants from other countries and from the U.S. countryside, thus paralleling the experiments we performed on the "foreign-born myth" at the national level. The data for doing so were not available at time of writing, however.

26. Lampman's modern estimates for 1922 are to be preferred, of course, but King (1927, p. 152) estimated a wealth distribution for 1921 from which it can be inferred that the top 1.4 percent of *persons* held 31.51 percent of total wealth. Lampman and King are remarkably close, it seems to us, and either estimate for the early 1920s implies the same mild upward drift in concentration following 1890.

27. Professor Lampman (1959, p. 388, note 14) was apparently in error when he rejected Holmes's estimate of the 1890 wealth concentration with the statement: "It is difficult to believe that wealth was actually that highly concentrated in 1890 in view of the 1921 and 1922 measures." This statement is apparently based on the mistaken impression that Spahr's (1896) allegation that the top 1 percent held 51 percent of 1890 wealth could be attributed to Holmes as well. On the contrary, Holmes's results are quite in line with Lampman's estimates.

28. In addition, the FTC sampled 540 estates of $1 million and over from New York, Philadelphia, and Chicago for 1918–23, using the earliest estate tax returns.

The data worksheets underlying the entire FTC income and wealth study are currently available in the Washington National Records Center in Suitland, Maryland. The 1912–23 probate sample has the file designation Tab 5 Cou 5. Our colleague Victor Goldberg has kindly sampled these files for us and reports that the counties sent varying details back to the FTC. While they all provided the size distributions the Commission requested, they did not provide the individual wealth data in all cases, and apparently there is no consistency in the degree of further detail volunteered by the county officers. Some gave the names of the decedents, some broke down wealth into asset categories, and so forth.

Scholars in serious pursuit of further historical wealth data should also consider two other potential sources in addition to the FTC data files. One is the Composition of Estates Survey of about 100,000 probated estates, collected by the WPA, but not analyzed by them because federal funds ran out (Mendershausen 1956, p. 279n). The other is an unsampled set of files at the National Bureau in New York marked "W. I. King data files," the existence of which was kindly reported to us by Geoffrey H. Moore of the Bureau.

29. We have a few time series of more limited scope, and they also give conflicting indications of trends across the late nineteenth century. The suggestion of a gentle rise in wealth inequality planted by Gallman's top 0.031 percent shares receives some slight support from the gentle rises in the Gini coefficients for Indiana real estate appraisals for 1870–1900 and for U.S. real estate mortgage values for 1880–89. On the other hand, Massachusetts probate and tax series fail to agree on any trend after 1860, and Soltow feels that wealth inequality in Wisconsin showed a net decline between 1860 and 1900 (1971b, pp. 11, 12). We cannot identify any trends between 1870 and World War I, either in these limited series or in the national wealth distributions available.

30. Using T. Paul Schultz's (1971) data on the log variance of 1950 incomes by age classes (males, aged 20 and above), we also computed the effect of the 1930–50 age distribution shift on *income* inequality. Whether one excludes those under 25, over 65, or both, the effect of age distribution changes is to *raise* income inequality. We conclude that the observed post-1929 equalization tends to understate the equalization of both life cycle income and wealth.

31. We are considering the *total* population of potential wealthholders, not those at or in retirement. If the latter age class were the sole focus, human capital would, of course, be irrelevant.

32. All of this assumes, of course, that human and conventional capital are equally fungible and perfect substitutes so that dollar values of both may be aggregated without further adjustment. Readers may wish to quarrel with that assumption.

33. While net rates of return for human and nonhuman wealth were roughly identical in 1929, the rates (with the sole exception of 1948) have diverged in favor of human capital since. The figures are reproduced below (Kendrick 1976, p. 240; 1974, p. 465):

|      | Human Capital | Nonhuman Capital |
|------|---------------|------------------|
| 1929 | 10.1%         | 10.0%            |
| 1937 | 9.6           | 8.9              |
| 1948 | 12.6          | 14.2             |
| 1953 | 14.8          | 11.4             |
| 1957 | 13.4          | 9.9              |
| 1960 | 12.9          | 9.2              |
| 1969 | 12.2          | 8.9              |

Elsewhere we have attempted to model the determinants of these rates of return (Williamson and Lindert 1978) and thus to emerge with a full analytical accounting of American twentieth-century distribution experience.

34. This argument implies that the covariance between human and nonhuman wealth holdings has weakened since 1929.

35. While Peter Drucker (1976, p. 12) and others have guessed that the inclusion of pension plans would result in a "distribution of total wealth [that] would probably turn out to be be very similar to . . . the distribution of personal income," no one to our knowledge has attempted for pensions a calculation like Feldstein's for social security. In any case, it is not clear how such an accounting would affect the post-1929 trends in income and wealth distribution. Lampman's (1962, table 97, p. 209) total wealth variant, upon which the trends in top shares are based, *includes* reserves of private pensions, although the 1962 Projector and Weiss estimates do not.

# References

Ahluwalia, Montek. 1976. "Inequality, Poverty, and Development." *Journal of Development Economics* 3:307–42.

Anderson, Terry L. 1975. "Wealth Estimates for the New England Colonies, 1650–1709." *Explorations in Economic History* 12:151–76.

Atkinson, A. B. 1970. "On the Measurement of Inequality." *Journal of Economic Theory* 2:244–63.

Atkinson, A. B., and A. J. Harrison. 1978. *The Distribution of Personal Wealth in Britain*. Cambridge: Cambridge University Press.

Ball, Duane E. 1976. "Dynamics of Population and Wealth in Eighteenth Century Chester County, Pennsylvania." *Journal of Interdisciplinary History* 6:621–44.

Barro, Robert J. 1977. "Social Security and Private Saving—Evidence from the U.S. Time Series." Mimeograph, Department of Economics, University of Rochester.

Bridenbaugh, Carl. 1955. *Cities in Revolt: Urban Life in America, 1743–1776*. New York: Knopf.

Clemens, Paul G. 1974. "From Tobacco to Grain: Economic Development on Maryland's Eastern Shore, 1660–1750." Ph.D. dissertation, Department of History, University of Wisconsin.

Daniels, Bruce. 1973/74. "Long Run Trends of Wealth Distribution in in 18th Century New England." *Explorations in Economic History* 11:123–36.

Denison, Edward F. 1962. *The Sources of Economic Growth in the United States*. New York: Committee for Economic Development.

Drucker, Peter F. 1976. "Pension Fund Socialism." *The Public Interest*, 42, pp. 1–14.

Feldstein, Martin. 1974. "Social Security, Induced Retirement, and Aggregate Capital Accumulation." *Journal of Political Economy* 82:905–26.

———. 1976. "Social Security and the Distribution of Wealth." *Journal of the American Statistical Association* 71:800–07.

Gallman, Robert E. 1969. "Trends in the Size Distribution of Wealth in the Nineteenth Century: Some Speculations," in Lee Soltow, ed., *Six Papers on the Size Distribution of Wealth and Income.* Studies in Income and Wealth 33. New York: National Bureau of Economic Research.

———. 1974. "Equality in America at the Time of Tocqueville." Unpublished paper, Department of Economics, University of North Carolina.

Henretta, James A. 1965. "Economic Development and Social Structure in Revolutionary Boston." *William and Mary Quarterly* 22:75–92.

Holmes, George K. 1893. "The Concentration of Wealth." *Political Science Quarterly* 8, no. 4, pp. 589–600.

Jones, A. H. 1970. "Wealth Estimates for the American Middle Colonies, 1774." *Economic Development and Cultural Change* 18, no. 4, part 2.

———. 1971. "Wealth Distribution in the American Middle Colonies in the Third Quarter of the Eighteenth Century." Paper read to the Organization of American Historians, New Orleans.

———. 1972. "Wealth Estimates for the New England Colonies about 1770." *Journal of Economic History* 32:98–127.

———. 1977a. *American Colonial Wealth: Documents and Methods.* New York: Arno Press.

———. 1977b, forthcoming. *Wealth of the Colonies on the Eve of the American Revolution.* New York: Columbia University Press.

Kendrick, John W. 1961. *Productivity Trends in the United States.* New York: National Bureau of Economic Research.

———. 1976. *The Formation and Stocks of Total Capital.* New York: National Bureau of Economic Research.

King, Willford I. 1915. *The Wealth and Income of the People of the United States.* New York: Macmillan.

———. 1927. "Wealth Distribution in the Continental United States at the Close of 1921." *Journal of the American Statistical Association,* 22, no. 158, pp. 135–53.

Koch, Donald W. 1969. "Income Distribution and Political Structure in Seventeenth Century Salem, Massachusetts." *Essex Institute Historical Collections* 105.

Kolodrubetz, Walter W. 1975. "Employee Benefit Plans, 1973." *Social Security Bulletin* 38:22–29.

Kulikoff, Allan. 1971. "The Progress of Inequality in Revolutionary Boston." *William and Mary Quarterly* 28:375–412.

Kuznets, Simon. 1953. *Shares of Upper Income Groups in Income and Savings.* New York: National Bureau of Economic Research.

————. 1955. "Economic Growth and Income Inequality." *American Economic Review* 45:1–28.

Lampman, Robert J. 1959. "Changes in the Share of Wealth Held By Top Wealthholders, 1922–1956." *Review of Economics and Statistics* 41, no. 4, pp. 379–92.

————. 1962. *The Share of Top Wealth-Holders in National Wealth, 1922–1956.* Princeton: Princeton University Press.

Lebergott, Stanley. 1976. "Are the Rich Getting Richer? Trends in U.S. Wealth Concentration." *Journal of Economic History* 36, no. 1, pp. 147–62.

Lemon, James T., and Gary B. Nash. 1968. "The Distribution of Wealth in Eighteenth Century America: A Century of Changes in Chester County, Pennsylvania, 1693–1802." *Journal of Social History* 2:1–24.

Lillard, Lee A. 1977. "Inequality: Earnings vs. Human Wealth." *American Economic Review* 67:42–53.

Lindert, P. H., and J. G. Williamson. 1976. "Three Centuries of American Inequality," in P. Uselding, ed., *Research In Economic History,* vol. 1. Greenwich, Conn.: Johnson Associates.

Lockridge, Kenneth A. 1970. *A New England Town the First Hundred Years: Dedham, Massachusetts, 1636–1736.* New York: Norton.

————. 1972. "Land, Population and the Evolution of New England Society, 1630–1790," S. N. Katz, ed., *Colonial America: Essays in Politics and Social Development.* Boston: Little, Brown.

Lydall, Harold, and James B. Lansing. 1959. "A Comparison of Distribution of Personal Income and Wealth in the United States and Great Britain." *American Economic Review* 49:43–67.

Main, Gloria. 1976. "Inequality in Early America: The Evidence of Probate Records from Massachusetts and Maryland." Paper presented to Cliometrics Conference, Madison, Wisc.

Main, Jackson T. 1965. *The Social Structure of Revolutionary America.* Princeton: Princeton University Press.

————. 1971. "Trends in Wealth Concentration Before 1860." *Journal of Economic History* 31:445–47.

————. 1976. "The Distribution of Property in Colonial Connecticut," in James Kirby, ed., *The Human Dimensions of Nation Making.* Madison, Wisc.: State Historical Society.

Massachusetts Bureau of Statistics of Labor. 1895. *Twenty-Fifth Annual Report.* Massachusetts Public Document 15, vol. 11. Boston: Wright and Potter.

Menard, Russell R. 1973. "Farm Prices of Maryland Tobacco, 1659–1710." *Maryland Historical Magazine* 68:80–85.

Menard, Russell R., P. M. G. Harris, and Lois G. Carr. 1974. "Opportunity and Inequality: The Distribution of Wealth on the Lower Western Shore of Maryland, 1638–1705." *Maryland Historical Magazine* 69:169–84.

Mendershausen, Horst. 1956. "The Pattern of Estate Tax Wealth," in R. W. Goldsmith, et al., *A Study of Saving in the United States,* vol. 3. Princeton: Princeton University Press.

Mereness, Newton D., ed. 1916. *Travels in the American Colonies.* New York: Macmillan.

Munnell, Alicia H. 1976. "Private Pensions and Saving: New Evidence." *Journal of Political Economy* 84:1013–32.

Nash, Gary B. 1976a. "Urban Wealth and Poverty in Pre-Revolutionary America." *Journal of Interdisciplinary History* 6:545–84.

———. 1976b. "Poverty and Poor Relief in Pre-Revolutionary Philadelphia." *William and Mary Quarterly* 33:3–30.

Paglin, Morton, 1975. "The Measurement and Trend of Inequality: A Basic Revision." *American Economic Review* 65:598–609.

Pessen, Edward. 1973. *Riches, Class and Power before the Civil War.* Lexington, Mass.: D. C. Heath.

Projector, Dorothy S., and Gertrude A. Weiss. 1966. *Survey of Financial Characteristics of Consumers.* Washington, D.C.: Federal Reserve Board.

Robinson, Sherman. 1976. "A Note on the U Hypothesis Relating Income Inequality and Economic Development." *American Economic Review* 66:437–40.

Schultz, T. Paul. 1971. "Long Term Change in Personal Income Distribution: Theoretical Approaches, Evidence and Explanations." Mimeograph, Rand, Santa Monica, Calif.

Schultz, Theodore W. 1961. "Education and Economic Growth," in N. B. Henry, ed., *Social Forces Influencing American Education.* Chicago: University of Chicago Press.

———. 1963. *The Economic Value of Education.* New York: Columbia University Press.

Shattuck, L. 1846. *Report to the Committee of the City Council Appointed to Obtain the Census of Boston for the Year 1845.* Reprint, New York: Arno Press, 1976.

Smith, Daniel S. 1973. "Population, Family, and Society in Hingham, Massachusetts, 1635–1880." Unpublished Ph.D dissertation, University of California, Berkeley.

———. 1975. "Underregistration and Bias in Probate Records: An Analysis of Data from Eighteenth-Century Hingham, Massachusetts." *William and Mary Quarterly* 32.

Smith, James D. 1974. "The Concentration of Personal Wealth in America, 1969." *Review of Income and Wealth*, series 20, no. 2.

Smith, James D., and Stephen D. Franklin. 1974. "The Concentration of Personal Wealth, 1922–1969." *American Economic Review* 64:162–167.

Soltow, Lee. 1969. "Evidence on Income Inequality in the United States, 1866–1965." *Journal of Economic History* 29: 279–86.

————. 1971a. "Economic Inequality in the United States in the Period from 1790 to 1860." *Journal of Economic History* 31:822–39.

————. 1971b. *Patterns of Wealthholding in Wisconsin since 1850.* Madison, Wisc.: University of Wisconsin Press.

————. 1975. *Men and Wealth in the United States, 1850–1870.* New Haven: Yale University Press.

Spahr, Charles B. 1896. *An Essay on the Present Distribution of Wealth in the United States.* New York: Crowell.

Thomas, Robert P., and Terry Anderson. 1973. "White Population, Labor Force, and the Extensive Growth of the New England Economy in the Seventeenth Century." *Journal of Economic History* 33:634–67.

Tocqueville, Alexis de. 1963. *Democracy in America.* New York: Knopf.

U.S. Bureau of the Census. 1976. *Historical Statistics of the United States, Colonial Times to 1970,* parts 1 and 2. Washington, D.C.: Government Printing Office.

U.S. Bureau of Labor Statistics. 1929. *History of Wages in the United States from Colonial Times to 1928.* Bulletin no. 604. Washington, D.C.: Government Printing Office.

U.S. Internal Revenue Service. 1967, 1973, 1976. *Statistics of Income, 1962, 1969, and 1972, Supplemental Reports. Personal Wealth Estimated from Estate Tax Returns.* Washington, D.C.: Government Printing Office.

Vinovskis, Maris A. 1972. "Mortality Rates and Trends in Massachusetts before 1860." *Journal of Economic History* 32:202–13.

Warden, Gerard B. 1976. "Inequality and Instability in Eighteenth-Century Boston: A Reappraisal." *Journal of Interdisciplinary History* 6:585–620.

Wells, Robert. 1975. *The Population of the British Colonies in America before 1776.* Princeton: Princeton University Press.

Williamson, Jeffrey G. 1977. "Strategic Wage Goods, Prices and Inequality." *American Economic Review* 67:29–41.

Williamson, Jeffrey G., and Peter H. Lindert. 1978, forthcoming. *American Inequality: A Macroeconomic History.*

Wright, Gavin. 1970. " 'Economic Democracy' and the Concentration of Agricultural Wealth in the Cotton South, 1850–1860." *Agricultural History* 44:63–93.

# 2　The Wealth of Testators and Its Distribution: Butler County, Ohio, 1803–65

William H. Newell

The paucity of data and the weakness of distribution theory have long kept economists out of the study of the distribution of wealth in nineteenth-century America. We have relied in this field largely on assiduous quotes from Tocqueville, sociological explanations of class formation and class conflict, and historical inferences from the nature of Jacksonian Democracy, the existence of a frontier safety valve, the blossoming of the Industrial Revolution, and the upheavals of the Civil War. Economists and social historians have now begun to tap two rich data sources which show promise of providing a solid empirical base from which to develop a clear picture of the distribution of wealth across time and regions. More intriguing is the prospect of using these data to test hypotheses about the sources of the observed variations in wealth and its distribution.

The first data base came with the rediscovery of the manuscript census schedules, providing wealth data for 1860 and 1870 (see esp. Soltow 1969, 1971), and providing the prospect of a delightful array of socioeconomic information on individuals whose wealth records can be successfully linked to the census. More recently, probate records have gained recognition by scholars as a source of wealth data covering most of the nineteenth century in the Midwest and extending well into the eighteenth century and even earlier in New England (see, e.g., G. Main

William H. Newell is associate professor in the School of Interdisciplinary Studies, Miami University, Oxford, Ohio.

Much of the data underlying this study were collected by Alex Echols, Keith Johnson, Rebecca Kennard, Debra Kocar, Anastasia Peterson, and Christine Pryately under a grant from the National Science Foundation (SOS-07995). Supplementary data were collected by Peter Mehas. Esther Benzing, Butler County Archivist, provided innumerable hours of assistance over a two-year period, as well as extra-ordinary access to archival materials.

1976; J. Main 1976; and Menard 1974). This study combines the full range of available county archival data with the manuscript censuses of 1850 and 1860 to examine the wealth of testators in Butler County, Ohio, from its organization in 1803 through the Civil War. Probate data were collected on all 1,151 decedents whose wills were filed in the county during this period, although only testators dying after 1850 could be linked to the census.

Each of these sources has its drawbacks, of course. As provocative as census studies of nineteenth-century wealth and wealth distributions are, they leave one curious about the other ninety-eight years not covered by the 1860 and 1870 censuses. And in the absence of checks of census data against other wealth information, one wonders if the former director of the Bureau of the Census, Francis Walker, was really unjustified in removing wealth questions from the 1880 census.

Probate records of estate inventories may provide an accurate picture of the personal property of decedents, but decedents have a peculiar age distribution which makes unclear the relevance of their wealth distribution for the younger live population. Jackson Main (1976) has attempted to adjust the wealth distribution of decedents to give a better reflection of the age composition of the live population, but the dubious quality of mortality data renders this procedure more suggestive than definitive. A study such as the present one, which is further restricted to testators (or those leaving wills), has even greater problems of generalizability. These problems are discussed at more length in part 2.4.

An even more serious problem with antebellum probate records outside of New England is that they generally cover personal property but not real property. Less than half a dozen of the 1,151 testators in this study had the value of their real property included in testamentary records. The task of wading through volumes of inventory and testamentary records (or worse, through individual estate papers) is sufficiently tedious to make it tempting to restrict one's attention to personal property. In a predominantly agricultural society, however, real property can be expected to form a substantial portion of wealth; indeed, as late as 1860 the census lists real property in Butler County as eighty percent of total wealth.

It is understandable that scholars have resisted entry into deed records and tax duplicates in search of individual holdings of real property. In Butler County, at least, land transfers from decedent to heir are never recorded in the deed records at all, leaving determination of individual landholdings and their value at any one point in time to a complicated process described in appendix 1. This study gleans information on real property from tax duplicates in the county archives and from deed records and township deed indexes in the county recorder's office. The time requirements for determining wealth in real property are an order of magnitude more than for that in personal property. As dismal as the prospect may be, there appears to be no alternative to building up local studies of the distribution of real as well as personal property, for it is on such studies that we must ultimately construct a national picture for the decades prior to the 1860 census and eventually test the accuracy of the wealth declarations in the 1860 and 1870 censuses.

The study is limited to testators, instead of including all decedents, for several reasons. First, the date of death cannot be estimated for most intestators, and county death records (which provide date of death) are available only for 1856 and 1857. The date the will was filed provides a good proxy of date of death for testators: comparison with actual dates of death in the 1856–57 records reveals that wills were filed an average of less than a month after death. The names of legatees mentioned in the will also prove valuable in identifying some landholdings of the testator, and in linking the testator to the census (see appendix 1). Finally, a focus on testators should permit the study to capture most wealthy decedents without gathering data on all decedents: testators are generally conceded to be more wealthy on the average than decedents in general (G. Main 1976). However sound the reasons for limiting the sample to testators, there are substantial difficulties in generalizing the findings of this study, even to all wealthholders in Butler County through the Civil War. These difficulties are discussed in part 2.4.

Butler County proved a fruitful choice for a local study of wealth. Complete sets of records of wills, land transactions, tax duplicates, inventory records, and testamentary records are available from the day the county was organized, and in the case of some wills and land transactions, even earlier. Consequently the distribution of wealth can be traced from frontier to mature settlement. Butler County contains two small manufacturing centers, the cities of Hamilton and Middletown, which boasted combined populations of over 9,000 in 1860, and which allow urban effects to be disentangled from the effects of rural settlement. Too many studies of wealth in the nineteenth century have been exclusively urban (often of large cities) for a country which was predominantly rural and agricultural (see Pessen 1973, and Soltow 1975). And much of the use of county records for wealth studies has been confined to East Coast communities prior to the nineteenth century. This study seeks to redress the balance.

## 2.1  Overview of Testator Wealth and Its Distribution

### 2.1.1  The Data

Included within personal property are the assessed value of household inventory, debts receivable, and debts payable. Sale value is used when inventory was not recorded. Sale value is a less desirable measure than inventory for two reasons. First, inventories were assessed promptly after the death of the decedent, averaging six months after the will was filed, while sales might not take place until years later, especially if the will was contested. Second, inventories were meticulous in their coverage, down to separate itemization of cracked drinking glasses, while sales excluded items earmarked in the will for specific legatees. In spite of the difficulties with sale value as a proxy for inventory, a comparison of inventory and sale when both are available for a testator shows that the discrepancy between them averages between two and three percent. Both sale and inventory also include the contents of wholly owned retail stores, as well as the cattle, implements, and seed stores of farms.

Debts receivable include stocks and bonds as well as cash lent to individuals. "Desperate debts" as bad debts were termed are excluded from debts receivable. In most cases the judgment about the probability of repayment was recorded by the executor. In a few instances debts judged collectible by the executors were excluded because subsequent entries in the testamentary records proved otherwise. Debts payable include all legally binding financial obligations of the testator at the time of death. Excluded are all funeral expenses, even though they may have been stipulated in the will, and all expenses incurred in the settlement of the estate.

Real property includes the value of all township land, out-lots and in-lots owned by the testator at death. It also includes the value of all buildings on that land. The attempt was made to determine the value of real property at the time of death (see appendix 1 for procedure). Real property owned outside the county is not included unless it happened to be valued in the testamentary record.

Data on personal property were found for two-thirds of the testators, and real property was found for a similar percentage. These figures probably understate the coverage of the data. While data on both real and personal property are undoubtedly missing for a number of testators, only rarely, for example, was real property mentioned in the will but not found in the land records, and all of these cases occur in wills filed before 1820. In some of those cases, the will was written several years before the death of the testator, leaving open the possibility that the land was sold before the death of the testator. Some of the testators for whom personal property data are unavailable were women whose wills specified the distribution only of items such as bed, bedding, or favorite dress, items with more sentimental than market value. The decision was made to assume that a testator had no real or personal property if none was found, rather than deleting the observation or replacing it with some mean value. Still, legal records of the time were demonstrably incomplete, and there is no doubt that the coverage of wealth is incomplete and that the mean wealth of testators is understated as a result.

Even more disconcerting is the possibility that improved coverage over time might have the effect of overstating the growth in wealth. Luckily, an examination of the data for 1803–19 lays at least that fear to rest. Personal property data for this earliest period are available for 81 percent, more than the average of 67 percent for the entire sixty-three years. Real property was found for 64 percent of the testators between 1803 and 1819, quite comparable to the 66 percent found for the study as a whole.

Current dollar wealth was converted to constant 1967 dollars using the Bureau of Labor Statistics Consumer Price Index. Because the value of real property was often estimated using data a few years removed from the date of death of the decedent, the deflator was constructed by passing a three-year moving average through the price index.

### 2.1.2 Overall Trends in Wealth and Its Distribution

Figure 2.1 shows that testator wealth grew rapidly during the antebellum decades. After an initial decline from 1803–19 to 1820–29, constant dollar wealth grew rapidly and relatively steadily to 1860–65, nearly quadrupling in four decades.

Figure 2.2 shows that most of the period of rapid growth in mean wealth was characterized by high and increasing inequality in the distribution of that wealth. The measure of inequality employed in this study is the proportion of testators who own the top fifty percent of all testator wealth. In the absence of any straightforward comparison between the wealth distribution of testators and the wealth distribution of the county's wealthholders, it seems appropriate to forego inequality measures (which might be misconstrued as applying to the total population) in favor of a measure best suited to the distributions under analysis. The choice of the cutoff between the wealthy (testators owning the top fifty percent of the wealth) and the nonwealthy was determined pragmatically by the need for enough observations on the wealthy to allow statistically significant comparisons of the characteristics of the two groups.

Initially inequality moved in the opposite direction from wealth. The decline in wealth from 1803–19 to 1820–29 was accompanied by an increase in inequality, as a smaller proportion of testators owned the top half of testator wealth. And the return of wealth in 1830–39 to the level of 1803–19 was accompanied by a reduction in inequality, with the proportion of testators owning the top fifty percent increasing to over sixteen percent. After the 1830s, however, wealth and inequality moved sharply and steadily in the same direction. While constant dollar wealth

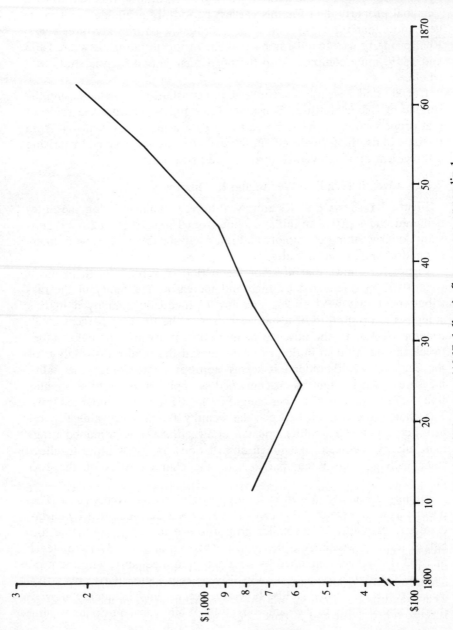

**Fig. 2.1**  Mean Wealth of Testators (1967 dollars). Source: see appendix 1.

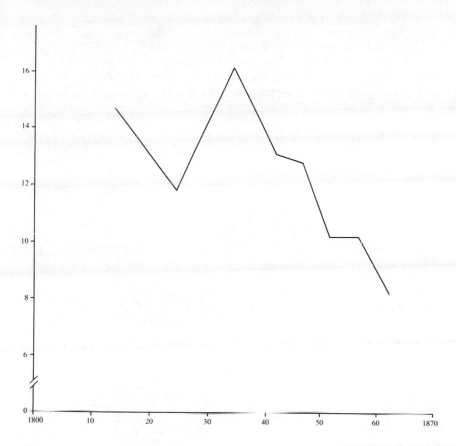

**Fig. 2.2**            Percent of Testators Owning Top 50% of Wealth, 1803–65.
                        Source: see appendix 1.

nearly tripled between 1830–39 and 1860–65, inequality doubled, the proportion of testators owning the top fifty percent falling from just over sixteen percent to just over eight percent.

Each of these trends, the growth in wealth and the growth in inequality, merits explanation in its own right. Beyond the interest inherent in the individual trends, it would be interesting to discover if the two are related. One might conjecture, for example, that the industrialization of the urban areas of the county was responsible for both trends, or that increasing concentration of land under a few large, efficient farms produced more wealth even as it concentrated that wealth in fewer hands. The rest of this study focuses on the underlying sources of the trends in wealth and its distribution, and the relationship between the two trends is reexamined at the end of part 2.3.

## 2.2    The Sources of the Growth in Wealth

Figure 2.3 sets out the relative importance of real and personal property in explaining the growth in wealth. Both real and personal property grow rapidly up to the 1840s, whereupon real property continues to grow at a rapid pace while personal property grows more slowly and then

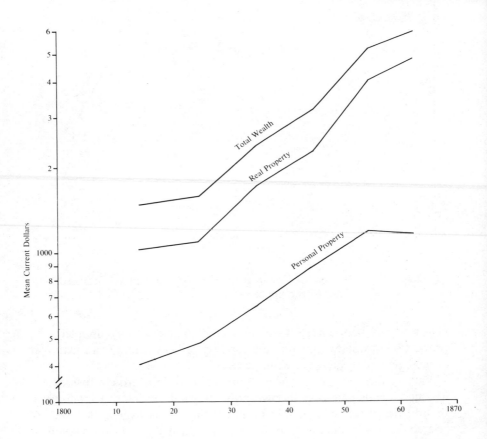

**Fig. 2.3**            Wealth and Its Components. Source: see appendix 1.

levels off. But the growth in wealth, especially the rapid growth after 1830, is dominated by growth in real property, which constitutes a high proportion of wealth, between 60 and 70 percent depending on the decade. While real property is responsible for most of the growth in wealth, personal property at least contributes to that growth up through the 1850s.

Figure 2.4 displays the relative importance of the components of personal property in explaining its growth. Inventories and debts receivable take turns dominating the trend in personal property. Overall, debts receivable grow much more than inventories, raising the question of whether the growth in wealth might be partly attributable to growing ownership of stocks and bonds, and thus to nonagricultural economic

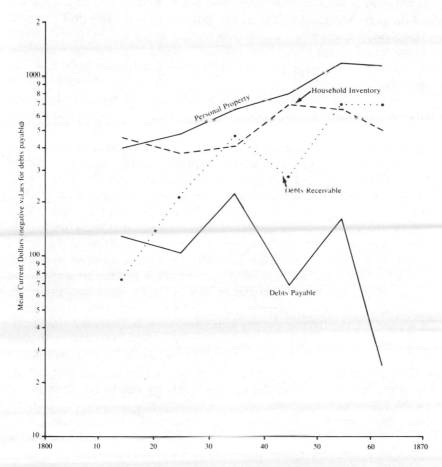

**Fig. 2.4**    Personal Property and Its Components. Source: see appendix 1.

growth. However, that argument appears weak. Personal property accounts for only 30 to 40 percent of wealth, and inventories dominate its trend at least as much as debts receivable. More importantly, the period of most rapid growth in debts receivable ends in the 1830s, when wealth has succeeded only in recovering its 1803–19 level and its important growth is yet to occur. More likely, the growing debts receivable of the wealthy reflect the financial problems in the county in the 1820s.

A more promising hypothesis is that the source of the growth in wealth is the same as those for real property. Figure 2.5 shows that the growth in value of real property results entirely from increases in land prices and not from any increase in the acreage held by testators. In fact, median (and mean) farm size of testators fell by roughly a third from 1803–19 to 1860–65. Appendix 1 describes how land prices were determined. The conclusion is not new that rising land prices were responsible for much of the growth in rural wealth on the frontier. Paul Gates (1960) argued that "the pioneer farmer was well aware that in the end his profits would come largely from rising land values." Indeed, Gates argued that for states such as Ohio the growth in land values continued its importance into the 1860s.

The source of rising land prices is not immediately apparent, however. If Gates is correct for Ohio, then we must expect to look beyond the explanation that probably first comes to mind, namely that land prices grew because the products grown on the land increased in value. To test the hypothesis, crop production and improved acreage figures for Butler County were gathered from the agricultural censuses of 1840, 1850, 1860, and 1870, and the production figures were aggregated using 1861 prices. (See appendix 2 for details.) The resulting constant dollar land productivity indexes were combined with a wholesale price series to construct a current dollar land productivity series. This current dollar series is compared with current dollar land prices in figure 2.6. Land productivity did grow on balance between 1840 and 1865, but the growth was an order of magnitude less than the growth in land prices: land prices increased at around six percent per year, while land productivity grew between 0.5 and 0.6 percent per year. And while land prices grew steadily, productivity fell almost as much between 1840 and 1850 as it grew between 1850 and 1860. The pattern of productivity growth does not fit the steady growth in land prices which we wish to explain. What little land productivity increase did exist was entirely due to increases in the wholesale price index: real land productivity was virtually constant. At best, then, growth in the value of the products of the land made a weak and uneven contribution to the growth in land prices, and thus to the growth in real property and ultimately to the growth in wealth.

The search for the source of the increase in land prices may be clarified by viewing farms as purely competitive firms and by making explicit reference to the theory of the firm. Land is a factor of production whose value should be derived from the value of the agricultural products grown on it. If we start with firms in equilibrium, the demand for (and thus the price of) land should grow if average costs of farm operation fall or average revenue rises, both from old firms increasing production and from new firms entering the market in response to increasing profits.

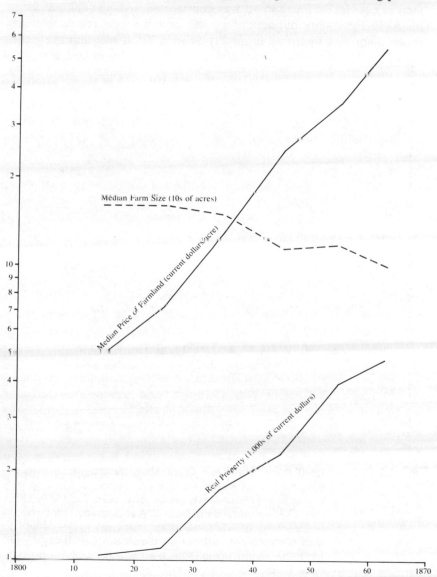

**Fig. 2.5**    Real Property, Price of Farmland, and Median Farm Size.
Source: see appendix 1.

The slow and uneven growth in wholesale prices shown in figure 2.6 largely eliminates increases in average revenue as the source of growth in land prices. And the constant productivity of land eliminates most possibilities for reductions in average costs.

It is still conceivable, though, that decreases in transportation costs might have reduced average costs and brought about some increase in land prices. Indeed, a railroad was constructed and a canal was completed in the county during this period, and it seems reasonable that roads might have improved in quality as well. Yet it seems unlikely that

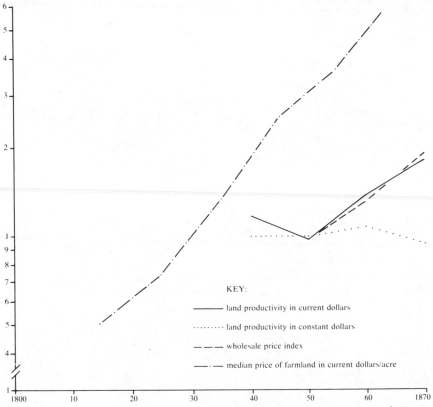

KEY:

————— land productivity in current dollars

·········· land productivity in constant dollars

— — — wholesale price index

—·— median price of farmland in current dollars/acre

**Fig. 2.6**    Land Prices and Land Productivity. Source: land prices—deed records of Butler County (see appendix 1); crop output—see appendix 2; wholesale price index for 1840, 1850, and 1860—constructed from 3-year average (centered on census year) of wholesale price index (of prices identified with northern agriculture) for Cincinnati (see Berry 1943); for 1870—constructed from Warren and Pearson wholesale price index (see *Historical Statistics of the United States* 1975) and Berry (1943). Crop output in current dollars is the product of price index and crop output in constant dollars.

transportation costs were initially high enough and fell fast enough to account for much of the growth in land prices. The next county south of Butler County is Hamilton County which contains Cincinnati. A wagonload of produce could reach Cincinnati from almost anywhere in the county in one day, and a farmer could deliver a load from almost anywhere in the county to the city of Hamilton and return home in the same day. Hamilton had inexpensive water transportation to Cincinnati via the Great Miami River from early on. Thus it seems implausible that any reduction in transportation costs could have been great enough to have had a substantial impact on land prices. Nonetheless, good data on transportation costs in the county are not available, and the impact of transportation costs on land prices must remain conjectural.

If average costs do not appear to have fallen or average revenues to have risen enough to account for the increase in land prices, and if there is no reason to believe that growing nonagricultural uses of farmland bid up its price, then there remains the possibility that the initial assumption of equilibrium was incorrect. If farmers enjoyed economic profits throughout the period, and barriers to entry were low, then we could expect the price of land to be bid up. Indeed, Bateman and Atack (1978) make the argument that Ohio farmers enjoyed substantial economic profits in 1860. In the absence of data series needed to measure farm profits, figure 2.7 provides an indirect approach to the question. In a largely agrarian county, the growth of the male labor force may be a crude proxy for the growth in entrepreneurs who are potential farm owners. The substantial growth in males aged 15 to 69 lends at least some credence to the conjecture that farmers enjoyed economic profits which attracted other entrepreneurs, and that the growth in land prices was the consequence of the growing demand of entrepreneurs for land.

The proportion of land area held in farms, which is also included in figure 2.7, allows us to construct the following plausible scenario. When the county was formed in 1803 it was largely unsettled frontier. Agricultural entrepreneurs moved rapidly in response to cheap land and high profits. In a couple of decades most of the good agricultural land was in farms. Because economic profits persisted, entrepreneurs continued to come into the county, bringing marginal lands into farms and bidding up the price of land. What is disconcerting about this scenario is that entrepreneurs continued to come into the county and bid up land prices for several decades after all available land was in farms. One wonders how long economic profits could persist in the face of the ever-increasing cost of purchasing a farm: at some point, increasing land prices should have caused new entrepreneurs to expect no more than normal profits. Of course, farming represented a way of life as well as a business, and it is possible that migrants continued to enter the county after all the available land was in farms because they sought the noneconomic amenities

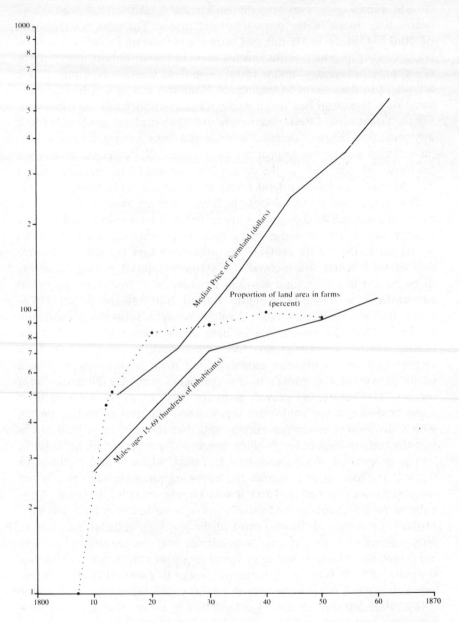

**Fig. 2.7**     Male Labor Force, Land Use, and Land Prices. Sources:
Males—U.S. census of population for 1810, 1830, 1840,
1850, 1860; land area—U.S. Census of Agriculture for
1840, 1850, Butler County tax duplicates for 1807, 1812,
1813, 1820; price—see appendix 1.

of that lifestyle. To purchase land after all available land was under farms, they would have to secure it from other farmers, which might account for the declining average farm size observed in figure 2.5. The large number of land transactions of many testators supports this picture of farmer-speculators reaping capital gains from their land. Whatever the eventual profitability of raising crops, it seems reasonable to hypothesize that the growing number of agricultural entrepreneurs entering the county in search of farmland and bidding up the price of land was what contributed to the growing wealth of testators.

## 2.3   The Distribution of Wealth

### 2.3.1   The Contribution of Testator Characteristics to Differences in Wealth

Table 2.1 sets out the mean wealth of testators for a number of standard socioeconomic characteristics. Data on the sex, place of residence, literacy, and number of surviving children come from probate records which are available for all testators. Age, occupation, and place of birth come from the census, however, and these data are available only for testators dying after mid-1850. Because wills did not always specify the residence of the testators, and testators often owned more than one tract of land, we have occasionally supplemented the probate and deed records by the census to determine place of residence. The measure of literacy used is signature literacy, determined by whether the testator signed or x-ed the will. This measure has the difficulty that some testators may have been literate but physically unable to sign their name at the time the will was written. The judgment was made to use this measure, however defective, for testators dying after 1850, in place of the declared literacy available from the census: signature literacy yields a literacy rate of around 75 percent in 1850, whereas the declared literacy rate of all Butler County adults in the 1850 census is an unlikely 96 percent. The number of surviving children is determined by the number of children mentioned in the will. A comparison of children mentioned in the will with children listed in the genealogies available at the Butler County Historical Society found that every will tested listed all children still living at the date the will was written. The complete coverage of children in the will is not surprising: children were legal heirs, and any legal heir not granted at least one dollar could contest the will. Age actually refers to the testator's age when the will was filed, and it is computed from the testator's declared age in the census. County death records available for 1856 and 1857 reveal that wills were filed an average of less than a month after the death of the testator and none of the wills was filed more than three months after death, making age at the filing of the will a good estimate of age at death. Only about 56 percent of the testators filing wills after mid-1850 were successfully linked to the censuses of 1850 or 1860. The biases introduced by incomplete linkage are unclear, but the data on age, occupation, and place of birth should still be viewed with special caution.

**Table 2.1**    **Mean Wealth of Testators (in tens of 1967 dollars; number of testators in parentheses)**

|  | 1803–29 | | 1830–59 | | 1860–65 | | 1803–65 | |
|---|---|---|---|---|---|---|---|---|
| *Sex* | | | | | | | | |
| Male | 70 | (231) | 122 | (604) | 232 | (151) | 127 | (986) |
| Female | 29 | (18) | 28 | (114) | 112 | (33) | 45 | (165) |
| *Urbanization* | | | | | | | | |
| Nonurban | 66 | (243) | 105 | (665) | 224 | (136) | 111 | (1044) |
| Rural | 66 | (240) | 108 | (616) | 175 | (115) | 105 | (971) |
| Towns | 113 | (3) | 65 | (49) | 496 | (21) | 191 | (73) |
| Urban | 106 | (6) | 138 | (53) | 170 | (48) | 151 | (107) |
| *Literacy* | | | | | | | | |
| Literate | 77 | (174) | 123 | (535) | 238 | (137) | 132 | (846) |
| Illiterate | 42 | (69) | 61 | (169) | 130 | (40) | 66 | (278) |
| *Occupation* | | | | | | | | |
| Farmer | | | 213 | (92) | 300 | (38) | 238 | (130) |
| Prof/Major prop | | | 289 | (9) | 345 | (9) | 317 | (18) |
| Other | | | 283 | (16) | 199 | (17) | 240 | (33) |
| None | | | 73 | (51) | 122 | (26) | 90 | (77) |
| *Place of birth* | | | | | | | | |
| Foreign | | | 175 | (17) | 201 | (20) | 189 | (37) |
| Native | | | 182 | (149) | 247 | (69) | 203 | (218) |
| Middle Atlantic | | | 188 | (78) | 316 | (35) | 228 | (113) |
| Ohio | | | 301 | (17) | 179 | (20) | 235 | (37) |
| Tidewater | | | 114 | (33) | 245 | (9) | 147 | (42) |
| Other | | | 150 | (21) | 134 | (5) | 140 | (26) |
| *No. of children* | | | | | | | | |
| 0 | 23 | (32) | 44 | (158) | 100 | (65) | 56 | (255) |
| 1 | 61 | (16) | 67 | (51) | 158 | (17) | 84 | (84) |
| 2–3 | 51 | (41) | 139 | (114) | 195 | (34) | 130 | (189) |
| 4–5 | 69 | (43) | 140 | (117) | 329 | (32) | 155 | (192) |
| 6–7 | 77 | (42) | 125 | (101) | 374 | (15) | 136 | (158) |
| 8+ | 108 | (56) | 139 | (114) | 534 | (9) | 149 | (179) |
| *Age* | | | | | | | | |
| 20–39 | | | 349 | (12) | 154 | (13) | 248 | (25) |
| 40–49 | | | 114 | (11) | 60 | (10) | 88 | (21) |
| 50–59 | | | 187 | (31) | 243 | (13) | 204 | (44) |
| 60–69 | | | 208 | (41) | 227 | (25) | 215 | (66) |
| 70+ | | | 146 | (73) | 322 | (30) | 197 | (103) |

*Source*: See appendix 1.

Men were considerably more wealthy than women, with differences which are significant at least at the .01 level (using a standard two-tailed $t$-test) for all three periods. Women failed completely to share in the growth in wealth between 1803–29 and 1830–59, and their rapid gains by 1860–65 still left them with less than half the mean wealth of men. The lack of growth in women's wealth in the antebellum decades raises the possibility that women may have held more of their wealth in household inventories and less in real property than men, because real property accounted for most of the growth in wealth during those decades. In fact, women held only 41 percent of their wealth in real property, compared with 69 percent for men.

Testators living in rural areas were significantly less wealthy (at the .0001 level) than testators living in small towns and cities. The difference is not significant in the first two periods, however, perhaps because the observations on nonrural testators are so limited. A few unusually wealthy testators account for the high mean wealth of small town testators in 1860–65. Overall, nonurban wealth grew much faster than urban wealth, partly from those unusually wealthy small town testators in 1860–65, but mostly from growth in the price of farmland. If we combine small towns and cities into nonrural areas, mean nonrural wealth remained constant between 1803–29 and 1830–59 and then grew more than 2.5 times between 1830–59 and 1860–65, reaching a mean wealth which was significantly higher (at the .0001 level) than the mean wealth of rural areas.

Testators with more surviving children tended to own more wealth. Testators with two or more children, for example, were significantly more wealthy (at the .0001 level) than testators with no or only one child, and the differences remain as significant for all three periods. The correlations of number of children with wealth (.15) and logwealth (.27) are also significant at the .0001 level. While it is easy to conjecture ways in which literacy (or education) might have contributed to wealth, it is less obvious why testators with larger families were more wealthy. Several explanations are available: (1) wealthier testators may have been able to afford more children; (2) they may have had more land which children might help farm; (3) relatively poor testators might not have been able to afford even to get married; (4) the children of wealthier parents may have enjoyed lower mortality rates, and thus been more likely to be alive when the will was written; or (5) wealthier parents may have been healthier, and enjoyed higher fecundity. All these explanations assume that the direction of causation was from wealth to children, with the possible exception of (2), where the direction of causation is unclear.

Differences between the wealth of literate and illiterate testators are highly significant (at the .0001 level) for all three time periods. Literate

testators remained roughly twice as wealthy as illiterate testators throughout the study.

The wealth of the different age groups did not follow the pattern one
would expect from a life cycle model of accumulation, deaccumulation,
and bequest, although the small number of observations available on
each age group makes any generalizations tentative. From such a model
one would expect average wealth to rise steadily from entry into the labor
force to the middle earning years and then stabilize until withdrawal
from the labor force caused it to decline slowly (Gallman 1974). The
timing of bequests to the next generation may complicate the picture,
but the general pattern should remain intact. The data depart from the
expected pattern for testators in their twenties and thirties when average
wealth is higher than predicted, and for testators in their forties when
wealth is lower than predicted. It turns out that the unexpectedly high
mean wealth for the youngest group of testators has a much higher
standard error (of $101 for a mean of $248) than for the other age
groups, produced by a couple of extremely wealthy young testators in
1850–59. But the mean wealth of the youngest testators was still over
twice as great as for the forty-year-olds in 1860–65, when the standard
error is within the normal range. Conceivably the overstatement of
wealth for the youngest testators was combined with some unusual situation at a critical point in the wealth accumulation of the cohort of testators who were in their forties in the 1860s which restricted their opportunities to accumulate wealth. After all, the life cycle model refers
to the wealth profile of individuals over time, and not to the wealth profile of a group at a point in time. Still, if this cohort explanation holds,
then testators in their thirties in the 1850s should have had much less
wealth then testators in their forties in the 1850s. Even after allowing
for the large standard error of the mean wealth of the young testators in
the 1850s, the data do not support this interpretation. Still, the numbers
of observations are few, the sample possibly biased by incomplete linkage with the census, and the results inconclusive. Yet it seems reasonable
to conclude that the data do raise some questions about the validity of
the life cycle model of wealth accumulation for Butler County in the
antebellum decades and the Civil War.

The only significant occupational differences in wealth were between
the relatively poor testators who were not in the labor force and the
wealthier labor force participants. These differences are significant for
both periods at the .01 level or better. Three distinct groups comprise
the category of testators not in the labor force. A little over half (57%)
are seventy years of age or more and presumably retired. Just under
half (49%) are females, who are presumed by the census to be not in
the labor force as long as they live with an adult male. After allowing
for overlap in these two groups, 13 percent remain who are males under

seventy but not in the labor force. None have sufficient wealth to qualify as wealthy; indeed, a majority of them possess scant wealth. Almost half are sixty years of age or more and may be retired as well. In short, few of them are independently wealthy members of a leisure class: only one testator listed his occupation with the census taker as "gentleman." The low wealth of women tends to depress the mean wealth of the not-in-the-labor-force category, but the high mean wealth of testators aged seventy and older would lead one to expect a higher average wealth than actually obtains for testators not in the labor force. It may be that the ability of the elderly to achieve relatively high mean wealth was partly a reflection of the ability of most of them to continue to generate income late in life.

It comes as no surprise that some of the wealthiest testators were found among professionals and major proprietors. Lawyers and owners of major businesses could be expected to accumulate more wealth than testators in other occupations, but beyond that, the professions have long attracted those already wealthy. While farmers had the same mean wealth overall as other nonprofessional members of the labor force, their wealth grew more rapidly between 1850–59 and 1860–65 than either of the other labor force groups. The more rapid growth of farmers' wealth probably represents their relatively large investment in real property which grew rapidly in value.

Native-born testators averaged more wealth than their foreign-born counterparts, as one might expect, but the differences remained small and insignificant. Among the native born, testators originating from the Middle Atlantic states (especially New York and Pennsylvania) and Ohio enjoyed significantly more wealth (at the .03 level or better) than those from the Tidewater or other states.

It remains unclear from the preceding analysis which characteristics of testators have a direct association with wealth, and which are merely associated with those causally related to wealth. It might be the case, for example, that the apparent relationship between literacy and wealth is only the result of a real connection between sex and wealth, and a greater tendency for males to be literate than for females. The independent links between testator characteristics and wealth were tested using multiple regression analysis. Number of children, age, and dummy variables for sex, literacy, place of residence (rural/nonrural), labor force participation, occupation (farmer/nonfarmer), and place of birth (native/foreign born) were all entered as explanatory variables of wealth. Wealth is measured in logarithms because of the skewness of its distribution.

No matter what other variables were entered into the analysis, or the order in which they were entered, sex, literacy, and number of children were the only testator characteristics which were significantly related to (log) wealth at the .05 level or better. The following regression equation isolates the significant variables. (standard errors are in parentheses):

$$\text{Logwealth} = 2.27 + 1.68 \text{ Male} + 0.18 \text{ Children} + 0.50 \text{ Literate}$$
$$\qquad\qquad\quad (0.23) \qquad\quad (0.02) \qquad\qquad (0.18)$$

$$R^2 = .13 \qquad N = 1032$$

All three independent variables are significant at better than the .01 level. Standardized regression coefficients are .22 for children and males, and .08 for the literate, showing that the relationship of literacy and wealth is weaker than the relationship of wealth with either number of children or sex.

Logwealth also has zero-order correlations with labor force participation ($r = .31$) and farmers ($r = .28$) which are significant at the .0001 level. Each variable loses its significance when sex is included in the regression. Labor force participation is correlated with wealth because men predominated in the labor force and women formed half of the non-participants, and men had significantly more wealth than women: the correlation between males and labor force participation is .56. Similarly, the correlation between farmer and male is .40: males are relatively numerous among farmers while women are relatively frequent among the other occupations. The other variables do not even have a significant zero-order correlation with wealth.

### 2.3.2   Changes in Testator Characteristics and the Growth in Inequality

If some characteristics of testators change substantially during the decades covered by this study, and those characteristics are strongly linked to wealth, then changes in the characteristics of testators might account for some of the growth in inequality in the distribution of the wealth of testators. Table 2.2 sets out the frequency of each testator characteristic for 1803–65 and three subperiods. Age, occupation, and place of birth, of course, are available only for the years after 1850. Focusing our attention on the variables significantly linked with wealth, we find that changes in the sex composition and the relative number of children show some promise of contributing to the explanation of the growth in inequality. Literacy, which is less strongly associated with wealth, maintains fairly constant proportions, and cannot be expected to contribute to growing inequality. Sex and number of children show promise because the relatively poor females and testators with few children grow in relative numbers, increasing the proportion of testators at the bottom of the wealth distribution.

Tables 2.3 and 2.4 assess the quantitative importance of structural changes in the characteristics of testators. Essentially these tables are exercises in counterfactual history, asking, for example, how much the proportion of wealthy individuals (those owning the top 50 percent of the wealth) would have changed if the only other change had been in the proportion of men and women. If we assume that the proportion of females who are wealthy and that of males who are wealthy remain constant at their 1803–65 average level, then we can use the relative proportions of males to females in 1803–29 to compute what the wealth distribution would have been in 1803–29. Similarly, we can compute what

**Table 2.2**        **Characteristics of Testators (%)**

| | 1803–29 | 1830–59* | 1860–65 | 1803–65** |
|---|---|---|---|---|
| *Urbanization* | | | | |
| Nonurban | 98 | 93 | 74 | 91 |
|   Rural | 96 | 86 | 62 | 84 |
|   Towns | 1 | 7 | 11 | 6 |
| Urban | 2 | 7 | 26 | 9 |
| *Sex* | | | | |
| Male | 93 | 84 | 82 | 86 |
| Female | 7 | 16 | 18 | 14 |
| *Literacy* | | | | |
| Literate | 72 | 76 | 77 | 75 |
| Illiterate | 28 | 24 | 23 | 25 |
| *Age* | | | | |
| 20–39 | | 7 | 14 | 10 |
| 40–49 | | 7 | 11 | 8 |
| 50–59 | | 18 | 14 | 17 |
| 60–69 | | 24 | 27 | 25 |
| 70+ | | 43 | 33 | 40 |
| *Occupation* | | | | |
| Farmer | | 55 | 42 | 50 |
| Prof/Major prop | | 5 | 10 | 7 |
| Other | | 10 | 19 | 13 |
| None | | 30 | 29 | 30 |
| *Place of birth* | | | | |
| Foreign | | 10 | 22 | 15 |
| Native | | 90 | 78 | 85 |
|   Middle Atlantic | | 47 | 39 | 44 |
|   Ohio | | 10 | 22 | 15 |
|   Tidewater | | 20 | 10 | 16 |
|   Other | | 13 | 6 | 10 |
| *No. of children* | | | | |
| 0 | 14 | 24 | 38 | 24 |
| 1 | 7 | 8 | 10 | 8 |
| 2–3 | 18 | 17 | 20 | 18 |
| 4–5 | 19 | 18 | 19 | 18 |
| 6–7 | 18 | 15 | 9 | 15 |
| 8+ | 24 | 17 | 5 | 17 |

*Source*: See appendix 1.
  *1850–59 for age, occupation, and place of birth.
**1850–65 for age, occupation, and place of birth.

**Table 2.3    Testator Contributions to Decline in Equality, 1803–29 to 1860–65**

| | 1803–65 | 1803–29 | | 1860–65 | | | 1803–29/ 1860–65 | |
| | (1) Actual % Wealthy | (2) Actual % Testators | (3) Predicted % Wealthy | (4) Actual % Testators | (5) Predicted % Wealthy | (6) Predicted Amount Change | (7) Predicted Percent Change | (8) Predicted/ Actual (%) |
|---|---|---|---|---|---|---|---|---|
| *Sex* | | 100% | 10.304% | | 9.288% | 1.016 | 9.86 | 25.248 |
| Male | 10.99 | 92.771 | | 82.065 | | | | |
| Female | 1.5 | 7.229 | | 17.935 | | | | |
| *Residence* | | 100% | 9.246 | | 10.662 | −1.416 | −15.315 | −39.216 |
| Rural | 9.101 | 96.386 | | 62.500 | | | | |
| Small town | 9.532 | 1.205 | | 11.413 | | | | |
| City | 14.897 | 2.410 | | 26.087 | | | | |
| *Literacy* | | 100% | 9.525 | | 9.881 | −.356 | −3.738 | −9.571 |
| Literate | 11.272 | 71.605 | | 77.401 | | | | |
| Illiterate | 5.118 | 28.395 | | 22.599 | | | | |
| *No. of children* | | 100% | 10.477 | | 8.599 | 1.878 | 17.925 | 45.900 |
| 0 | 3.455 | 13.913 | | 37.791 | | | | |
| 1 | 7.932 | 6.957 | | 9.884 | | | | |
| 2–3 | 11.782 | 17.826 | | 19.767 | | | | |
| 4–5 | 14.623 | 18.696 | | 18.605 | | | | |
| 6–7 | 9.775 | 18.281 | | 8.721 | | | | |
| 8+ | 11.603 | 24.348 | | 5.233 | | | | |
| Actual % wealthy all testators | 9.676 | 13.477 | | 8.214 | | | | |

*Source:* See appendix 1.

*Notes:* Total "explained," 22.361%. Percent of testators wealthy uses all-testator standards for wealth. Predicted percent wealth computed by applying 1803–65 proportions wealthy to the actual proportions of testators in each category. Thus, column 3 applies weights from column 2 to the proportion wealthy in column 1. Similarly, column 5 is computed by applying weights from column 4 to the proportion wealthy in column 1. Column 6 = column 3 − column 5. Column 7 = column 6/column 3. Column 8 = column 7/39.052, the actual percent change in proportion wealthy for all testators.

the wealth distribution would have been in 1860–65 utilizing the relative proportions of males to females for those years. The difference between 1860–65 and 1803–29 with respect to the proportion of wealthy testators is the extent of inequality produced by changes in the sex composition of testators. The ratio of the predicted percent change in inequality to the actual percent change is the contribution of the change in sex composition to the growth in inequality. Table 2.4 focuses on the contributions to inequality of age, occupation, and place of birth for testators dying after 1850.

Sex and number of living children have a substantial impact on inequality as predicted, accounting for 25 percent and 46 percent of the increased inequality respectively. The shift in place of birth toward a greater proportion of foreign born, which might be expected to promote inequality, has a negligible impact (6 percent) because the differences in wealth between native and foreign born are slight. Interestingly, a number of shifts in the mix of testator characteristics actually tend to produce less inequality. Cities, for example, have wealthier testators at the beginning of the period than do nonurban areas, and the proportion of urban testators grows during the years of the study, leading to the prediction of a 39 percent decrease in inequality. And nonfarm occupations with their relative wealth grow in importance, as do the proportions of testators from the relatively wealthy Middle Atlantic states and Ohio, leading to the prediction of decreases in inequality of 18 percent and 46 percent respectively. On balance, even though structural changes in sex and number of children tend to predict the expected changes in inequality, the changing characteristics of testators overall provide little explanation of the sources of growing inequality in the distribution of wealth. Even those structural changes in sex and number of children predicting more inequality are not particularly satisfying. While the sex ratio of testators may have changed, the sex ratio of decedents in general or of the total population probably did not, making generalizations from this study difficult. And changing numbers of children seem an unsatisfactory explanation for changes in inequality when they appear to be the effect, not the cause, of wealth.

### 2.3.3 The Composition of Wealth and the Growth in Inequality

If changes in testators' characteristics fail to account for increasing inequality, the composition of wealth may hold the key. Part 2.2 concluded that the preponderance of wealth was in real property, and that the source of growth in the value of real property was increasing land prices. If wealthy testators held a higher percentage of their wealth in real property than less wealthy testators, then the nearly ninefold increase in land prices might contribute substantially to the increase in inequality as well as to the growth in average testator wealth. In fact, the propor-

**Table 2.4    Contributions to Decline in Equality, 1850–59 to 1860–65**

| | 1850–65 | 1850–59 | | 1860–65 | | 1850–59/1860–65 | | |
| | (1) Actual % Wealthy | (2) Actual % Testators | (3) Predicted % Wealthy | (4) Actual % Testators | (5) Predicted % Wealthy | (6) Predicted Amount Change | (7) Predicted Percent Change | (8) Predicted/ Actual (%) |
|---|---|---|---|---|---|---|---|---|
| *Country of birth* | | 100% | | 100% | | | | |
| Foreign | 10.386 | 10.241 | 11.358 | 22.472 | 11.226 | 0.132 | 1.162 | 6.240 |
| Native | 11.469 | 89.759 | | 77.528 | | | | |
| *State of birth* | | 100% | | 100% | | | | |
| Middle Atl. & Ohio | 13.335 | 63.758 | 11.167 | 79.710 | 12.121 | −.954 | −8.543 | −45.869 |
| Other | 7.353 | 36.242 | | 20.290 | | | | |
| *Occupation* | | 100% | | 100% | | | | |
| Farmer | 14.248 | 78.632 | 14.803 | 59.375 | 15.303 | −.500 | −3.378 | −18.135 |
| Other | 16.846 | 21.368 | | 40.625 | | | | |
| *Labor force participation* | | 100% | | 100% | | | | |
| Participant | 14.980 | 69.643 | 11.098 | 71.111 | 11.286 | −.188 | −1.694 | −9.095 |
| Nonparticipant | 2.193 | 30.357 | | 28.889 | | | | |
| *Age* | | 100% | | 100% | | | | |
| 20–59 | 8.294 | 32.143 | 9.243 | 39.560 | 9.222 | .021 | 0.227 | 1.219 |
| 60–69 | 10.614 | 24.405 | | 27.473 | | | | |
| 70+ | 9.176 | 43.452 | | 32.967 | | | | |
| Actual % wealthy all testators | 9.086 | 10.094 | | 8.214 | | | | |

*Source and notes:* See table 2.3. Total explained, 65.64%.

tion of wealth held in real property varied dramatically from under 20 percent for testators in the bottom half of the wealth distribution to over 70 percent for the ten percent of testators at the top of the wealth distribution.

Table 2.5 tests the quantitative importance of these differentials in the proportion of wealth in real property for the growth in inequality. The procedure is similar to that employed in tables 2.3 and 2.4. By assuming that the 1803–29 proportion of wealth held in real property by each decile of the wealth distribution remained the same throughout the decades, and by assuming that the value of real property grows in proportion to land prices while the value of personal property remains constant, one can compute the projected wealth distribution for 1860–65 and compare it with the actual wealth distribution. Table 2.5 predicts a 31 percent decline in the proportion of testators owning the top 50 percent of wealth, whereas the actual decline was around 39 percent. Thus, increasing land prices accounted for almost 80 percent of the increase in inequality as well as most of the growth in wealth.

### 2.4    The Representativeness of Testators for All Decedents

This paper has limited its discussion to testators, reserving comparisons of testators with all decedents for this final section in order to discourage overly eager generalizations of these findings. The study of testators is of interest in its own right, as testators have considerable say in the distribution of wealth across generations as well as having attendant social (and possibly political) status. Nonetheless, it is desirable to determine how the characteristics of Butler County testators compare with those for county decedents in general.

Data on all decedents in Butler County are readily available during the years covered by this study only for 1856–57, when the county experimented briefly with recording cause of death and other socioeceonomic information on all decedents. Information is available not only on date, place, and cause of death, but on age, sex, color, marital status, occupation, place of birth, place of residence, and names of parents as well. While these data provide no insight into relative changes over time in the characteristics of testators and intestators (those who died without wills) they do provide a statistical peek at how well and in what ways testators represent all decedents.

Table 2.6 sets out the comparison of testators and intestators for 1856–57. The largest differences appear in the age distribution, as one might expect. Only one of the fifteen testators was under age forty (7%) compared with the 75 percent of intestators under forty: infant and child mortality was high, and minors could not legally write a will. The sex ratio of testators was higher than for intestators. With so few obser-

**Table 2.5    Effect of Growth in Land Prices on Wealth Distribution**

| Decile | Real Property/ Wealth (in %) | 1803–29 | | 1860–65 | | 1803–29/1860–65 | | |
|---|---|---|---|---|---|---|---|---|
| | | Actual Wealth | Predicted Wealth | Actual Wealth | Predicted Wealth | Actual | Predicted | Predicted/ Actual |
| 1–5 | 19 | $ 143.41 | | | $ 402.83 | | | |
| 6 | 47 | 468.05 | | | 2,219.12 | | | |
| 7 | 44 | 623.61 | | | 2,808.18 | | | |
| 8 | 48 | 857.80 | | | 4,135.77 | | | |
| 9 | 64 | 1,195.82 | | | 7,287.81 | | | |
| 10 | 71 | 2,847.31 | | | 18,939.17 | | | |
| Percent owning top 50% of wealth | | 13.477% | 14.244% | 8.214% | 9.875% | | | |
| Percent decline in equality | | | | | | 39.05 | 30.67 | 79 |

*Source:* See appendix 1.

*Notes:* Predicted wealth in 1860–65 for each decile is computed for each 1803–29 wealth decile by multiplying its mean wealth held in real property by 8.96 (the actual growth over that period in land prices) while holding the value of personal property constant. The proportion of testators owning the top 50% of wealth is computed by assuming all members of a decile own its mean wealth. The predicted proportion wealthy in 1803–29 is higher than the actual proportion because relatively few testators own much of each decile's wealth, in violation of the preceding assumption.

vations on testators for 1856–57, the chi square test is not significant, although we know that high sex ratios persist throughout the sixty-three years of the study. Presumably we would find highly significant differences in the sex ratio if we had data on intestators for more years. The proportion Black is quite comparable for the two groups—very low. Differences in marital status are significant (at the .002 level), but the high

**Table 2.6**     **Comparison of All Testators and Intestators, 1856–57**

| | Testators | | Intestators | |
|---|---|---|---|---|
| Variable | % | (N) | % | (N) |
| *Age* | 100 | (15) | 100 | (216) |
| <1 | 0 | (0) | 20 | (43) |
| 1–9 | 0 | (0) | 29 | (62) |
| 10–19 | 0 | (0) | 7 | (15) |
| 20–29 | 7 | (1) | 13 | (29) |
| 30–39 | 0 | (0) | 6 | (13) |
| 40–49 | 13 | (2) | 9 | (19) |
| 50–59 | 20 | (3) | 6 | (12) |
| 60–69 | 27 | (4) | 2 | (5) |
| 70+ | 33 | (5) | 8 | (18) |
| *Sex* | 100 | (15) | 100 | (220) |
| Male | 74 | (11) | 51 | (112) |
| Female | 27 | (4) | 49 | (108) |
| *Color* | 100 | (15) | 100 | (220) |
| Black | 7 | (1) | 4 | (8) |
| White | 93 | (14) | 96 | (212) |
| *Marital status* | 100 | (15) | 100 | (217) |
| Married | 47 | (7) | 29 | (62) |
| Single | 27 | (4) | 65 | (141) |
| Widowed | 27 | (4) | 6 | (14) |
| *Occupation* | 100 | (15) | 100 | (214) |
| Farmers | 27 | (4) | 13 | (27) |
| Professional | 13 | (2) | 2 | (4) |
| Other occ. | 7 | (1) | 7 | (14) |
| Not in LF | 53 | (8) | 79 | (169) |
| *Place of birth* | 100 | (14) | 100 | (177) |
| Butler County | 29 | (4) | 65 | (115) |
| Middle Atlantic | 50 | (7) | 11 | (20) |
| Tidewater | 7 | (1) | 7 | (13) |
| Other natives | 7 | (1) | 7 | (13) |
| European | 7 | (1) | 12 | (22) |
| *Place of residence* | 100 | (15) | 100 | (204) |
| Rural | 53 | (8) | 60 | (123) |
| Small town | 5 | (1) | 14 | (29) |
| City | 40 | (6) | 25 | (52) |

*Source*: Butler County death records for 1856 and 1857, and appendix 1.

proportion single in the intestate population may simply reflect its children. Similarly the high proportion of intestators not in the labor force (significantly higher at the .02 level) may reflect its children. Differences in place of residence, on the other hand, are quite insignificant, with a few more testators living in cities and a few more intestators living in small towns. It appears that testators provide a poor representation of all decedents, but the differences appear to be largely related to differences in the age (and probably sex) distributions.

To test this hypothesis, table 2.7 limits the comparison of testators and

**Table 2.7    Comparison of Testators and Intestators over Forty, 1856–57**

| | Testators | | Intestators | |
|---|---|---|---|---|
| Variable | % | (N) | % | (N) |
| *Age* | 100 | (14) | 100 | (54) |
| 40–49 | 14 | (2) | 35 | (19) |
| 50–59 | 21 | (3) | 22 | (12) |
| 60–69 | 29 | (4) | 9 | (5) |
| 70+ | 36 | (5) | 33 | (18) |
| *Sex* | 100 | (14) | 100 | (54) |
| Female | 29 | (4) | 52 | (28) |
| Male | 71 | (10) | 48 | (26) |
| *Color* | 100 | (14) | 100 | (54) |
| Black | 7 | (1) | 6 | (3) |
| White | 93 | (13) | 74 | (51) |
| *Marital status* | 100 | (14) | 100 | (54) |
| Married | 43 | (6) | 63 | (34) |
| Single | 29 | (4) | 17 | (9) |
| Widowed | 29 | (4) | 20 | (11) |
| *Occupation* | 100 | (14) | 100 | (51) |
| Farmer | 29 | (4) | 31 | (16) |
| Professional | 7 | (1) | 0 | (0) |
| Other | 7 | (1) | 16 | (8) |
| None | 57 | (8) | 53 | (27) |
| *Place of birth* | 100 | (13) | 100 | (49) |
| Butler County | 31 | (4) | 18 | (9) |
| Middle Atlantic | 46 | (6) | 33 | (16) |
| Tidewater | 8 | (1) | 10 | (5) |
| Other states | 8 | (1) | 10 | (5) |
| European | 8 | (1) | 29 | (14) |
| *Place of residence* | 100 | (14) | 100 | (49) |
| Rural | 57 | (8) | 69 | (34) |
| Small town | 7 | (1) | 12 | (6) |
| City | 36 | (5) | 18 | (9) |

*Source*: See table 2.6.

intestators to decedents aged forty and older. Differences in the age distribution persist, with a few more intestators in their forties and a few more testators in their sixties, but the differences are insignificant (at least with the number of observations available on testators). The differences in the sex ratio persist unabated, although they fail to achieve significance at even the .10 level; but, again, the high sex ratio through out the antebellum decades makes it likely that more observations would prove the sex ratios different. The proportions Black remain low and virtually identical for the two groups. With the removal of the under-forty set, the proportion single becomes less instead of greater for intestators, though none of the differences is significant. Differences in occupation narrow, with only a few more professionals among the testators and a few more intestators in the residual occupations category, and the proportion not in the labor force is now almost identical (even though a lower proportion of testators are women). A higher proportion of testa tors were born in the county and a lower proportion were foreign born, although again the differences do not attain significance. Differences in the proportion living in cities remain, although as was the case in table 2.6, differences do not achieve significance. It is possible that with a a larger sample, more differences would become significant, especially in the proportions female, professional, foreign born, and urban, but on the basis of this two-year sample alone, we must conclude that testators and intestators aged forty and older are not significantly different in these characteristics.

It remains possible, even likely, that testators and intestators differ in the extent of their wealth. Unfortunately, with the data available for Butler County, there is no simple way to test the extent of the difference. If the date of death were available for intestators, it would be possible to take a sample of intestators who died shortly after 1860, find their declared real property in the 1860 census, and combine that with the value of their personal property listed in inventory records to estimate their total wealth. Since we lack information on date of death of intestators (which was estimated from the date the will was filed for testators), the relative wealth of testators and intestators remains conjectural.

Similarly important and elusive is the difference in the proportions of wealth held in real property by testators and intestators. This study shows that the growth in inequality in the antebellum decades is largely attributable to the differential effect of rapidly growing land prices on testators holding different proportions of their wealth in real property. The extent to which the declining equality of testators reflects the experience of all Butler County decedents is heavily dependent upon the proportion of wealth in real property held by wealthy decedents. In the absence of data on the proportion of wealth held in real property by the different wealth groups of decedents, changes in the wealth distribution of decedents cannot be inferred from changes in the wealth distribution of testators.

What this study must conclude with is a hypothesis: that the process of settling the frontier by farmers in search of farm sites drove up the price of land; that swelling capital gains from the land contributed most of the growth in wealth; and that it was because the wealthy held a higher proportion of their wealth in land that inequality in the distribution of wealth grew. It remains for studies of other frontier areas, where different kinds of data are available, to test this hypothesis.

# Appendix 1: Data Gathering Procedures

What follows is a brief guide to county records used in this study. While records and their organization vary with the county, materials for Butler County are summarized in the hopes that they will assist scholars in search of data to test the hypotheses in this paper.

*Will Records* are handwritten bound copies of all wills filed in (or remanded to) the county from 1803 when the county and state were founded up to the present. They are arranged in order of month (or term) and year filed, and indexed in a *General Decedents' Index*. The *Index* with its alphabetical listing of decedents also provides a list of the documents available in the original estate papers. Wills provide the following information used in this study: name; date written (useful for determining if some data were obsolete by the date the will was filed); date filed (proxy for date of death); place of residence (varies from a blank to "Butler County" to the township to the town if appropriate); names and relations of legatees (useful in tracing real property, and in linking to other records when the decedent's name is common and to the census when it is faded beyond legibility); real property bequeathed to legatee (may specify range, town, and section which can be looked up in a *Township Deed Index,* or may say, more generally, "the property on which John Smith now resides"—which still allows a check of the data-gathering procedures for real property); signature or X or signature of witness on behalf of decedent (a crude measure of literacy confounded by literate but feeble testators who also sign with an X); and the executor (useful in tracing real property after the testator's death).

*Testamentary Records* are handwritten bound copies of documents relating to the settlement of estates, appointment of guardians, and the like, recorded in the order they were received by the court. The index in the front of each volume is as likely to refer to the executor as to the decedent. These may contain value of inventory, proceeds from sale, debts receivable and payable, net value of personal property and, rarely, the distribution of the balance of the estate to the heirs. The county archivist advised us to examine testamentary records extending up to fifteen years after the filing of the will in search of data on each testator, and even then she estimated that as little as three-quarters of the estates may have been settled. Inventories were also copied into *Inventory Records* which are more accessible because extraneous material is excluded. Because inventories were carried out quite promptly after the will was filed, we searched inventory records only for three years before turning to testamentary records.

*Tax Duplicates* are annual listings by township ostensibly covering all taxable property, which is generally real property although depending on the year it may include personal property, cattle, carriages, houses (brick or frame), or financial paper. Tax duplicates are sometimes divided into resident and nonresident owners, but this is rare. Within each township, parcels of land are divided into township (rural) land and in-lots (town or city property). Within each category, landowners are listed in alphabetical order with the following information on each parcel: range, town, section and part section; acres (often divided into first, second, and third-quality land); and amount of each tax. Because of the incompleteness of the coverage, three years of records were checked for each testator centered on the year the will was filed (because land continued to be listed in the decedent's name until that part of the estate was settled). These records provide the best available list of each decedent's real property, and the location provides access to the records in the recorder's office. These records need to be supplemented by judicious use of deed indexes.

*Township Deed Indexes* for each township are organized by range, town (not to be confused with towns or townships), and section, and within each section they list transactions chronologically. One side of each page is devoted to deeds and the other side to mortgages. Deed pages include the fraction of the section, acres, names of buyers and sellers, date, and volume and page of the *Deed Record* where the sale price is recorded. In theory, one should be able to trace the ownership of any parcel of land back to its original owner, although in practice many transactions were never recorded. Because testators who owned more than one parcel tended to buy them in the same geographical area, the deed indexes proved a useful supplement to the tax records.

The attempt was made to find a transaction within five years of the date the will was filed to provide a market value for the property. Because no deed recorded the transfer of ownership from decedent to heir, property would be variously listed after the death of the testator: in the name of the executor or administrator of the estate, of "the heirs of" the testator (unnamed), or simply in the name of the heir who inherited the property. If no transaction occurred close enough to the death of the decedent the property was valued at the average price of township land for that date.

*City* and *Village Indexes* are arranged within each municipality by in-lot or out-lot number, and provide a chronological listing of transactions similar to the township indexes, with names of buyer and seller, date, and volume and page of deed record. As cities grow, out-lots become in-lots, township land is annexed, and in-lots get renumbered when most transactions take place in small fractions of the original lots. *In-Lot* and *Out-Lot Schedules* provide the necessary conversion from original lot number to revised lot number.

## Appendix 2: Measurement of Productivity

Table 2.A.1 summarizes the data used in calculating the productivity of land for figure 2.6. In the absence of data on animal production, the analysis is restricted to use of farmland for crops. And because no information is available on the land devoted to individual crops, the decision was made to measure the constant dollar value of crops per improved acre of farmland as the best available measure of land productivity. In effect, grazing of animals or other farm production is assumed to take place on unimproved land, or to utilize only a relatively small proportion of improved land. For 1840 even the luxury of this assumption is unavailable because the agricultural census does not provide land data. In its stead, one may turn to the tax duplicates of the county for township land assessed for taxes, as most rural (or township) land taxed was in farms, where the land is conveniently categorized by extent of improvement. While the tax duplicates may overstate farm acreage because they include rural nonfarm land, they also may have a tendency to understate farm acreage because of the incentive for farmers to underdeclare land holdings and thereby reduce their taxes. The net bias is unclear. All one can say for sure is that the resulting productivity measure for 1840 will be even more crude than the measures for later years. The specific crops covered by the census vary from year to year, so the productivity measures in table 2.A.1 are constructed so that comparison can be made between years on the basis of comparable crops.

*Sources to Table 2.A.1:* Land inputs, crop outputs, and value of market garden production from *1840 Butler County Tax Duplicates* and *U.S. Census of Agriculture*, 1840, 1850, 1860, and 1870. Prices for wheat, oats, rye, corn, peas and beans, barley, hops, and flaxseed from Berry (1943, pp. 595–96). Prices for potatoes from 1880 Census, vol. 20; Weeks [1883, p. 77, "Prices in Hamilton, Ohio, furnished by W. C. Fretchling" (linked by butter and cheese prices to the Cincinnati market).]. Prices for hay from The Cincinnati Daily Gazette, April 11, 1862. For buckwheat, the price of rye was used, as closest comparable crop.
*Hops in pounds, hay in tons, all other crops in bushels.

**Table 2.A.1   Land Inputs, Crop Outputs, and Productivity: Butler County, 1840–70**

| | 1840 | | 1850 | | 1860 | | 1870 | | 1861 |
|---|---|---|---|---|---|---|---|---|---|
| **Farmland (acres)** | | | | | | | | | |
| Improved | 165,532 | | 172,345 | | 207,985 | | 191,028 | | |
| Total | 284,908 | | 274,349 | | 308,033 | | | | |

| Crops | Output* | CDV | Output* | CDV | Output* | CDV | Output* | CDV | Price |
|---|---|---|---|---|---|---|---|---|---|
| Wheat | 318,720 | 299,597 | 291,782 | 274,275 | 682,823 | 641,854 | 627,823 | 590,154 | $ .94 |
| Oats | 550,990 | 132,238 | 336,717 | 80,812 | 216,064 | 51,855 | 229,621 | 55,109 | .24 |
| Rye | 29,291 | 14,353 | 12,213 | 5,984 | 4,246 | 2,081 | 1,863 | 913 | .49 |
| Corn | 2,243,561 | 628,197 | 2,732,734 | 765,166 | 2,396,323 | 670,970 | 1,716,862 | 480,721 | .28 |
| Potatoes | 46,035 | 13,350 | 92,845 | 26,925 | 97,734 | 28,343 | 113,135 | 32,809 | .29 |
| Peas & beans | | | 620 | | 733 | | | | 1.22 |
| Barley | 12,656 | 6,328 | 5,896 | 28,948 | 337,064 | 158,532 | 277,016 | 138,508 | .50 |
| Buckwheat | 1,760 | 862 | 771 | 2,338 | 6,452 | 3,161 | | | .49 |
| Hay | 12,769 | 159,612 | 10,494 | 131,175 | 7,377 | 92,212 | | | 12.50 |
| Hops | 110 | 25 | 51 | 11 | 84 | 19 | | | .22 |
| Flaxseed | | | 825 | 825 | 1,430 | 1,430 | | | 1.00 |
| Market gardens | | 12,290 | | 3,866 | | 8,692 | | | |
| Total CDV | | 1,266,852 | | 1,321,081 | | 1,670,043 | | 1,298,214 | |

| For comparison with: | CDV/ Imp. Acre | Total CDV | CDV/ Imp. Acre | Total CDV | CDV/ Imp. Acre | Total CDV | CDV/ Imp. Acre | Total CDV | |
|---|---|---|---|---|---|---|---|---|---|
| 1840 | | | 7.656 | 1,319,500 | 8.030 | 1,670,043 | 6.796 | 1,298,214 | |
| 1850 | 7.653 | 1,266,852 | | | 8.030 | 1,670,043 | 6.796 | 1,298,214 | |
| 1860 | 7.653 | 1,266,852 | 7.665 | 1,321,081 | | | 6.796 | 1,298,214 | |
| 1870 | 6.609 | 1,094,063 | 6.859 | 1,182,110 | 7.518 | 1,563,635 | | | |
| Productivity index | 100.0 | | 100.0 | | 100.8 | | 94.7 | | |

## Comment on Chapters 1 and 2    Robert E. Gallman

The two papers on which I am to comment are, at first blush, worlds apart. Newell is concerned with the distribution of wealth among those who died and left a will in the sixty-two year period, 1803–65, in Butler County, Ohio—clearly, a microstudy. On the other hand, Lindert and Williamson are interested in the broad changes in the distribution of wealth among residents of the United States and their colonial forbears, from the seventeenth century to the present—clearly, a macrostudy. Furthermore, Newell and the numerous research assistants whom he generously thanks in his notes have been at work on primary, archival sources. They have assembled their evidence from wills, estate inventories, other testamentary records, tax lists, the original manuscripts of the U.S. census enumerators in Butler County, and genealogical records. And when I say "assembled," I mean that they have been obliged to match materials from these disparate sources, going from John Doe's will to his estate inventory, to his landholdings according to the local tax duplicate, to the notes concerning him in the manuscript census, to the information concerning the Doe family collected by the genealogists of Butler County. Williamson and Lindert, on the other hand, have carried out a synthesis, using estimates put together by others. There are no primary materials in their paper, although they have spared no pains in manipulating and testing the data drawn from secondary sources.

Despite these patent differences, the two papers have a good deal in common. In the first place, both are concerned with measuring and explaining changes in the size distribution of wealth, and here and there they even use similar analytical devices. But they are related in yet another way. Williamson and Lindert bring together and analyze data from previous studies that are very similar to Newell's. And when they ask for more work to illuminate the history of change between 1774 and 1860 and between 1860 and 1914, it is precisely the type of study Newell has done that they have in mind. On the other hand, when Newell attempts to relate his results to the wider experience of American economic development, it is the type of paper that Williamson and Lindert have produced that he seeks. Thus the links between these two fine papers are very close.

Newell begins with a brief, lucid account of the types of evidence available to him and the chief strengths and weaknesses of each source. Here, and in a short appendix, he also describes the main kinds of data adjust-

Robert E. Gallman is professor of economics at the University of North Carolina, Chapel Hill.

ment and estimation in which he and his colleagues have engaged. It is obvious that Butler County has extraordinarily rich sources of evidence for the period in question, but that these sources yield their record only to exceptionally patient, industrious, and imaginative researchers. The research effort underlying this paper is really quite remarkable.

Newell then turns to the two principal empirical findings of his work. First, the mean wealth per testator, deflated by the Bureau of Labor Statistics cost of living index, declined from a level of just over $750 (in 1967 prices) in the period 1803–19 to about $575 in the period 1820–29, when it began to rise, steadily and rapidly, reaching a level of about $2,100 in 1860–65. Second, the distribution of wealth became less equal between the first and the second period, more equal between the second period and 1830–39, and then moved persistently and quite dramatically in the direction of greater inequality down to the period 1860–65. (The measure of distribution used is the fraction of testators owning the top 50 percent of wealth. Thus in 1830–39 just over 16 percent of testators owned 50 percent of wealth, while by 1860–65 the figure had fallen to just over 8 percent.)

Newell then asks how one might account for these developments. As to the first, he argues that real property comprised between 60 and 70 percent of total testamentary wealth and that real property per testator grew much faster than personal property per testator. Thus the growth of wealth per testator, after 1820–29, was chiefly a consequence of the increase in the value of real property. Furthermore, arguing on the basis of the evidence on farm real property   which, presumably, was the chief form of real estate in Butler County—Newell asserts that the increase in the value of real estate per testator was entirely a consequence of an increase in the price of land, the volume of land per testator actually declining during the period. To put the matter another way, the "real" value of property per testator increased chiefly because the price of land rose relative to the consumer price index, the index used by Newell as the deflator for testamentary wealth.

Newell next seeks to explain the course of land prices. He first tests the possibility that improved farm revenues account for the phenomenon, the test being restricted to data assembled for the four census dates between 1840 and 1870. The results of the test lead him to discard this possibility. Physical productivity did not rise—indeed, it may have declined a little—and while farm prices went up, their impact on revenues could not have been adequate to have produced the observed results with respect to farm land values. Land values went up an average of 6 percent per year; revenues, by about 6/10 of one percent per year. Newell concludes that the farm land market must have been out of equilibrium through the entire period, farm revenues being high relative to land values. Thus through the period in question, potential farmers were migrating into Butler County to acquire the cheap agricultural land. Their bidding drove the price of agricultural land up.

Newell next turns to changes in the size distribution of wealth among testators, focusing on the growth of inequality after 1830–39. By cross-section regression analysis he establishes those variables that appear to have been associated with wealthholding. He then designs and carries out an index number procedure to isolate the impacts of structural changes in the population of testators on inequality of wealthholding. As it turns out, the effects of these changes are compensatory, so that the net effect of changes in the composition of population is to produce no change in the size distribution of wealth. The analysis turns up a number of other interesting and, in some measure, puzzling results. Of the variables Newell tested, only three—sex, number of children, and literacy—yield significant results in the multiple regression. Age is not significant, nor does it yield significant zero-order correlation.

Finally Newell considers the possibility that the growing wealth inequality was due to the concentration of real estate holdings in the wealth of the rich. This explanation turns out to be the correct one. Thus both the growth in the wealth of testators and the increasing concentration of wealthholdings were due to the rise in the prices of land relative to other prices. Newell argues that we may have a pattern here that was repeated in each new frontier community as it aged, and he asks for further research on the subject.

Newell's paper is certainly an impressive one and I have just a few suggestions to make.

To begin with, I think the decision to deflate wealth by the Bureau of Labor Statistics cost of living index needs some further discussion. I did not have the opportunity to look up the source notes to the index, but if the nature of the twentieth-century component has been preserved in the nineteenth-century component, then we have here an index relevant to urban lower middle class families. My guess is also that the cities involved are large eastern cities. In what sense is such an index relevant to the predominantly rural types of Butler County?

Before we can answer that question, we have to ask why Newell wants to deflate. I presume that he wants to know what happened to the material circumstances of that class of wealthholders which wrote wills. One possible answer to that question is that the material well-being of such wealthholders changed very little over time. The *volume* of land they held (per wealthholder) actually declined and the income received per acre changed very little, in current prices, at least. Perhaps the volume of personal property held went up a little bit. But on the whole, the situation of these wealthholders changed little.

Newell, clearly, does not like that answer. The *price* of land went up and, therefore, landholders may have been better off even if the *amount* of land they held declined. How much better off? In order to answer that question, we need to know what happened to the prices of other goods that wealthholders might have converted their land into. Newell's selection of the BLS cost of living index for his deflator involves an implicit judgment about this matter. But one could argue that a farmer selling out in Butler County would likely shift farther west and buy more land (or send his sons out to do so). In which case, the deflator we want for his wealth is the price index of land farther west. The point is that I think Newell should incorporate in his paper a clearer account of why he selected the BLS index and a defense of that choice.

Second, I am not altogether certain that the measure of the rate of change of revenues per acre can be trusted. Newell was obliged to compute the value of revenue (in current prices) in an indirect way. First, he valued farm output in each of the years 1840, 1850, 1860, and 1870 in Cincinnati prices of 1861, taken from Berry. Then he inflated the series, using a price index of Berry's, which describes changes in the prices of goods which were the product of Northern agriculture or derived from the product of Northern agriculture. Thus the index probably includes such items as bacon, salted beef, leather, tobacco, and whiskey, none of which figures as part of the agricultural output employed by Newell. The point may conceivably have some importance. I ran a quick test, accepting Newell's figure of 1860 output in 1861 prices as a fair estimate of current price output in 1860. Next I valued 1840 product in Ohio farm prices of 1840, provided by Tucker (1855). Using the Tucker figure for 1840, one finds that the value of output per acre in Butler County increased by all of 2.8 percent per year between 1840 and 1860, and if the rather dubious data on oats production are dropped, the rate of increase rises to 3.2 percent. (There is a dramatic drop in oats production between 1840 and 1850, and no subsequent, significant rise. See, also, Gallman, 1963). If, as may very well have been the case, the rate of interest fell between 1840 and 1860, it may be possible to reconcile the increase in land prices with the data on revenues (i.e. return to an equilibrium analysis).

It is possible, of course, that my estimates will not bear up under close scrutiny. For example, Tucker intended to estimate *farm* prices in 1840, whereas Berry's data refer to prices in Cincinnati. Thus my reestimate of the rate of change may be biased in an upward direction. Nonetheless, I think it would be worthwhile for Newell to reconsider his interpretation of rising land prices. In particular he probably has interest rate data, drawn from his evidence on debts. Unless these figures are only pro forma, he may be able to obtain some feel for the effect of the interest rate on land prices.

Third, I find the fact that wealth and age are unrelated in this sample very odd, indeed. I don't know how to account for it, and I don't know exactly what it means. I think Newell might give this a little more thought.

Finally, I agree with Newell that the pattern he finds in Butler County is most interesting and may reflect a common, rural development pattern in the U.S., and I look forward to Newell's future work on the subject. In particular, while I think Newell was wise to focus on the wealth distribution among decedent testators, obviously it would be more interesting to know how wealth was divided among the living (testators and nontestators), and I hope Newell will look into that matter.

The principal conclusions of Williamson and Lindert are easily summarized: the size distribution of wealth during colonial times probably changed very little; between 1774 and 1860, however, there was what can only be called a distributional revolution, wealth becoming very much more unequally distributed. It may very well be that the revolution was actually confined to only some part of that period, say 1820 to 1850. Across the Civil War, inequality was reduced, but thereafter it grew, perhaps reaching a maximum in 1914, at a level approximating that of 1860. Across World War I, once again there was a pronounced movement toward greater equality, a movement reversed in the 1920s. The end of the 1920s marks another peak of inequality, but from then until the early 1950s there is a pronounced movement toward greater equality, a movement previously documented by Kuznets and Lampman. From then until the present, little change in wealth or income size distribution has occurred. What engage Williamson and Lindert chiefly are the efforts to defend these generalizations and elicit their meaning. I will now attempt to summarize these efforts and to offer a few suggestions.

Williamson and Lindert review the now very substantial list of local colonial wealth studies, most of which have been produced within the last fifteen or twenty years. They point out that many of them show growing inequality of wealthholding from the seventeenth century down to the Revolution. The social historians who have carried out these studies (working chiefly from probate and property tax data) interpret their work variously, but according to Williamson and Lindert, two important schools conclude that, in fact, wealth was becoming more closely held in the American colonies, at least during the six or seven decades before the Revolution.

Williamson and Lindert argue, however, that at the macro level, wealth was not becoming more unequally distributed; indeed, there may have been a trend toward greater equality. The point is that while inequality may have grown in the cities (partly as a result of the immigration of young adults) and in the old rural communities (perhaps following a pattern similar to the one found by Newell), new, egalitarian rural communities were persistently being created, and population persistently shifted into them. Thus the changing population weights produced, at the macro level, little change in wealth concentration, even if at the micro level inequality persistently grew. This is a good point, and Williamson and Lindert are entirely correct in supposing that it has been largely (although not entirely) ignored by the social historians working in the field. I believe that they are wise to underline it.

A second point that I think might be made here is that the local colonial studies may very well overstate the degree to which inequality increased, even at the local level. For example, Greven's study shows that as the agricultural land of Andover was occupied and population continued to grow, there were pressures toward the fragmentation of farms, pressures that were quite strongly resisted. Thus excess children were either sent off to a frontier community, or were trained to a trade or profession. If one measures wealth in Andover in terms of real estate and personal property, no doubt the holding of wealth was concentrated in the hands of an ever-diminishing fraction of the population. But if we were to take human capital into account, that tendency would no doubt be moderated.

Finally, it comes as a surprise to find that the two authors have virtually ignored the institution of slavery. After all, it was during the eighteenth century that slavery came to dominate the Southern economy. In 1690, Africans accounted for no more than 8 percent of the population; by 1770, they were very nearly 20 percent. We know that wealth inequality was greater in the South than elsewhere, and one may suppose that there is a connection here to the institution of slavery. Might it not, then, have been true that the expansion of slavery produced a growing inequality in the South? And might not Southern developments have produced growing inequality at the macro, all-colonies level? This does not emerge in the Southern data consulted by Williamson and Lindert, but they have looked at data for only six counties in Maryland. One wonders what was happening in the rest of the South (especially South Carolina).

Williamson and Lindert base their identification of a wealthholding revolution between 1774 and 1860 on comparisons of wealth distributions derived by them for 1774, from data supplied by Alice Jones, and wealth distributions for 1860, published by Lee Soltow. They consider these two sets of estimates with great care and quite properly point out that both are of high quality. This point is worth underlining. There is some tendency to think of old data as necessarily weaker than modern evidence. But in certain important respects the Jones and Soltow data are actually better than modern data, as Williamson and Lindert point out.

On the other hand, it is also true that the two bodies of evidence were gathered from quite different sources, which, in turn, depended upon quite different methods of data collection. The Jones figures are also heavily processed, as is true of any set of estimates of wealth distribution among the living derived from probate data. Clearly, then, it would be desirable to find other evidence confirming the distributional change that can be inferred from the Jones and Soltow figures. But the data Williamson and Lindert examine yield quite a mixed picture and, indeed, the series which they find that confirm the change are subject to the same type of criticism they have previously made with respect to the colonial series. One wonders, therefore, whether or not they are premature to declare a distributional revolution.

Williamson and Lindert seek the sources of the putative revolution in various directions. First they ask whether or not changes in the age structure, rural-urban division, or native-foreign composition of the population might have produced a marked change in the size distribution of wealth between 1774 and 1860. They carry out various tests, the results of which indicate that the effects of changes in population structure on wealthholding were probably largely compensatory.

They turn next to an earlier work by Williamson on the structure of wage rates. In this work, Williamson (1976) argues that there is a high correlation between changes in the distribution of income and changes in the ratio of the wage of skilled workers to the wage of unskilled workers. Since the relevant ratios increased dramatically in the antebellum period, there is a good chance that income inequality—and its correlate, wealth inequality—also increased dramatically. He argues also that unbalanced technical change and the associated marked decline in the relative prices of capital goods lay behind these developments.

I find this argument ingenious, exciting and most attractive, but by no means convincing, at least so far as the macro distributions are concerned. First, the wage rate ratios refer to urban workers and the data are probably restricted to some small set of workers in some small set of urban places. But in any case, the urban population of the U.S. accounted for only between 8 and 17 percent of the total population during the relevant period. It may be, of course, that the wage structure is still a good predictor of aggregate income and wealth distributions, but I would require a little more evidence before I were willing to agree.

I also do not find the evidence for unbalanced technical change and the decline in the relative price of capital at all compelling. As to the latter, it is my strong impression that the price decline was much more pronounced *after* 1860 than before. As to the former, Williamson cites in support of his judgment that the period was one of unbalanced technical change some data on total factor productivity change in agriculture and in cotton textiles. But there are two reasons why this comparison is not proper and one reason for believing that it ill serves Williamson and Lindert. First, the agricultural estimates are in fact calculations intended to show the implications of the existing data series on output and factor supplies, with the object of arguing that these implications *are not plausible*. Second, the comparison is between a *sector* and an *industry*. Clearly, an industry experiencing technical change and growth will normally and usually show a higher rate of productivity advance than will a sector. Finally, Williamson wants to show that unbalanced technical change favored skilled workers. But the technical developments in the cotton textile industry, after all, were developments that permitted employers to substitute children and inexperienced young women for prime workers. It is very difficult to see this type of development as favorable to "skill." Indeed, a major theme in labor history during this period has to do with labor opposition to the substitution of children, young women, and convicts for prime workers. A second, related theme has to do with the dilution of skill by the factories and the decline of the aristocrats of labor, the artisans. The process is typically described as one that had leveling tendencies *among* laborers, providing new opportunities for large numbers with limited skill, while restricting the opportunities of the highly skilled artisans.

Finally, Williamson and Lindert devote most of their attention to the period 1820–50. I wish that they had considered the years 1774–1820 more carefully, and particularly the years of the Revolution and just after it. We sometimes forget the enormous number of Americans who either chose to leave or were driven out during the period, people whose property was frequently expropriated. How did these developments affect the distribution of wealth? Williamson and Lindert do not essay an answer to this question and, unfortunately, I don't have one to offer, either.

The period between the Civil War and World War I Williamson and Lindert refer to as a statistical wasteland, an apt description. They call for more work on the period and, in the meantime, offer a clear-sighted appraisal of the evidence available. In particular, I am delighted to see that they make good use of the work of G. K. Holmes, which is too often neglected in such discussions. They conclude, with no great feeling of certainty, that wealth inequality probably peaked in 1914, although the entire period from 1860 to 1914 is best regarded as a plateau of high inequality, with a few instances of deviations, such as the period of the Civil War. For my part, I would not want to rule out an *increase* in inequality from 1860 (1870) down to the 1890s, but I agree with them that it is difficult to establish much about this period with great certainty (see Gallman 1968).

I have concentrated on the earlier sections of their paper, where I had a critical word or two to contribute. Unfortunately, my decision has probably given my comments a rather negative tone. That is too bad, since I think this is a first rate paper. In particular, the sections devoted to testing the effects of changes in demographic structure on the wealth distribution are marvelous. The last sections seemed to me to be quite straightforward (there are some nice ones reconciling seemingly inconsistent estimates), and my impressions of them were altogether favorable.

## Further Comment    William H. Newell

Gallman's comments are helpful in tightening and clarifying my paper, and in some cases they suggest useful lines of future research. My responses follow in the order of his criticisms.

1. Gallman fears that my choice of the Bureau of Labor Statistics cost of living index may bias the measured trend in wealth because that index reflects the price experience of urban families. For the years 1851–65 his fears may be justified because the prices are taken from Ethel Hoover's consumer price index which she constructed according to modern definitions. For 1803–50, however, the BLS series turns out to be constructed from the "Index of Prices Paid by Vermont Farmers for Family Living." While Gallman's fears prove unfounded for most of the period under study, he is correct in pointing out that the choice of deflator merits further scrutiny.

2. Gallman makes a series of criticisms of my rough estimate of changes over time in revenue per acre. I view the test set out in appendix 2 as a crude first approximation, nothing more. After all, four annual observations are scarcely enough evidence to draw any firm conclusions about a thirty-year trend in productivity. Nonetheless, it seems worthwhile to follow up on Gallman's suggestions.

First, he correctly points out that Berry's annual price series includes a number of animal products which were excluded from the output estimate in appendix 2, and which might cause an understatement of productivity growth by their omission. In particular, hogs were a major product of Butler County farms and a major component of Berry's price series. Cattle and sheep account for the remaining excluded commodities. However, if roughly constant proportions were slaughtered and average weights remained fairly constant over time, the inclusion of slaughtered animals would tend to *reduce* the measured growth in productivity because numbers of hogs, cattle, and sheep all *fell* steadily between 1840 and 1870.

Second, when Gallman compares 1840 production valued in farm prices from Tucker with 1860 production valued in city prices from Berry, he finds a growth rate of 2.8 percent or more, a rate substantially higher than my estimate. Gallman recognizes that his estimation procedure tends to bias upward the rate of growth in productivity by measuring from farm prices to higher city prices. It would be preferable to reconstruct consistent price series for each crop instead of relying on the annual movement of an aggregate index. A check of Berry's sources, however, reveals that the crop prices underlying his index are spotty, particularly, it seems, for the relevant census years. Thus the indirect procedure employed in this study (modified to include animal products) may provide as sound an estimate as the underlying data will support.

Finally, Gallman reasonably observes that mortgage interest rates might account for some of the growth in land prices. However, a preliminary check of interest rates from the late 1840s (when mortgages first began to appear in substantial numbers) to the late 1860s reveals no apparent trend, either up or down, in mortgage interest rates.

3. When females are dropped from the sample, no new variables achieve significance and none of the old variables changes relative importance. Indeed, it would be surprising if the regression analysis were to turn up other testator characteristics which were significantly associated with wealth. One of the findings of the subsequent index number analysis is that other testator characteristics had minimal impact on changes in the wealth distribution.

4. I, too, find the lack of association between age and wealth perplexing.

# References

Bateman, Fred, and Jeremy Atack. 1978, forthcoming. "Northern Agricultural Profitability: Some Preliminary Estimates." *Research in Economic History* 4.

Berry, Thomas S. 1943. *Western Prices before 1861*. Cambridge, Mass.: Harvard University Press.

Gallman, Robert E. 1963. "A Note on the Patent Office Crop Statistics." *Journal of Economic History*, vol. 23.

———. 1968. "The Social Distribution of Wealth in the United States of America." *Third International Conference of Economic History*, Paris.

———. 1969. "Trends in the Size Distribution of Wealth in the Nineteenth Century: Some Speculations," in Lee Soltow, ed., *Six Papers on the Size Distribution of Wealth and Income*. Studies in Income and Wealth 33. New York: National Bureau of Economic Research.

Gates, Paul. 1960. *The Farmer's Age, 1815–1860*. New York: Holt, Rinehart & Winston.

Main, Gloria L. 1976. "Inequality in Early America: The Evidence of Probate Records from Massachusetts and Maryland." Paper presented to Cliometrics conference, Madison, Wisc.

Main, Jackson T. 1976. "The Distribution of Property in Colonial Connecticut," in James Kirby Martin, ed., *The Human Dimensions of Nation Making*. Madison, Wisc.: State Historical Society.

————. 1965. *The Social Structure of Revolutionary America*. Princeton: Princeton University Press.

Menard, Russell, et al. 1974. "Opportunity and Inequality: The Distribution of Wealth on the Lower Western Shore of Maryland, 1638–1705." *Maryland Historical Magazine* 69:169–84.

Pessen, Edward. 1973. *Riches, Class, and Power before the Civil War*. Lexington, Mass.: D. C. Heath.

Soltow, Lee. 1969. "Evidence on Income Inequality in the United States, 1866–1965." *Journal of Economic History* 29:279–86.

————. 1971. "Economic Inequality in the United States in the Period from 1790 to 1860." *Journal of Economic History* 31:822–39.

————. 1971. *Patterns of Wealthholding in Wisconsin since 1850*. Madison, Wisc.: University of Wisconsin Press.

————. 1975. *Men and Wealth in the United States, 1850–1870*. New Haven: Yale University Press.

Tucker, George. 1855. *Progress of the United States in Population and Wealth*. New York.

U.S. Bureau of the Census. 1975. *Historical Statistics of the United States: Colonial Times to 1970*, part 2. Washington, D.C., Government Printing Office.

Weeks, Joseph D. 1883. *Report on the Statistics of Wages in Manufacturing Industries, with Supplementary Reports*. Washington, D.C., Government Printing Office. From the U.S. Census of Population, vol. 20.

Williamson, Jeffrey. 1976. "American Prices and Urban Inequality since 1820." *Journal of Economic History*, vol. 36.

# 3 The Perpetuation of Wealth: A Simulation Model

Michael Patrick Allen

Inequality of wealth is a persistent characteristic of American society. Historical comparisons of the distribution of wealth over the past two centuries suggest that an extremely small segment of the total population has invariably owned a disproportionately large share of the total wealth (Lampman 1962; Soltow 1975; Pessen 1973; Smith and Franklin 1974). Specifically, one percent of the population has typically owned between twenty and thirty percent of the total personal wealth in the United States. In general, it is possible to distinguish between two types of wealth; original and inherited. Original wealth, on the one hand, is wealth that has been accumulated over the course of a single generation. If this wealth is very large, then the rate of accumulation must be very rapid. Indeed, Thurow (1975) refers to original wealth as "instant" or "spontaneous" wealth. On the other hand, inherited wealth is wealth that has been accumulated over the course of several generations. One of the most important theoretical issues raised by the persistence of the inequality of wealth is the extent to which this distribution of wealth is attributable to inheritance rather than the creation of original wealth.

The present analysis represents somewhat of a departure from previous studies of the intergenerational transmission of wealth (Ward and Beuscher 1950; Dunham 1962). Indeed, it proceeds from the assumption that the intergenerational transmission of wealth is only one element, albeit an integral one, of a more general process responsible for the perpetuation of wealth. In particular, this analysis addresses the problem of whether or not it is possible for the members of a wealthy family to perpetuate their wealth over several generations. There are, of course, factors which operate to perpetuate the wealth of a family as well as factors

Michael Patrick Allen is associate professor in the Department of Sociology, Washington State University, Pullman.

which operate to reduce this wealth. Wealth is perpetuated by intergenerational transfers of wealth, while it is reduced by the imposition of progressive inheritance and estate taxes. The present analysis attempts to examine the effects of these and other factors on the perpetuation of wealth within families over the course of several generations. Therefore, the unit of analysis is the individual as a member of a kinship group defined as the lineal descendents of an original wealthholder.

It must be noted at the outset that the presently available information on wealthholding and the intergenerational transmission of wealth does not permit a direct empirical analysis of this problem. Even if information on patterns of wealthholding and intergenerational transfers were available on any systematic basis, a longitudinal analysis spanning several decades would be required to examine the problem of the perpetuation of wealth in any detail. For these reasons, this analysis employs a simulation model of the perpetuation of wealth. The purpose of this model is to generate projections concerning the transmission, distribution, and accumulation of wealth among the members of a family over the course of several generations. Whenever possible, the parameters of this model are derived from empirical research. For example, estimates of the intragenerational and intergenerational transfers of wealth by deceased wealthholders are obtained from an analysis of the estate tax returns filed in 1972. Other parameters of the model are based upon the findings of other researchers. However, some of the parameters required by this model have not been the subject of much empirical research. Therefore, the simulation model must rely, at least in part, upon certain assumptions. As a result, the empirical adequacy of this model and its projections rests upon the validity of these assumptions as well as the accuracy of these parameters.

## 3.1  The Perpetuation of Wealth

This analysis assumes that the perpetuation of wealth is the result of three conceptually distinct but empirically related processes. These three processes involve the transmission of wealth from one generation to succeeding generations, the distribution of this wealth among the lineal descendents of a deceased wealthholder, and the accumulation of this inherited wealth over the course of a generation until the death of the inheritor. Indeed, these three processes form a cycle which is repeated with each succeeding generation. Any systematic analysis of the problem of the perpetuation of wealth must consider each of these three processes and their relationship to one another. The simulation model employed in this analysis incorporates each of these processes.

It is apparent that the process of the intergenerational transmission of wealth is a central component of any systematic model of the perpetuation of wealth. Without any inheritance or estate taxes, virtually all of the wealth held by a deceased wealthholder, reduced only by funeral and administrative expenses, could be transferred to his or her descendants. However, inheritance and estate taxes, at the state and federal levels, ensure that only a portion of the wealth owned by one generation is transferred to succeeding generations. Typically, these taxes are progressive so that large estates are taxed at higher rates than small estates. The federal estate tax in effect until 1976, for example, reached a maximum marginal rate of 77 percent on taxable estates in excess of $10 million. Conversely, a taxable estate of $100,000 was taxed at a rate of only 21 percent. Clearly, inheritance and estate taxes represent the major barriers to the intergenerational transmission of wealth, particularly for large estates.

In addition to the intergenerational transmission of wealth, a systematic model of the perpetuation of wealth must consider the distribution of any intergenerational transfers of wealth among the lineal descendants of the deceased wealthholder. Obviously, for any given intergenerational transfer of wealth, the wealth inherited by each descendant depends both upon the number of descendants and upon the proportional distribution of the aggregate transfer of wealth among these descendants. If there is only a single descendant, then he will inherit the entire residual estate available for distribution after deductions for funeral and administrative expenses, debts, charitable contributions, and taxes. However, if there are four descendants, each receiving an equal share of the estate, each will inherit only one-quarter of the residual estate available for distribution after deductions. Moreover, there is the possibility that the aggregate intergenerational transfer is to be distributed over more than one generation. It is not uncommon for deceased wealthholders to bequeath part of their estates to their grandchildren.

Finally, the third process in the perpetuation of wealth is the accumulation of wealth over the course of a generation. One of the most important characteristics of both inheritance and estate taxes is that these taxes are ordinarily imposed upon wealth only once each generation. In short, they are taxes on the transfer of wealth from one generation to succeeding generations and not taxes on the ownership of wealth or property as such. An estate is taxed upon the death of a wealthholder, and is not subject to taxation again until the death of the descendant. In the interim, a period equivalent to a generation, this wealth is generally free from taxation except as it is received by the descendant in the form of income or realized capital gains. During this generation, it can accumulate at some annual rate which is related to the average rate of return on investment. As a result, there is the possibility that the wealth inherited by each descendant will accumulate enough over the course of a generation to offset the reduction attributable to estate taxes and other expenses.

These three processes can be concatenated to construct a simulation model of the perpetuation of wealth. This model is presented in schematic form in figure 3.1. It begins with the initial wealth of an original wealthholder. This initial wealth corresponds to the net estate of a wealthholder at the time of death. The model continues with the transfer process which determines the aggregate wealth, for any given level of initial wealth, that is transferred from one generation to succeeding generations. In other words, this transfer results in a residual estate which is equal to the initial net estate minus deductions for funeral and administrative expenses, charitable contributions, and taxes. Next, there is the distribution process which determines how much of the aggregate wealth transferred from the original wealthholder is received by each descen-

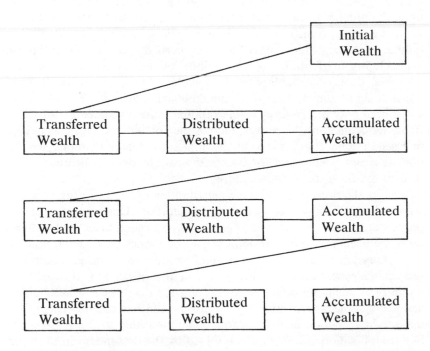

**Fig. 3.1**          Simulation Model of the Perpetuation of Wealth

dant. This process depends upon the number of descendants and distribution of the residual estate among these descendants according to the bequest pattern established by the deceased wealthholder or by the succession pattern established by state law. Finally, there is the accumulation process which determines the value of the inherited wealth after the period of a generation. This process depends upon both the annual rate of accumulation for wealth and the number of years in the accumulation period. This sequence of processes can be iterated to determine the wealth of the individual members of a family after each generation.

In order to demonstrate the logic of this model, a graph of the rise and fall of the aggregate wealth of a family over the course of three generations, showing the effects of estate taxes and the accumulation of inherited wealth, is presented in figure 3.2. In this hypothetical example, the rate of wealth accumulation just offsets the rate of estate taxation, so that the aggregate wealth of the family remains relatively constant at any given point in the cycle. The model of the perpetuation of wealth represented by this graph does not involve any distribution process, since the graph depicts the wealth of a family and not the wealth of its individual members. It must be noted that this graph is adapted from a similar graph presented by Tait (1967). Indeed, this model for the perpetuation of wealth is based, in large part, upon his discussion of the effects of capital accumulation upon the effectiveness of estate taxes.

## 3.2 Parameters of the Model

The central process in this model of the perpetuation of wealth is the transfer of wealth from one generation to succeeding generations. This process involves two related quantities: the initial wealth of the original wealthholder prior to death, and the total wealth inherited by his or her descendants. The first quantity can be referred to as the "net estate" of a wealthholder and corresponds to his or her net worth. Specifically, it is equal to the gross estate of the wealthholder minus deductions for debts and mortgages. The second quantity can be referred to as the "residual estate" and represents the total wealth inherited by the various descendants of the original wealthholder. It is equal to the net estate minus deductions for funeral and administrative expenses, charitable bequests, and taxes. The federal estate tax returns contain information on all of these deductions with only one exception, the state death taxes paid by an estate. Almost all states have some form of inheritance or estate tax. However, the federal estate tax does permit a limited credit for the payment of state death taxes. The best available estimate of the total tax liability of an estate, based upon the federal estate tax return, is provided by the federal estate tax liability before any credits for the

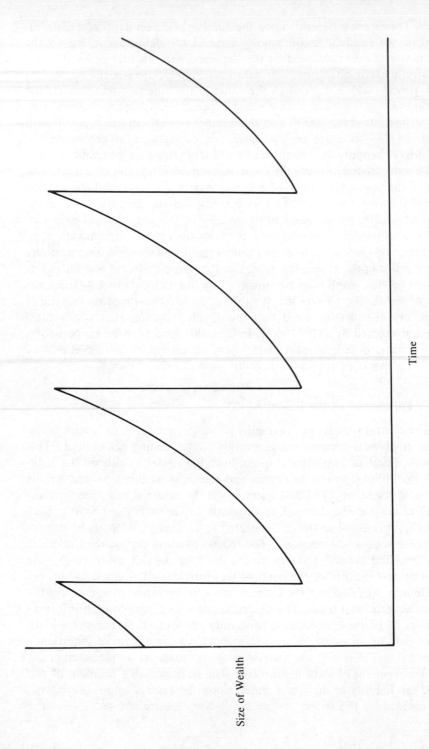

**Fig. 3.2**    Rise and Fall of Family Aggregate Wealth over the Course of Three Generations

payment of state death taxes. To the extent that the state death tax may exceed the maximum credit permitted by the federal estate tax, this procedure may underestimate the total tax liability of an estate.

Given the net estate and the corresponding residual estate for a representative sample of deceased wealthholders, it is possible to estimate a function which predicts the size of the residual estate for any given size of net estate. A function which estimates the residual estate from a net estate can be referred to as a "transfer function." This function estimates the total wealth that is transferred to the heirs of an estate. One major complication arises from the fact that the federal estate tax contains a marital deduction which permits a deceased wealthholder to transfer one-half of his or her adjusted gross estate, defined as the gross estate minus deductions for debts and expenses, to a surviving spouse without any estate tax liability. Therefore, it is necessary to construct separate transfer functions for deceased wealthholders with and without surviving spouses. Once again, the federal estate tax return contains information on the actual bequests to surviving spouses.

The present analysis relies upon three separate transfer functions. The first function estimates the size of the intergenerational transfer for any given size of net estate for those deceased wealthholders without surviving spouses. In this case, the intergenerational transfer is defined as the residual estate of the deceased wealthholder. An analysis of the estate tax returns filed in 1972 indicates that 41.6 percent of decedents with net estates in excess of $100,000 were not survived by their spouses. The two remaining transfer functions pertain to deceased wealthholders with surviving spouses. One is an intragenerational transfer function which estimates the size of the bequest to the surviving spouse from the size of the net estate. The other function estimates the size of the intergenerational transfer, defined as the residual estate minus the bequest to the surviving spouse, for any given size of net estate. These functions were established using the regression of each type of transfer on the net estate for the 75,608 deceased wealthholders in 1972 with net estates in excess of $100,000.

The estimation of these transfer functions entails certain methodological difficulties. Given the fact that the federal estate tax is highly progressive, it might be expected that the sizes of both the intergenerational and intragenerational transfers would be nonlinearly related to the size of the net estate. Consequently, several nonlinear transformations of the variables were employed in an attempt to identify the transfer functions with the best fit. Contrary to expectations, the size of both the intergenerational and the intragenerational transfer were approximately linearly related to the size of the net estate for the case of a deceased wealthholder with a surviving spouse; the linear correlation is 0.779 in the first case, 0.892 in the second case.

However, a simple linear function is not appropriate for predicting the size of the intergenerational transfer from the size of the net estate for those deceased wealthholders without surviving spouses. Several non-linear functions, involving various monotonic transformations of the variables, were examined but they yielded inappropriate estimates of the size of the intergenerational transfer for net estates of less than $1 million. Therefore, the function adopted represents a concatenation of three separate linear functions, each appropriate for a limited range of net estates. Although this is not a particularly elegant solution to the estimation problem, it does provide reasonable estimates of the size of the inter-generational transfer for every size of net estate. The correlation between the size of the intergenerational transfer and the size of the net estate is 0.799 for the case of decedents without surviving spouses.

Although these intergenerational transfer functions predict the aggregate wealth that is available for distribution among the descendants of a deceased wealthholder, there is little direct evidence on the actual distribution of this wealth among these descendants. This information is not available on the estate tax returns filed in 1972. Therefore, this stage of the analysis requires a series of assumptions concerning the distribution of the aggregate transfer of wealth among the lineal descendants. It must be recalled that this analysis is specifically concerned with the ability of wealthholders to perpetuate their wealth among their descendants over several generations. Consequently, the distributions of transferred wealth employed here assume that all of the residual estate not transferred to a surviving spouse is transferred to the children of the deceased wealthholder. This analysis does not consider the possibility of intergenerational transfers of wealth to grandchildren, although this contingency is amenable to analysis using a more complex simulation model. Moreover, it does not consider the possibility of bequests to individuals other than members of the immediate family. In general, this last assumption is supported by the available evidence on patterns of inheritance (Sussman, Cates, and Smith 1970).

The intergenerational transfer and distribution of wealth among the descendants of a deceased wealthholder represent only two elements of a systematic model of the perpetuation of wealth. The third element involves the accumulation of inherited wealth over the course of a generation. It has been noted that estate and inheritance taxes are ordinarily imposed upon wealth only once each generation. In the interim, this inherited wealth generally accumulates without significant taxation, except for the taxable income that it returns to the wealthholder. For the purposes of this analysis, it is assumed that the period of wealth accumulation for each generation is approximately twenty-two years. This period represents a somewhat low estimate of the average age of parents at the birth of their first child.

This analysis also examines the effects of the accumulation of wealth on the overall perpetuation of wealth using different estimates of the annual rate of wealth accumulation. To simplify matters, the rate of wealth accumulation can be stated in real terms adjusted for inflation. Specifically the analysis uses two different real annual rates of wealth accumulation: 1 percent and 3 percent. These estimates of the real annual rate of wealth accumulation are well within the limits suggested by the real annual rates of return for alternative types of investments over the past several decades (Brittain 1967). Since the wealth of top wealthholders is disproportionately concentrated in corporate stocks, these rates are certainly conservative, and are employed because they correspond to real rates of wealth accumulation after deductions for the living expenses of the wealthholder. It is implicitly assumed that wealthholders with relatively small net estates also receive supplemental incomes from other sources.

It is possible to demonstrate the basic operation of the model of the perpetuation of wealth using a simple example, the case of a deceased wealthholder with a net estate of $1 million. To simplify the analysis, it will be assumed that for each generation there is no surviving spouse and only a single descendant. According to the intergenerational transfer function for deceased wealthholders without spouses, the estimated intergenerational transfer for a net estate of this size is $584,380. The remainder of the net estate goes to funeral and administrative expenses, charitable contributions, and taxes. The distribution function for this example dictates that the entire intergenerational transfer goes to a single descendant; The accumulation function, that the inherited wealth accumulates at a real annual rate of 3 percent for a period of 22 years. The accumulated interest on $584,380 compounded annually at a rate of 3 percent for 22 years is $535,330. Therefore, the accumulated wealth of the single descendant is estimated to be $1,119,710. This process can be repeated for each successive generation. Using these assumptions, the accumulated wealth of the third-generation descendant is $1,310,060.

### 3.3 Simple Models of the Perpetuation of Wealth

The simplest possible model for the perpetuation of wealth over the course of several generations is the case of a deceased wealthholder without a surviving spouse and only a single descendant. It involves only the intergenerational transmission of wealth and the accumulation of wealth processes. The distribution of wealth process is not required in the case of a single descendant. The results of this model are presented in table 3.1 for several different levels of initial wealth and the two different rates of wealth accumulation. The estimates of wealth represent the accumulated wealth of the third-generation descendant of the original wealth-

Table 3.1    Estimated Wealth after Three
Generations by Initial Wealth and
Rate of Accumulation for Case of
No Spouse and One Descendant

| Initial Wealth | 1 Percent per Annum | 3 Percent per Annum |
|---|---|---|
| 100 | 132 | 374 |
| 200 | 166 | 500 |
| 300 | 209 | 657 |
| 400 | 252 | 814 |
| 500 | 295 | 939 |
| 600 | 338 | 1,039 |
| 800 | 411 | 1,184 |
| 1,000 | 469 | 1,310 |
| 1,200 | 516 | 1,436 |
| 1,400 | 560 | 1,561 |
| 1,600 | 595 | 1,687 |
| 1,800 | 629 | 1,813 |
| 2,000 | 663 | 1,938 |
| 3,000 | 836 | 2,567 |
| 4,000 | 1,008 | 3,195 |
| 5,000 | 1,171 | 3,790 |
| 10,000 | 1,319 | 4,147 |
| 50,000 | 1,917 | 4,560 |
| 75,000 | 2,044 | 4,640 |
| 100,000 | 2,172 | 4,720 |

Note: Amounts are expressed in thousands of dollars.

holder. This is the wealth held by the single descendant after three intergenerational transfers of wealth and three generations of wealth accumulation. This is the simplest possible model because the wealth is passed from a single individual in one generation to a single individual in the next generation. Although this process obviously concentrates the wealth of the original wealthholder in the hands of a single descendant, it also serves to maximize the tax liability of each successive estate, since no use is made of either the marital deduction or the distribution of wealth among several descendants.

The estimates of the wealth accumulated by the third generation descendant of the original wealthholder presented in table 3.1 demonstrate a pattern which obtains in more complex models of the perpetuation of wealth. Specifically, there is the tendency for relatively small wealthholdings to increase over time and for relatively large wealthholdings to decrease, especially with higher rates of wealth accumulation. This general pattern is a logical consequence of a tax structure which levies a progressive tax on the intergenerational transmission of wealth but does not tax the accumulation of wealth over the course of a generation. Among relatively small wealthholdings, the effective estate tax rate permits the growth of these wealthholdings. Conversely, among relatively large wealthholdings, the effective estate tax rates result in the diminution of these wealthholdings. It is important to note that differences in the level of initial wealth yield significant differences in the wealth held by the third-generation descendants. These results suggest that it may require several generations, certainly more than three, to eliminate the differences in the wealthholdings of descendants of top wealthholders.

It has been noted that the model of wealth perpetuation involving no surviving spouse and only one descendant serves to maximize the tax liability of each successive estate because it does not use the marital deduction. It is interesting to compare the results obtained for the case of a single descendant and no surviving spouse with those obtained for that of a single descendant and a surviving spouse. The case of a surviving spouse and a single descendant is presented in table 3.2. It must be noted that in this case the intergenerational transfer of wealth occurs in

| Table 3.2 | Estimated Wealth after Three Generations by Initial Wealth and Rate of Accumulation for Case of Spouse and One Descendant | |
| --- | --- | --- |
| Initial Wealth | 1 Percent per Annum | 3 Percent per Annum |
| 100 | 193 | 455 |
| 200 | 228 | 535 |
| 300 | 231 | 547 |
| 400 | 245 | 596 |
| 500 | 258 | 644 |
| 600 | 272 | 693 |
| 800 | 299 | 791 |
| 1,000 | 325 | 889 |
| 1,200 | 352 | 987 |
| 1,400 | 379 | 1,085 |
| 1,600 | 406 | 1,183 |
| 1,800 | 432 | 1,277 |
| 2,000 | 455 | 1,362 |
| 3,000 | 571 | 1,702 |
| 4,000 | 677 | 2,016 |
| 5,000 | 777 | 2,329 |
| 10,000 | 1,237 | 7,149 |
| 50,000 | 3,317 | 9,997 |
| 75,000 | 4,163 | 11,933 |
| 100,000 | 5,009 | 13,970 |

*Note*: Amounts are expressed in thousands of dollars.

two stages. First, there is the intergenerational transfer of wealth which occurs simultaneously with the intragenerational transfer of wealth to the surviving spouse. Second, there is the intergenerational transfer of wealth which occurs with the death of this surviving spouse. Without loss of generality, it can be assumed that both spouses die within the same year. It is apparent from a comparison of the estimates of wealth provided by each model that the existence of a surviving spouse facilitates the perpetuation of wealth at the highest levels of initial wealth. The effect of a surviving spouse on the perpetuation of wealth is much less pronounced and even somewhat inconsistent at the lower levels of initial wealth.

The assumption that there is only one descendant in each generation serves a certain analytical purpose, but it is patently unrealistic in terms of the demographical characteristics of the population of top wealthholders. It is somewhat more realistic to assume that there are two descendants in each generation. This model requires a simple distribution process which divides the aggregate intergenerational transfer of wealth for each generation between both descendants. The results of this model are presented in table 3.3 for the case of no surviving spouse and two descendants. The estimates of wealth represent the accumulated wealth of the third-generation descendant of the original wealthholder. A comparison of these results with those obtained for the case of no surviving can be drawn from a comparison of the case of a surviving spouse and significantly reduces the wealth of each descendant. Similar conclusions spouse and only one descendant indicates that this distribution process two descendants with the case of a surviving spouse and only one descendant. The results of the model assuming a surviving spouse and two descendants are presented in table 3.4. In general, the wealth of each descendant is reduced when there are two descendants in each generation instead of one.

These models of the perpetuation of wealth have been concerned solely with the accumulated wealth of the individual descendants of the original wealthholder. However, these individual descendants can also be considered as members of the same family. In this case, the family is defined as the lineal descendants of the original wealthholder. Given the assumption of two descendants in each generation, there are two siblings in the first generation of descendants, four first cousins in the second generation, and eight second cousins in the third generation. Therefore, the aggregate wealth of the family comprising third-generation descendants of the original wealthholder is simply eight times the wealth accumulated by each third generation descendant. The estimates of the aggregate wealth accumulated by the third-generation descendants, in the case of no surviving spouses from preceding generations and two descendants each generation, are presented in table 3.5 by the different levels of ini-

| Table 3.3 | Estimated Wealth after Three Generations by Initial Wealth and Rate of Accumulation for Case of No Spouse and Two Descendants | |
|---|---|---|
| Initial Wealth | 1 Percent per Annum | 3 Percent per Annum |
| 100 | 24 | 88 |
| 200 | 36 | 90 |
| 300 | 41 | 110 |
| 400 | 50 | 129 |
| 500 | 58 | 149 |
| 600 | 60 | 169 |
| 800 | 68 | 202 |
| 1,000 | 76 | 231 |
| 1,200 | 83 | 260 |
| 1,400 | 91 | 285 |
| 1,600 | 99 | 306 |
| 1,800 | 107 | 327 |
| 2,000 | 115 | 349 |
| 3,000 | 146 | 448 |
| 4,000 | 175 | 526 |
| 5,000 | 203 | 601 |
| 10,000 | 228 | 668 |
| 50,000 | 389 | 1,113 |
| 75,000 | 482 | 1,171 |
| 100,000 | 506 | 1,230 |

*Note*: Amounts are expressed in thousands of dollars.

tial wealth. Similar estimates of the aggregate accumulated wealth of the family, in the case of a surviving spouse and two descendants each generation, are presented in table 3.6. It is apparent that, although the existence of two descendants in each generation reduces the wealth accumulated by each individual descendant, it increases the aggregate wealth accumulated by the family. In short, the distribution of wealth among more than one descendant serves to preserve the aggregate wealth of the family by reducing the tax liability of each individual estate.

Finally, it is apparent from an examination of these various estimates of the wealth accumulated by the third-generation descendant that the perpetuation-of-wealth model is very sensitive to changes in the real annual rate of wealth accumulation. A two percent difference in the rate of wealth accumulation, from one percent per annum to three percent, yields estimates of accumulated wealth which differ by a multiple of three for all but the highest levels of initial wealth. For these highest levels, this same percentage difference produces estimates of accumulated wealth which differ only by a multiple of two instead of three. This differential

| Table 3.4 | Estimated Wealth after Three Generations by Initial Wealth and Rate of Accumulation for Case of Spouse and Two Descendants | |
|---|---|---|
| Initial Wealth | 1 Percent per Annum | 3 Percent per Annum |
| 100 | 24 | 88 |
| 200 | 48 | 148 |
| 300 | 51 | 155 |
| 400 | 60 | 161 |
| 500 | 63 | 168 |
| 600 | 66 | 171 |
| 800 | 75 | 179 |
| 1,000 | 83 | 190 |
| 1,200 | 91 | 202 |
| 1,400 | 99 | 214 |
| 1,600 | 107 | 226 |
| 1,800 | 115 | 238 |
| 2,000 | 120 | 249 |
| 3,000 | 122 | 301 |
| 4,000 | 133 | 354 |
| 5,000 | 148 | 404 |
| 10,000 | 215 | 632 |
| 50,000 | 538 | 1,688 |
| 75,000 | 707 | 2,120 |
| 100,000 | 849 | 2,506 |

*Note*: Amounts are expressed in thousands of dollars.

impact of a two percent change in the rate of wealth accumulation over the course of a generation is attributable largely to the progressive nature of the estate tax, particularly among the largest estates. Moreover, it must be noted that these two estimates of the real annual rate of wealth accumulation represent relatively conservative estimates of the historical rate of capital accumulation adjusted for inflation, especially since the wealthholdings of the top wealthholders are disproportionately concentrated in corporate stocks.

## 3.4   Conclusions

The general simulation model of the perpetuation of wealth presented in this analysis yields results which are important even though they are not entirely unexpected. They are important because they demonstrate, in some detail, the relationships among the processes governing the transmission, distribution, and accumulation of wealth over the course of several generations. They are not entirely unexpected because each of these processes has been the subject of prior research. This model provides results which are simply the logical consequences of the interaction among these separate processes. The value of such a simulation model is that it attempts to integrate these different processes into a more general model which can provide projections concerning the perpetuaton of wealth over several generations.

In general, the federal estate tax reduces the wealth held by the descendants of the original wealthholder, particularly those with relatively large estates. At the other extreme, the federal estate tax does not, at least by itself, reduce the wealth held by the descendants of those wealthholders with relatively small estates. The distribution process, involving the distribution of intergenerational transfers of wealth among more than one descendant, accounts for much of the reduction in the wealth held by the descendants of the original wealthholders. Finally, the federal estate tax, since it taxes the estates of individuals, does not reduce the aggregate wealth of a family, comprising the lineal descen-

| Table 3.5 | Estimated Aggregate Wealth of Family after Three Generations by Initial Wealth and Rate of Accumulation for Case of No Spouse and Two Descendants | |
|---|---|---|
| Initial Wealth | 1 Percent per Annum | 3 Percent per Annum |
| 100 | 192 | 704 |
| 200 | 288 | 720 |
| 300 | 328 | 880 |
| 400 | 400 | 1,032 |
| 500 | 464 | 1,192 |
| 600 | 480 | 1,352 |
| 800 | 544 | 1,616 |
| 1,000 | 608 | 1,848 |
| 1,200 | 664 | 2,080 |
| 1,400 | 728 | 2,280 |
| 1,600 | 792 | 2,448 |
| 1,800 | 856 | 2,616 |
| 2,000 | 920 | 2,792 |
| 3,000 | 1,168 | 3,584 |
| 4,000 | 1,400 | 4,208 |
| 5,000 | 1,624 | 4,808 |
| 10,000 | 1,824 | 5,344 |
| 50,000 | 3,112 | 8,904 |
| 75,000 | 3,856 | 9,368 |
| 100,000 | 4,048 | 9,840 |

*Note*: Amounts are expressed in thousands of dollars.

dants of a wealthholder, except for those wealthholders with the largest estates. In short, the federal estate tax facilitates the accumulation of relatively small wealthholdings and inhibits the accumulation of relatively large wealthholdings among individual descendants of the orignal wealthholder.

The present analysis represents only a preliminary attempt to construct a comprehensive model of the perpetuation of wealth. Any conclusions drawn from it must be tempered by a consideration of its inherent limitations. The models examined were extremely simple. The assumptions employed can be considered as plausible hypotheses at best. Moreover, many of the parameters require further research. Indeed, one of the major contributions of this kind of analysis is that it suggests potentially productive directions for new research. Although each of the three processes comprising this model require additional research and refinement, the one which requires the most attention is the distribution process. There is the need for detailed research on the actual distribution of

| Table 3.6 | Estimated Aggregate Wealth of Family after Three Generations by Initial Wealth and Rate of Accumulation for Case of Spouse and Two Descendants | |
|---|---|---|
| Initial Wealth | 1 Percent per Annum | 3 Percent per Annum |
| 100 | 192 | 704 |
| 200 | 384 | 1,184 |
| 300 | 408 | 1,240 |
| 400 | 480 | 1,288 |
| 500 | 504 | 1,344 |
| 600 | 528 | 1,368 |
| 800 | 600 | 1,432 |
| 1,000 | 664 | 1,520 |
| 1,200 | 728 | 1,616 |
| 1,400 | 792 | 1,712 |
| 1,600 | 856 | 1,808 |
| 1,800 | 920 | 1,904 |
| 2,000 | 960 | 1,992 |
| 3,000 | 976 | 2,408 |
| 4,000 | 1,064 | 2,832 |
| 5,000 | 1,184 | 3,232 |
| 10,000 | 1,720 | 5,056 |
| 50,000 | 4,304 | 13,504 |
| 75,000 | 5,656 | 16,960 |
| 100,000 | 6,792 | 20,048 |

*Note*: Amounts are expressed in thousands of dollars.

wealth among lineal descendants and others. Once the empirical parameters governing the transmission, distribution, and accumulation of wealth have been established, it will be possible to develop more complex and more accurate models of the perpetuation of wealth. These models may provide projections which might suggest changes in the present federal estate tax.

## Comment    Thad W. Mirer

I have three points to raise about Michael Allen's interesting simulation analysis of the perpetuation of wealth over several generations. The first two are brief and regard what is not in the paper; the third is more substantial and regards what is.

First, as this paper presents only the preliminary work on a more comprehensive model, I feel free to suggest that Allen go on to determine transfer functions for estates smaller than $100,000, and then combine his model with a sample of initial wealthholders so that he can simulate changes in the size distribution of wealth over time.

Second, I was disappointed that he did not elaborate on the results of his estimation of the three transfer functions. Of the three elements in his simulation (i.e., the transfer function, the division rule, and the rate of accumulation), only the transfer function embodies the results of Allen's own empirical research. These functions are of considerable interest in themselves, because they measure the real impact of inheritance tax laws. They estimate the "effective" inheritance tax, and are comparable to the work that others have done measuring the effective tax rates in the personal income tax and in the Aid to Families with Dependent Children program, for example.

Also, it would be helpful to have the characteristics of the transfer functions analyzed, so that the reader could make his own evaluation of the simulations. For example, we are told that in the case where there is never a surviving spouse, the transfer function is composed of three linear segments. One has to presume that this is a concave function. In the case where there is a surviving spouse, the two linear transfer functions interact to yield a grand intergenerational transfer function that is also linear, as I understand it. We have no clear idea from the paper of how the effective tax compares to the nominal rate structure. It would be especially interesting to see how high the rates actually get.

My third point addresses the conclusion that the federal estate tax "inhibits the accumulation of relatively large wealthholdings among in-

Thad W. Mirer is associate professor in the Department of Economics, State University of New York at Albany.

dividual descendants of the original wealthholder." This certainly is supported by a quick glance at the tables in the paper. In none of the cases illustrated does a great-grandson of a man with $100 million end up with more than 14 percent of the initial wealth. There would seem to be a tremendous decrease in wealthholdings as a result of taxation and distribution over three generations. I see the possibility of the opposite conclusion, however.

One way to examine the effect of the inheritance tax in Allen's simulation model is to determine the "break-even" levels of wealth—i.e., the levels of initial wealth that are just maintained through the system. For initial wealth levels above the break-even levels, the wealth of the third generation is smaller than that of first, while for initial wealth levels below the break-even level the wealth of the third generation is larger. Examining Allen's tables 3.1 and 3.2 for cases of one descendant, we find that if wealth accumulates at 1 percent annually, then the break-even levels of wealth are roughly $150 thousand if there is no spouse and $225 thousand if there is one. At 3 percent growth, the break-even levels are roughly $1,850 thousand and $775 thousand in the cases of no spouse and spouse, respectively. These are all large amounts of money—especially those at 3 percent—and the simulations show us that only above these levels does the inheritance tax serve to diminish wealthholdings. (In tables 3.3 and 3.4, for cases of two descendants, the break-even levels occur below $100 thousand—the smallest levels given.)

If higher rates of accumulation (i.e., rates of growth of wealth) had been chosen for illustration, the break-even levels would be higher. How much higher? This is impossible to determine fully from the paper, because the transfer functions are not specified. It is possible to make some inferences, however. For a given transfer function, each level of wealth is associated with a particular (average) effective rate of inheritance "taxation," which includes both true tax and administrative costs. Presumably, the transfer function shows that this effective rate would increase with the wealth level. Simple calculations will enable one to determine what rate of accumulation is necessary if the wealth level that has associated with it an effective tax rate of $X$ percent is to be the break-even level. We shall examine only high tax rates, which might be associated with very large levels of wealth.

In the case where there is one descendant, if the (average) effective tax rate were 50 percent, then wealth would have to double during each generation span of 22 years in order for the wealth level to exactly "break even." This would call for an annual growth rate of only 3.2 percent. If the effective tax rate were 75 percent, the required rate of growth would be 6.5 percent. If the effective tax rate were 90 percent—which would have to include high administrative costs—the required rate of growth would be about 11 percent.

When we consider cases involving two descendants, the rates of growth (accumulation) necessary for the break-even condition are higher. If the effective tax rate were 50 percent, then the wealth held by each descendant would have to quadruple in order for his wealth to break even with his father's; this would require a growth rate of 6.5 percent. If the effective tax rate were 75 percent the required rate of growth would be 9.9 percent, and if the tax rate were as high as 90 percent the required growth rate would be 14.6 percent.

If we assume that only the largest estate is subject to an (average) effective tax as high as 75 percent, then the required rates of growth are 6.5 and 9.9 percent, in the cases of one and two descendants, respectively. Are these "reasonable"? As Allen mentions, the rate of accumulation is determined by consumption out of interest income, as well as by the rates of interest and capital appreciation. Additionally, if the holding of inherited wealth makes the creation of "spontaneous" wealth easier, then the simulated rate of accumulation might be adjusted upward to measure this opportunity. Although I have no data to present, rates of accumulation between 6 and 10 percent strike me as reasonable and these could lead to the conclusion on the basis of the simulations that all descendants end up better than their benefactors. The line of logic leading to this conclusion contains many assumptions, and hence the real point that I have to make is that one must use care in accepting the result of any simple simulation model as a measure of reality.

# References

Blinder, Alan S. 1974. *Toward an Economic Theory of Income Distribution*. Cambridge, Mass.: M.I.T. Press.

Brittain, John A. 1967. "The Real Rate of Interest on Lifetime Contributions toward Retirement under Social Security." *Old Age Income Assurance*. Part 3: Public Programs. U.S. Congress, Joint Economic Committee.

Dunham, Allison. 1962. "The Method, Process and Frequency of Wealth Transmission." *Chicago Law Review* 30: 241–85.

Kolko, Gabriel. 1962. *Wealth and Power in America*. New York: Praeger.

Lampman, Robert J. 1962. *The Share of Top Wealth-Holders in National Wealth, 1922–1956*. Princeton: Princeton University Press.

Lebergott, Stanley. 1975. *Wealth and Want*. Princeton: Princeton University Press.

Meade, J. E. 1976. *The Just Economy*. London: George Allen and Unwin.

Pessen, Edward. 1973. *Riches, Class, and Power before the Civil War.* Lexington, Mass.: D. C. Heath.

Shoup, Carl S. 1966. *Federal Estate and Gift Taxes.* Washington, D.C.: Brookings.

Smith, James D., and Stephen D. Franklin. 1974. "The Concentration of Personal Wealth, 1922–1969." *American Economic Review* 64: 162–67.

Soltow, Lee. 1975. *Men and Wealth in the United States, 1850–1870.* New Haven: Yale University Press.

Sussman, Marvin B., Judith N. Cates, and David T. Smith. 1970. *The Family and Inheritance.* New York: Russell Sage Foundation.

Tait, Alan C. 1967. *The Taxation of Personal Wealth.* Urbana, Illinois: University of Illinois Press.

Thurow, Lester C. 1975. *Generating Inequality: Mechanisms of Distribution in the U.S. Economy.* New York: Basic Books.

Ward, Edward, and J. H. Beuscher. 1950. "The Inheritance Process in Wisconsin." *Wisconsin Law Review,* pp. 393–426.

# 4      The Importance of Material Inheritance: The Financial Link between Generations

Paul L. Menchik

There seems to have been a recent revival of scholarly interest in the distribution of privately held material wealth and in the transmission of wealth inequality across generations. Impressive analytical and simulation models have been devised to study these issues and predict the outcomes of various social policy changes. (Blinder 1973, 1976a, 1976b; Oulton 1976; Atkinson 1971; Stiglitz 1969; Smith, Franklin, and Orcutt 1978). Empirical evidence, however, is necessary to provide the building blocks of simulation models, and to test the validity of the predictions of analytical models. In this field, as in so many other areas of the social sciences, empirical advances have unfortunately failed to keep pace with nonempirical developments.

I examine two questions in this paper. First, a specific one: To what extent does the material inheritance received by the children of wealthy parents "account" for their own wealth? Second, a more general one: What is the relationship between the lifetime resources (both inheritance and earnings) of individuals and the amount they fail to consume themselves—that is, the amount they leave to others—in a life cycle sense?[1]

## 4.1   Does Material Inheritance Matter?

There is ample evidence that privately held wealth is more concentrated than earnings in the United States. The pioneering work done by

Paul L. Menchik is assistant professor of economics, Michigan State University.

The research reported here was supported by funds granted to the Institute for Research on Poverty of the University of Wisconsin-Madison by the Department of Health, Education, and Welfare pursuant to the provisions of the Economic Opportunity Act of 1964. Particularly helpful suggestions were received from A. Blinder, A. Goldberger, J. Heckman, F. Modigliani, M. David, and J. Williamson.

Colin Harbury (1962) showed a strong positive relationship, at least for the U.K., between the wealth of wealthy individuals and that of their parents. Though Harbury was not able to obtain information on the bequests from specific parents to their children, the implication of his study is that material inheritance does indeed transmit inequality across generations. This paper relates inheritance and gifts received by a sample of children to their wealth at death, using probate record data.

There has been previous empirical research into a question somewhat similar, though not identical, to the first question I have posed. In a survey of 957 high-income people, having an income of $10,000 or more in 1964, Barlow et al. (1966) asked each individual if he had received an inheritance. Three-fifths of the group responded in the negative. After making assumptions about the growth of the value of assets, the authors concluded that more than four-fifths of the total wealth of this high-income group was derived from saving out of income (not earnings), and less than one-fifth from inheritances and gifts plus their appreciation.

In a Federal Reserve study by Projector and Weiss (1966), respondents were asked what portion of total assets was inherited. The choice of answers was: none, small, and substantial. The percent answering "none" falls as wealth class rises, and the percent answering "substantial" rises from zero in the $1 to $999 wealth class to 34 percent in the $500,-000 and over wealth class in the cross-section. The percent responding "substantial" was, overall, 5 percent, rising with age from 1 percent for those under 34 to 9 percent for those 65 and over.

One problem with these surveys, if the focus of concern is intergenerational transfers, is that they do not take account of the effects of the death of both parents. One would expect reported inherited wealth to be small as long as one's parents were living. I shall present evidence on the ratio of the real present value of inheritance from parents and the real value of wealth for individuals both of whose parents are dead.

### 4.1.1   The Relationship between Lifetime Resources and Transfers

The unknown relationship between lifetime resources and the amount transferred to others is quite important in inter and intragenerational models, and its character has important policy implications.

*Macroeconomic Theory and Policy*

Does aggregate consumption vary with the degree of income inequality in an economy? Does the marginal propensity to consume out of *lifetime* resources vary with one's resources? While it was first thought that equalizing the income distribution would increase consumption, the models of Friedman (1957) and Modigliani and Brumberg (1954) indicate no such distributional effect. A recent paper by Blinder (1975) reconsiders the effect of resource inequality on consumption in a life cycle framework.

In Blinder's model, the consumer chooses his time path of consumption $c(t)$ in order to maximize lifetime utility and is subject to the constraint that the present discounted value of both consumption and terminal wealth or bequests (if any) equals lifetime resources, $W$. Formally, the budget constraint is

$$\int_0^T c(t)e^{-rt}\mathrm{d}t + K_T e^{-rt} = W$$

with $r$ the rate of interest, $t$ the consumer's age, $K_T$ the bequest, and $W$ the sum of the present value of earnings and bequests received (*inter vivos* gifts are treated as discounted bequests in the model). $T$ is the certain length of life.[2] A lifetime utility function, the isoelastic function, is specified. The isoelastic function has the following property: when lifetime resources increase, $c(t)$ increases in the same proportion for all $t$. Yaari (1964) has demonstrated that if this property is preserved and the consumption plan does not dictate equal consumption at each instant, then the utility function must be isoelastic. The lifetime utility function is,

$$U - \int_0^T \frac{c(t)^{1-\delta}}{1-\delta} e^{-\rho t}\mathrm{d}t + \frac{bK^{1-\beta}_T}{1-\beta}$$

where $\delta, \beta > 0$

and $b \geq 0$

and $\rho$ is the subjective rate of time preference for consumption. Strict proportionality between consumption and resources follows from this model if one of two parameter relations holds. If $b = 0$, individuals derive no utility from bequests and proportional consumption holds.[3] If $b > 0$ but $\delta = \beta$, proportionality holds. (This result is mentioned by Modigliani and Ando [1957].)

Blinder shows that if $b > 0$ the lifetime marginal propensity to consume (MPC) is less than unity; it decreases with $W$ if $\delta > \beta$ and increases with $W$ if $\beta > \delta$. Hence, the notion that the lifetime MPC is constant over the income distribution is a special case (when $\delta = \beta$) of a general model in which the MPC can either rise or fall with one's resources: the answer hinges on the relative magnitude of $\beta$ and $\delta$. Furthermore, Blinder shows that the effect of permanent inequality (though mean preserving) changes in the income distribution will alter aggregate consumption, and consequently aggregate saving, depending on the relative magnitude of $\beta$ and $\delta$. A reduction in inequality will increase, leave unchanged, or decrease aggregate consumption according to whether $\delta$ is greater than, equal to, or less than $\beta$. Though the relative magnitude of $\beta$ and $\delta$ is unknown, the ratio $\delta/\beta$ is approximately the resource elasticity of bequests. This elasticity has never been estimated; in this paper I will offer an estimate of its magnitude, using data from two sources.

The relationship between lifetime resources and transfers is important in models of income and wealth distribution. If the elasticity of transfers with respect to resources exceeds unity, higher income parents will leave a greater proportion of their income to their children than lower income parents. Assuming that the correlation between parent and child earnings is not negative,[4] this effect would be a force for greater inequality in wealth and nonearned income across generations. The disequalizing effect of nonproportional transfers is shown formally in the intergenerational model presented by Meade (1964) and discussed in detail in Atkinson and Harrison (1978, chap. 8).

Pryor (1973) simulates the distribution of income in a multigenerational context. He specifies an "intergenerational saving function" which relates bequests to lifetime resources. Two forms of the function are used, one function assuming that the elasticity of bequests with respect to resources is unity, the other that bequests are luxury goods, implying an elasticity in excess of unity. His results show that the second function will yield a substantially greater degree of income inequality than the first function.

The magnitude of the resource elasticity of transfers has implications concerning aggregate factor shares and earnings inequality. If the elasticity exceeds unity, a growing economy will experience a rising capital-output ratio, since the aggregate saving rate will rise. If the aggregate elasticity of substitution between capital and labor is less than one, labor's share in the national income will increase over time. However, if capital intensity increases, the degree of inequality of labor income may also increase. A model by Michael Sattinger (1977) generates earnings inequality as an increasing function of capital intensity—a result that depends upon capital-skill complementarity. If Sattinger's analysis is correct (he presents supporting empirical evidence), the distributive consequences of a resource elasticity in excess of unity, in a growing economy, will be an increasing share of national income to labor *and* increasing inequality in the division of that share among earners.

Economic mobility across generations should be influenced by the relationship between lifetime resources and transfers to children. If economic immobility is defined as the degree of similarity in economic position of parents and children, mobility would be the lack of similarity across generations. Material inheritance affords parents the opportunity to influence their children's economic positions. Since higher wealth parents can be expected to make a larger financial bequest to their children than lower wealth parents, this bequest effect would reinforce the positive correlation between parent-child earnings (Sewell and Hauser, 1975) and reduce intergenerational economic mobility.

### The Burden of a Consumption Tax

The U.S. Treasury (1977) has recently been considering the imposition of a consumption tax to replace the income tax. An annual tax on consumption, with a lifetime averaging scheme in which each year's tax is based on the average of present and past years, is tantamount to a a lifetime consumption tax. If transfers are an untaxed good, as I understand them to be in the proposal, the relationship between lifetime resources and transfers is critical in determining the burden of the tax. If, for example, transfers were a luxury good having a resource elasticity in excess of unity, a proportional consumption tax would be regressive with respect to lifetime economic resources. In fact, without knowledge of the elasticity of transfers with respect to total resources, we cannot say *a priori* what the rate schedule would have to be to ensure progressivity or even proportionality.

### Some Prior Expectations

Though the elasticity of transfers or of bequests with respect to lifetime resources is still unknown, some rather strong *a priori* arguments have been made about its magnitude. Gary Becker (1974) presents a a model of intergenerational transfers in which the elasticity of bequests with respect to lifetime resources must exceed unity. His model assumes that family heads act as if they were maximizing a utility function as composed of the wealths of the present and *all* future generations descending from the family head. An assumption of homothetic preferences for all generations, present and future, is sufficient to guarantee that only a small fraction of an increment in the head's resources will be consumed by him, the rest going to his heirs. However, if the head's utility function is not homothetic with respect to the present and all future generations, and if the head does not act as if he is allocating his dynasty's income but only his own, Becker's conclusions need not follow.

Taking quite a different tack, Lester Thurow's (1975) model implies conclusions similar to Becker's concerning the resource elasticity of bequests. In Thurow's model, individuals do not hold or accumulate wealth with the bequest motive or an interdependent utility function motive in mind. In fact, Thurow dismisses the latter reason, citing the "mysterious" fact that large wealthholders do not fully utilize the opportunities to transfer property by making gifts, which are subject to lower rates of taxation than are bequests. A possible explanation for this apparent mystery is that the transfer of appreciated assets by gift is subject to capital gains taxation that uses original cost as the basis while transfer by bequest allows the basis to be stepped up to the value at death of the testator.

In Thurow's formulation, the motive for accumulating and holding wealth is economic power. Individuals enjoy the power that accrues from wealthholding until their death, at which time the wealth passes to heirs. since consumption of market goods and services is subject to diminishing marginal utility, while power, he asserts, is not, wealth and consequently bequests will rise disproportionately with lifetime resources.

However, the elasticity of bequests with respect to lifetime resources will exceed unity under much weaker conditions than those invoked by Thurow. Blinder (1974) points out that the bequest elasticity will exceed unity as long as the marginal utility of consumption declines at a faster rate than the marginal utility of bequests—a condition that I find quite reasonable.

### Some Problems in Estimation

The absence of knowledge about the relationship between lifetime resources and transfers in general, or even bequests alone, is due to the lack of appropriate data. As Blinder states (1976b, p. 92): "To date, lack of either time series or cross-section data on lifetime income and bequests has precluded direct measurement of the wealth elasticity of bequests. . . . it must be admitted that we know relatively little about the wealth elasticity of bequests." It should be pointed out that the data base required to answer the questions posed above would match individual earnings histories and inheritances received with *actual* bequests, not notional or planned bequests (unless plans are perfectly realized, an unlikely occurrence when the time and costs of death are not known with certainty and capital markets are less than perfect). Furthermore, efforts to estimate the relationship between earnings histories and net worth held by living individuals as reported in a survey might be quite imprecise because of nonresponse and response error. There is evidence that high income and high wealth individuals are more likely not to respond than others (Projector and Weiss 1966, p. 58; Ferber 1965, 1969). It has also been found that response bias has the effect of overstating small asset holdings and understating large holdings. (Ferber 1905, 1969). If these factors are operating, the bias would be predictable. The regression coefficient of reported earnings on reported net worth would be *biased downward* if the data base was not adjusted for nonresponse and response error.[5]

### 4.2   Two Simple Models

I formulated two simple models for my analysis, a linear form and a nonlinear form. Each will be described in turn.

### 4.2.1    The Linear Form

Let us say that net worth $A$ is a linear function of "full wealth" $W$, such that,

$$A = \alpha_0 + \alpha_1 W + \epsilon$$

with $\epsilon$ the stochastic error term. Full wealth, $W$, is the sum of two components: the present value of potential lifetime earnings, $E$, and the present value of inherited wealth, $I$.

Since $W = E + I$, we get

$$A = \alpha_0 + \alpha_1 E + \alpha_1 I + \epsilon$$

as the basic linear specification.[6] Net worth in this paper is measured at a very specific point, death, when its magnitude is revealed in the probate records. Hence, we are analyzing a particular net asset holding function. It is the function relating full wealth—potential earnings and inheritance—to terminal wealth or bequests. The present value of *inter vivos* transfers made and received should, of course, be included in both $A$ and $I$. Gifts, to the extent that they were revealed in the probate records, were therefore included in my empirical work.

It is important to note that potential rather than actual earnings are specified in the model. Since potential earnings (average wage rate multiplied by a "standard" number of hours) are independent of variations in leisure time consumed, this formulation avoids a possible source of endogeneity between inheritance received and labor supply, and consequently actual earnings.

In the primary data base used in this study only two of the three variables are observable, $A$ and $I$. Earnings (both potential and actual) are unobservable. If $E$ and $I$ are positively correlated, that is, if inheritors of large amounts are able to earn more than inheritors of small amounts, the estimate of $\alpha_1$ (as well as the intercept $\alpha_0$) from the regression equation is biased upward. There are many possible reasons to think earnings and inheritance are positively correlated: more schooling, which is a result of wealth and leads to high wage rates; genetic endowments that influence earnings (this hypothesis is controversial); family background effects on tastes; and, quite simply, either family or "class" nepotism. If $E$ and $I$ are positively correlated, for whatever reason, the estimated coefficient $\alpha_1$ must be adjusted downward. The unbiased estimate, $\alpha_1$, is related to the biased observed estimate, $\alpha_1$, by the equation

$$\alpha_1 = \alpha_1 / 1 + \frac{\text{COV}(E,I)}{\text{VAR}(I)}$$

In this paper, I try to correct for this omitted variable bias in two ways: first, by using occupational groupings as proxies for earnings, and second, by using extraneous information (data from another sample) to estimate the covariance-variance ratio.

One definition of $\alpha_1$ is the marginal propensity to bequeath. The elasticity of the dependent variable with respect to the independent variables depends, of course, on where along the function the elasticity is evaluated. Standard procedure is to evaluate the elasticity at the mean, since we know that the function goes through that point. Since we do not know mean full wealth in this sample, this specification cannot reveal the full wealth elasticity of bequests.

### 4.2.2    The Double Log Form

Let us now assume that terminal wealth is related to full wealth as follows:

$$A = e^{\gamma_0} W^{\gamma_1} e^{\epsilon}$$

where $W = E + I$, with $\epsilon$ the stochastic error term. We may decompose $W$ to get

$$A = e^{\gamma_0} \left[ I \left( 1 + \frac{E}{I} \right) \right]^{\gamma_1} e^{\epsilon}$$

Taking natural logs we get,

$$\ln A = \gamma_0 + \gamma_1 \ln I + \gamma_1 \ln \left( 1 + \frac{E}{I} \right) + \epsilon$$

In this constant elasticity specification, $\gamma_1$ is the full wealth elasticity of bequests. In this model the omitted variable is $\ln [(1 + E/I)]$ and the unbiased estimate of $\gamma_1$ is related to the biased estimate by

$$\hat{\gamma}_1 = \tilde{\gamma}_1 / 1 + \frac{\text{COV} \left[ \ln I, \ln \left( 1 + \frac{E}{I} \right) \right]}{\text{VAR} \ln I}$$

with $\hat{\gamma}_1$ the unbiased and $\tilde{\gamma}_1$ the observed coefficient. One would expect a negative correlation between $\ln I$ and $\ln [1 + (E/I)]$ since the inheritance term appears in the numerator of one variable and in the denominator of the other. Consequently, it is expected that to correct for the bias, the estimated coefficient $\gamma_1$ would have to be adjusted upward in magnitude. Data from another sample (as already mentioned) will be used to correct for omitted variable bias.

At this stage it is appropriate to consider the implication of these alternative functional forms. The linear form assumes that given increments in full wealth evoke constant incremental changes in bequests (and in lifetime consumption), without regard to the preincremental full wealth position.

The double log form assumes constant proportional responses, with the constant of proportionality being the parameter of interest. The assumption of proportional effects embodied in the double log model seems more plausible to me on *a priori* grounds. Individuals with low full wealth are restricted by their budget constraint in their ability to bequeath; hence variations around the mean would tend to be restricted. Higher full wealth individuals would be less constrained by their budget and the variation in their bequests would tend to be higher. This question is analogous to the issue of error structure in cross-section budget studies. Findings by Prais and Houthakker (1955) support the view that the error variance rises with income in the cross-section studies of expenditure patterns. Furthermore, if the interest rate used to compute the value of full wealth had an error component in it, we would expect the size of the discrepancy between actual and predicted bequest to vary directly with full wealth. In the linear model, simple additivity of the error term, combined with an assumption of a constant error variance, would not yield a discrepancy that increases with full wealth. However, since the error enters the double log specification in a multiplicative fashion, discrepancies that increase in size with full wealth are allowed. In any case, this paper uses two statistical procedures in an effort to determine which form is more appropriate.

## 4.3  The Data

The starting point for my study was a master file of 1,050 Connecticut residents who died in the 1930s and '40s leaving estates of $40,000 or more in current dollars—obviously a very wealthy group.[7] In approximately half the cases, obituary column data was also available. There were 614 cases in which children were indicated by the death records. These 614 parents had 1,458 children, for an average of 2.37 children per family.

The number of children whose probate records were actively searched for was reduced to 1,182, for two reasons: (a) in certain cases, names were illegible or were not given; (b) it was assumed that daughters who were unmarried at the time of the parent's death would eventually marry and change names. (I eventually searched for some of the unmarried daughters and found a small subsample.)

### 4.3.1  Bequests

In order to find the probate records of the children, I first searched the index of deaths in the Connecticut Department of Vital Records. If a name from my active list turned up, I checked the actual death certificate, which listed the name of the child's parents (information I also had from the parent's probate records) and allowed me to make a positive match between parent and child. I then tracked down the estate of the children in the probate files, and using similar methods, I tracked down the estate of the spouse of the parent in the original sample. Connecticut does not have an annual index of deaths before 1948, and I located only 191 cases in which both parents' estates are known; I have used this subsample here.

The 1,182 cases searched are accounted for as follows:

| | |
|---|---:|
| Cases found | 300 |
| Women listed by husband's first name and therefore lost to the sample | 12 |
| Search error (estimate) | 100 |
| Individuals still alive (estimate) | 150–200 |
| Individuals who died out of state (estimate) | 570–620 |

The estimate that 150–200 individuals were alive in 1976 (the last year that was searched) is based on the age distribution of the children. The considerable search error came in making matches based on death data. In order to approximate the magnitude of this error, I ran through my entire list of 1,182 at a designated probate district, and found a number of children in the probate files that I had overlooked in the death index. The proportion of my sample that fell within this district gave me an estimate of 100 cases lost by search error.

If the heirs of a child in my sample did not file because the child in my sample had no wealth or negative wealth, truncation of the dependent variable might bias my results. According to Connecticut statutes, however, records for estates of *any* positive size must be filed, even if only a small estates affidavit is made. The Connecticut Probate Administration has recently begun to tabulate the number of estates in which records are filed on a yearly basis. In 1975, the first year of tabulation, they reported 19,939 cases filed. The total number of deaths of adult Connecticut residents in 1975 is 24,466; we thus can estimate a filing ratio of 81.5 percent (State of Connecticut 1977).

How likely is it that one of the children in my sample fell in the bottom 18.5 percent (those who did not file because there was no estate), after having been born to parents in roughly the upper 2 percent of the wealth distribution? Projector and Weiss (1966) report, by wealth class, the proportion of consumer units for whom inherited assets constitute a "substantial" proportion of total assets. The bottom wealth class (less than $1,000) constitute 26 percent of the consumer units. Since my sample was drawn from inheritors, the inherited portion of total wealth for any low wealth member of that sample should be substantial. The number of the group that reported the answer "substantial" is zero. This does not, of course, prove lack of truncation bias, but it does suggest that the problem is minimal in this particular sample.

A potentially more serious problem is the lack of data for those who moved out of state. If the movers earn more than the stayers, the measured ratio of inheritance to terminal wealth will be biased upward. (The danger of bias is much less for the coefficient estimates, since the market for capital is a national market.) If it is true that movers earn more than stayers, the measured ratio of inheritance to terminal wealth will be biased upward in this study. However, I do not think we can say on *a priori* grounds that movers will earn more than stayers; we can only argue that those who move do so because they think their earnings opportunities will be greater after moving than they would have been if they had chosen to stay.[8] Furthermore, the decision to move from an area can be expected to depend on prospects at both the destination and the origin. Connecticut is the richest state in per capita income in the continental United States.[9] Prosperous or soon-to-be-prosperous people are more likely to move from relatively poor states, for instance, Mississippi, to wealthy areas. The mover/stayer issue might, therefore, cause biases in intergenerational studies centering on these states. Since Connecticut is a wealthy state the danger of bias is not nearly so great as it would be for other states.

An additional argument for assuming that the mover-stayer issue is not a problem in my sample is that the people I studied tended to own businesses or were corporate executives and successful professionals. Individuals operating their parents' businesses would tend to be stayers. Corporate executives outside Connecticut are unlikely to be more successful than Connecticut corporate executives, given the agglomeration of high corporate executives residing in Fairfield County. The same argument would hold for successful professionals. Wealthy lawyers, for instance, who work in the New York metropolitan area are likely to live outside it, and Connecticut has never had an income tax (New York has one). Finally, the median estate for the sixteen out-of-state decedents that I was able to find was only 1 percent higher than that of the in-state decedents.

### 4.3.2    Inter Vivos Transfers

If a gift is made "in contemplation of death," it is treated as a bequest for Connecticut death tax purposes. However, whether or not a particular gift is made in contemplation of death is a matter for the probate authorities to decide, and all gifts are supposed to be revealed to the authorities, whether they will ultimately be considered taxable or not. I incorporated the information on gifts revealed in the probate records, using rates of return discussed below, in my definitions of inheritance received and terminal wealth.

### 4.3.3    Contingent Bequests

When a testator bequeaths the life interest of an asset to an heir, with the asset itself passing to a subsequent heir (the remainderman) after the initial heir dies, the present value of the contingent bequest is allocated to the remainderman. The present value is calculated using the age and life expectancy of the initial heir and an appropriate discount rate (4% was used by the Connecticut authorities). The difference between the current value of the asset and the present value of the contingent interest is allocated to the life tenant.

## 4.4 Empirical Results

What is the proportion of material wealth attributable to inheritance among the people in this sample of inheritors? A simple answer to this question, following in the tradition of the two previous studies cited, would be to compute the ratio of the present value of inheritances received to wealth held when the data are revealed to us, i.e., upon the death of the inheritor.

Inheritance is defined in this paper as including only bequests and gifts (as revealed in the probate records) from both parents. It excludes inheritances received from others (grandparents, spouse, siblings, and so on) and is, therefore, a lower bound estimate of total inheritances received by the child. We should use the present value, at death, of inheritance received, since a dollar of wealth received in the past would potentially grow at the market rate of return over time; its present value would, therefore, indicate its current command over resources. If the ratio of the present value of inheritance received and terminal wealth is less than unity for an individual, we can say that in a life cycle sense he was a net saver out of his own earnings. Conversely, if the ratio exceeds unity, he was a net "depleter."

There are several possible complications in this approach. If individual net worth reaches a peak and then declines with age, the denominator of the ratio (net worth at death) would be understated relative to the lifetime peak. Moreover, if the rate of return was positive in the period after the individual's peak wealth position, the ratio of inheritance and wealth would tend to be overstated (relative to the peak) for both of these reasons. There is, however, an increasing body of evidence that suggests that wealthholding rises monotonically with age, and that individuals die at or near their lifetime peak (Mirer 1979; Smith 1975; Shorrocks 1975). Within my sample I found no significant effect of age at death or age at death squared on terminal wealth or the log of terminal wealth. Since, as Shorrocks points out, a flat age-wealth relation in the cross-section implies an increasing individual profile over time if real productivity is growing, these data imply that wealth is at a lifetime peak at death.

Another possible complication would occur if there were changes over time in the share of full wealth that parents expend on human capital investments in their children. For example, suppose the parents in the sample purchased only a high school education for the children, while the children purchased a college education for their own children. In such a case, children who were identical to their parents in every respect, except for a difference in the composition (not total amount) of their intergenerational transfer, would more likely be classified as "depleters" than their parents, since human-capital-augmenting expenditures are not measured in this study.

The real value (in 1967 dollars) of the terminal wealth of the 191 children in my sample is highly skewed, with a mean of $1,086,000, a median of $156,520, and a standard deviation of $3,811,848.[10] The value of inheritance received from parents in *real* (not present-value) units has a mean of $205,077, a median of $57,846, and a standard deviation of $386,098. The ratio of real inheritance received and terminal wealth for each child is distributed as follows:

| Percentile | |
| --- | --- |
| 5th | .030 |
| 25th | .125 |
| 50th (median) | .293 |
| 75th | .810 |
| 95th | 7.548 |

These ratios, generally less than unity, indicate the proportion of terminal wealth attributed to inheritance *only* from parents in a world in which the real rate of return is zero. Using this method, we see that at the median the ratio of inheritance to terminal wealth is approximately .30, implying that inheritance accounts for 30 percent of terminal wealth. A more realistic technique is to compute these ratios with positive real rates of return.

In order to compute present values it is necessary to choose appropriate measures of the market rate of return, i.e., that rate at which wealth would grow from the time the bequest was received to the time of death of the child. I used four different rates: an interest rate (the rate on prime commercial 4–6 months paper),[11] and three stock market rates. The stock market rates were constructed from the Fisher and Lorie (1977) stock index, using three alternative tax treatments of the dividends yielded.[12] (Since I want the total rate of return I use the rates that assume all dividends are reinvested.) The first assumption is that no tax was paid, the second that tax was paid at a medium rate (the rate on an individual with taxable income of $10,000 in 1960), and the third that tax was paid at a high rate (the rate at the $50,000 level in 1960).

The interest rate on prime commercial 4–6 months paper kept only slightly ahead of inflation. Over the period 1926 to 1960, for example, an asset growing at this interest rate would have increased in market value by 197 percent. But during the same period prices rose by 167 percent. The value of stocks using the high tax rate index grew 1,737 percent between 1926 and 1960, and the growth rates of the other two series were even greater. We may thus think of the interest rate return as a conservative return that only modestly augments the real value of the portfolio.

Table 4.1 presents the size distribution of the ratio of present value of inheritance received and terminal wealth, using four asset price indexes. There is substantial variation in the ratio for each index used. The interest rate index implies that at the median, about 50 percent of the child's terminal wealth can be attributed to parental inheritance. If this index is the appropriate rate of return, we can say that most of the children were net savers out of own earnings. The results using the three stock price indexes are quite different. Index 2, for example, assumes a value of 4.40 at the median. This implies that the median child not only consumed all his own earnings, but most of the yield from his inheritance (dividends as well as capital appreciation), and still left an estate more than three times that left to him by his parents, in constant dollars (since the median ratio of the real value of inheritance to terminal wealth is about .3). Let me add as qualifications, that the stock price indexes do not take capital gains taxation into account and that the typical portfolio may have included less productive but perhaps less risky assets than shares on the New York Stock Exchange. In any case, the results in column 1 indicate that if the median child's inheritance grew only as fast as the interest rate index, parental inheritance alone would amount to one-half of the child's terminal wealth. If higher rates of return are used, parental inheritance would amount to a much greater share of terminal wealth and, in fact, exceed unity.

### 4.4.1 The Demand to Bequeath: Uncorrected Estimates

In this section regression results relating terminal wealth to inheritance received are presented. Recall that these estimates are biased due to the

**Table 4.1**    **Ratio of Real Present Value of Inheritance Received from Parents and Real Terminal Wealth**

| Distribution (percentile) | Asset Price Indexes | | | |
|---|---|---|---|---|
| | Index 1 Interest Rate | Index 2 Stocks–High Tax | Index 3 Stocks–Med. Tax | Index 4 Stocks–No Tax |
| 5 | .05 | .36 | .42 | .46 |
| 25 | .25 | 1.40 | 1.74 | 2.01 |
| 50 | .51 | 4.40 | 6.15 | 7.86 |
| 75 | 1.48 | 12.50 | 16.50 | 21.30 |
| 95 | 11.26 | 154.00 | 180.00 | 260.00 |

omission of lifetime earnings from the regression. First, the results from the linear model are presented, then the double log results.

The dependent variable in these regression equations is the value of terminal wealth (in constant 1967 dollars) of the children. If a child made a gift, its value is added to terminal wealth after it has been inflated with one of the four indexes mentioned above. Four versions of the major independent variable, present value (also in 1967 dollars) of inheritance received from mother and father, were constructed using the four indexes. The bivariate regression results appear in table 4.2. As can be seen, the coefficient estimates are quite sensitive to the asset price index used.

The wide range in coefficient estimates is a consequence of the scaling of the independent variable. The higher the rate of return used the greater the real present value of the inheritance received, and the lower the value of its coefficient estimate. In a case like this, the $\bar{R}^2$ tells us something about the appropriate results to rely upon. The independent variable is constructed from three components, nominal inheritance received, the time between the child's death and that of his parents, and the rate of return. Only the third factor varies across regressions, and the $\bar{R}^2$ tells us that the first index provides the least information in explaining the variation of the dependent variable. The $\bar{R}^2$ for the last three regressions implies that for this group nearly 60 percent of the variation in terminal wealth is explained by variation in inheritance received.

In table 4.3 the loglinear regression results are presented; they indicate that the uncorrected full wealth elasticities cluster between .32 and .38.

**Table 4.2**     **Regression Results: Real Terminal Wealth (RWLTH) as a Linear Function of Real Present Value of Inheritance Received (RPVNHER)**

|  | Independent Variable | | | | | |
| --- | --- | --- | --- | --- | --- | --- |
| Dependent Variable | RPVNHER #1 | RPVNHER #2 | RPVNHER #3 | RPVNHER #4 | Constant | $\bar{R}^2$ |
| RWLTH #1 | 2.801 (10.5) | | | | −74,234.6 | .358 |
| RWLTH #2 | | .1860 (16.7) | | | 60,649.0 | .595 |
| RWLTH #3 | | | .1253 (16.6) | | 95,800.1 | .591 |
| RWLTH #4 | | | | .0939 (16.3) | 120,828.5 | .582 |

*Note*: "*t*" ratio in parentheses; $n = 191$.

Table 4.3          Regression Results: Log of Terminal Wealth (LWLTH) on
                   Log of Inheritance (LPVNHER)

| | Independent Variable | | | | | |
|---|---|---|---|---|---|---|
| Dependent Variable | LPVNHER #1 | LPVNHER #2 | LPVNHER #3 | LPVNHER #4 | Constant | $\bar{R}^2$ |
| LWLTH #1 | .3833 (6.63) | | | | 7.642 | .185 |
| LWLTH #2 | | .3388 (7.28) | | | 7.502 | .215 |
| LWLTH #3 | | | .3346 (7.37) | | 7.466 | .219 |
| LWLTH #4 | | | | .3287 (7.36) | 7.482 | .219 |

*Note*: "*t*" ratio in parentheses, $n = 191$.

Additional explanatory variables were added to the regression equations. SEX is a dummy variable assuming a value of unity for males, zero for females. Three marital status dummies were added, MAR, WIDOW, and NEV MAR. These assume a value of unity if the subject was married (at time of death), widowed, or never married. Divorced persons constitute the excluded basis. SIBSHIP is the number of the child's siblings plus one. Birth cohort dummies were added to the regression to link the subject's wealth accumulation behavior to history, since people born at different times faced different economic environments during their lives. BC1, BC2, BC3, BC4, and BC5 assume values of unity if the subject was born before 1876, from 1876 to 1885, from 1886 to 1895, from 1896 to 1905, and from 1906 to 1915 respectively. The excluded basis consists of those born after 1915. UBC consists of those whose birth cohort could not be determined with the available data (there are eight such cases). Occupational dummies were added as well: $OCC_1$ has a value of unity for those owning a business; $OCC_2$ for business executives, $OCC_3$ for those engaged in domestic duties, $OCC_5$ for those whose occupations could not be determined from the available data, $OCC_6$ for those who were independent professionals. ($OCC_4$, the excluded basis, assumes a value of unity for those in all other occupations.) The regression results are presented in tables 4.4 and 4.5. This battery of demographic and occupational variables adds little in terms of $\bar{R}^2$ or statistical significance (with the possible exception of $OCC_1$ in table 4.5, implying that business owners save at higher rates than others).[13] Inclusion of these variables has a negligible effect on the coefficient estimates of the inheritance variable. I also experimented with additional variables: age (at death), age squared, and the number of children of the inheriting child. These added nothing in terms of statistical sig-

**Table 4.4**  Regression Results: Effect of Explanatory Variables on Terminal Wealth

| Independent Variable | Dependent Variable | | | |
|---|---|---|---|---|
| | RWLTH #1 | RWLTH #2 | RWLTH #3 | RWLTH #4 |
| RPVNHER #1 | 2.747 (9.49) | | | |
| RPVNHER #2 | | .187 (11.14) | | |
| RPVNHER #3 | | | .126 (15.86) | |
| RPVNHER #4 | | | | .095 (15.57) |
| | | In 000s | | |
| SEX | −382.3 (−.518) | 178.3 (.305) | 190.9 (.324) | 208.1 (.349) |
| MAR | 465.0 (.423) | 485.2 (.526) | 463.2 (.526) | 458.1 (.513) |
| WIDOW | −81.5 (.068) | −397.1 (−.419) | −405.7 (−.424) | −422.4 (−.435) |
| NEV MAR | −25.4 (.020) | −172.4 (−.173) | −194.3 (.193) | −191.1 (−.187) |
| SIBSHIP | −34.4 (−.234) | 22.3 (.154) | 16.6 (.143) | 12.4 (.105) |
| BC$_1$ | −810.6 (−.325) | 100.5 (.051) | 210.9 (.107) | 267.7 (.133) |
| BC$_2$ | −486.0 (−.207) | −283.5 (−.154) | −214.4 (−.115) | −177.2 (−.094) |
| BC$_3$ | −434.9 (−.185) | −374.2 (−.202) | −345.3 (−.185) | −316.7 (−.167) |
| BC$_4$ | −235.4 (−.099) | 8.49 (.005) | 30.0 (.016) | 50.7 (.027) |
| BC$_5$ | 16.2 (.007) | 748.0 (.394) | 719.6 (.375) | 708.3 (.364) |
| UBC | 444.7 (.271) | −1,390.2 (−1.07) | −1,471.3 (1.13) | −1,479.5 (−1.16) |
| OCC$_1$ | 981.7 (1.25) | 462.0 (.744) | 467.5 (.746) | 488.0 (.768) |
| OCC$_2$ | −104.2 (.114) | −202.8 (−.253) | −226.3 (.313) | −246.4 (−.336) |
| OCC$_3$ | −428.4 (.499) | −81.2 (−.120) | 72.4 (.106) | 60.4 (−.087) |
| OCC$_5$ | −318.1 (.364) | 34.9 (.051) | 63.4 (.091) | 54.8 (.078) |
| OCC$_6$ | 1,342.2 (.364) | 780.6 (.920) | 851.1 (1.06) | 888.2 (1.09) |
| CONSTANT | 275.6 | −227.1 | −209.0 | −208.2 |
| $\bar{R}^2$ (adj.) | .325 | .506 | .599 | .588 |

*Note*: "$t$" ratio in parentheses.

**Table 4.5    Regression Results: Effect of Explanatory Variables on Log of Terminal Wealth**

| Independent Variable | Dependent Variable | | | |
|---|---|---|---|---|
| | LWLTH #1 | LWLTH #2 | LWLTH #3 | LWLTH #4 |
| LPVNHER #1 | .358 (5.85) | | | |
| LPVNHER #2 | | .321 (6.61) | | |
| LPVNHER #3 | | | .318 (6.74) | |
| LPVNHER #4 | | | | .313 (6.75) |
| | | In 000s | | |
| SEX | −.326 (−.751) | −.271 (−.635) | −.285 (−.668) | −.284 (−.665) |
| MAR | .387 (.586) | .375 (.579) | .363 (.561) | .362 (.559) |
| WIDOW | .250 (.351) | .212 (.303) | .198 (.283) | .188 (.268) |
| NEV MAR | .137 (.182) | .147 (.199) | .108 (.147) | .104 (.141) |
| SIBSHIP | −.076 (−.873) | −.112 (−1.34) | −.114 (−1.35) | −.116 (−1.38) |
| $BC_1$ | −1.33 (−.908) | −1.50 (−1.04) | −1.47 (−1.02) | −1.46 (−1.01) |
| $BC_2$ | −1.04 (−.749) | −1.26 (−.926) | −1.26 (−.930) | −1.26 (−.932) |
| $BC_3$ | −1.18 (−.849) | −1.34 (−.983) | −1.38 (−1.01) | −1.39 (−1.02) |
| $BC_4$ | −1.61 (−1.15) | −1.67 (−1.22) | −1.70 (−1.24) | −1.71 (−1.24) |
| $BC_5$ | −.978 (−.688) | −.958 (−.684) | −1.01 (−.721) | −1.03 (−.739) |
| UBC | .275 (.285) | .496 (.522) | .431 (.455) | .409 (.432) |
| $OCC_1$ | .972 (1.99) | .953 (2.10) | .968 (2.14) | .976 (2.16) |
| $OCC_2$ | .547 (1.02) | .549 (1.04) | .563 (1.07) | .564 (1.07) |
| $OCC_3$ | −.177 (−.351) | −.148 (−.298) | −.168 (−.339) | −.172 (−.347) |
| $OCC_5$ | .347 (.676) | .392 (.776) | .439 (.870) | .446 (.883) |
| $OCC_6$ | .551 (.929) | .509 (.871) | .529 (.908) | .539 (.924) |
| CONSTANT | 8.94 | 8.98 | 8.96 | 8.98 |
| $\bar{R}^2$ (adj.) | .162 | .199 | .205 | .205 |

*Note*: "*t*" ratio in parentheses, $n = 191$.

nificance, did not increase $\bar{R}^2$, and did not alter the coefficient of inheritance or log of inheritance received.[14]

### 4.4.2    Correcting for Omitted Variable Bias

I used information from another data base, that in Morgan et al. (1962), to estimate the covariance/variance ratio between the excluded and included variables. This survey asked if the respondent received an inheritance. If the answer was yes, it asked how much, and when. There were also questions about earnings and hours worked. I used a subsample of respondents aged 55 to 64. Since my interest was in matching results from my sample with those having the same attributes in the Morgan study, I used only those 124 families reporting that they had received positive inheritances. Annual earnings were divided by annual hours to generate wage rates. Positive wage rates were assigned to those with zero wages (both husband and wife), using a potential earnings code based on age, sex, and education. Since the year of inheritance was reported, I was able to calculate the present value of inheritance received, assuming a 5 percent discount rate. The observed correlation between wage and inheritance received for this group of inheritors was positive, .17.

To estimate a value for $E$, potential lifetime earnings, I used the lifetime age-earnings profile presented by Mincer (1974), and discounted lifetime earnings to age 59.5 at a 5 percent rate. I assumed a working life beginning at 18 years of age and ending at 65. The correction factor in the linear model is the covariance of $E$ and $I$, divided by the variance of $I$, plus one. The estimated covariance/variance ratio came to 1.139, implying a correction factor of 2.139. Hence, the unbiased coefficient estimates of inheritance on terminal wealth are less than one-half the biased estimates. The unbiased coefficient estimate, $\alpha_1$ in the linear model (using the results from table 4.1), is 1.31 when the interest rate of return is used. When the stock price indexes are used to compute present value of inheritance received, the $\alpha_1$ estimates are .087, .059, and .044 for the high tax, medium tax, and low tax rates of return respectively. If we select the rates of return that maximize the proportion of explained to total variance of the dependent variable in the regression equations, the coefficients that we obtained when using the stock price rates are chosen. The coefficient .087, corresponding to the high tax rate index, is consequently the most preferred estimate of the marginal propensity to bequeath out of full wealth when the model is constrained to be linear.

I found the correlation between the omitted and excluded variables in the loglinear model—recall that these were $\ln I$ and $\ln [(1 + E/I)]$—to be sharply negative: $-.883$. The covariance was $-2.225$ and the variance of $\ln I$, 2.586. Hence, the covariance/variance ratio is computed to be —.86. The correction factor is therefore .14, implying that the true full wealth elasticity is more than seven times the biased estimates obtained in the loglinear models. The unbiased elasticity estimates $\gamma_1$, using the interest and stock price rates of return, were computed to be 2.75, 2.42, 2.40, and 2.36 respectively. Hence, regardless of the choice of discount rate, the estimates of the elasticity of bequests are in the elastic range when the double log form is used.

### 4.4.3  Determination of Functional Form

Maximum likelihood methods have been devised by Box and Cox (1964) for choosing among alternative function forms. Heckman and Polachek (1974) have utilized this technique to choose among alternative forms of the earnings/schooling relationship.[15] Using a transformation of the sum of squared residuals, I selected the double log form over its alternative, the linear specification. As an additional test, the parametric test developed by Goldfeld and Quandt (1965) was used to select between the linear and double log form. Applying this procedure, I find that the linear specification fails to yield homoscedastic residuals. The residuals from the double log form do indeed exhibit homoscedasticity. Thus, the assumption of constant proportional effects assumed in the double log form is supported by these two tests.

### 4.4.4  Computing Confidence Intervals

As I mentioned in section 4.1, the magnitude of the elasticity of bequests with respect to lifetime resources has theoretical and policy implications. It is most important to know if this elasticity exceeds unity. On the basis of the Goldfeld-Quandt test, it was determined that the disturbances in the double log model are homoscedastic and that therefore the estimated variance of $\hat{\gamma}_1$, the full wealth elasticity, is unbiased. Consequently we can construct confidence intervals around $\hat{\gamma}_1$, and test hypotheses using standard procedure.

The unbiased estimate of the full wealth elasticity is a function of two components, the biased estimate of $\gamma_1$ and the correction factor (call this factor $\beta$). Hence $\hat{\gamma}_1 = f(\tilde{\gamma}_1, \beta)$. Using the Taylor expansion for $f$ the variance of $\hat{\gamma}_1$ can be approximated as

$$VAR(\hat{\gamma}_1) \approx \left(\frac{\partial f}{\partial \tilde{\gamma}_1}\right)^2 VAR(\tilde{\gamma}_1) + \left(\frac{\partial f}{\partial \beta}\right)^2 VAR(\beta)$$

$$+ 2\left(\frac{\partial f}{\partial \tilde{\gamma}_1}\right)\left(\frac{\partial f}{\partial \beta}\right) COV(\tilde{\gamma}_1, \beta)$$

The covariance term is zero since the estimates were taken from independent samples. In this case $f(\tilde{\gamma}_1, \beta) = \tilde{\gamma}_1/\beta^2$, so $(\partial f/\partial \tilde{\gamma}_1)^2 = 1/\beta^2$ and $(\partial f/\partial \beta)^2 = \tilde{\gamma}_1^2/\beta^4$.

Using the estimated variances, the standard errors of $\hat{\gamma}_1$ are easily computed and are presented in table 4.6. Given the size of the standard errors we can reject the null hypothesis that our elasticity is unity at the .025 level for each of the four estimates. These data support the hypothesis that bequests are luxury goods.

### 4.4.5  Are the Results Believable?

Though 2.5 may at first seem like a high elasticity of bequests with respect to lifetime resources, it is plausible if we keep the Engels aggregation property in mind. This property states that, for a consumer, the weighted sum of income elasticities for each good is unity, with the weights being the share of one's budget expended on each good. In the lifetime context of my model there are two goods, lifetime consumption and bequests, and lifetime resources (full wealth) constitute the income measure. Hence,

$$\alpha_C E_C + \alpha_B E_B = 1$$

with $E_C$ and $E_B$ the elasticities of lifetime consumption and bequests with respect to lifetime resources, and $\alpha_C$ and $\alpha_B$ the respective budget shares. Since, for the overwhelming majority of people, bequests constitute a small portion of lifetime resources, $\alpha_C$ would tend to dominate $\alpha_B$ in magnitude; hence the weighted sum of $E_C$ and $E_B$ would be unity even with seemingly high values of $E_B$. For example, if as estimated in this paper $E_B = 2.5$, we get

$$\alpha_C = \frac{1.5}{2.5 - E_C}$$

Though an estimate of the elasticity of consumption with respect to lifetime resources has not appeared in the literature, a measure that is conceptually very similar to it has been estimated: the permanent income elasticity of consumption. Permanent income has been defined as the perpetual flow yield of an asset equal in value to lifetime resources. Since the annual yields of perpetual and life annuities of equal present value

| Table 4.6 | Estimates of the Full Wealth Elasticity of Bequests | |
| --- | --- | --- |
| Asset Price Index | Unbiased Elasticity | Standard Error |
| Interest rate | 2.75 | .840 |
| Stock price high tax | 2.42 | .645 |
| Stock price medium tax | 2.40 | .593 |
| Stock price low tax | 2.36 | .633 |

are quite similar, the permanent and lifetime income elasticities of consumption should be quite similar.[16] Estimated permanent income elasticities of consumption fall in the range of .85 to .95.[17] Using the above relationship, elasticities of .85, .90, and .95 predict lifetime consumption budget shares of .9090, .9375, and .9677 respectively. Hence my bequest elasticity of 2.5 is quite consistent with existing estimates of the permanent income elasticities of consumption as long as budget shares for bequests are less than 10 percent—a requirement that is plausible for the overwhelming majority of consumers.

## 4.5    Conclusion

This paper estimates the ratio of inherited to total wealth at death for a sample of children of wealthy parents. This ratio is quite sensitive to the choice of discount rate used. If the interest rate or prime commercial paper 4-6 months is used, the median ratio is .5. If the rate of return on stocks is used, the ratio is substantially greater, exceeding unity.

Two models, a linear and a double log model, were estimated for the relationship of net worth at death to "full wealth," the sum of potential lifetime earnings and inheritance received (both expressed in present value units). Statistical methods determined that the double log model was more appropriate to this set of data. The implication of this functional form is that lifetime saving is generated by constant proportional, not absolute, responses. Since the constant of proportionality, the full wealth elasticity, clusters around 2.5 we can say that a 1 percent increase in full wealth will result in a 2.5 percent increase in lifetime saving. Consequently a more egalitarian state will have a lower savings rate (in a life cycle sense) than a less egalitarian state, other things being the same. One must, however, be careful about concluding that a consequence of equalizing income redistribution will necessarily be to reduce the rate of total capital formation. If income is redistributed in ways that augment people's productive abilities, the rate of increase of total capital, both physical and human, need not be diminished. For example, if as a consequence of income inequality children born to low income parents are less likely to achieve their earning potential than other children, then income redistribution in cash or in kind may augment human capital, and offset the reduction in the growth of nonhuman capital.[18]

There is a further reason for caution in concluding that an equity–capital formation tradeoff exists. Equalizing the income distribution need not reduce macro capital formation if other policy adjustments are made as well. Use of monetary or fiscal policy, i.e., increased government saving or expanded use of investment incentives, can prevent the rate of capital formation from falling.

If it is true that the elasticity of bequests with respect to life resources is 2.5, the lifetime marginal and average propensities to consume fall with life income in the cross-section; this implies that a lifetime consumption tax having a proportional rate structure will be regressive with respect to life resources. Furthermore, as long as the intercorrelation between the earnings of parents and children is positive, intergenerational transfers will reduce economic equality within a generation and reduce economic mobility across generations.

Closing on a note of caution, I must add that the parameter estimates presented in this paper depend on the correction factors used, correction factors that used only one year of earnings information to construct a lifetime earnings estimate. To obtain results resting on firmer ground we need new data sources that link multiyear earnings histories with either inheritance received, terminal wealth, or both.

Impressive analytical and simulation models have been devised to study the distribution of wealth and the intergenerational transmission of wealth inequality. It is now up to empirical research to keep pace with these impressive advances.

# Notes

1. John Brittain (1978) is attempting to answer a question similar to the first question, using an indirect approach.

2. Levhari and Mirman (1977) have analyzed the saving-consumption decision when length of life is uncertain. Uncertainty can either increase or decrease lifetime consumption; the net effect is not known *a priori*.

3. If $b = 0$, people would not bother to change wills as a consequence of changes in death taxation in which the level of death taxation varies with the form of estate devolution. In fact, one could argue that if $b = 0$, people would not write wills at all since the legal fees associated with will writing can be a costly expenditure diverting resources from consumption.

4. In fact, evidence presented by Sewell and Hauser (1975) reveals a positive correlation of about .2 between the earnings of parent and child. This would tend to strengthen the disequalizing effect of transfers that proportionately increase with increasing resources.

5. An example of an unadjusted data base is the Retirement History Survey of the Social Security Administration (Ireland et al. 1976).

6. Present values are calculated to the point in time when $A$ is measured.

7. I am indebted to William McKinstry for making this data base available to me.

8. To check the probable magnitude of this problem, we estimated the ratio of the earnings of Wisconsin high school graduates who moved out of state to the earnings of the stayers, 17 years after graduation. It revealed that movers earned 26 percent more than stayers. However, for those whose parents were in the top 10 percent of the income distribution, the ratio was only 9.6 percent, which sug-

gests that the differential falls as we move up the parental income distribution. This tabulation was done for me by Robert Hauser using the Sewell and Hauser (1975) sample.

9. In fact, it could be argued that mover/stayer bias could run in the opposite direction, if lower earners move to less expensive or affluent areas outside Connecticut.

10. The price deflator used is the Consumer Price Index compiled by the Bureau of Labor Statistics.

11. The annual index was computed using the series presented in the U.S. Bureau of the Census (1975) and updated in the annual series, *Statistical Abstract of the United States.*

12. Fisher and Lorie's rates of return are based on the behavior of all stocks listed on the New York Stock Exchange and constitute the most comprehensive stock index ever constructed. I constructed an asset price time series from their annual rates. Since their annual rates include only one digit past the decimal, the cumulative effects of rounding can be substantial. The procedure inflates the value of an inheritance received at a time $t_o$, $N_{t_o}$, to a value at time $T$, $PV_T$, in the following way:

$$\frac{PV_T}{N_{t_o}} = \prod_{i = t_o}^{T} (1 + r_i) \text{ with } r_i \text{ the rate of return in year } i.$$

For the rates used see Fisher and Lorie (1977, pp. 24–25, 28–29, and 32–33).

13. I was suprised that WIDOW, a dummy assuming a value of unity if the person was a widow or widower, was not positive and significant. Since I do not have the interspousal transfers of children in the data base, I though that surviving spouses, having an opportunity to inherit from their mates, would possess more terminal wealth than others in the sample.

14. Could it be that for this group, only inheritance matters?

15. Discussions of this technique are presented in econometrics textbooks by Zarembka (1974) and Rao and Miller (1971).

16: For example, with a 10 percent interest rate the annual yield of a 50-year annuity is less than 1 percent greater per annum than the yield of a perpetual annuity of equal present value.

17. See Mayer (1972) for income elasticities estimated by Friedman and others.

18. Examples of such policies would include expenditures on health and education as well as general redistributive policies that strengthen (not weaken) the family and provide work incentives and opportunities.

# References

Atkinson, A. 1971. "The Distribution of Wealth and the Individual Life Cycle." *Oxford Economic Papers,* n.s., vol. 23.

Atkinson, A., and A. Harrison. 1978. *The Distribution of Personal Wealth in Britain.* Cambridge: Cambridge University Press.

Barlow, R., H. Brazer, and J. Morgan. 1966. *Economic Behavior of the Affluent.* Washington, D.C.: Brookings.

Becker, G. 1974. "A Theory of Social Interactions." *Journal of Political Economy* 82:1063–94.

Blinder, A. 1973. "A Model of Inherited Wealth." *Quarterly Journal of Economics* 87:608–26.

————. 1974. *Toward an Economic Theory of Income Distribution.* Cambridge, Mass.: M.I.T. Press.

————. 1975. "Distribution Effects and the Aggregate Consumption Function." *Journal of Political Economy* 83:447–76.

————. 1976a. "Inequality and Mobility in the Distribution of Wealth." *Kyklos* 29–Fasc. 4:607–38.

————. 1976b. "Intergenerational Transfers and Life Cycle Consumption. Papers and Proceedings of the American Economic Association 66, no. 2, pp. 87–93.

Box, G., and D. Cox. 1964. "An Analysis of Transformations." *Journal of the Royal Statistical Society* Ser. D 26, no. 2, pp. 211–52.

Brittain, J. 1978. *Inheritance and the Inequality of Material Wealth.* Washington, D.C.: Brookings.

Ferber, R. 1965. "The Reliability of Consumer Surveys of Financial Holdings: Time Deposits." *Journal of the American Statistical Association* 60:148–63.

————, et al. 1969. "Validation of Consumer Financial Characteristics: Common Stock." *Journal of the American Statistical Association* 64: 415–32.

Fisher, L., and J. Lorie. 1977. *A Half Century of Returns on Stocks and Bonds.* Chicago: University of Chicago Press.

Friedman, M. 1957. *A Theory of the Consumption Function.* Princeton: Princeton University Press.

Goldfeld, S., and R. Quandt. 1965. "Some Tests for Homoscedasticity." *Journal of the American Statistical Association* 60:539–47.

Harbury, C. 1962. "Inheritance and the Distribution of Personal Wealth in Britain." *Economic Journal* 72:845–68.

Heckman, J., and S. Polachek. 1974. "Empirical Evidence on the Functional Form of the Earnings-Schooling Relationship." *Journal of the American Statistical Association* 69:350–54.

Ireland, L., et al. 1976. *Almost 65: Baseline Data from the Retirement History Study.* U.S. Department of Health, Education, and Welfare. Washington, D.C.: Government Printing Office.

Levhari, D., and J. Mirman. 1977. "Savings and Consumption with an Uncertain Horizon." *Journal of Political Economy* 85:265–82.

Mayer, T. 1972. *Permanent Income, Wealth and Consumption.* Cambridge, Mass.: Harvard University Press.

Meade, J. 1964. *Efficiency, Equality and the Ownership of Property.* Cambridge, Mass.: Harvard University Press.

Mincer, J. 1974. *Schooling, Experience and Earnings*. New York: National Bureau of Economic Research.

Mirer, T. 1979. "The Wealth-Age Relationship among the Aged." *American Economic Review* 69:435–43.

Modigliani, F., and Ando, A. 1957. "Tests of the Life Cycle Hypothesis of Saving." *Bulletin of the Oxford Institute of Statistics* 19:99–124.

Modigliani, F., and R. Brumberg. 1954. "Utility Analysis and the Consumption Function: An Interpretation of Cross-Section Data." In K. K. Kurihara, ed., *Post-Keynesian Economics*. New Brunswick, N.J.: Rutgers University Press.

Morgan, J.; M. David; W. Cohen; and H. Brazer. 1962. *Income and Welfare in the United States*. New York: McGraw-Hill.

Oulton, N. 1976. "Inheritance and the Distribution of Wealth." *Oxford Economic Papers*, n. s. 28:86–101.

Prais, S. and H. Houthakker. 1955. *The Analysis of Family Budgets*. Cambridge: Cambridge University Press.

Projector, D., and G. Weiss. 1966. *Survey of Financial Characteristics of Consumers*. Washington, D.C.: Federal Reserve Board.

Pryor, F. 1973. Simulation of the Impact of Social and Economic Institutions on the Size Distribution of Income and Wealth." *American Economic Review* 63:50-72.

Rao, P. and R. Miller. 1971. *Applied Econometrics*. Belmont, California: Wadsworth.

Sattinger, M. 1977. "Capital Intensity and Labor Earnings Inequality." Paper presented at the American Economics Association meetings.

Sewell, W., and R. Hauser. 1975. *Education, Occupation, and Earnings*. New York: Academic Press.

Shorrocks, A. 1975. "The Age-Wealth Relationship: A Cross-Section and Cohort Analysis." *Review of Economics and Statistics* 57:155–63.

Smith, J. 1975. "White Wealth and Black People: The Distribution of Personal Wealth in Washington, D.C., in 1967." In J. Smith, ed., *The Personal Distribution of Wealth*. New York: National Bureau of Economic Research.

Smith, J., S. Franklin; and G. Orcutt. 1978. "The Intergenerational Transmission of Wealth: A Simulation Experiment." In F. Thomas Juster, ed., *The Distribution of Economic Well-being*. Cambridge, Mass.: National Bureau of Economic Research.

State of Connecticut. 1977. *Registration Report of Births, Marriages, Divorces and Deaths for the Year Ended December 31, 1975*. State Department of Health, Hartford.

Stiglitz, J. 1969. "Distribution of Income and Wealth Among Individuals." *Econometrica* 37:382–97.

Thurow, L. 1975. *Generating Inequality*. New York: Basic Books.

U.S. Bureau of the Census. 1975. *Historical Statistics of the United States, Colonial Times to 1970. Bicentennial Edition.* Washington, D.C.: Government Printing Office.

U.S. Bureau of the Census, Annual Series. *Statistical Abstract of the United States.* Washington, D.C.: Government Printing Office.

U.S. Treasury. 1977. *Blueprints for Basic Tax Reform.* Washington, D.C.: Government Printing Office.

Yaari, M. 1964. "On the Consumer's Lifetime Allocation Process." *International Economic Review* 5:304–17.

Zarembka, P. 1974. *Frontiers in Econometrics.* New York: Academic Press.

# 5 The Bequest Process and the Causes of Inequality in the Distribution of Wealth

Michael C. Wolfson

## Introduction

The objective of this paper is to assess, in a reasonably realistic manner, the quantitative importance of various patterns of intergenerational wealth transmission on the overall level of wealth inequality. The basic ingredients of the analysis are: a set of models of the main processes involved in the evolution of the size distribution of wealth; detailed micro-data drawn from two Statistics Canada surveys for the distribution of wealth and the pattern of saving; and a specially developed computer simulation program.

The analysis starts with the distribution of wealth as observed in Canada in May, 1970, and projects it to the year 2000 under a range of alternative assumptions.

The model developed for the analysis involves a new methodological approach. For example, it is not based on the Orcutt, et al. (1976) style of microsimulation which operates at the level of individuals and families. Instead, the population density function representing the wealth distribution for each age/family size group is the basic building block or object of analysis. As a result, the model consists of a set of component processes that are defined, in mathematical terms, directly as operations on distributions. In this way, restrictive assumptions such as omission of age specific distributional detail (e.g., Atkinson 1971) and reliance on specific inequality measures or fixed function forms (e.g., Oulton 1976; Blinder 1973) can be avoided. At the same time, the

Michael C. Wolfson is an economist associated with the Department of Finance, Ottawa.

This paper is based on chapters 8 and 9 of my Ph.D. thesis, "The Causes of Inequality in the Distribution of Wealth: A Simulation Analysis."

simulation model is considerably smaller and less costly to run than that developed by Orcutt, et al. (1976). The model constitutes a development of the "continuum" approach to models of size distributions rather than the "fixed identity" approach as described by Vaughan (1975) and Wolfson (1977).

The plan of the paper is as follows: First, the general structure of the model will be described. Then the component processes specifically associated in the intergenerational transmission of wealth will be developed. Finally, the results of a set of computer simulations focusing on the bequest process will be presented and discussed. The interested reader is referred to Wolfson (1977) for a detailed discussion of the model, data, and other simulation results.

## 5.1    General Structure of the Model

The time series model of the evolution of the distribution of wealth starts with an "observation" of this distribution. This observation is drawn from the 1970 Statistics Canada Survey of Consumer Finance. The population was divided into two family size groups—one-adult families (including single parent families) and two-or-more adult families (all of which are assumed to be exactly two-adult nuclear families) —and twelve five-year age groups, the youngest being 20–24 and the eldest 85–89. For each of these twenty-four age/family size groups, a wealth density function was tabulated using thirty given wealth intervals. The twenty-four wealth densities then constituted the starting point for the model.

The time series model projects this disaggregated wealth distribution five years at a time. Figure 5.1 displays the general structure of the model where $W_{at}$ represents the wealth densities for age group $a$ ($1 \leq a \leq A$) at time $t$. (A subscript for family size has been omitted for notational convenience.) It should be noted that the ordering of these processes is somewhat arbitrary; for example, marriage could precede divorce. It is assumed that reordering would not affect our results significantly.

The first step in the evolution of the set of wealth densities is the saving process. This process is quite complex. Actual saving rates and distributions of saving by age, family size, and wealth category were obtained by special analysis and tabulation of the microdata from the 1970 Statistics Canada Survey of Family Expenditures. These observed saving patterns as well as assumed rates of return are combined with the wealth densities in a complex of operations that include scaling and convolution.

In the growth step, the two main concerns are to keep the wealth densities in constant dollars and to account for population growth. It is assumed that population is growing at 10 percent, nominal saving at 25

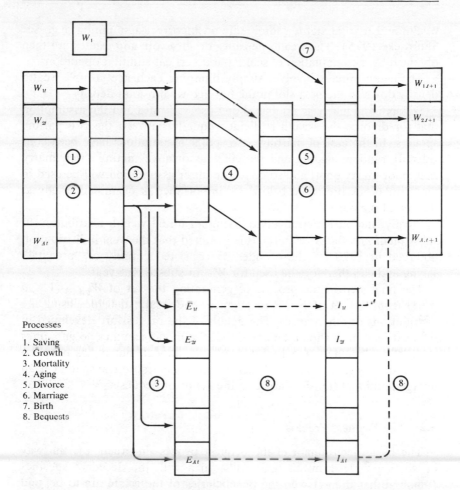

**Fig. 5.1**     General Structure of the Time Series Model. Variables: $W_{at}$ = distribution of wealth; $E_{at}$ = distribution of estates; $I_{at}$ = distribution of inheritance.

percent, and prices at 12.5 percent, all per five years. The pattern of saving (i.e., the "shapes" of the saving density functions by age, family size, and wealth category) is assumed fixed as observed in 1970. The growth process therefore involves a set of vertical and horizontal scaling operations on the wealth and saving densities.

The mortality step is based on observed age and sex specific mortality rates. Note that when only one spouse in a two-adult family dies, it becomes a one-adult family; if both spouses die it becomes an estate. (The annual mortality rates have been appropriately transformed into five-year rates.) The mortality rate for the 85–89 age group is assumed to be 100 percent. Mortality has also been assumed to be independent of wealth and marital status (admittedly an incorrect assumption, e.g., see Shorrocks 1975). The wealth densities of survivors and estates are then obtained by a combination of scaling and vertical addition operations.

The aging process involves simply bumping each age group's wealth. density down to the next slot in the full age-wealth joint density.

Divorce and marriage are based on observed rates and the assumption that for divorce the wealth is divided equally between the two parting spouses. In the case of marriage, two polar assumptions have been considered: random mating and perfectly assortative mating (rich marry rich, poor marry poor, and so on). The latter assumption will be used in the simulations presented below. Its importance is examined briefly at the end of the paper.

Finally, the birth step involves giving an initial wealth distribution to subsequent "newborn" cohorts. It is assumed that the wealth distribution observed in 1970 for those under 25 consisted entirely of "prenatal" saving and can therefore be used for $W_{1t}$ in subsequent years.

The final step in the process of generating the set of $W_{a,t+1}$ ($1 \leq a \leq A$) from the set of $W_{at}$ is to augment the wealth densities using the distributions of inheritances. The details of the process are developed in the next section. It should be noted that the model assumes no gifts *inter vivos*. They could be incorporated into the model, but it has been assumed that as a first step, the analysis would be more transparent if all intergenerational transfers arose as the result of bequests.

## 5.2    The Bequest Process

The basic determinant of the bequest process in practice is the way in which people draw up their wills. In a will, the decedent specifies (among other things) who the beneficiaries of the estate are to be, and how much each will receive. Our intent here is to describe this process in such a way that it is easy to pose hypothetical questions of the following form: What would the distribution of wealth be like if will writing behavior differed from the usual pattern with regard to some aspect such as x?

There are two basic difficulties that must be overcome, however. The first is a general lack of data (see, e.g., Shoup 1966; Jantscher 1967; Cheng, Grant, Ploeger, no date). For example, it is not well known how the average number of heirs varies with the size of the estate. In cases like this, our strategy will be to define a set of polar cases. These cases are ones that would be expected, intuitively, to constitute bounds on the kinds of behavior most likely to be observed.

This procedure of constructing bounding assumptions is like that used for the pattern of marriage above where, in the absence of reasonable data, we identified assortative and random mating as *a priori* bounding polar cases.

A second difficulty is that where polar assumptions regarding bequests have already been discussed in the theoretical literature, they are not stated in a form suitable for our methodological approach. This problem stems from the distinction between the "fixed identity" and "continuum" approaches. For example, we just referred to the division of an estate among the heirs. The conventional polar assumptions are primogeniture and equal division. But these cases are typically defined for an average or representative estate—the fixed identity approach. Our problem will be to define corresponding polar cases directly in terms of distributions of estates—the continuum approach.

The starting point for the bequest process in the context of figure 5.1 is the set of estate distributions $\{E_{at}(x)\}$, where $a$ indicates the age of the decedents. The end point of the process is the set of wealth distributions $\{W_{a,t+1}(x)\}$ that have been augmented by inheritance. The basic assumption to begin with is that between these two endpoints, the bequest process can be divided into three broad steps which are independent of each other. These steps will then form the framework within which the polar assumptions will be constructed. These three steps are: the transformation of estates into bequests (how each estate is divided); the transformation of bequests into inheritances (how the ages of decedents and inheritors are related); and the association of inheritances and inheritors (how within age groups the size of the inheritance tends to be related to the wealth level of the inheritor).

Clearly, any detailed description of how these steps operate in reality is necessarily very complex. The requirement for our model then is to construct a concise and relatively simple set of assumptions. These assumptions should be formulated in accordance with three main objectives: they should span the full range of behavior likely to be observed within each step; they should be easily translated into simple and efficient computer algorithms; and they should be parameterized in such a way that a relatively small number of "points" span or fully explore all possible combinations of polar cases.

We turn now to a discussion of each of the three main steps of the bequest process and the particular assumptions that will be employed.

## 5.2.1    Estates to Bequests

Recall that it has already been assumed that if only one spouse in a family dies, all wealth passes to the surviving spouse. Thus estates arise only when individuals, or both spouses in a family, die. There are two basic assumptions that will be made to start. First, we will make no distinction between estates coming from deceased individuals and those coming from "deceased" families. Thus, a preliminary step of the bequest process is actually to combine the estates (i.e., vertically add the two distributions) for the two family size groups within each age interval. The second assumption concerns legal practice by which it is impossible to inherit debt. The "estates" of individuals or families dying in debt are therefore ignored. However, the plight of these (negative) estates' creditors is also ignored (less than 0.04 percent of aggregate net worth in 1970–74).

The polar possibilities with regard to disequalizing or equalizing tendencies, in the case of a single estate (the fixed identity approach), are that it is either left intact and passed to a single heir (age and sex are ignored), or divided equally among some larger number of heirs, $h$. These two cases will be called primogeniture and equal division, respectively. Perhaps a more realistic situation is what might be called "modified primogeniture." In this case, some proportion $p$ of the estate goes to one heir while the remaining part $(1-p)$ is divided equally among the remaining $h$-1 heirs. Note that $p = 1/h$ corresponds to equal division, and $p = 1$ to primogeniture. It would also seem realistic to expect some relationship between the size of the estate and the way it is divided. For example, if only the very wealthy were concerned about keeping their estates intact, one might expect more primogeniture at the upper end of the wealth spectrum than at the lower end. (A more formal way to describe this last example is "differential division," the assumption that the size range of estates is partitioned into a set of wealth intervals, and within each interval a different pattern of division occurs: primogeniture in one, equal division among $h$ heirs in another.)

The discussion so far has been in terms of single or representative estates. But our concern is to formulate these assumptions directly in terms of distributions. To this end, let $B_a(x)$ be the density function of bequests coming from the estates of decedents age $a$. We then seek ways of relating $B_a(x)$ to $E_a(x)$. (The time subscript has been dropped for notational convenience only.)

Let us consider five such relationships, based on the discussion above of the possibilities with regard to a single estate:

a. Primogeniture: $B_a(x) = E_a(x)$

b. Equal Division: $B_a(x) = h^2 E_a(hx)$

c. Modified Primogeniture, i.e., a bequest of size $x$ may have come either from an estate of size $x/p$, or from an estate of size $(h-1)$ $x/(1-p)$: $B_a(x) = E_a(x/p) + (h-1)^2 E_a[(h-1) \ x/(1-p)]$

d. Class Primogeniture, i.e., below some wealth level $w$ there is equal division while above it there is primogeniture:

$$\text{Let } E_a^1(x) = \begin{cases} E_a(x) \text{ for } x < w \\ 0 \qquad \text{otherwise} \end{cases}$$

$$E_a^2(x) = \begin{cases} E_a(x) \text{ for } x \geq w \\ 0 \qquad \text{otherwise} \end{cases}$$

Then $B_a(x) = h^2 E_a^1(hx) + E_a^2(x)$

e. Differential Division, i.e., the wealth spectrum is divided into $k$ intervals; within each interval there is equal division among $h_i$ heirs; $h_i = 1$ implies primogeniture in the $i$th interval:

$$\text{Let } E_a^i(x) = \begin{cases} E_a(x) \text{ for } c_i < x \leq c_{i+1} \\ 0 \qquad \text{otherwise} \end{cases}$$

Then $B_a(x) = \sum_{i=1}^{k} h_i^2 E_a^i(h_i w)$

From these descriptions it is clear that $a$ and $b$ are special cases of $c$, indeed polar cases of $c$ with regard to their equalizing or disequalizing tendencies. Also, $a$, $b$, and $d$ are special cases of $e$. Because of its relative flexibility $e$, differential division, has been chosen as the general parametric form for the model of this part of the bequest process. The parameters are then:

> $k =$ the number of distinct wealth classes from the point of view of bequest behavior (this number has nothing to do with the wealth classes used by the cross-sectional saving function);
>
> $c_i =$ the lower limit (in dollars) of the $i$th wealth class (assumed fixed in real terms); and
>
> $h_i =$ the number of heirs in the $i$th wealth class.

In the simulation runs described below, only two wealth classes ($k = 2$) will be used with a wealth cutoff of $c_2 = \$40,000$ in 1970 and $h_i$ taking values in the set $\{1, 2, 4, 6\}$. Specific assumptions for this step will be denoted "heirs = $h_1$, $h_2$." Since the number of heirs in each wealth class is the parameter of greatest interest, $c_2$ is not included in this shorthand notation. Given this value of $c_2$, $i = 1$ can be interpreted as a reference to poor or middle class families, and when $i = 2$ the reference is to the rich.

The situation with heirs = 2,1 ($h_1 = 2$ and $h_2 = 1$) is illustrated in figures 5.2 and 5.3, in terms of the population density function and Lorenz curve, respectively. It seems clear from the comparison between figures 5.3a and 5.3b that the distribution of bequests is more unequal after this differential division than after "universal primogeniture" where $h_1 = h_2 = 1$. However this conclusion is complicated by the fact that the number of bequests is different in the two cases. If $n_1$ is the number of "poor" estates and $n_2$ is the number of rich estates, then differential division in this particular case results in $n_1$ more more bequests than universal primogeniture. As an alternative, if the Lorenz curves for bequests for heirs $= 2,1$ and heirs $= 1,1$ with a suitable number ($n_1$ in this case) of zero inheritances included are compared, then it is clear that differential division (heirs $= 2,1$) results in a *more* equal distribution of bequests ("higher" Lorenz curve) than universal primogeniture. This point is illustrated in figure 5.3c.

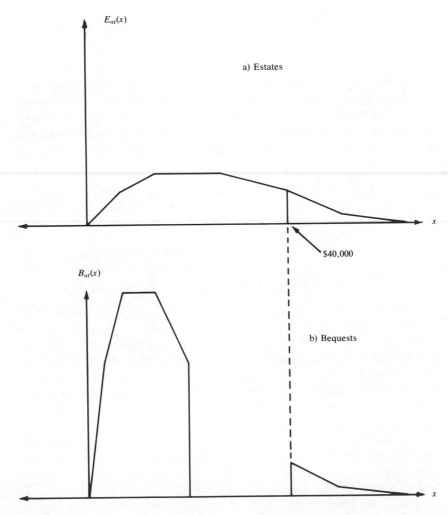

**Fig. 5.2**          Population Densities for Estates and Bequests Given Differential Division. Hypothetical case: heirs $= 2,1$.

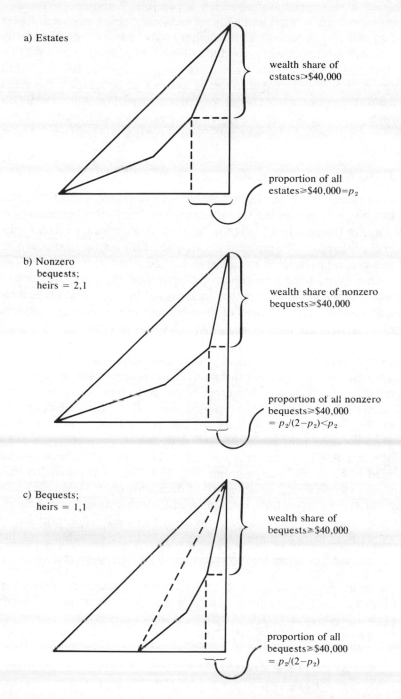

a) Estates

wealth share of
estates≥$40,000

proportion of all
estates≥$40,000=$p_2$

b) Nonzero
bequests;
heirs = 2,1

wealth share of nonzero
bequests≥$40,000

proportion of all nonzero
bequests≥$40,000
= $p_2/(2-p_2) < p_2$

c) Bequests;
heirs = 1,1

wealth share of
bequests≥$40,000

proportion of all
bequests≥$40,000
= $p_2/(2-p_2)$

**Fig. 5.3**     Hypothetical Lorenz Curves for Differential Division

In fact, a more general proposition is possible. If the two alternative assumptions heirs $= g_1,g_2$ and heirs $= h_1,h_2$ are being compared, where $g_1 \leq h_1$ and $g_2 \leq h_2$ and strict inequality holds at least once, then heirs $= h_1,h_2$ will result in a more equal distribution of bequests provided that the distribution of bequests from heirs $= g_1,g_2$ is "padded out" with enough zero bequests so that the total number of bequests is the same for the two distributions. (This proposition is proved in Wolfson 1977.) However, it is not possible to say in general which distribution of bequests is more equal, for example, when comparing heirs $= 1,4$ and heirs $= 4,1$.

### 5.2.2  Bequests to Inheritances

In our model, the basic distinction between bequests and inheritances lies in the significance of the age subscript. The "age" of a bequest refers to the age of the decedent, while the "age" of an inheritance refers to the age of the inheritor. The problem in this step of the bequest process is to define a general parametric relationship between the two sets of distributions. One major issue here concerns "generation skipping." It appears that many of the wealthy, to reduce total tax liability over several generations, leave substantial portions of their estates (in the form of trusts) to their grandchildren (Shoup 1966, p. 41). Lampman (1962, p. 239) suggests that this behavior has an equalizing effect. It also appears that many estates are divided among heirs of two or three different generations.

Given this range of bequest behavior, it seems important to be able to examine the effects of age differences between decedents and inheritors. This will be done in a highly simplified way: all the heirs of decedents aged $a$ will be assumed to be the same age, and this age will be $d$ years less than the age of the decedent. And if decedents are age $a \leq d$ (i.e., their heirs would be in age group $a - d < 20$), then their heirs will be assumed to be in the first age group (20–24). Thus, the possibility that heirs of the same estate, or generally of decedents of the same age, may be of different ages has been ignored. And by implication, the possibility that heirs of certain ages may be more likely to inherit larger portions of the estate than heirs of other ages (e.g., children versus siblings of the decedent) will also be ignored, since all the heirs of any given estate will be in the same age group. But as a starting point, this assumption still allows an interesting range of "polar" cases to be examined, defined in terms of the single parameter $d$. More formally, the assumption will be:

$$I_1(x) = \sum_{a=1}^{d+1} B_a(x)$$

$$I_a(x) = B_{a+d}(x) \text{ for } 2 \leq a \leq A - d,$$

$$I_a(x) = 0 \qquad \text{for } A - d < a \leq A,$$

where $I_a(x)$ is the density function of inheritances destined for inheritors aged $a$ and $0 \leq d < A$. In general, this assumption will be denoted "age-diff $= d$." The values that will be examined are 0, 25, 45, and 65. This assumption is illustrated in figure 5.4. Note that if one set of distributions of bequests by age group is more equal than another (in the general sense of their all having higher Lorenz curves) then the corresponding set of distributions of inheritances by age group will also be more equal (see Wolfson 1977).

### 5.2.3   Inheritances to Inheritors

There are actually three parts to this step in the bequest process: allocating inheritances between the two family size categories; choosing the subset of each age/family size category who will inherit; and associating inheritances by size with the wealth levels of inheritors. Given

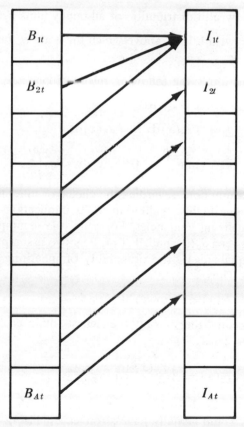

**Fig. 5.4**          Bequests to Inheritances

the general objectives of comprehensiveness and simplicity, the following assumptions will be made:

a. Inheritances are divided between the two family size groups in proportion to the number of family units in each. Thus, if $p_{au}$ is the number of unattached individuals aged $a$ and $p_{af}$ is the number of families aged $a$, then $(p_{au}/(p_{au}+p_{af}))\,I_a(x)$ is the distribution of inheritances destined for unattached individuals aged $a$.

b. Two main methods for choosing inheritors will be distinguished. In both it is assumed that no inheritor receives more than one inheritance.[1]

Let $p_a$ = number of family units aged $a$ (ignoring family size for notational convenience);

$q_a$ = number of inheritances destined for inheritors aged $a$, assumed less than $p_a$;

$J_a(x)$ = wealth distribution of inheritors aged $a$;

$W_a(x)$ = wealth distribution of all family units aged $a$; and

$w_a$ = wealth level above which there are $q_a$ family units aged $a$.

These definitions imply the following relationships:

$$p_a = \int W_a(x)\,\mathrm{d}x$$

$$q_a = \int I_a(x)\,\mathrm{d}x = \int J_a(x)\,\mathrm{d}x$$

$$w_a = \min\left\{ w: \int_w^\infty W_a(x)\,dx \le q_a \right\}$$

Two polar assumptions regarding the choice of inheritors can now be easily defined, one highly egalitarian in its implications and the other implying disequalizing tendencies. Formally, the assumptions require a relationship between $J_a(x)$ and $W_a(x)$. The two assumptions are:

*Random* (equalizing)—the probability of inheriting is independent of wealth level. Thus,

$$J_a(x) = (q_a/p_a)\,W_a(x)$$

*Select-R* (disequalizing)—only the richest within each age group become inheritors. Thus,

$$J_a(x) = \begin{cases} W_a(x) & \text{for } x \ge w_a \\ 0 & \text{otherwise} \end{cases}$$

Figure 5.5 illustrates these two alternatives. Note that there is a third possibility that would actually have stronger equalizing tendencies than random choice of inheritors—namely if the poorest $q_a$ were always chosen to inherit. However this possibility seems as unlikely as the assumption of "perfectly perverse assortative mating" (rich systematically marrying poor) and it will not be considered further.

c. The final part of this step of the bequest process is the manner in which the distributions of inheritances $I_a(x)$ and inheritors $J_a(x)$ are combined (ignoring family size for notational convenience). We shall again define two polar cases:

*Random* (equalizing)—the probability of inheriting any particular amount of wealth, given that one inherits, is independent of current wealth.

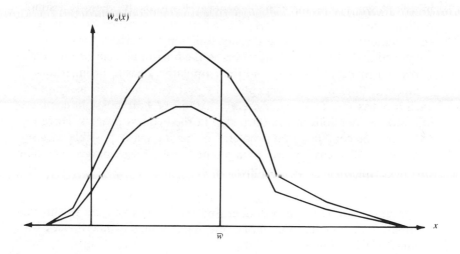

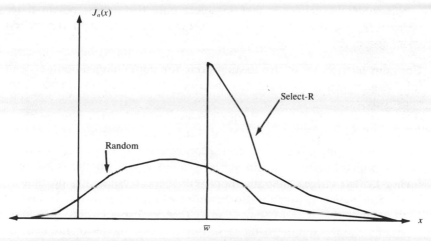

**Fig. 5.5**          Hypothetical Example of Polar Cases for the Selection of Inheritors

*Assortative* (disequalizing)—the richest inheritor receives the largest inheritance, the second richest inheritor receives the second largest inheritance, and so on.

The random case corresponds to the mathematical operation of convoluting $I_a(x)$ and $J_a(x)$, and it can therefore use the algorithm already developed for the saving process and random mating. However, the assortative case here does not correspond to the case of assortative mating in the demographic model. There, it was possible to make use of the fact that the wealth distributions of prospective husbands and wives were identical.[2] But the shapes of the distributions of inheritances and inheritors will not be the same in general. Fortunately, there is a simple mathematical operation corresponding to this process of assortative combination: the cumulative density function of perfectly assortatively combined inheritances and inheritors is the horizontal sum of the cumulative density of inheritances and the cumulative density of inheritors.

Given a total of one assumption in part (a), and two assumptions each in parts (b) and (c), there are a total of four possible combinaations of assumptions in this third step of the bequest process. However, to reduce the combinatorial problems of having many possible assumptions, we shall focus on two (compound) polar assumptions regarding the receipt of inheritances by inheritors:

*Equal*—The most equalizing case for combining inheritors and inheritances is first to choose inheritors randomly from the wealth distribution of potential inheritors, and then to match inheritances with inheritors in a random manner.

*Unequal*—The most disequalizing polar case for combining inheritors and inheritances is first to select only the richest potential inheritors, and then to match the largest inheritances with the richest inheritors assortatively.

For convenience, these two assumptions for combining inheritors with inheritances will be denoted "comb = equal" and "comb = uneq," respectively.

It is clear that for any particular distribution of inheritances, comb = equal will result in a more equal "post inheritance" distribution of wealth than comb = uneq. But consider a second question. Suppose it is known that one distribution of inheritances is more equal (in the sense of a higher Lorenz curve) than another. Will the corresponding postinheritance distribution of wealth also be more equal? The answer is yes for both comb = equal and comb = uneq (see Wolfson 1977).

We have now completed the description of the model of the bequest process. There are three main steps. First, estates are divided into bequests. A general structure allowing differing numbers of heirs by wealth class is used. Second, bequests are transformed into inheritances by considering the differences in age between decedents and inheritors. Third, and finally, inheritors are selected and their wealth is augmented by inheritances in either an equalizing or a disequalizing manner.

Formally, any particular assumption for the bequest process can be summarized in terms of the following parameters:

$k$ = number of wealth classes for bequest behavior of decedents;

$c_i$ = lower limit (in 1970 dollars) of $i$th wealth class;

$h_i$ = number of heirs in $i$th wealth class;

$d$ = age difference between decedents and inheritors; and

$\left\{ \begin{array}{l} \text{Equal} \\ \text{Unequal} \end{array} \right\}$ = polar methods for matching inheritances and inheritors

However, we shall always assume $k = 2$ and usually assume that $c_2 =$ \$40,000 (in 1970). (More wealth classes could have been simulated, but it was not felt that any further interesting results would emerge.) The shorthand notation for the three assumptions will then be:

heirs = $h_1, h_2$, for $h_i \in \{1,2,4,6\}$;

age-diff = $d$, for $d \in \{0,25,45,65\}$; and

comb = equal or comb = uneq.

## 5.3  Computer Simulation Results

Before launching into a discussion of the simulation results, it is first necessary to explain how these results will be summarized. Typically, a single simulation of the time series model will cover a period of thirty years. It therefore generates a sequence of six age/family size/wealth joint densities, in addition to the initial joint density for 1970. Furthermore, an anlysis of a particular parameter may involve as many as five or six such simulated wealth sequences at a time. There is, as a result, a nontrivial problem of "data reduction"—selecting the key indicators of the results of any simulated sequence of wealth distributions.

Our approach to the problem is the following. First, the primary concern will be with the aggregate wealth distribution, i.e., the distribution for all age/family size groups combined. Second, for any wealth distribution the focus will be on six summary statistics: the mean level of net worth, three summary measures of inequality, and two inequality indicators. The three inequality measures are the well-known Gini coefficient and squared coefficient of variation (CV), and a specially designed measure we have called the exponential measure (EXP). The two inequality indicators are the wealth shares of the top 1 percent and next 4 percent of the population.[3] Finally, the main interest will be in the wealth distribution at the end of the sequence, in the year 2000. This approach is clearly a dramatic simplification. From a total of 168 (2 family size groups, 14 age groups, 6 years) wealth densities, six scalar magnitudes will be distilled. However, when it is necessary to the discussion of various simulation results we shall refer to the more disaggregated data.

The model of the bequest process has three basic parameters: heirs, age-diff, and comb. For each of these parameters, a range of values was specified. Both the number of parameters and the number of values each would take was kept small so that the total number of combinations did not grow too large. The main reason for concern over the number of possible combinations is the expectation that there could well be significant interaction among the parameters. This expectation affects the experimental strategy. If there were no significant interactions among the main parameters, it would be possible to proceed by first defining a "base run" of the simulation model. Then variations around it, one parameter at a time, could be explored. But in the case of the bequest process, this approach is unacceptable. We must be able to check whether or not there is significant interaction. Having a relatively small set of parameter combinations makes this task easier.

Given the three main parameters and their range of values, it is possible to display the set of combinations as nodes on a three-dimensional grid—or two two-dimensional grids, one each for comb = equal and comb = uneq. The two 2-D grids are displayed in figure 5.6 below. The nodes marked by heavy dots indicate the combinations of parameters which have been simulated. For example, (heirs = 1,1; comb = uneq; age-diff = 45) has been simulated, while (heirs = 4,1; comb = uneq; age-diff = 25) has not. This diagram, therefore, displays the program of experiments with the bequest model. This set of simulations will be analyzed in two stages.

The first parameter that will be examined is "heirs," with the set of "experimental values" corresponding to the two horizontal rows of dots for age-diff = 45 in figure 5.6. The results of these simulations are displayed in table 5.1, collected into three groups.

A preliminary observation concerns the level of inequality in the year 2000 compared with 1970. Even with universal primogeniture (heirs = 1,1) and unequal combination (comb = uneq), when age-diff = 45 inequality in the upper tail of the distribution is reduced by the year 2000 (CV = 5.0 versus CV = 5.8, and top 1% = 17.0 versus top 1% = 20.3, comparing run 1 and the 1970 values), though inequality increases in the lower and middle ranges of the wealth spectrum (EXP

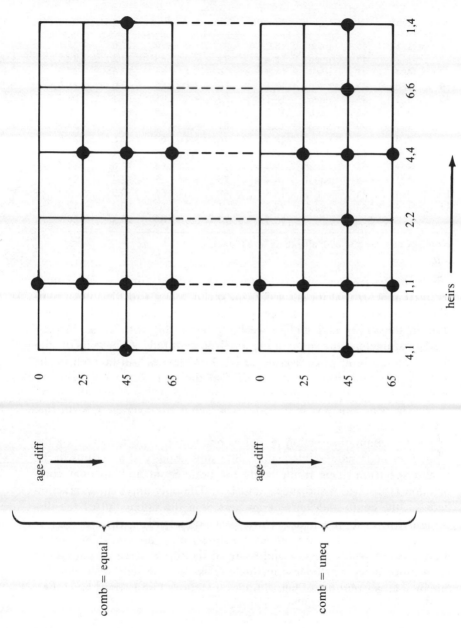

**Fig. 5.6**   Space of Parameters for the Bequest Model

Table 5.1                Time Series Results, Bequests Part 1

| Run | Heirs | Age-Diff | Comb | Mean Wealth | Inequality | | | Wealth Shares | |
|---|---|---|---|---|---|---|---|---|---|
| | | | | | Gini | CV | Exp | Top 1% | Next 4% |
| 1 | 1, 1 | 45 | uneq | 18.2 | .81 | 5.0 | .70 | 17.0 | 25.1 |
| 2 | 2, 2 | 45 | uneq | 18.4 | .79 | 4.0 | .68 | 14.2 | 24.2 |
| 3 | 4, 4 | 45 | uneq | 18.5 | .76 | 3.4 | .66 | 12.6 | 22.6 |
| 4 | 6, 6 | 45 | uneq | 18.5 | .74 | 3.1 | .65 | 12.0 | 21.6 |
| 5 | 4, 1[a] | 45 | uneq | 18.1 | .79 | 4.8 | .68 | 17.1 | 23.4 |
| 6 | 4, 1 | 45 | uneq | 18.2 | .78 | 4.6 | .68 | 16.7 | 22.5 |
| 1 | 1, 1 | 45 | uneq | 18.2 | .81 | 5.0 | .70 | 17.0 | 25.1 |
| 3 | 4, 4 | 45 | uneq | 18.5 | .76 | 3.4 | .66 | 12.6 | 22.6 |
| 7 | 1, 4 | 45 | uneq | 18.4 | .79 | 3.7 | .68 | 13.1 | 24.6 |
| 8 | 4, 1 | 45 | equal | 18.3 | .72 | 3.2 | .64 | 12.5 | 21.4 |
| 9 | 1, 1 | 45 | equal | 18.4 | .75 | 3.3 | .65 | 12.4 | 21.8 |
| 10 | 4, 4 | 45 | equal | 18.3 | .68 | 2.6 | .61 | 10.9 | 19.3 |
| 11 | 1, 4 | 45 | equal | 18.5 | .71 | 2.7 | .63 | 10.9 | 19.8 |
| | 1970 | | | 15.4 | .75 | 5.8 | .65 | 20.3 | 20.9 |

Note: [a]Cutoff at $25,000; all others at $40,000.

= .70 versus EXP = .65, and Gini = .81 versus Gini = .75). Intuitively, it appears that the dispersion in saving along with the other components of the model is sufficient to generate increasing inequality over time in the lower and middle wealth ranges. But with these bequest model parameters, the share of the top 1 percent falls. (These inequality results do not hold when age-diff = 25, however, as will be seen in the next set of simulation results.) It is also the case that with the given growth rate assumptions and no taxation, average "real" wealth grows slowly over the thirty-year period. (The geometric average growth rate is 0.56% per year.)

The first main observation is that as one would expect, increasing the number of heirs reduces inequality quite substantially at all points in the wealth spectrum. This result holds for both equal and unequal combination (runs 1 to 4 and runs 9 and 10). The only apparent interaction between the comb and heirs parameters is in the upper tail of the distribution: runs 1 and 3 do not show a consistently larger or smaller change in inequality values, either absolutely or relatively, than do runs 9 and 10 except for the CV and share of the top 1 percent. This result (that more heirs implies less inequality) is as expected, since division among a larger number of heirs implies that more family units have their wealth augmented by smaller amounts.

The second main observation is that differential division (heirs = 4, 1) does not always lead to unambiguously (i.e., in terms of Lorenz curves) lower inequality than universal primogeniture. It appears to be the case for run 6 versus run 1. This result is what one would expect, given the earlier theoretical analysis. But in run 5 versus run 1, the share of the top 1 percent is higher. The explanation must be that despite the fact that (initially, in 1970–74) the postinheritance distributions of wealth are more equal in run 5 than in run 1 (i.e., the upper tail of the distribution is not so elongated), more family units are moved above the cutoff dividing middle and rich for the saving process. Thus, the disequalizing tendencies of the saving and yield differences outweigh, in this case, the effects of a more equal postinheritance distribution of wealth. A similar result (the share of the top 1% increases) occurs in run 8 versus run 9 with comb = equal.

If we turn to the interactions between the heirs and comb parameters, we find that in the case of comb = equal, all three summary measures agree on the ranking heirs = 1,1 > heirs = 4,1 > heirs = 1,4 > heirs = 4,4 (runs 8 to 11). The same ranking holds when comb = uneq for the CV; but the EXP is equal for heirs = 1,4 and heirs = 4,1 (runs 6 and 7); and the Gini reverses their order. However, a more important interaction between the heirs and comb parameters would seem to be revealed by the CV and share of the top 1 percent. When comb = uneq, having fewer heirs (e.g., heirs = 1,1 versus heirs = 4,4) has a much more pronounced effect in the upper tail of the distribution than when comb = equal (runs 1 and 3 versus runs 9 and 10). These results correspond to the intuition that the disequalizing effects of primogeniture (relative to equal division) are highlighted and concentrated in the upper tail of the distribution when comb = uneq, but muted and spread throughout the distribution when comb = equal.

We turn now to focus on the effects of age-diff, the age difference between decedents and inheritors. As figure 5.6 indicates, there are four sets of runs that can be assembled to explore the age-diff parameter for alternative heirs and comb assumptions. The results of these runs are set out in table 5.2 (runs 2, 6, 9, and 12 have already appeared in the previous table as runs 1, 3, 9, and 10, respectively).

As a preliminary observation, note that both run 3 and run 4 have all indicators showing greater inequality than the 1970 values. But the main observation to be drawn from these simulation results is that almost without exception, lower values of age-diff are associated with higher levels of inequality. (The only exception is the share of the top 1% in runs 12 and 13.) In other words, a general shift to more generation skipping would decrease the level of inequality over the next thirty years, in agreement with Lampman's (1962, p. 239) suggestion.

A range of factors must be combined to explain this phenomenon. The first fact to be kept in mind is that almost 80 percent of the (nonnegative) estates in the model are from decedents aged 70–89. The average size of these estates is about $16,000 in 1970–74. Their average level of inequality is relatively low (Gini = .56, CV = 1.8, EXP = .53,

Table 5.2          Time Series Results, Bequests Part 2

| Run | Heirs | Age-Diff | Comb | Mean Wealth | Inequality | | | Wealth Shares | |
|---|---|---|---|---|---|---|---|---|---|
| | | | | | Gini | CV | Exp | Top 1% | Next 4% |
| 1 | 1, 1 | 65 | uneq | 18.2 | .76 | 3.5 | .66 | 13.2 | 22.2 |
| 2 | 1, 1 | 45 | uneq | 18.2 | .81 | 5.0 | .70 | 17.0 | 25.1 |
| 3 | 1, 1 | 25 | uneq | 17.8 | .83 | 6.0 | .71 | 21.4 | 25.1 |
| 4 | 1, 1 | 0 | uneq | 17.5 | .83 | 8.8 | .71 | 24.7 | 21.8 |
| 5 | 4, 4 | 65 | uneq | 18.1 | .68 | 2.7 | .61 | 11.4 | 19.7 |
| 6 | 4, 4 | 45 | uneq | 18.5 | .76 | 3.4 | .66 | 12.6 | 22.6 |
| 7 | 4, 4 | 25 | uneq | 18.0 | .81 | 4.5 | .70 | 15.6 | 24.8 |
| 8 | 1, 1 | 65 | equal | 18.2 | .73 | 3.2 | .64 | 12.4 | 21.1 |
| 9 | 1, 1 | 45 | equal | 18.4 | .75 | 3.3 | .65 | 12.4 | 21.8 |
| 10 | 1, 1 | 25 | equal | 18.3 | .77 | 3.5 | .67 | 12.7 | 22.7 |
| 11 | 1, 1 | 0 | equal | 17.5 | .80 | 4.2 | .69 | 14.5 | 24.8 |
| 12 | 4, 4 | 65 | equal | 18.1 | .66 | 2.5 | .59 | 11.0 | 18.9 |
| 13 | 4, 4 | 45 | equal | 18.3 | .68 | 2.6 | .61 | 10.9 | 19.3 |
| 14 | 4, 4 | 25 | equal | 18.4 | .72 | 2.8 | .64 | 11.2 | 20.4 |
| | 1970 | | | 15.4 | .75 | 5.8 | .65 | 20.3 | 20.9 |

top 1% = 10, next 4% = 18) compared with both overall inequality and levels of inequality within most age groups. When age-diff is high, most of these bequests are concentrated in the younger age groups rather than being spread among more and older age groups (recall figure 5.4). Since these young age groups tend to have below average wealth, the main effect of the inheritances is to raise their average level of wealth. By bringing it closer to the overall mean, the between-age-group component of aggregate inequality is reduced. Had these bequests been spread among older age groups, more wealth would have gone to age groups already owning closer to average or above average wealth. Thus, lower values of age-diff tend to distribute inheritances in such a way that "between group" inequality is reduced less or even increased. This point is illustrated by the figures given in table 5.3.

A second point is that as age-diff decreases (e.g., from 65 to 45), bequests are spread among a wider range of age groups. In the case of unequal combination (of inheritors and inheritances) this means, for example, that an eightieth-percentile family unit in the 20–24 age group may no longer be an inheritor while a ninety-seventh-percentile family unit in the 35–39 age group (who is typically wealthier) may become an inheritor—clearly a disequalizing change.[4] And as table 5.2 shows, with primogeniture (heirs = 1,1) and comb = uneq, the decrease in age-diff has a much more pronounced effect on the upper tail of the distribution, indicated by the CV and share of the top 1 percent, than in the other cases (runs 1 to 4 versus runs 5 to 14).

Equal rather than unequal combination has the anticipated equalizing effect on the aggregate wealth distribution, for all combinations of heirs and age-diff assumptions. Similarly, four-way equal division rather than primogeniture continues to show equalizing effects for all combinations of age-diff and comb assumptions.

However, the relative impact of these two pairs of specific alternatives depends on age-diff. If the "distance" covered by each inequality measure in moving from unequal combination and primogeniture to equal combination and four-way division is examined, more of this distance is covered by the move to four-way division when age-diff = 65. But when age-diff is 45 or 25, more of the distance is covered by moving from unequal to equal combination. This point is illustrated in figure 5.7. If $A, B, C$, and $D$ are the differences in the values of a particular inequality measure for the given pairs of runs, it is clear that $A + D = B + C$. What the figure shows *is* that $A > B$ and thus $D < C$ when age-diff = 65 for the Gini, CV, EXP, and share of the top 1 percent and 5 percent. But when age-diff = 45 or 25, $B > A$.

Intuitively, the explanation is that the number of heirs has a greater impact on overall inequality than the manner of combination when all these heirs are concentrated in the 20–24 age group. However, as the heirs are spread among a wider range of age groups, the move to comb = equal has a greater effect in reducing overall inequality than the move

**Table 5.3**  **Numbers and Sizes of Estates Compared with 1970 Age-Wealth Distribution**

| Age Group | Family Size 1 | | Family Size 2+ | | Estates | |
|---|---|---|---|---|---|---|
| | Number | Mean ($000s) | Number | Mean ($000s) | Number | Mean ($000s) |
| 20–24 | .0741 | .6 | .0775 | 2.2 | .0002 | 2.3 |
| 25–29 | .0333 | 1.2 | .0869 | 6.7 | .0001 | 3.8 |
| 30–34 | .0248 | 8.7 | .0812 | 13.0 | .0001 | 12.6 |
| 35–39 | .0217 | 10.0 | .0738 | 16.9 | .0001 | 14.9 |
| 40–44 | .0210 | 11.7 | .0658 | 21.7 | .0002 | 15.1 |
| 45–49 | .0206 | 10.4 | .0582 | 33.4 | .0004 | 15.1 |
| 50–54 | .0216 | 16.6 | .0502 | 27.0 | .0006 | 22.1 |
| 55–59 | .0218 | 13.2 | .0426 | 37.8 | .0010 | 19.2 |
| 60–64 | .0227 | 15.2 | .0347 | 25.1 | .0016 | 22.7 |
| 65–69 | .0237 | 13.8 | .0266 | 31.7 | .0025 | 17.4 |
| 70–74 | .0248 | 13.3 | .0183 | 26.3 | .0040 | 15.8 |
| 75–79 | .0237 | 14.4 | .0110 | 23.4 | .0056 | 16.3 |
| 80–84 | .0198 | 14.4 | .0051 | 23.4 | .0068 | 16.1 |
| 85–89 | .0131 | 14.4 | .0016 | 23.4 | .0114 | 16.2 |
| All | .3666 | 9.4 | .6334 | 18.9 | .0346 | 16.6 |

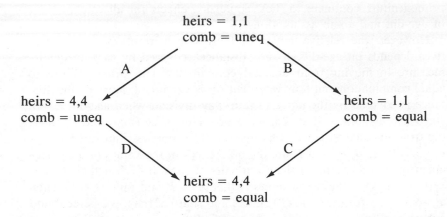

**Fig. 5.7**          Movement of Inequality Measures

from heirs = 1,1 to heirs = 4,4. Since the 20–24 age group has average wealth substantially below the overall average, the implication is that (obviously) the main factor in accounting for the level of inequality is the wealth position of inheritors in the overall distribution. An inheritor in the upper tail of the distribution for the 20–24 age group (comb = uneq, age-diff = 65) may well own less wealth than the average family unit in the 60–64 age group (comb = equal, age-diff = 25).

As a final point, the average level of wealth in the year 2000 is influenced by two main factors: the extent to which inheritances go to age/wealth groups with higher accumulation rates (saving rate × yield) and the extent to which inheritances cause inheritors to move up to the next wealth class. For example, if the effect of a lower value of age-diff is to redirect an inheritance from a middle class aged 20–24 family unit well below the wealth cutoff to an aged 30–34 family unit just below this cutoff, average wealth should increase because the inheritance will be subject to a higher accumulation rate with the latter family unit.

As a matter of further interest the pattern of marriage will be considered. Three pairs of simulation runs will be examined, corresponding to three sets of assumptions regarding the bequest process. The three sets of assumptions are: A) there are no capital transfers at all (i.e., 100%

estate tax); B) there are no wealth taxes and all heirs are in the 20–24 age group (age-diff = 65); and C) there are no wealth taxes and the age difference between decedents and inheritors is always twenty-five years (age-diff = 25).

In addition, except for the first pair of runs, it is assumed that all estates have exactly one heir (heirs = 1,1) and that inheritors and inheritances are combined in a "disequalizing" manner (comb = uneq). Otherwise, the simulation runs use identical inputs. The results for the aggregate wealth distributions in the year 2000 are displayed in table 5.4.

**Table 5.4**    **Time Series Results, Pattern of Marriage**

| Pattern of Marriage | Bequest Assumption | Mean Wealth | Inequality | | | Wealth Share | |
|---|---|---|---|---|---|---|---|
| | | | Gini | CV | EXP | Top 1% | Next 4% |
| Assort. | A | 14.3 | .80 | 3.9 | .70 | 13.8 | 22.5 |
| random | A | 14.3 | .79 | 3.8 | .68 | 13.4 | 22.3 |
| Assort. | B | 18.2 | .76 | 3.5 | .66 | 13.2 | 22.2 |
| random | B | 18.1 | .74 | 3.2 | .65 | 12.5 | 21.6 |
| Assort. | C | 17.8 | .83 | 6.6 | .71 | 21.4 | 25.1 |
| random | C | 17.8 | .82 | 6.4 | .70 | 20.8 | 25.1 |

The pattern of marriage, unlike the pattern of bequests, appears to be of small quantitative significance, in contrast to Blinder's (1973, p. 624) conclusion. Its quantitative effect is strongest in the second pair of runs. Intuitively, this observation is quite plausible: concentrating all inheritance in the youngest age group gives the greatest chance, of the three runs, for the pattern of marriage to have an effect. The reason, of course, is that the youngest age group has the most marrying yet to do.

## 5.4  Summary and Conclusions

In this paper, the general structure of the time series model developed in Wolfson (1977) has been briefly described and the basic structure of the bequest submodel has been specified. The task of the bequest part of the time series model is to transform the distribution of estates generated by mortality into a set of wealth distributions of survivors where inheritors have been found and their wealth has been augmented by the amounts of their inheritances. This process has been divided into three main steps: transforming estates into bequests, transforming bequests into inheritances, and matching inheritances with inheritors. Correspondingly, three main parameters of the bequest process have been defined: the heirs parameter describes the way in which estates are divided into bequests, using either primogeniture or equal division for either of two wealth classes; the age-diff parameter gives the age difference in years between decedents and their heirs, as an indication of the extent of generation skipping; and the comb parameter determines whether inheritors are to be selected and matched (combined) with their inheritances in an equalizing or disequalizing manner.

The basic conclusions are:

a. Equal division among a large number of heirs reduces inequality. This effect is most pronounced in the upper tail of the distribution when there is unequal combination. When there is equal combination, the strength of this effect is relatively unaffected by the extent of generation skipping (age-diff). When there is unequal combination, the effect is stronger in the upper tail of the distribution (CV and share of the top 1%) but weaker elsewhere (Gini and EXP) when there is less generation skipping (age-diff is lower).

b. Differential division generally results in less inequality than universal primogeniture, and more inequality than equal division. Exceptions can arise because of differential yields and saving behavior by wealth class.

c. More extensive generation skipping reduces inequality. This effect is strongest when there is unequal combination. Given unequal combination, the strongest effect in the upper tail occurs with universal primogeniture. Given equal combination, the strength of this effect is relatively unaffected by the pattern of division.

d. Unequal rather than equal combination results in greater inequality. For both primogeniture and equal division, this effect is much stronger when there is no generation skipping. For various amounts of generation skipping, this effect is not greatly affected by the pattern of division (heirs = 1,1 versus heirs = 4,4).

e. The levels of inequality generated for the year 2000 fall on both sides of the levels observed in 1970.

f. With no capital transfer taxes, real average wealth increases from 1970 to 2000 by about 0.6 percent per year.

g. The pattern of marriage appears relatively unimportant.

# Notes

1. Note that this assumption implies a constraint on the acceptable values of the parameters $\{h_i\}$ and $d$ defined above—so that the number of inheritances never exceeds the number of potential inheritors. These parameter values will always be chosen so that this constraint is not binding.

2. In that case, the "assortatively married" distribution was simply the husbands' (or wives') distribution horizontally scaled by a factor of two (and scaled vertically by one-half and again by one-half).

3. The Gini is most sensitive to inequality near the mode; the CV is relatively more sensitive in the upper tail of the distribution; while the EXP is relatively

more sensitive to inequality at the lower end of the wealth spectrum. An inequality measure always obeys the Pigou-Dalton condition of transfer, while an inequality indicator satisfies only the weaker condition of never violating the Pigou-Dalton condition. These five statistics have been chosen to give the most complete picture of the aspects of the "shape" of a wealth density in which we are most interested. For a more complete discussion, see Wolfson (1977, chap. 3), and Love and Wolfson (1976).

4. More precisely, when heirs = 1,1, age-diff = 65 implies that 22.8 percent of the 20–24 age group inherit. But age-diff = 45 implies that 7.1 percent of the 20–24 age group inherit and 11.9 percent of the 35–39 group inherit. These figures can be computed from table 5.3.

## Comment     Martin David

Michael Wolfson should be complimented for a major breakthrough in understanding the process of intergenerational wealth transmission and its impact on inequality of wealth. His approach is commendable for working with distributions, for keeping the number of parameters in his simulation to a minimum, and for exploring the sensitivity of results with a number of extreme cases.

Before embarking on a critique of the specific simulation that Wolfson has developed, it is useful to categorize the kinds of information that can be obtained from simulation and to answer the question, What do we wish to know about the process of transfer of wealth between generations? Five areas of research appear to be relevant:

(1) the concentration and deconcentration of wealth; (2) the share of wealth held by the very rich that represents taxable capacity and the share of wealth held by the poor that represents a resource which should be considered in transfer payment programs; (3) the transmission of wealth through human capital investments; (4) the transmission of entrepreneurial activity through family enterprises; and (5) the maintenance of economic power in a kinship grouping through purposive creation of family dynasties.

Wolfson's paper tells us about the first two areas for a sample of Canadian families. The technique that he develops appears useful for investigation of at least some aspects of the other three categories.

There appears to be particularly little concern over these five areas, in this conference. While intellectual curiosity may be satisfied by a view into the affairs of the wealthy, support for serious study of the wealth distribution requires that we indicate clearly how knowledge of wealth

Martin David is professor of economics at the University of Wisconsin, Madison.

can increase the target efficiency of government redistribution programs, and that we relate the consequences of changes in the progression of taxation on the wealthy to the level of investment in human and physical capital.

I would like to organize my remarks into two classes: those that can be handled within the limited framework describing the bequest process that has already been outlined; and those that require the addition of one or more new routines in the simulation process, but which would appear to add greatly to the realism of the results.

## Alterations of the Model

### Savings Rates

A major flaw in the work presented is that we have no data on the sensitivity of the findings to the savings rates assumed for the age/wealth/family size groups. Table C5.1 reproduces the savings rates on which Wolfson bases the accumulation that occurs in the simulation. These rates were extracted from the Statistics Canada FAMEX expenditure study for 1969. Several aspects of the table are troublesome. The savings are derived as a residual from income and expenditure reports in the survey and are therefore subject to the response errors that are well known (and carefully discussed by Ferber [1966] and Modigliani and Ando [1960]). The author also had available separate estimates of net change in assets and liabilities, and it would have been desirable to incorporate those estimates into alternative simulations.

**Table C5.1    Average Propensity to Save Out of Disposable Income (%)**

| Age Category | Family Size = 1 | | | | Family Size ≥ 2 | | | | All FS |
|---|---|---|---|---|---|---|---|---|---|
| | Poor | Middle | Rich | All $W$* | Poor | Middle | Rich | All $W$* | All $W$* |
| < 25 | | | | 0.0 | 1.8 | 8.5 | | 2.7 | 1.9 |
| 25–29 | | | | 0.9 | 5.5 | 9.5 | | 6.8 | 6.2 |
| 30–34 | | | | 6.3 | 4.4 | 6.7 | 17.5 | 6.2 | 6.2 |
| 35–39 | | | | 10.2 | 1.5 | 5.4 | | 4.8 | 5.1 |
| 40–44 | | | | 5.3 | 2.5 | 6.6 | 14.0 | 6.3 | 6.3 |
| 45–49 | | | | 8.0 | 4.2 | 10.2 | 12.2 | 8.7 | 8.7 |
| 50–54 | 5.6 | 13.8 | | 8.6 | 7.1 | 9.9 | 12.6 | 9.5 | 9.4 |
| 55–59 | 7.0 | 12.2 | | 9.4 | 6.2 | 11.5 | 11.2 | 10.1 | 10.0 |
| 60–64 | .1 | − .3 | | − .1 | 8.2 | 9.8 | 9.9 | 9.4 | 8.2 |
| 65–69 | 3.5 | −3.5 | | −1.1 | 4.7 | 1.3 | 8.3 | 4.0 | 3.0 |
| 70–74 | 2.5 | 2.5 | | 2.5 | 1.2 | 1.6 | 10.0 | 4.0 | 3.6 |
| ≥ 75 | −2.3 | 1.1 | | −1.6 | 4.3 | −1.0 | 11.9 | 3.3 | 1.7 |
| All ages | 3.0 | .4 | 16.0 | 3.5 | 4.3 | 7.8 | 12.1 | 7.0 | 6.6 |

Source: Wolfson (1977, p. 128).
*$W$ defined by investment income classes.

A second problem with the table is that from age 60 to age 70 there is a peculiar trough of low savings or dissavings that disappears in most groups at age 75. I would guess that this is in part a phenomenon of aggregation. As Shorrocks (1976) has pointed out, the mortality risks tend to be less for persons with higher incomes. Thus cross-sectional age differences in the table show differential selection (within each wealth class) of those with higher earnings and higher savings rates. The difference between savings rates of those aged 65–69 and those aged 70–74 is thus more likely to reflect differences in individuals and their income level than a shift in behavior.

Both of the foregoing problems might be attacked by using an explicit model of the lifetime accumulation pattern to generate a savings function that is smoothed across age groups and wealth groups. The same model could then more explicitly deal with a richer family size classification. A second advantage of the use of a model on group mean average savings data is that it would overcome one of the difficulties that Wolfson faced in deriving savings rates: the expenditure survey did not contain data on net worth. The table actually classifies families by amount of income from investment rather than by net wealth. With an identical matrix of cells defined on the net worth survey, it would be possible to validate a wealth effect from an aggregated model.

One strength of the savings rate should be noted. The savings rate is net of any gifts, so that *inter vivos* transfers to children are properly excluded from the amounts accumulated into the estates of decedents by the simulation.

### Number of Heirs

A demographer would gasp at the manner in which Wolfson selects the number of heirs. We have a choice of 1, 2, 4, or 6 uniformly across the population. No rationale is offered for the choice of these numbers, except in the case of primogeniture. It seems apparent that some effort should be made to tie the number of heirs to the distribution of eligible persons. Failing that, some effort should be made to relate the number of heirs and their age to some likely expectations in the population. Fortunately, Menchik (1976) offers some evidence on the distribution of heirs by category of relationship to the head (see table C5.2). An average of 7.6 bequests are made in each estate (over $40,000) included in the sample. Roughly one-third are bequests to spouses, children, and grandchildren. Another six percent go to brothers or sisters. Thus data on completed family size are useful for distributing about four-tenths of the total number of bequests. U.S. data from Blau and Duncan (1967) indicate that there would thus be approximately 2.45 children per completed family and therefore eligible to receive bequests from each of the two natural parents.

Table C5.2     Proportion of Beneficiaries by Relationship to Decedent

| Beneficiary's Relationship to Decedent | Ratio of Number of Beneficiaries to Number of Estates ($\times$ 100) |
|---|---|
| Spouse | 43.1 |
| Child | 126.0 |
| Grandchild | 78.4 |
| Total | 247.5 |
| Brother | 20.0 |
| Sister | 27.7 |
| Niece or nephew | 135.5 |
| Total all beneficiaries | 763.5 |

Source: Menchik (1976, p. 144).

Perhaps more interesting, and a useful factor to consider in simulating the inequality of wealth distribution, is that expected completed family size is inversely related to socioeconomic status (see tables C5.3 and C5.4). While Blau and Duncan point out that the differential fertility associated with education has diminished in more recent cohorts, the differentials shown for farm and nonfarm residents are large and could be significant factors in changing the inequality of wealth distribution. Since Wolfson's data include information on occupation, education, and place of residence, it would be easy to vary the number of heirs according to such variables and assess changes in the inequality of the results.

## Primogeniture

Wolfson offers simulations in which bequests are concentrated on a single heir as one polar extreme. I find that possibility very unlikely, and would like to see some evidence that primogeniture is still a factor in the bequest process. (Menchik (1976) finds little evidence of primogeniture in his Connecticut probate sample.) The principal motivation for

Table C5.3     Children Ever Born According to Husband's Father's Occupation

| Husband's Father's Occupation | Children Ever Born per Wife |
|---|---|
| All couples | 2.45 |
| Higher white-collar | 1.98 |
| Lower white-collar | 1.99 |
| Higher manual | 2.39 |
| Lower manual | 2.33 |
| Farm | 2.84 |
| N.A. | 2.45 |

Source: Blau and Duncan (1967, p. 366).

Table C5.4    **Children Ever Born per Wife by Educational Attainment of Wife and Farm Residence and Background of Couple**

| Years of School Completed by Wife | Total | Nonfarm Residence | | Farm Residence |
|---|---|---|---|---|
| | | Nonfarm Background | Farm Background | |
| Total | 2.45 | 2.21 | 2.58 | 3.34 |
| *Elementary* | | | | |
| 0 to 4 | 3.96 | 2.30 | 4.24 | 5.15 |
| 5 to 7 | 3.07 | 2.39 | 3.39 | 3.85 |
| 8 | 2.71 | 2.43 | 2.77 | 3.53 |
| *High school* | | | | |
| 1 to 3 | 2.47 | 2.38 | 2.46 | 3.26 |
| 4 | 2.11 | 2.09 | 2.02 | 2.70 |
| *College* | | | | |
| 1 to 3 | 2.14 | 1.99 | 2.24 | 2.62 |
| 4 or more | 1.98 | 1.98 | 1.91 | 2.18 |

*Source*: Blau and Duncan (1967, p. 382).

primogeniture is the indivisibility of assets involved in some closely held family enterprise, a farm or a business. Thus it might be of use to separate the share of wealth that is in such enterprises and allocate it to a single heir, while dividing the remaining estate among several beneficiaries. Table C5.5 gives some indication of the importance of a primo-

Table C5.5    **Mean Net Worth and Equity in Business within 1969 Income Class (all households, Canada, 1969)**

| 1969 Income Group (lower bound of interval in $000s) | Average Net Worth | | Percent with Equity in Business | Median Equity in Business (holders only) | Ratio: Bus. Equity to Total Net Worth |
|---|---|---|---|---|---|
| | Excluding Business Equity | Including Business Equity | | | |
| − ∞ | 4.0 | 7.4 | 13.5 | 19.9 | 45.9 |
| + 1 | 6.9 | 8.9 | 7.2 | 12.6 | 22.5 |
| 2 | 8.4 | 11.1 | 15.6 | 15.5 | 24.3 |
| 3 | 10.2 | 12.8 | 17.2 | 13.7 | 20.3 |
| 4 | 10.2 | 13.6 | 16.6 | 11.1 | 25.0 |
| 5 | 9.6 | 11.3 | 11.2 | 10.8 | 15.0 |
| 6 | 10.8 | 12.8 | 13.5 | 8.4 | 15.6 |
| 7 | 12.7 | 14.8 | 11.1 | 10.6 | 14.2 |
| 10 | 18.1 | 20.8 | 13.2 | 13.9 | 13.0 |
| 15 | 33.9 | 39.4 | 21.6 | 16.6 | 14.0 |
| 25 | 94.8 | 205.2 | 53.4 | 60.0 | 53.8 |
| Total | 14.4 | 18.4 | 14.0 | 13.3 | 21.7 |

*Source*: Statistics Canada (1973b, tables 73, 93, 97).

geniture relating only to business assets. For Canada as a whole about one-fifth of net wealth is in business equity (proprietorships, partnerships, or closely held corporations). The percent is particularly high in the top income group and the lowest income group, suggesting that the proposed modification of the rule could lead to substantial differences from the bounding simulations that Wolfson shows in table 5.1.

One last suggested alteration of Wolfson's model is that wealth be divided between the surviving spouse and children at the time of death of the first marriage partner. As far as I can see, this would be possible within the framework that Wolfson has already derived. Table C5.6 delineates the nature of Wolfson's assumption that assets pass exclusively to the surviving spouse. The options marked w can be simulated within Wolfson's assumptions, depending upon the age difference assumed between decedent and beneficiary. The asterisks indicate additional possibilities for splitting the estate, possibilities which may do nothing to lessen the inequality of wealth among family dynasties, but which may go a great length to lessening the degree of inequality in the distribution of wealth among households (see Menchik 1976, chap. 4). These additional possibilities are important in several ways. Table C5.7 addresses the question of how much present value is left to children when the spouse is provided for by a generation skipping trust through which the spouse has a lifetime interest while the children have a remainder interest. The table shows, given the distribution of age at death, that the trust mechanism passes a healthy percent of the decedent's wealth to the children. Considering the infrequency with which the principal of trusts is invaded, the value of the conditional wealth represented by the present value of the remainder interest ought to be counted part of the wealth of the children rather than wealth of the surviving spouse. This would generally produce an equalizing change in the simulation outcomes.

Table C5.8, taken from Menchik's sample of Connecticut probate records, indicates the proportion of the estate going to spouse, children, and grandchildren by wealth class of the estate. (The values passed to

**Table C5.6    Alternative Beneficiaries for the Estate**

| Case | Decedent Ever Married? | Surviving Spouse? | Children Ever Born? | Eligible Heirs | | | |
|------|------------------------|-------------------|---------------------|--------|----------|--------------|--------|
|      |                        |                   |                     | Spouse | Children | Grandchildren | Others |
| A | No |     |     |   |   |             | w |
| B | Yes | Yes | No  | w |   |             | * |
| C |     |     | Yes | w | * | *(possibly) | * |
| D |     | No  | No  |   |   |             | w |
| E |     |     | Yes |   | w | w           | w |

children and grandchildren are present values of remainder interests, such as those contained in table C5.7 when the bequest is in trust.) Confirmation of this pattern was reported by Jantscher (1967), who shows that trusts involving spouse-children, and children-grandchildren as income and remaindermen account for a large share of the total wealth passing

**Table C5.7**      **Present Value of a Remainder Interest in an Estate Left to the Children, with a Life Interest to the Surviving Spouse**

| | Age at Death of Spouse | | | |
|---|---|---|---|---|
| | 25 | 45 | 65 | 75 |
| *Widower* | | | | |
| Life expectancy | 45.6 | 27.4 | 13.0 | 8.1 |
| Present value of the principal interest discounted at | | | | |
| 5% | .108 | .267 | .530 | .674 |
| 7% | .046 | .157 | .415 | .578 |
| *Widow* | | | | |
| Life expectancy | 51.8 | 32.9 | 16.3 | 9.6 |
| Present value of the principal interest discounted at | | | | |
| 5% | .079 | .201 | .452 | .626 |
| 7% | .030 | .108 | .332 | .522 |

**Table C5.8**      **Mean Bequest and Share of Bequest to Beneficiaries within Wealth Class (Connecticut probate sample)**

| | Wealth Class | | | | | |
|---|---|---|---|---|---|---|
| | 1 | 2 | 3 | 4 | 5 | 6 |
| Mean bequest ($000) | 48.8 | 77.8 | 138.9 | 278.5 | 615.0 | 1,941.6 |
| *Share of bequest given to* | | | | | | |
| Spouse | .23 | .24 | .20 | .23 | .17 | .15 |
| Children | .42 | .34 | .35 | .27 | .31 | .30 |
| Grandchildren | .03 | .04 | .04 | .05 | .07 | .06 |
| Total | .68 | .62 | .59 | .55 | .55 | .51 |
| Brothers | .05 | .06 | .04 | .03 | .01 | .02 |
| Sisters | .07 | .05 | .04 | .05 | .02 | .04 |
| Nieces and nephews | .09 | .11 | .12 | .13 | .12 | .09 |

*Source*: Menchik (1976, pp. 148, 149).

218     Michael C. Wolfson

into trusts at death (see tables C5.9 and C5.10). Both Menchik's and Jantscher's studies show that the number of heirs increases with increasing estate size, and that there is an increased tendency to generation skipping (which Menchik demonstrates to be tax induced). While these findings, peculiar to U.S. institutions in transfer taxation, may not be directly applicable to the Canadian tax environment, they suggest that several extensions of the model are highly desirable: variable numbers of heirs should be generated by a distribution of completed family size; estates should be divided among persons from several generations; the number of generations involved in a single transfer should be made conditional on the size of the estate. Each extension appears to be a desir-

Table C5.9     Bequests in Spouse-Children and Children-Grandchildren Trusts and Value of Such Bequests, as a Percentage of Total Bequests, All Decedents, 1957 and 1959, by Size of Estate

| | Estate Size | | |
|---|---|---|---|
| Trust Type | Small | Medium | Large |
| *Spouse-children* | | | |
| All decedents bequeathing property | 5.2 | 10.4 | 9.0 |
| Trust-creating decedents bequeathing property | 34.6 | 26.8 | 16.1 |
| Total value of bequests in trust | 35.0 | 24.7 | 11.2 |
| *Children-grandchildren* | | | |
| All decedents bequeathing property | 2.0 | 6.2 | 13.4 |
| Trust-creating decedents bequeathing property | 13.1 | 16.0 | 24.2 |
| Total value of bequests in trust | 13.4 | 16.1 | 25.8 |

*Source*: Jantscher (1967, p. 68).

Table C5.10     Bequests in Spouse-Children and Children-Grandchildren Trusts and Value of Such Bequests, as a Percentage of Total Bequests, Husbands, 1957 and 1959, by Size of Estate

| | Estate Size | | |
|---|---|---|---|
| Trust Type | Small | Medium | Large |
| *Spouse-children* | | | |
| All husbands bequeathing property | 9.8 | 19.8 | 17.4 |
| Trust-creating husbands bequeathing property | 53.8 | 44.2 | 29.4 |
| Total value of bequests in trust | 52.9 | 41.8 | 22.0 |
| *Children-grandchildren* | | | |
| All husbands bequeathing property | 0.5 | 3.4 | 11.0 |
| Trust-creating husbands bequeathing property | 2.6 | 7.7 | 18.5 |
| Total value of bequests in trust | 1.3 | 6.4 | 16.9 |

*Source*: Jantscher (1967, p. 71).

able and more realistic specification of the bequest process than what can be captured in the bounding simulations involving award of bequests to a single age difference in relation to the decedent and a uniform number of heirs within each of two wealth classes.

Finally, no simulation is complete without an accounting of the transmission of human capital. Inclusion of an algorithm for intergenerational transmission of education would be extremely valuable, as it is the joint distribution of human and nonhuman capital that is of the greatest policy significance.

## Further Comment     Michael C. Wolfson

Professor David, in his comment, has indicated a number of useful points and directions for further work. Let me first reply to some of his specific criticisms. He suggests that a major flaw in my paper is the absence of a sensitivity analysis with respect to the saving rates used in the simulations. In fact, in my thesis on which this paper is based (Wolfson 1977), a fairly extensive sensitivity analysis was performed. The results showed, for example, that assuming a uniform 10 percent saving rate for all age/wealth/family size groups made almost no difference to the simulation results.

Considerations of space did not permit any explanation in the paper of the saving process actually used in the model. It is the case, however, that the saving rates displayed in Professor David's table C5.1 comprise only one part of the saving function. The general saving function used in the model is given by the following equation (all items disaggregated by the two family size categories; time subscript omitted for convenience).

$$W_{a+s}(x) = \sum_{i=1}^{k} \int_{V_i}^{V^{i+1}} W_a(z) \, S_{ai}^E [x$$
$$- (1 + s_{ai} r_{ai}) z] dz$$

where $a$ = age group
$i$ = wealth class
$V_i$ = lower limit of $i$th wealth class
$W_a(x)$ = wealth density before saving
$W_{a+s}(x)$ = wealth density after saving
$s_{ai}$ = saving rate out of income
$r_{ai}$ = yield on wealth after tax
$S_{ai}^E (y)$ = probability distribution for saving out of earnings

The saving rates in Professor David's table C5.1 refer only to the $s_{ai}$, though his comments about the definition of saving apply equally to the derivation of the $s_{ai}$ and the $S_{ai}^{E}(y)$.

A second concern raised by Professor David is the definition of saving. The difference between the definition actually used and net change in assets and liabilities less net capital receipts (gifts received less gifts given), an alternative suggested by Professor David, is indicated by the following sum: payments for insurance, annuities, and private and registered pension plans + net accumulation of motor vehicles — one-half of pension and private annuity income. These items were included in our definition of saving first to eliminate the difference in the definition of wealth between the SCF(1973) and the FAMEX (1973) in the case of motor vehicles, and second to capture pension saving and dis-saving.

With regard to the patterns shown by the saving rates in Professor David's table C5.1, it is not clear that Professor David's concerns are entirely appropriate. His point about mortality selection is obviously relevant. However, it is not necessarily a correct interpretation of the table to infer a peculiar trough in savings in the 60 to 70 age range. For all wealth groups combined, there is a fairly clear pattern of declining but always positive saving rates from age 55 on. There is greater variability within the columns associated with specific family size/wealth categories. However, this could be the result of movement of family units from family size group 2 to size group 1 as they age as a result of mortality, or from movement from higher to lower wealth classes, both of which actually occurred (see Wolfson 1977, p. 124).

In my paper, I used quite arbitrary choices for the number of heirs in the simulations, as Professor David has pointed out. The Menchik data he cites are certainly interesting in this regard, though I was unaware of them when the simulations were being run. In any case, the range of simulations actually run gives results that are clear enough, and the range chosen is not unreasonable given the figures presented in Professor David's table C5.2.

Finally, Professor David has indicated a number of directions in which the model could be extended. Of course, in any exercise like that of my thesis, a number of choices must be made regarding the areas where more or less detailed effort should be applied—everything cannot be done at once. It is hoped that some of the extensions to the model that he has suggested can be incorporated sometime in the future.

# References

Atkinson, A.B. 1971. "The Distribution of Wealth and the Individual Life-Cycle." *Oxford Economic Papers,* n.s., vol. 23.

Blau, Peter, and Dudley Duncan. 1967. *The American Occupational Structure.* New York: John Wiley.

Blinder, A. S. 1973. "A Model of Inherited Wealth." *Quarterly Journal of Economics* 87:608–26.

Cheng, K.; J. A. Grant, and H. M. Ploeger. No date. *Ontario Estates in 1963–64: A Tabular Analysis of Personal Wealth Held in Estates Out of Which Ontario Succession Duties Were Paid.* Ontario Committee on Taxation. Toronto: Queen's Printer.

Ferber, Robert. 1966. *The Reliability of Consumer Reports of Financial Assets and Debts.* Urbana: Bureau of Economic and Business Research, University of Illinois.

Jantscher, Gerald. 1967. *Trusts and Estate Taxation.* Washington, D.C.: Brookings.

Lampman, Robert J. 1962. *The Share of Top Wealth-Holders in National Wealth 1922–1956.* Princeton: Princeton University Press.

Love, R., and M. C. Wolfson. 1976. *Income Inequality: Statistical Methodology and Canadian Illustrations.* Statistics Canada, cat. no. 13–559 occasional. Ottawa: Government Printer.

Menchik, Paul. 1976. *A Study of Inheritance and Death Taxation.* Ph.D. dissertation, University of Pennsylvania.

Modigliani, Franco, and A. Ando. 1960. "The 'Permanent Income' and the Life Cycle Hypotheses of Saving Behavior: Comparison and Tests," in Irwin Friend and Ronald Jones, eds., *Proceedings of the Conference on Consumption and Saving,* vol. 2 pp. 51–73. Philadelphia: University of Pennsylvania Press.

Orcutt, G.; S. Caldwell; and R. Wertheimer. 1976. *Policy Exploration through Microanalytic Simulation.* Washington, D.C.: Urban Institute.

Oulton, N. 1976. "Inheritance and the Distribution of Wealth," *Oxford Economic Papers,* n.s. 28:86–101.

Shorrocks, A. F. 1975. "The Age-Wealth Relationship: A Cross-Section and Cohort Analysis." *Review of Economics and Statistics* 5, no. 57, pp. 155–163.

Shoup, C. S. 1966. *Federal Estate and Gift Taxes.* Washington, D.C.: Brookings.

Statistics Canada. 1973a. *Family Expenditure in Canada. Vol. 1: All Canada, Urban and Rural, 1969.* cat. no. 62–535 occasional. Ottawa: Government Printer.

———. 1973b. *Income, Assets and Indebetedness of Families in Canada, 1969,* cat. no. 13–547 occasional. Ottawa: Government Printer.

Vaughan, R. N. 1975. *A Study of the Distribution of Wealth*. Ph.D. Thesis, Cambridge University.

Wolfson, M. C. 1977. *The Causes of Inequality in the Distribution of Wealth—A Simulation Analysis*. Ph.D. Thesis, Cambridge University.

# 6     Estimates of the 1969 Size Distribution of Household Wealth in the U.S. from a Synthetic Data Base

Edward N. Wolff

This paper presents a description, as well as some new estimates, of the size distribution of household wealth for the United States in 1969, from a synthetic data base called MESP. This data base was developed at the National Bureau of Economic Research as part of a project called Measurement of Economic and Social Performance (MESP), under the direction of Richard Ruggles, from October 1972 to October 1977.[1] The data base is the product of three statistical matches and two sets of imputations and contains asset and liability information, as well as detailed demographic data, for a sample of 63,457 households.

Some justification may be required for developing a new (and synthetic) data base for estimating household wealth distributions. There are four major sources of household wealth data. The first consists of administrative records, in particular tax returns required of wealthholders for paying wealth taxes. Unfortunately (or fortunately), the U.S. has not imposed a wealth tax, and such a data source is not available in the U.S. However, Sweden and several other Western European countries do have a general wealth tax and this data source. This type of data is probably the best for wealth distribution analysis. Even so, there are three major problems in using it. First, there is usually a minimum level of wealth required for filing the return; thus the coverage of the popu-

Edward N. Wolff is associate professor in the Department of Economics, New York University.

The original version of this paper was presented at the 1977 Conference on Research in Income and Wealth in Williamsburg, Virginia. This is a revised version and, as such, embodies many of the valuable suggestions of Mr. Vito Natrella, the paper's discussant. Most of the credit for the development of this data base must go to Nancy and Richard Ruggles, who originally conceived the idea and directed its execution. The research for this paper was funded by NSF Grant No. SOC74–21391.

lation is incomplete. Second, not all assets are normally included in this type of tax return (particularly, consumer durables), and for those that are, there are usually problems of underreporting (both from ignorance of current market value and for tax reasons). Thus, the coverage of asset values is normally deficient. Third, there are quite often disclosure problems in releasing this type of data for research use.

The second major source of wealth data consists of estate tax records. These, too, are administrative records, but unlike wealth tax records they cover decedents, not the living. In the United States the use of estate tax data as a means of making wealth distribution estimates has been largely developed by James Smith (see Smith 1974 and Smith and Franklin 1974 for a description of the methodology used). There are five main problems associated with this source of data. First, the sample is limited to the top of the wealth distribution (decedents with gross estates of $60,000 or more in 1969). Second, asset coverage is also limited, with consumer durables and household inventories omitted. In addition, there is a tendency for assets, particularly business equity, to be undervalued for tax reasons. Third, very limited demographic detail is available on the decedent and none on his family. Fourth, developing full population estimates from the sample of decedents depends on assumptions about relative mortality rates (though the overall size distribution estimates are fairly robust with respect to different assumptions). Fifth, there is almost no way of determining the effect of *inter vivos* transfers (gifts before death) and the establishment of trust funds on the size distribution of wealth estimated from this data source.

The third major source of wealth data comes from direct surveys of households. This might come from a full census or from a sample survey. Perhaps the most well known example of this type in the United States is the Federal Reserve Board's 1962–63 Survey of Financial Characteristics of Consumers (see Projector and Weiss 1966). As in all surveys, deficiencies arise because of the limited time and budget allocated to complete them. For this survey, 2,557 consumer units were given questionnaires to report their assets and liabilities, as well as other household information. The asset coverage is fairly complete, except for consumer durables. The main problem with this survey is the severe underreporting of liquid assets and installment debt (Projector and Weiss 1966, p. 61). For example, in comparison with Flow of Funds data, only 51 percent of savings accounts, 55 percent of U.S. Government securities, 39 percent of state and local government securities, and 58 percent of installment debt were reported in the survey. Another problem with this survey is that due to its relatively small sample size, wealth distribution estimates for subgroups of the population, particularly the poor and the rich, are not very reliable.

The fourth major source of wealth data is income flows. Essentially, the technique involves "capitalizing" interest, dividends, business profits, and the like into corresponding asset values. An early example of such a set of estimates for the U.S. is contained in Stewart (1939). A more recent set of estimates is provided in Lebergott (1976). To date, the technique has been used on aggregate income flow data. MESP, in effect, uses the same technique on a micro–data base. There are both advantages and disadvantages to this technique (See Friedman 1939). First, the resulting asset estimates are only as good as the income flow estimates. In Stewart, Lebergott, and the MESP data base, the underlying income flows come from Internal Revenue Service tax returns. This is probably the most accurate source of income information in the U.S., particularly for nonwage income. Moreover, the income data contained in the tax returns are probably far more reliable than survey wealth data. A second advantage is that the resulting wealth imputations automatically balance with the national totals, because the capitalizing ratio is the ratio of the national total for a given asset to the sample total of the corresponding income flow. A possible disadvantage is that the resulting wealth estimates are sensitive to the yield ratios used. In Stewart, Lebergott, and the MESP data base, it was implicitly assumed that the yield on each asset was the same for each income class, race, region of the country, and the like. If there were a systematic relation between yield and some demographic characteristics (for example, higher income classes may receive a higher dividend yield on stock equity), then a bias would be introduced into the wealth imputations. But the advantages outweigh the disadvantages. Since a capitalization procedure is not "tied" to a particular survey or set of administrative records, it can be applied to any sample frame. Thus, as in the MESP data base, full coverage of the population is possible. Also, the technique is a relatively open one, so that assets not normally covered by this approach, like consumer durables, can be added to household portfolios. This approach thus makes possible full coverage of assets and liabilities.

The bulk of this paper will present a description of the techniques used in the construction of the MESP data base (section 6.1). Section 6.2 will present some new estimates of wealth holdings for different social and economic classes in 1969. Section 6.3 will present some concluding remarks as well as cautions in the use of this data base. It should be noted that no attempt has been made here to compare wealth estimates from the MESP data base with those from other sources. This is done in Wolff (1978). However, it might be noted that the results of the comparison are encouraging and indicate reasonably close sets of estimates. Most of the discrepancies that exist can be traced to differences in concept or sampling frame.

## 6.1    The Formation of the MESP Data Base

The MESP data base was formed by combining information from the 1970 Census Public Use sample with the Internal Revenue Service tax return data and by imputing asset and liability values based on income flows and other available household information. The sample frame of the MESP data base is the 1970 state 15 percent Census 1/1000 Public Use Sample (PUS), which contains personal and household information for a randomly drawn sample of 63,457 households. Statistical matching procedures were used to add household information from three other data sets: the 1970 Internal Revenue Service Tax Model (IRS 70), the 1969 Internal Revenue Service Tax Model (IRS 69), and the 1970 state 5 percent Census 1/1000 Public Use Sample (PUS5). Asset and liability information was then imputed to each household based on its extended set of demographic and income data. Household asset and liability estimates were then adjusted to align with national balance sheet totals of household wealth.

### 6.1.1    The Statistical Matches

A statistical matching procedure developed by Nancy and Richard Ruggles (see Ruggles and Ruggles 1974; Ruggles, Ruggles and Wolff 1977) was used to combine information from the two census and the two tax return files. In all, three separate matches were performed (See appendix). The first match was between the 1969 and 1970 IRS files. This was done because a special 1970 IRS file had been developed by the Social Security Administration containing the race and age of the head of household on each tax return,[2] as well as more detailed information on the deductions taken in each tax return, particularly mortgage and other interest payments and state, local, sales, and property tax payments, than the 1969 IRS file. For the match, the two files were first divided into single and joint returns. The single filers were then divided into four cohort groups: males under 65, males 65 or over, females under 65, and females 65 or over. The joint filers were also divided into four cohorts: both under 65, both 65 or over, husband under 65 and wife 65 or over, and husband 65 or over and wife under 65. Each of these groups was then subdivided again, depending on the number of children in the family. Tax returns within each of these finely divided groups were then matched between the IRS69 and IRS70 file, depending on how close the two records were with respect to the following thirteen items: adjusted gross income (AGI); wage and salary earnings/AGI; interest income/AGI; long-term capital gains/AGI; rental income/AGI; dividends/AGI; farm income/AGI; trust income/AGI; royalty income/AGI; business and professional earnings/AGI; pension income/AGI; property sale gains/AGI; and total deductions/AGI.

Race, age, and itemized deductions were then transferred from the IRS-70 record to the corresponding IRS69 record.

The second and major match was between this "augmented" IRS69 file and the 1970 PUS file, containing income and earnings information for the year 1969. The purpose of this match was to combine the detailed income information of the IRS69 file with the detailed demographic information of the PUS. Moreover, the PUS contains information on the value of owner occupied housing as well as stocks of durables held. Both sets of information were thus required to construct household balance sheets.

The two files were first divided into cohort groups on the basis of the following four (common) variables: marital status (single vs. married); sex (for singles); age of head of household; and race of head of household. Within each cohort group the two files were matched depending on how close the two records were with respect to the following six characteristics: number of children; homeowner vs. renter; wage and salary earnings; business earnings; farm income; total income. The detailed income information, as well as data on itemized deductions, was then transferred from the IRS69 file to the 1970 PUS file.

The last match was that of the PUS5 file to the PUS. The reason for this match was that only the PUS5 file has information on the televisions, radios, and clothes washers and dryers owned by each household. The two files were first divided into cohorts on the basis of the following five variables: marital status; age of head of household; sex of head of household; race of head of household; homeowner vs. renter. Records from the two files were matched depending on how close they were with respect to the following five characteristics: number of children; value of property or gross monthly rental; wage earnings of head of household; wage earnings of spouse; total family income. Information on the stocks of consumer durables was then transferred from the PUS5 file to the PUS.[3]

### 6.1.2   Alignment of Income Flows

Since tax returns were imputed to households in the PUS, some error was expected in the total income flows computed from this sample. This is documented in table 6.1, which compares the MESP totals with those of the IRS *Statistics of Income*. The adjusted gross income (AGI) and wage and salary totals were quite close. The interest, dividend, business and professional net income, and rental income totals were all higher in the unadjusted MESP file than in the IRS totals. The main reason for the discrepency is evident from the second column of table 6.1: the matching procedure assigned too many tax returns containing these income items to households in the PUS sample frame.[4]

Table 6.1          Comparison of 1969 Income Flows between the Unadjusted
                   MESP Totals and Statistics of Income

| Item | National Totals (billions of dollars) | | | Percent Receiving the Item | |
|---|---|---|---|---|---|
| | MESP | IRS | MESP/IRS | MESP | IRS |
| Adjusted gross income | $629.6 | $603.6 | 1.04 | | |
| Wages and salary | 573.1 | 499.0 | 1.15 | | |
| Interest | 44.5 | 19.6 | 2.27 | 65.1% | 42.3% |
| Dividends | 38.4 | 16.9 | 2.27 | 30.7 | 16.0 |
| Business and profes- sional net income | 42.6 | 30.4 | 1.40 | 32.7 | 8.0 |
| Partnership net income | −17.2 | 2.0 | | 5.7 | 2.7 |
| Farm net income | −10.0 | 3.6 | | 16.5 | 4.1 |
| Rental income | 4.0 | 2.6 | 1.54 | 20.6 | 8.4 |
| Estates and trust income | − 1.2 | 1.4 | | 1.9 | 0.8 |

Source: U.S. Internal Revenue Service 1971.

Our fix-up procedure was straightforward. In the case of interest, dividends, business and professional net income, and rental income, we randomly eliminated these entries so that the percent of households receiving each item in the MESP file would be equal to the IRS percent.[5] We then adjusted the remaining income entries by a constant multiple so that they would sum to the IRS total. In the case of partnership, farm, and trust income, where the signs for the totals differed, we used a somewhat different procedure. We randomly eliminated a certain percent of positive entries and a certain (though different) percent of negative entries, so that the percent receiving the income item and the total income flow would equal the IRS total.[6]

### 6.1.3   Asset and Liability Imputations

Our next step was to "build up" balance sheet information for each household based on the stock and flow data already contained in the (now adjusted) MESP data base. The imputation procedures differed for different assets and liabilities. However, in all the procedures the resultant stock totals were aligned with the national balance sheet totals for the household sector (see table 6.2).

### Owner-occupied Housing

House values were provided in the PUS, though they were coded in 11 intervals. The midpoints of each interval were used, except for the last, open-ended interval of $50,000 or more. For this we chose a value of $77,538 so that the total would agree with the aggregate balance sheet.

## Consumer Durables

Ownership, though not values, was provided for the following set of durables in the PUS: number of automobiles (0, 1, 2, 3 or more), air conditioning unit, washing machine and clothes dryer, dishwasher, home food freezer, television, and radio. To construct a balance sheet for each household, it was necessary to increase the coverage of durables and to impute a *dollar* value for each durable owned by the household.

Estimates of the total value of consumer durables held by households were obtained from the Bureau of Economic Analysis (see table 6.3). Moreover, from the 1960–61 Bureau of Labor Statistics Consumer Expenditure Survey (CES), information was provided about the annual expenditure by families on each of the following durables for 1960–61: automobiles, washer/dryer combinations, refrigerators, other major ap-

Table 6.2    **Aggregate National Balance Sheet of Household Wealth for the U.S., 1969, by Item (billions of current dollars)**

| Item | Value | |
|------|------:|------:|
| *Assets* | 3,612.8 | |
| Tangible Assets | 1,220.3 | |
|   Owner-occupied housing | | 635.0 |
|   Other real estate | | 175.8 |
|   Automobiles | | 89.5 |
|   Other consumer durables | | 227.3 |
|   Inventories | | 92.7 |
| Financial Assets | 2,392.6 | |
|   Demand deposits and currency | | 104.9 |
|   Time and savings deposits | | 381.4 |
|   Federal securities | | 101.4 |
|   State and local governments securities | | 34.8 |
|   Corporate and foreign bonds, mortgages, open market paper, other instruments | | 85.6 |
|   Corporate stock | | 635.9 |
|   Farm business equity | | 218.1 |
|   Unincorporated nonfarm equity | | 314.5 |
|   Trust fund equity | | 132.8 |
|   Insurance and pension reserves | | 383.1 |
| *Liabilities* | 450.2 | |
|   Mortgage debt | | 276.6 |
|   Consumer credit | | 121.1 |
|   Other debt | | 52.5 |
| *Net Worth* | 3,162.6 | |

*Source*: Estimates prepared by Raymond Goldsmith in Ruggles (1977). Consumer durables were split into autos and others from Bureau of Economic Analysis worksheets provided by John Musgrave.

Table 6.3    Net Stocks of Consumer Durables Held by Households in 1969 (billions of current dollars)

| Item | Value |
|------|-------|
| Automobiles | $ 89.5 |
| Other motor vehicles | 9.5 |
| Appliances | 30.8 |
| Radios, televisions, phonographs, etc. | 30.9 |
| Furniture | 52.3 |
| Textiles and other durable home furnishings (excluding china and utensils) | 68.4 |
| Other (including china and utensils, jewelry, books, and toys) | 35.4 |
| Total | $316.8 |

*Sources*: Bureau of Economic Analysis Worksheets, provided by Mr. John Musgrave. (See Young and Musgrave, [1976] for methods.)

pliances, small appliances, televisions, radios and phonographs, furniture, textiles, floor coverings, and housewares. For the imputation of consumer durable values, it was necessary to combine the information contained in these three sources of data. This was done in three successive steps. First, ownership of durables not included in the PUS inventory was imputed to households, and the purchase price and year of purchase of each durable were estimated for each household. Second, the current market value (as of 1969) of each durable was estimated by depreciating the purchase price of the durable according to its age and the life span of the durable. Third, the total value of durables held by households in the sample was aligned to the BEA net stock estimates.

*Imputing the Ownership of Durables.* Using the CES we computed the percent of households falling within predefined demographic categories who purchased each of eleven durables during the survey year. We initially used nine demographic characteristics. The categories of each of these, as well as the marginal percent who purchased each durable are shown in table 6.4. Using the nine-dimensional breakdown would have resulted in 43,336 ($2 \times 4 \times 2 \times 3 \times 3 \times 2 \times 7 \times 3 \times 7$) categories—far in excess of the 13,728 families in the CES. We therefore chose the three most important demographic characteristics out of the nine—income, age, and urban/rural residence—and added a fourth homeowner/renter category.[7] This resulted in a small enough number of cells to obtain reliable estimates of the proportion who purchased each durable by demographic group.[8]

We treated the proportion of each group purchasing each durable in 1960–61 as the *probability* of each group's purchasing the good in cal-

**Table 6.4**  Percent of Families of the Indicated Type Purchasing Each of Eleven Durables in the CES Survey Year

| | Textiles | Furniture | Floor Coverings | Refrigerator | Washing Machine | All Other Major Appliances | Small Appliances | Housewares | Automobile | Television | Radio |
|---|---|---|---|---|---|---|---|---|---|---|---|
| *Urbanization* | | | | | | | | | | | |
| Urban | 75.9 | 45.1 | 29.9 | 8.2 | 9.3 | 20.3 | 26.8 | 68.3 | 23.2 | 54.3 | 46.5 |
| Rural | 77.0 | 39.8 | 31.9 | 10.9 | 11.0 | 20.3 | 26.6 | 74.6 | 27.0 | 52.4 | 37.5 |
| *Region* | | | | | | | | | | | |
| Northeast | 76.4 | 43.8 | 32.4 | 7.2 | 8.8 | 18.4 | 25.4 | 66.8 | 23.7 | 55.1 | 45.9 |
| North Central | 77.1 | 45.0 | 31.7 | 9.1 | 10.8 | 21.3 | 26.7 | 69.5 | 24.9 | 56.0 | 45.6 |
| South | 74.8 | 41.0 | 30.2 | 10.1 | 9.0 | 19.4 | 27.8 | 74.3 | 23.5 | 50.2 | 36.8 |
| West | 77.3 | 44.4 | 26.0 | 9.3 | 11.0 | 23.0 | 26.8 | 69.3 | 26.2 | 54.2 | 50.0 |
| *Sex of head* | | | | | | | | | | | |
| Male | 79.4 | 46.6 | 32.5 | 9.9 | 10.9 | 22.4 | 28.5 | 73.2 | 27.3 | 56.5 | 47.0 |
| Female | 60.4 | 27.1 | 20.6 | 4.8 | 4.1 | 9.8 | 17.8 | 55.5 | 9.5 | 39.6 | 27.2 |
| *Race of head* | | | | | | | | | | | |
| White | 77.1 | 44.2 | 30.8 | 9.1 | 10.1 | 21.2 | 26.8 | 70.2 | 25.4 | 55.1 | 44.6 |
| Negro | 70.2 | 38.2 | 30.4 | 8.2 | 6.7 | 12.1 | 28.2 | 71.2 | 15.0 | 42.9 | 35.3 |
| Other | 69.4 | 32.2 | 18.2 | 9.7 | 10.1 | 21.7 | 16.7 | 70.9 | 24.0 | 46.5 | 48.4 |
| *Education of head* | | | | | | | | | | | |
| Less than H.S. grad | 72.9 | 37.2 | 30.1 | 8.8 | 9.1 | 17.5 | 25.1 | 67.9 | 22.3 | 50.5 | 34.6 |
| H.S. grad | 80.7 | 48.8 | 32.1 | 9.6 | 10.8 | 23.0 | 29.1 | 72.8 | 28.2 | 59.0 | 52.3 |
| Some college | 82.2 | 55.3 | 30.7 | 9.3 | 10.8 | 25.4 | 29.1 | 74.6 | 26.6 | 57.8 | 61.0 |
| *Marital status* | | | | | | | | | | | |
| Married | 82.4 | 49.1 | 34.2 | 10.3 | 11.6 | 23.7 | 29.7 | 76.2 | 28.5 | 58.5 | 48.7 |
| Not married | 56.3 | 24.8 | 18.6 | 5.0 | 4.1 | 9.1 | 17.2 | 51.1 | 11.1 | 38.1 | 27.2 |

**Table 6.4**—*continued*

| | Textiles | Furniture | Floor Coverings | Refrigerator | Washing Machine | All Other Major Appliances | Small Appliances | Housewares | Automobile | Television | Radio |
|---|---|---|---|---|---|---|---|---|---|---|---|
| *Age of head* | | | | | | | | | | | |
| Under 25 years | 78.0 | 59.5 | 34.8 | 12.6 | 18.8 | 27.2 | 27.7 | 79.7 | 35.8 | 48.6 | 46.2 |
| 25–34 years | 83.2 | 57.1 | 35.2 | 12.0 | 14.9 | 27.5 | 30.0 | 80.9 | 32.7 | 57.4 | 53.1 |
| 35–44 ” | 85.7 | 51.0 | 35.3 | 10.2 | 11.5 | 23.4 | 32.0 | 78.6 | 29.9 | 60.2 | 60.0 |
| 45–54 ” | 79.9 | 44.1 | 32.5 | 8.9 | 9.0 | 20.1 | 29.5 | 72.5 | 27.0 | 57.2 | 50.9 |
| 55–64 ” | 72.5 | 34.9 | 26.1 | 7.8 | 6.7 | 16.2 | 23.9 | 64.3 | 18.9 | 49.7 | 31.1 |
| 65–74 ” | 60.5 | 26.4 | 23.4 | 5.3 | 4.5 | 12.7 | 18.7 | 53.5 | 10.2 | 47.2 | 19.4 |
| 75 years & over | 48.4 | 17.4 | 14.6 | 4.1 | 3.7 | 9.3 | 11.2 | 43.3 | 5.4 | 34.1 | 12.8 |
| *Occupational status* | | | | | | | | | | | |
| White collar (empl) | 83.3 | 53.2 | 32.6 | 8.9 | 10.8 | 24.1 | 29.3 | 74.9 | 27.6 | 58.7 | 59.6 |
| Blue collar (empl) | 79.4 | 46.6 | 33.7 | 10.4 | 11.3 | 21.7 | 29.2 | 73.9 | 28.8 | 56.2 | 45.2 |
| Retired | 56.1 | 24.5 | 19.9 | 5.3 | 4.1 | 11.2 | 15.8 | 49.4 | 8.8 | 42.8 | 17.6 |
| *Income of head* | | | | | | | | | | | |
| Under $1,000 | 40.6 | 12.0 | 12.2 | 4.6 | 3.8 | 8.2 | 8.4 | 45.2 | 4.8 | 19.5 | 14.3 |
| $1,000–2,999 | 58.6 | 24.5 | 20.9 | 6.5 | 5.3 | 9.8 | 17.1 | 58.0 | 11.1 | 39.0 | 18.3 |
| $3,000–4,999 | 75.4 | 39.5 | 29.6 | 9.1 | 10.1 | 18.0 | 26.7 | 71.1 | 23.3 | 52.7 | 35.4 |
| $5,000–6,999 | 81.5 | 49.3 | 33.5 | 9.9 | 11.8 | 22.2 | 28.0 | 73.3 | 27.2 | 58.3 | 48.3 |
| $7,000–9,999 | 86.9 | 55.1 | 37.2 | 10.5 | 11.5 | 26.4 | 32.0 | 76.7 | 31.4 | 63.0 | 59.6 |
| $10,000–14,999 | 88.7 | 58.3 | 36.0 | 10.6 | 12.7 | 29.2 | 35.0 | 79.3 | 35.1 | 64.5 | 69.2 |
| $15,000 & above | 89.9 | 59.7 | 36.5 | 9.0 | 9.0 | 32.3 | 38.2 | 78.8 | 37.3 | 66.5 | 71.5 |

*Source*: 1960–61 Bureau of Labor Statistics Consumer Expenditure Survey.

endar year 1960 and all successive years.[9] We let $q_{ij}$ be the probability of demographic group $j$'s purchasing durable $i$. We obtained information on $L_i$, the service life of each durable $i$ (table 6.5). Thus, the probability $r_{ij}$ that a person in group $j$ owns durable $i$ is $q_{ij}L_i$, under the assumption that no one in a group purchases a durable until its service life is over.[10] Probability $r_{ij}$ was then computed for each household in the PUS on the basis of its demographic characteristics and for all durables except cars, television, radios, and washer/dryer units.[11] A number $s_i$ between 0 and 1 was randomly picked (using a random number generator) from a uniform distribution for each household and each durable $i$. If $s_i < r_{ij}$, we assigned ownership of durable $i$ to the household; otherwise no ownership was imputed. The age $A_i$ of durable $i$ was also imputed to households for all durables owned by the household (including those in the PUS inventory). Let $T_{ij} = 1/q_{ij}$. $T_{ij}$ then indicates the average length of ownership of durable $i$ for demographic group $j$, where, if $T_{ij} > L_i$, the good has zero value in the $T_{ij} - L_i$ years of possession. The age $A_i$ of good $i$ is then given for each household by $A_i = s_i T_{ij} = s_i/q_{ij}$ (as long as $s_i < r_{ij}$).[12]

Table 6.6 compares the percent of households which purchased each of the eleven durables in 1960–61 according to the CES and our estimates of the percent which purchased each durable in 1969 (that is, those durables whose age is less than or equal to 1.0). The imputed purchase estimates were quite close to the actual CES figures for all durables except autos and televisions. Automobile and television purchases in the imputation for calendar year 1969 were probably overstated because of the occurrence of multiple ownership of each item in the PUS.[13]

*Imputing the Current Market Value of Durables.* The purchase price of each durable owned by households was imputed using regression analysis. Using the CES, we regressed family expenditure on each of the eleven durables, conditional on purchasing the durable, on the following set of variables common to the CES and PUS[14]: family income; years of schooling of head of household; age of head of household; family size; urban/rural/farm residence; region; sex of head of household; race of head of household; marital status; industry of employment of head of household; occupation of head of household; and homeowner/renter.

The regression results were used to impute a purchase price to all households in the PUS owning durables, as follows: for each household owning durable $i$, we computed $p_i = xb_i$, where $b_i$ are the regression coefficients for durable $i$ and $x$ the set of regressors. The estimate $p_i$ is the mean purchase price (in 1961 dollars) of durable $i$ for households with characteristics $x$. The variance was added back in by setting $p_i$, the purchase price of durable $i$, equal to $p_i + t\sigma$ where $\sigma$ is the estimated standard error for the regression and $t$ is a standard normal variate whose

Table 6.5        Service Life (in years) of Each of Eleven
                 Consumer Durables

| Item | Service Life (years) |
|------|----------------------|
| Automobiles | 10 |
| Televisions | 9 |
| Radios | 9 |
| Housewares | 11 |
| Small appliances | 11 |
| Textiles | 10 |
| Furniture | 14 |
| Floor coverings | 10 |
| Refrigerators | 10 |
| Washing machines/dryers | 10 |
| Other major appliances | 10 |

*Source*: Young and Musgrave 1976, table 1, p. 10.

Table 6.6        Comparison of the Percent of Households Purchasing Durables
                 and the Average Purchase Price between the 1960–61 CES and
                 the Imputed Value for the 1970 PUS

|  | % of Households | | Average Purchase Price (1961 dollars) | | |
|------|------|------|------|------|------|
| Item | 1960–61 CES | 1969 PUS (imputed) | CES | PUS | % Diff. |
| Textiles | 76% | 70% | $ 44 | $ 70 | 59% |
| Furniture | 44 | 44 | 173 | 274 | 58 |
| Floor coverings | 30 | 25 | 87 | 183 | 110 |
| Refrigerators | 9 | 10 | 240 | 275 | 15 |
| Washer/dryer units | 10 | 9 | 193 | 207 | 7 |
| Other major appliances | 20 | 23 | 135 | 168 | 24 |
| Small appliances | 27 | 25 | 28 | 37 | 32 |
| Housewares | 70 | 56 | 19 | 41 | 116 |
| Automobiles | 24 | 40 | 1,234 | 1,561 | 26 |
| Televisions | 54 | 74 | 71 | 90 | 27 |
| Radios & phonographs | 44 | 41 | 76 | 148 | 95 |

*Note*: Sample sizes CES 13,728; PUS 63,457.

value was obtained from a standard normal random number generator.[15]
Table 6.6 shows the mean purchase price of each of the eleven durables
in the CES and the mean (imputed) purchase price for the same durables
in the PUS. The PUS mean purchase prices are uniformly higher. This
is to be expected, since the PUS imputations use 1969 incomes. (In fact,
the mean income in current dollars is about 50 percent higher in 1969
than in 1961.)

To obtain the current market value $V_i$ of durable $i$, we assumed a
straight line depreciation schedule and computed $V_i$ as follows:

$$V_i = (L_i - A_i) \ p_i/L_i$$

where $A_i$ is the imputed age of durable $i$. In the case of autos and televisions, this valuation was done for each one owned by the household.

*Reconciling the Estimates with the BEA Net Stock Totals.* The final step was to reconcile our valuation of consumer durables with the aggregate BEA totals of household owned stocks (table 6.3). There are two major sources of error in our estimates. First, the estimates are still in 1961 dollars, though adjusted for 1969 incomes. Second, purchase decisions and expenditure behavior may have changed between 1961 and 1969.

To balance our estimates of the stock of household durables, we applied "adjustment factors," shown in table 6.7, so that the stock of durables in the PUS sample would sum to the BEA totals. Automobile and major appliances required minor adjustment. Furniture and home furnishings required a large adjustment, presumably because the CES coverage of these groups was considerably smaller than the BEA coverage. The television category required a large adjustment, probably because of the introduction of color televisions during the 1960s.

The MESP coverage of consumer durables included all BEA categories except the "other durable" group (china, utensils, jewelry, books, toys, etc.). The PUS coverage thus amounted to $248.4 billion, or 78 percent of the BEA total.

*Time Deposits, Bonds (excluding state and local government securities), Notes and Other Interest-Earning Securities*

Capitalization techniques were used for the valuation of the remaining assets in the household balance sheet. Ideally, information providing differential yields by demographic and income characteristics of households for different asset types would have been desirable. Thus, for example if we knew that high income households had an average yield of

| Table 6.7 | Adjustment Factors for the Alignment of Consumer Durable Totals in the PUS with the BEA Totals |
|---|---|
| BEA Group | Adjustment Factor |
| Automobiles | 0.99 |
| Appliances (washer/dryer units, refrigerators, other major appliances, small appliances) | 1.37 |
| Televisions, radios, and phonographs | 2.49 |
| Furniture | 4.04 |
| Home furnishings (textiles, floor coverings, housewares) | 2.80 |

8.0 percent on bonds, and low income households an average yield of 6.0 percent, different capitalization ratios could be provided for low and high income households. Such information, however, was not available except for stock equity (see below). We therefore provided uniform capitalization ratios for each of the remaining assets in the portfolio.

In the case of financial securities, interest on time and savings deposits is not distinguished from that on bonds, notes, mortgages, and other financial securities in the tax return. Time and savings deposits were therefore aggregated with the other financial securities to form one category. Moreover, state and local government bonds were excluded, since interest received from these bonds is nontaxable and, as a result, not recorded in the tax return. The average yield on this group of securities for 1969 was 3.4% (19.6/568.4), which was used to capitalize the interest into stock estimates. There are two offsetting biases in this procedure. First, the fact that savings accounts normally have lower interest rates than bonds and other securities implies that our imputation procedure is overstating the asset values of bond holders relative to those with savings accounts. We are therefore overestimating the financial security holdings of the upper income classes relative to the lower ones. Second, the fact that state and local government bonds have been excluded implies that the financial security holdings of their owners, who are primarily upper income, are being understated.[16]

### Corporate Securities

Dividends received from corporate equities are recorded in the IRS tax return data. The average yield was 2.7% (16.9/635.9), which we used to capitalize dividends into corporate stock estimates. In the case of this asset, some information was available on the relation of dividend yield to household income for 1969 (Blume, et al., 1974, p. 26). Dividend yields were found to vary inversely with income. However, average dividend yields by AGI class varied only from 2.78 to 2.51 percent.[17] This range was so small compared with the likely error in the imputation that we ignored this correction.

### Investment Real Estate Holdings

Net rental income is reported in the IRS tax return data. A simple capitalization procedure was not possible here, since some of the income reported was negative.[18] In general, gross rents and costs[19] rise with the value of the property. Thus, the greater the discrepancy between gross rents and costs, the higher, in general, the value of the property. We therefore capitalized net rental income into real estate value proportional to the *absolute value* of net rental income. The average "yield" figure was 7.5% (13.2/175.8).

*Unincorporated Nonfarm Equity*

Net business and professional (including partnership) income is reported in the IRS tax return data. Like net rental income, both positive and negative entries occur. We therefore used the same procedure as for real estate holdings, and capitalized the absolute value of net income into unincorporated nonfarm equity, using an average "yield" figure of 18.7% (58.8/314.5).

*Farm Equity*

We used the same procedure as above to capitalize the absolute value of farm net income into farm equity value. The average "yield" figure was 4.8% (10.5/218.1).

*Mortgage Debt*

Considerably more information was available for the imputation of home mortgage debt. In the Public Use Sample, both home value and length of time of ownership ("When Moved In") were provided for each household. From other sources, we obtained information on average interest rates for home mortgages, average maturity of home mortgages, and a price index for residential housing (see table 6.8). Assum-

| Table 6.8 | Basic Data for Mortgage Debt Imputation | | |
|---|---|---|---|
| Period | Average Interest Rate on Home Mortgages[a] | Price Index for Residential Structures[b] (1970 = 100) | Average Maturity[c] (months) |
| 1946–49 | 4.34% | 60.8 | 231 |
| 1950–59 | 4.81 | 76.9 | 261 |
| 1960–64 | 5.69 | 80.9 | 318 |
| 1965–66 | 5.93 | 83.5 | 329 |
| 1967 | 6.56 | 87.7 | 334 |
| 1968 | 7.19 | 91.9 | 338 |
| 1969 | 8.26 | 100.0 | 338 |

*Sources*: [a]U.S. Department of Commerce, Bureau of Economic Analysis, *Business Conditions Digest* (February 1976), table C.118, p. 109 (FHA mortgages).

[b]U.S. Department of Commerce, Bureau of Economic Analysis, *National Income and Product Accounts of the United States, 1929–74*, table 7–13, pp. 294–95.

[c]For average maturity, we used a weighted average of FHA and conventional mortgages. Prior to 1964, the source is Guttentag and Beck, *New Series on Home Mortgage Yields*, NBER, 1970 (#92 General Series), tables C–2 and C–3. After 1963, the source is Department of Housing and Urban Development, *Housing and Urban Development Trends: Annual Summary* (May 1970), table A–61.

ing an average down payment of 25 percent and using standard mortgage amortization tables, we computed the outstanding home mortgage for each homeowner based on initial house value (current value multiplied by the price index) and time of ownership. Our initial estimates resulted in a total household mortgage debt of 273.8, compared with the balance sheet total of 276.6. We then adjusted our estimates by 1.0 percent (276.6/273.8).

### Other Household Debt

Interest payments for households itemizing their deductions are recorded in the IRS tax return data. In the MESP file, 40.9 percent of all households recorded some interest payment. The Survey of Financial Characteristics of Consumers reported that 56.0 percent of all households in 1962 had some form of debt other than mortgage debt. We assumed that 56.0 percent of all households in 1969 had some consumer debt, and that the remainder (56.0% — 40.9% = 15.1%) were households that did not itemize their deductions. We randomly selected this remaining 15.1% from households that did not itemize deductions and capitalized the resulting interest flows into household debt, using an average interest yield of 7.3% (12.6/173.6).

### Asset Coverage

Table 6.9 gives a summary of household information contained in the MESP data base. A comparison with the aggregate balance sheet in table 6.2 reveals the extent of our coverage. Owner occupied housing, other real estate, and automobiles are fully covered. 70% (158.9/227.3) of other consumer durables are included in the MESP data base but there is no coverage of inventories. The MESP coverage of tangible assets thus amounts to 87% (1059.2/1220.3). Coverage of financial assets is also incomplete. Time and savings deposits, federal securities, bonds, mortgages, and other securities, corporate stock, farm business equity, and unincorporated nonfarm equity are fully covered. However, demand deposits and currency, state and local government securities, trust fund equity, and insurance and pension reserves are not included. The coverage of financial assets amounts to 73% (1736.9/2392.6), and that of total assets equals 77% (2796.1/3612.8). Liabilities are fully covered in the data base.

## 6.2   Estimates of the Size Distribution of Household Wealth

This section presents some new estimates of the distribution of household wealth in the United States in 1969 from the MESP data base. Our basic definitions and concepts follow Goldsmith (as reported in Ruggles

1977). For illustrative purposes we have divided the household portfolio into five categories: owner occupied home (primary home only); automobiles and other consumer durables (excluding the Bureau of Economic Analysis "miscellaneous" category); financial securities, including time and savings deposits, federal securities, corporate and foreign bonds, mortgages, open market paper, other instruments (excluding state and local government bonds), and corporate stock; farm business equity, unincorporated nonfarm equity, and investment real estate (in-

**Table 6.9        Summary of Household Information in the MESP Data Base**

*Demographic Information*
Family and household size and composition
Location of household
Age, sex, race, education of each member

*Labor Force Information*
Employment status of each member
Industry and occupation of employment
Time worked for each member

*Income Information*
Wage and salary earnings
Self-employment earnings (including partnership and unincorporated
    business income)
Farm income
Social security income
Pension income
Welfare and public assistance transfers
Royalties
Interest
Dividends
Capital gains
Rental income
Trust income

*Balance Sheet Information*
Tangible assets
  owner occupied housing
  other real estate
  automobiles
  other consumer durables
Financial assets
  time and savings deposits, bonds (except state and local government),
      and other securities
  corporate stock
  farm business equity
  unincorporated nonfarm equity
Liabilities
  mortgage debt
  other household debt

cluding second homes); and debt, including mortgage debt, consumer debt, and other personal loans, but excluding debt secured by stock, investment real estate, or business equity. Total assets are the sum of the first four categories. Net worth is equal to total assets less debt (last category).

### 6.2.1   Estimates for the U.S. Population

The full sample consists of 63,457 households and is representative of the U.S. population as a whole for 1969 (table 6.10). In 1969 mean assets per household were estimated at $44,000 and mean net worth at $40,000. The concentration of ownership, as measured by the Gini coefficient, varied predictably by type of asset.[20] The Gini coefficient for consumer durables was quite low, at 0.30. That for owner occupied housing was 0.68. Financial securities were highly concentrated with a Gini of 0.91. Business equity was the most concentrated of all, as indicated by a Gini coefficient of 0.94. The distribution of total assets was more unequal than that of consumer durables but less unequal than that of financial securities or of business equity; its Gini coefficient was 0.69. The distribution of net worth was more unequal than that of total assets, indicating an overall negative correlation between assets and debt.

### 6.2.2   The Composition of Wealth by Demographic Group

The interesting differences are found when we disaggregate the sample by demographic group. Table 6.11 shows the composition of total assets for selected demographic groups, as well as debt, as a percentage of total assets. For the population as a whole, 22.7 percent of assets owned

| Table 6.10 | 1969 Summary Statistics for the Full Sample |
|---|---|
| Number of households | 63,457 |
| Mean asset value per household (current $) | $44,029 |
| Mean net worth per household (current $) | $39,926 |
| *Gini coefficients* | |
| Own home | 0.68 |
| Consumer durables | 0.30 |
| Financial securities[a] | 0.91 |
| Business equity[b] | 0.94 |
| Total assets | 0.69 |
| Net worth | 0.81 |

*Notes*: [a]This category includes time and savings deposits, stocks, bonds, government securities, mortgages, and other financial securities.

[b]This category includes both farm and nonfarm business equity and investment real estate.

**Table 6.11**    Composition of Wealth by Demographic Group, 1969

| | Number of Households | Own Home | Consumer Durables | Financial Securities[a] | Business Equity[b] | Debt |
|---|---|---|---|---|---|---|
| *AGI* | | | | | | |
| Negative | 1,852 | 7.5% | 2.6% | 34.1% | 55.7% | 28.4% |
| 0–$4,999 | 17,583 | 25.4 | 10.5 | 42.1 | 22.1 | 18.4 |
| 5,000–9,999 | 18,377 | 28.5 | 14.6 | 32.7 | 24.4 | 23.4 |
| 10,000–14,999 | 14,349 | 38.3 | 14.8 | 29.5 | 17.6 | 21.6 |
| 15,000–19,999 | 5,957 | 38.9 | 11.8 | 34.4 | 19.9 | 18.9 |
| 20,000–24,999 | 2,346 | 27.8 | 9.1 | 40.1 | 23.0 | 14.4 |
| 25,000–29,999 | 1,094 | 22.7 | 7.1 | 41.7 | 28.5 | 11.7 |
| 30,000–39,999 | 850 | 20.2 | 6.1 | 43.2 | 30.5 | 11.1 |
| 40,000–49,999 | 328 | 18.0 | 4.5 | 42.8 | 34.7 | 9.4 |
| 50,000–59,999 | 218 | 16.7 | 3.6 | 48.1 | 31.6 | 8.4 |
| 60,000–69,999 | 111 | 10.6 | 2.2 | 38.8 | 48.4 | 5.8 |
| 70,000–79,999 | 65 | 3.7 | 0.8 | 52.1 | 43.5 | 2.4 |
| 80,000–89,999 | 36 | 6.2 | 1.5 | 57.9 | 34.4 | 4.2 |
| 90,000–99,999 | 38 | 7.0 | 1.6 | 47.3 | 44.1 | 4.7 |
| 100,000 or more | 253 | 1.1 | 0.3 | 79.4 | 19.1 | 1.2 |
| *Age of household* | | | | | | |
| 24 years or less | 4,673 | 12.9 | 21.5 | 40.1 | 25.5 | 10.4 |
| 25–34 | 11,620 | 30.9 | 15.3 | 32.7 | 21.1 | 22.2 |
| 35–44 | 11,788 | 36.7 | 12.3 | 29.0 | 22.1 | 22.4 |
| 45–54 | 12,159 | 27.1 | 9.5 | 41.0 | 22.6 | 14.1 |
| 55–64 | 10,806 | 17.9 | 6.5 | 49.3 | 26.4 | 9.4 |
| 65 or more | 12,411 | 12.9 | 4.5 | 52.3 | 30.3 | 17.9 |
| *Race* | | | | | | |
| White | 56,600 | 23.7 | 9.0 | 41.9 | 25.4 | 16.4 |
| Nonwhite | 6,857 | 12.8 | 7.9 | 54.7 | 24.7 | 13.2 |

Table 6.11—continued

| | Number of Households | Own Home | Consumer Durables | Financial Securities[a] | Business Equity[b] | Debt |
|---|---|---|---|---|---|---|
| *Schooling of household head* | | | | | | |
| 0–8 years | 17,068 | 13.2 | 6.5 | 49.2 | 31.3 | 15.7 |
| 9–11 | 11,675 | 19.4 | 8.9 | 45.0 | 26.8 | 13.2 |
| 12 | 18,125 | 26.1 | 10.5 | 41.7 | 21.8 | 15.8 |
| 13–15 | 7,927 | 30.3 | 10.8 | 37.8 | 21.1 | 17.5 |
| 16 or more | 8,662 | 31.0 | 9.1 | 37.4 | 22.6 | 18.9 |
| *Region* | | | | | | |
| Northeast | 12,505 | 24.6 | 9.1 | 42.7 | 23.8 | 17.0 |
| North-Central | 10,563 | 20.6 | 8.8 | 45.4 | 25.3 | 14.1 |
| South | 22,257 | 21.5 | 8.7 | 44.4 | 25.5 | 16.0 |
| West | 18,132 | 24.4 | 9.1 | 40.5 | 26.1 | 16.9 |
| *Occupation of household head* | | | | | | |
| Professional and managerial | 13,902 | 29.5 | 9.0 | 38.1 | 23.6 | 17.8 |
| Clerical and sales | 9,501 | 26.6 | 9.9 | 41.5 | 22.2 | 15.9 |
| Craft | 10,665 | 26.6 | 10.9 | 39.4 | 23.2 | 17.8 |
| Operative | 10,218 | 23.8 | 12.1 | 40.8 | 23.3 | 17.8 |
| Service and unskilled | 10,970 | 13.4 | 7.8 | 49.9 | 29.0 | 12.6 |
| Not reported or not employed | 8,201 | 11.6 | 4.6 | 52.4 | 31.5 | 13.8 |
| *Industry of employment of head* | | | | | | |
| Agriculture | 2,743 | 6.6 | 5.7 | 55.4 | 32.3 | 9.7 |
| Mining | 648 | 20.4 | 8.7 | 53.4 | 17.5 | 18.6 |
| Construction | 4,729 | 22.5 | 9.2 | 43.5 | 24.8 | 16.4 |
| Manufacturing | 15,626 | 30.4 | 11.8 | 37.9 | 20.0 | 20.0 |
| Transportation | 4,460 | 28.8 | 11.4 | 35.2 | 24.6 | 17.9 |
| Trade | 9,737 | 23.5 | 8.9 | 46.9 | 20.8 | 15.3 |
| Finance, insurance and real estate | 2,467 | 29.7 | 9.4 | 37.9 | 23.0 | 18.2 |
| Services | 11,342 | 21.9 | 8.3 | 39.8 | 30.1 | 14.1 |

Table 6.11—continued

| | Number of Households | Own Home | Consumer Durables | Financial Securities[a] | Business Equity[b] | Debt |
|---|---|---|---|---|---|---|
| Public administration | 3,504 | 34.2 | 12.5 | 31.9 | 21.4 | 20.4 |
| Not reported or not employed | 8,201 | 11.6 | 4.6 | 52.4 | 31.5 | 13.8 |
| *Household composition* | | | | | | |
| Single, no children | 14,824 | 11.8 | 6.1 | 60.0 | 22.2 | 5.9 |
| Single, with children | 3,811 | 12.6 | 5.8 | 58.4 | 23.2 | 7.7 |
| Married, no children | 19,041 | 19.5 | 7.9 | 44.2 | 28.5 | 18.5 |
| Married, 1 child | 8,240 | 30.9 | 12.8 | 32.4 | 23.9 | 17.9 |
| Married, 2 children | 8,047 | 37.3 | 12.6 | 26.8 | 23.4 | 23.6 |
| Married, 3 or more children | 9,494 | 36.9 | 11.6 | 26.3 | 25.4 | 23.0 |
| *Net worth class* | | | | | | |
| 0–$4,999 | 17,161 | 14.4 | 67.4 | 11.5 | 6.8 | 78.1 |
| 5,000–9,999 | 9,671 | 49.4 | 36.2 | 11.2 | 3.2 | 33.5 |
| 10,000–14,999 | 8,441 | 53.3 | 20.8 | 10.8 | 5.2 | 36.9 |
| 15,000–19,999 | 5,838 | 52.7 | 18.0 | 13.3 | 6.1 | 32.6 |
| 20,000–24,999 | 4,023 | 55.5 | 15.9 | 19.3 | 9.3 | 25.9 |
| 25,000–29,999 | 2,797 | 51.0 | 13.4 | 24.4 | 11.2 | 22.2 |
| 30,000–39,999 | 3,634 | 40.8 | 10.7 | 28.9 | 19.6 | 18.3 |
| 40,000–49,999 | 2,420 | 31.7 | 8.5 | 36.9 | 23.0 | 15.0 |
| 50,000–59,999 | 1,745 | 23.1 | 6.9 | 43.3 | 26.6 | 11.2 |
| 60,000–69,999 | 1,272 | 22.6 | 6.0 | 47.6 | 23.8 | 9.7 |
| 70,000–79,999 | 1,063 | 20.2 | 5.2 | 46.7 | 27.9 | 9.3 |
| 80,000–89,999 | 743 | 18.8 | 4.8 | 41.0 | 35.5 | 7.9 |
| 90,000–99,999 | 615 | 14.6 | 4.3 | 47.7 | 33.4 | 7.8 |
| 100,000–199,999 | 2,640 | 11.3 | 3.3 | 49.8 | 35.7 | 5.1 |
| 200,000 or more | 1,394 | 2.7 | 0.8 | 62.4 | 34.1 | 1.4 |
| Full sample | 63,457 | 22.7 | 8.9 | 43.0 | 25.3 | 16.1 |

*Note:* The table shows the value of each asset (or debt) as a percent of the total assets held by the group.
[a]This category includes time and saving deposits, stocks, bonds, government securities, mortgages and other financial securities.
[b]This category includes both farm and nonfarm business equity and investment real estate.

by households was in the form of owner occupied housing, 8.9 percent in the form of durables, 43.0 percent in the form of financial assets, and 25.3 percent in the form of business equity. Moreover, the average debt-to-asset ratio was 16.1 percent. When we disaggregate the population by income class, we find that the share of housing and durables in total assets rose with income to about $15,000 and then fell continuously with income, while the share of financial assets and business equity generally rose with income. Moreover, debt as a fraction of assets rose with income until $10,000 and then declined almost continuously with income level.

The major difference in asset structure between whites and nonwhites was that the share of assets in owner occupied housing for whites was almost twice that for blacks. The debt-asset ratios were about the same. The percent of assets in home and durables rose with schooling level, as did the percent of debt. The asset and debt structure was very similar by region of the country and among occupational groups, except for (low-paid) service and unskilled workers. There was some variation by industry of employment. (Those in agriculture, for example, had a predictably large share of their assets in business equity and a low share in homeownership.) Singles with and without children and those married with no children had a large share of their assets in financial securities, a low share in housing and durables, and a small debt-to-asset ratio. The converse was true for married couples with children.

There was considerable variation in wealthholdings among wealth classes. The share of assets in homeownership increased with wealth through the first four wealth classes and then declined, while that in durables declined almost continuously with net worth. The share in financial securities rose almost continuously with wealth, while that in business equity increased through the first twelve wealth classes and then leveled off. The debt-to-asset ratio declined almost continuously with net worth.

### 6.2.3   Mean Wealth by Demographic Group

Table 6.12 shows the mean value of total assets and net worth for different groups in 1969. Household wealth rose consistently with household income, except between the first and second income classes and between the thirteenth and fourteenth income classes.[21] Moreover, net worth tended to rise considerably faster with income than income itself, particularly above $50,000 of income. Assets rose with age until age 65 and then leveled off, whereas net worth rose until age 65 and then fell by 9 percent.[22] The biggest increase in net worth occurred between the 35–44 and the 45–54 age groups. The 55–64 age group had mean assets 4.0 times as great as the youngest age group and a mean net worth 4.0 times as great. Mean assets were 20 percent greater for whites than nonwhites, and mean net worth 16 percent greater. There was relatively

**Table 6.12**        **Mean Household Assets and Net Worth by Demographic Group, 1969 (in current $1,000)**

| | Number of Households | Assets | Net Worth |
|---|---|---|---|
| *AGI* | | | |
| Negative | 1,852 | 102.5 | 73.4 |
| 0–$4,999 | 17,583 | 22.7 | 18.6 |
| 5,000–9,999 | 18,377 | 23.3 | 17.9 |
| 10,000–14,999 | 14,349 | 31.6 | 24.8 |
| 15,000–19,999 | 5,957 | 49.4 | 40.1 |
| 20,000–24,999 | 2,346 | 73.0 | 62.5 |
| 25,000–29,999 | 1,094 | 100.7 | 88.9 |
| 30,000–39,999 | 850 | 125.4 | 111.5 |
| 40,000–49,999 | 328 | 181.2 | 164.3 |
| 50,000–59,999 | 218 | 232.0 | 212.4 |
| 60,000–69,999 | 111 | 372.4 | 350.8 |
| 70,000–79,999 | 65 | 696.7 | 680.3 |
| 80,000–89,999 | 36 | 486.3 | 465.9 |
| 90,000–99,999 | 38 | 383.3 | 365.3 |
| 100,000 or more | 253 | 1,644.0 | 1,624.2 |
| *Age of household head* | | | |
| 24 years or less | 4,673 | 15.0 | 13.4 |
| 25–34 | 11,620 | 26.8 | 20.0 |
| 35–44 | 11,788 | 36.7 | 28.5 |
| 45–54 | 12,159 | 49.5 | 42.6 |
| 55–64 | 10,806 | 59.4 | 53.8 |
| 65 or more | 12,411 | 59.6 | 48.9 |
| *Race* | | | |
| White | 56,600 | 44.8 | 37.5 |
| Nonwhite | 6,857 | 37.4 | 32.4 |
| *Schooling of household head* | | | |
| 0–8 years | 17,068 | 45.4 | 38.3 |
| 9–11 | 11,675 | 40.6 | 35.3 |
| 12 | 18,125 | 38.9 | 32.8 |
| 13–15 | 7,927 | 41.9 | 34.6 |
| 16 or more | 8,662 | 58.8 | 47.7 |
| *Region* | | | |
| Northeast | 12,505 | 43.9 | 36.4 |
| North-Central | 10,563 | 43.0 | 37.0 |
| South | 22,257 | 44.0 | 37.0 |
| West | 18,132 | 44.8 | 37.3 |
| *Occupation of household head* | | | |
| Professional and managerial | 13,902 | 58.4 | 48.0 |
| Clerical and sales | 9,501 | 41.3 | 34.7 |
| Craft | 10,665 | 39.3 | 32.3 |
| Operative | 10,218 | 30.6 | 25.1 |
| Service and unskilled | 10,970 | 40.3 | 35.2 |
| Not reported or not employed | 88,201 | 51.3 | 44.3 |

**Table 6.12**—*continued*

|  | Number of Households | Assets | Net Worth |
|---|---|---|---|
| *Industry of employment of head* | | | |
| Agriculture | 2,743 | 59.3 | 53.5 |
| Mining | 648 | 46.6 | 38.0 |
| Construction | 4,729 | 45.3 | 37.8 |
| Manufacturing | 15,626 | 36.6 | 29.3 |
| Transportation | 4,460 | 36.9 | 30.3 |
| Trade | 9,737 | 46.0 | 38.9 |
| Finance, insurance, and real estate | 2,467 | 50.3 | 41.1 |
| Services | 11,342 | 47.4 | 40.7 |
| Public administration | 3,504 | 35.4 | 28.2 |
| Not reported or not employed | 8,201 | 51.3 | 44.3 |
| *Household composition* | | | |
| Single, no children | 14,824 | 41.7 | 39.3 |
| Single, with children | 3,811 | 45.8 | 42.3 |
| Married, no children | 19,041 | 54.4 | 44.3 |
| Married, 1 child | 8,240 | 36.8 | 30.2 |
| Married, 2 children | 8,047 | 37.8 | 28.9 |
| Married, 3 or more children | 9,494 | 38.1 | 29.3 |
| Full sample | 63,457 | 44.0 | 36.9 |

little variation in wealth by educational level, except for college graduates, who were considerably richer than other groups.

There was almost no variation of mean wealth by region. Professional and managerial workers were the wealthiest occupational group, while operatives were the poorest. There was considerable variation of wealth by industry of employment, with workers in agriculture by far the wealthiest. Married couples without children and singles with and without children were considerably wealthier than married couples with children. Married couples without children had considerably more assets (and debt) than singles. From this rather cursory analysis it would seem that age and income are the most important determinants of wealth. Household composition was less important than these two factors but more important than the remaining ones.

### 6.2.4    Inequality of Wealth within Demographic Groups

Our final table (table 6.13) shows the level of inequality in the size distribution of assets and net worth among households *within* each of the indicated groups.[23] The Gini coefficients for the full sample were 0.69 for assets and 0.81 for net worth. Thus, except for the first income class, the level of wealth inequality was lower within income class than for the whole population. Moreover, the level of wealth inequality generally declined over the first four income classes and then remained

**Table 6.13**    **Gini Coefficients of the Size Distribution of Assets and Net Worth by Demographic Group, 1969**

|  | Number of Households | Assets | Net Worth |
|---|---|---|---|
| *AGI* | | | |
| Negative | 1,852 | 0.87 | 0.93 |
| 0–$4,999 | 17,583 | 0.60 | 0.73 |
| 5,000–9,999 | 18,377 | 0.61 | 0.80 |
| 10,000–14,999 | 14,349 | 0.51 | 0.58 |
| 15,000–19,999 | 5,957 | 0.49 | 0.58 |
| 20,000–24,999 | 2,346 | 0.47 | 0.54 |
| 25,000–29,999 | 1,094 | 0.47 | 0.53 |
| 30,000–39,999 | 850 | 0.48 | 0.53 |
| 40,000–49,999 | 328 | 0.48 | 0.52 |
| 50,000–59,999 | 218 | 0.55 | 0.60 |
| 60,000–69,999 | 111 | 0.49 | 0.52 |
| 70,000–79,999 | 65 | 0.42 | 0.44 |
| 80,000–89,999 | 36 | 0.46 | 0.51 |
| 90,000–99,999 | 38 | 0.47 | 0.49 |
| 100,000 or more | 253 | 0.46 | 0.47 |
| | | | |
| *Age of household head* | | | |
| 24 years or less | 4,673 | 0.69 | 0.70 |
| 25–34 | 11,620 | 0.65 | 0.71 |
| 35–44 | 11,788 | 0.59 | 0.66 |
| 45–54 | 12,159 | 0.64 | 0.70 |
| 55–64 | 10,806 | 0.73 | 0.80 |
| 65 or more | 12,411 | 0.72 | 0.94 |
| | | | |
| *Race* | | | |
| White | 56,600 | 0.68 | 0.80 |
| Nonwhite | 6,857 | 0.77 | 0.89 |
| | | | |
| *Schooling of household head* | | | |
| 0–8 years | 17,068 | 0.74 | 0.94 |
| 9–11 | 11,675 | 0.70 | 0.81 |
| 12 | 18,125 | 0.66 | 0.75 |
| 13–15 | 7,927 | 0.64 | 0.71 |
| 16 or more | 8,662 | 0.67 | 0.75 |
| | | | |
| *Region* | | | |
| Northeast | 12,505 | 0.67 | 0.81 |
| North-Central | 10,563 | 0.71 | 0.81 |
| South | 22,257 | 0.70 | 0.83 |
| West | 18,132 | 0.68 | 0.80 |
| | | | |
| *Occupation of household head* | | | |
| Professional and managerial | 13,902 | 0.66 | 0.75 |
| Clerical and sales | 9,501 | 0.66 | 0.75 |
| Craft | 10,665 | 0.66 | 0.79 |
| Operative | 10,218 | 0.66 | 0.81 |
| Services and unskilled | 10,970 | 0.74 | 0.87 |
| Not reported or not employed | 8,201 | 0.73 | 0.91 |

**Table 6.13**—*continued*

|  | Number of Households | Assets | Net Worth |
|---|---|---|---|
| *Industry of employment of head* | | | |
| Agriculture | 8,743 | 0.78 | 0.90 |
| Mining | 648 | 0.75 | 0.94 |
| Construction | 4,729 | 0.71 | 0.84 |
| Manufacturing | 15,626 | 0.64 | 0.77 |
| Transportation | 4,460 | 0.65 | 0.75 |
| Trade | 9,737 | 0.70 | 0.79 |
| Finance, insurance, and real estate | 2,467 | 0.65 | 0.74 |
| Services | 11,342 | 0.71 | 0.79 |
| Public administration | 3,504 | 0.58 | 0.68 |
| Not reported or not employed | 8,201 | 0.73 | 0.91 |
| *Household composition* | | | |
| Single, no children | 14,824 | 0.74 | 0.77 |
| Single, with children | 3,811 | 0.72 | 0.75 |
| Married, no children | 19,041 | 0.71 | 0.94 |
| Married, 1 child | 8,240 | 0.64 | 0.71 |
| Married, 2 children | 8,047 | 0.61 | 0.70 |
| Married, 3 or more children | 9,494 | 0.61 | 0.70 |
| Full sample | 63,457 | 0.69 | 0.81 |

stable across the rest of the income ladder. The (unweighted) average level of wealth inequality within income class was 0.52 for assets and 0.58 for net worth, both surprisingly large.

The inequality of ownership of assets declined with age until age 45 and then increased with age, while inequality in net worth remained relatively constant until age 55 and then increased. The inequality in net worth was extremely high for those over 65. Wealth inequality was higher for nonwhites than for whites (or for the overall sample). Wealth inequality was somewhat higher for the less educated than for the more educated. The level of wealth inequality showed little variation by region of the country and was close to the overall level in all regions. Wealth inequality was somewhat greater for service and unskilled workers than for other occupational groups. Wealth inequality was greater among married couples with no children and singles than among married couples with children. In general, except within income classes, the level of wealth inequality was at approximately the same level within these demographic groups as in the whole population.

## 6.4   Conclusions and Cautions

The MESP data base, we believe, provides a valuable new resource tool for the analysis of wealth distribution in the United States. In particular, the vast array of demographic information made available by it will make possible work focusing on the wealth behavior of small subgroups of the U.S. population. More detailed work on size distributions, the composition of wealth, life cycle accumulation patterns, and simulation models can be undertaken with this new data base.

A word of caution should be noted in the use of this data base, even though general tests of its reliability have proved positive (see Wolff 1978). As with any new data base, there are certain problems and limitations in its use. Some can be corrected for or overcome with additional work and some cannot. In any synthetic data base created through statistical matching techniques, certain *conditional* joint distributions are not reliable. In this case, the joint distributions of noncommon variables in the PUS file and the IRS file conditional on a common variable cannot be used for estimation purposes, because this is the information that is lacking (and the rationale for performing the match). For example, the covariance of education (a PUS variable) and stock equity (an IRS variable) conditional on income (a common variable) will not be reliable in the MESP data base. However, the overall (unconditional) covariance of education and stock equity can be reliably estimated (see Ruggles, Ruggles and Wolff [1977] for more details).

Other deficiencies involve the estimation of household assets and liabilities. These estimates might be improved with additional work. With regard to *Owner occupied housing,* currently, house values are recorded in eleven interval codes; some attempt might be made to "smooth out" the distribution using a random number generator. The estimation procedure for consumer durables might be redone using the recently available 1972–73 Consumer Expenditure Survey; full coverage of durables might also be possible. It would also be desirable to add stocks of semidurables to the household portfolio using the new Consumer Expenditure Survey. The category of currency and demand deposits should also be added to the household portfolio (see Wolff [1978] for one attempt). With regard to financial securities, some attempt might be made to split time and savings deposits from bonds, mortgages, and other financial instruments, since the two groups of assets are currently aggregated into one category; it would also be desirable to add a separate imputation for nontaxed state and local government bonds, though appropriate data may be difficult to locate. Trust fund equity is not currently included in the household portfolio, and it would, of course, be desirable to include this, since much of the wealth of the rich is held in this form. One possible source for this imputation is the entry "trust fund income," which is currently in the IRS tax return data. Before this can be undertaken, the problem of whom to assign the assets of a trust to—whether the current beneficiary, the remainderman, or possibly the trustee—must be resolved. Pensions, too, should be added to the household portfolio, but here again important conceptual issues must first be resolved. For example, should only vested pensions be assigned to households? Should only redeemable pensions be imputed? How should one handle partially funded pensions? Should Social Security be included in pensions? Finally, the assignment of the cash surrender value of life insurance policies to households poses less serious conceptual problems than that of pensions. Here, the problem of obtaining pertinent data makes this imputation very rough, if not impossible.

Despite its limitations and deficiencies, the MESP data base is still the most complete in coverage of both households and assets of any now currently available. Moreover, unlike survey or administrative data sets, the MESP data base, thanks to its methodology, *allows* continual modification, improvement, and expansion of asset and liability estimates and coverage. Future use, it is hoped, will result in its gradual improvement as a research tool.

# Appendix: A Technical Description of the MESP Matches

## The Sort-Merge Matching Procedure

Six steps are involved in the sort-merge matching procedure we used in the creation of the MESP data base (see Ruggles and Ruggles 1974 and Ruggles and Wolff 1977). The first step is to select which of the two files is to be used as the sampling frame; the second data set, the "B File," is then matched onto the first data set, the "A File." The next step is to select the unit of the match; in the case of household data, the unit could be the household, the family, the individual, or some other composite. Information is then transferred from the B File to the A File on a unit by unit basis.

The variables in each of the two data sets are then divided into four kinds. The first are the "cohort" variables; the A and B samples are first divided into cohorts and the matches then performed within each cohort. The second are the $X$ or "matching" variables; the values of the $X$ variables are partitioned into intervals and the two files matched on the interval values of these variables. The third are the $Y$ variables, used to construct the intervals of the $X$ variables. The fourth are the remaining variables.

Matching intervals for each $X$ variable are then constructed by running cross-tabulations of $Y$ and $X$ and parsing the $X$ variable such that the conditional (frequency) distribution of $Y$ on $X$ is constant within intervals and different between intervals for each $Y$ variable according to a predetermined statistical criterion. $Y$ and $X$ are thus conditionally independent within intervals and significantly related across intervals. By varying the statistical criterion, we can generate different sets of matching intervals at different levels of statistical confidence.

Frequently, an $X$ variable will differ in concept or sampling distribution between the A and B files because of differences in definition or differences in sampling frame. Before the match is executed, the $X$ variable in the A file is adjusted or aligned to the corresponding $X$ variable in the B file to reconcile the differences between the two files.

Finally, the two files are each sorted into cohorts and within cohort by the matching intervals of the $X$ variables. Matches are first made at the highest level of statistical confidence. Records that fail to match at this level are then matched at successively lower levels of statistical confidence. This results in a distribution of matches by matching level, which is calibrated. For reasons of optimization, if the distribution is nonuniform over matching levels, new confidence levels are selected, new matching intervals computed, and the sort-merge match redone. A number of iterations may be required bfeore the distribution of matches is approximately uniform.

### The Construction of the MESP Data Base

*The Internal Revenue Service Tax File 1970–1969 Match*

The first match that was executed involved the 1969 and 1970 Internal Revenue Service Tax Files (IRS69 and IRS70). Both are samples of about 100,000 tax returns, heavily stratified on adjusted gross income.[24] The IRS69 file was used as the sample frame; the main purpose of the match was to transfer race and age information contained in the 1970 file to the 1969 file.

The tax return was used as the basic unit in the match. Joint returns from the IRS70 file were matched with joint returns in the IRS69 file, and IRS70 single returns with IRS69 single returns. The cohort, $X$, and $Y$ variables used in the match are shown in table 6.A.1. Sex was used as a cohort variable for single returns. Both data sets contained information indicating whether the filer(s) was 65 or over in age or less than 65 in age (since the former resulted in an added exemption). In the case of single returns, there were two categories: 65 or over in age; under 65 in age. In the case of joint returns, there were four categories: both filers 65 or over in age; husband 65 or over, wife under 65; husband under 65, wife 65 or over; both filers under 65 in age. The fourth cohort variable was the number of children, which we divided into four categories: zero, one, two, and three or more.

The first $X$ variable was the level of adjusted gross income (AGI). Because of the change in the size distribution of AGI between 1969 and

**Table 6.A.1     Structure of the IRS70–IRS69 Match**

*Cohort Variables*
Type of tax return
Sex
Age (over and under 65)
Number of children

*X Variables*
Adjusted gross income (AGI)
Wage and salary earnings as a percent of AGI
Interest income as a percent of AGI
Long-term capital gains as a percent of AGI
Rental income as a percent of AGI
Dividends as a percent of AGI
Farm income as a percent of AGI
Royalty income as a percent of AGI
Trust income as a percent of AGI
Business and professional earnings as a percent of AGI
Pension income as a percent of AGI
Property sale gain as a percent of AGI
Total deductions as a percent of AGI
    (only for those who itemize deductions)

*Y Variables (IRS70)*
Race (white or nonwhite)
Age (whites)
Age (nonwhites)

1970, it was necessary to align AGI in the two files before the match was executed (see below). The next eleven $X$ variables represented the major components of AGI. Since these items (particularly wage and salary earnings), as well as total deductions, are highly correlated with AGI, it would be redundant to match on the level of these income items as well as on the AGI level. We therefore matched on each income source and total deduction as a percent of AGI. The $Y$ variables are the age and race of the head of household recorded on the tax returns; these items were used as the $Y$ variables since these are the chief data to be transferred by the match.

Three iterations were necessary for a satisfactory match. Table 6.A.2 shows the final matching levels and the number of matching intervals for each $X$ variable by level. The matching intervals were generated on the IRS70 file. The number of matching intervals fell off sharply between the level of greatest confidence (level 1) and the level of least confidence. As is evident from table 6.A.2, the most important $X$ variable in the match was AGI, since it had consistently the highest number of intervals, except for level 6. Wage and salary earnings as a percent of AGI, dividends as a percent of AGI, business and professional income as a per-

Table 6.A.2     **Number of Matching Intervals by Matching Level in the IRS70–IRS69 Match**

| | Matching Level | | | | | |
|---|---|---|---|---|---|---|
| | 6 | 5 | 4 | 3 | 2 | 1 |
| X Variable | Corre-lation (.50) | Corre-lation (.95) | Corre-lation (.97) | Corre-lation (.99) | Chi-square (.995) | Chi-square (.50) |
| Adjusted gross income (AGI) | 1 | 13 | 15 | 16 | 21 | 93 |
| Wages and salary/AGI | 2 | 6 | 6 | 8 | 12 | 29 |
| Interest/AGI | 1 | 1 | 1 | 1 | 7 | 9 |
| Long term capital gains/AGI | 1 | 1 | 1 | 5 | 7 | 13 |
| Rental income/AGI | 1 | 1 | 1 | 1 | 5 | 8 |
| Dividends/AGI | 1 | 7 | 7 | 8 | 9 | 24 |
| Farm income/AGI | 1 | 1 | 1 | 1 | 1 | 10 |
| Royalty income/AGI | 1 | 1 | 1 | 1 | 1 | 9 |
| Trust income/AGI | 1 | 1 | 1 | 1 | 4 | 4 |
| Business and professional income/AGI | 1 | 2 | 3 | 6 | 7 | 19 |
| Pension income/AGI | 1 | 1 | 1 | 1 | 3 | 13 |
| Property sale gain/AGI | 1 | 1 | 1 | 1 | 1 | 4 |
| Total deductions/AGI | 1 | 4 | 10 | 10 | 12 | 24 |

cent of AGI, and deductions as a percent of AGI were also important matching variables. The remaining $X$ variables "washed out" at either the second, third, or fourth matching level.

As noted above, because of the general increase in income between 1969 and 1970, the IRS 69 and IRS70 files could not be matched directly on AGI level. Some alignment was required first. This was done on the basis of *percentile* rank. This meant, in effect, that the $n$th percentile AGI level in the IRS 70 file was treated as equivalent to the $n$th percentile AGI level in the IRS69 file. The matching intervals were then adjusted accordingly. Thus, if the $n$th percentile AGI level in the IRS70 file fell into matching interval $j$, the $n$th percentile AGI level in the IRS69 file was also mapped into matching interval $j$.[25]

Table 6.A.3 shows the distribution of matches by matching level in the third and final iteration of the sort-merge matching procedure. There were no nonmatches and no matches at the cohort level. Of the 95,288 tax returns in the IRS70 file, 38,211 (or 40.1%) were used in the match.

The following variables were transferred to the IRS69 file from the matched record in the IRS70 file: race of head of household; age of head of household; mortgage interest paid (only returns with itemized deductions); other interest paid (only for itemized deductions); and state and local taxes (only for itemized deductions).

Table 6.A.3    Final Calibration of the IRS70–IRS69
               Match

| Matching Level | Percent of Matches |
|---|---|
| 1. Chi-square (.50) | 13.2% |
| 2. Chi-square (.995) | 11.8 |
| 3. Correlation (.99) | 13.6 |
| 4. Correlation (.97) | 18.7 |
| 5. Correlation (.95) | 24.7 |
| 6. Correlation (.50) | 18.1 |
| 7. Cohort | 0.0 |

*The Internal Revenue Service Tax File 1969—*
*Public Use Sample 1970 Match*

The second and major match was between the IRS69 file, augmented with information from the IRS70 file, and the 1970 Census 1/1000 Public Use Sample (PUS).[26] This PUS file is a random sample of the U.S. population, with a sample size of 63,457 households. Both the IRS69 and the PUS file contain income information for calendar year 1969. The purpose of this match was to augment the income information in the PUS with the more detailed income breakdown in the IRS file.

The PUS file was used as the sample frame, and the IRS69 file was matched to the PUS. In effect, tax returns were imputed to households in the PUS. The reason for this is that the PUS is a representative sample of the U.S. population, while the IRS file is heavily stratified on income. By matching the IRS file to the PUS, we could assure that the tax information would be given its appropriate population weight.

We chose the tax return as the unit of the match. This required the creation of tax units from the information in the PUS. In the PUS, the basic unit is the household, but the household is broken down into family and individual observations. By assuming that all married couples file joint returns and all others file single returns, we constructed tax return units from the individuals in the PUS file.

The cohort, $X$, and $Y$ variables used in the match are shown in table 6.A.4. Both the race and age variables on the IRS69 file were imputed in the IRS70–IRS69 match. Only two categories were used for race: white and nonwhite.

For the number of children, we used the number who were listed as dependents (exemptions) in the IRS file, and the number under age 18 in the PUS file. Homeowner status is directly indicated in the PUS. In the case of the IRS sample, we used the mortgage interest deduction as a proxy for homeownership.[27] Wage and salary earnings of both spouses were summed in the case of married couples, and the sum matched against the corresponding entry in the IRS file. This was likewise done

Table 6.A.4        Structures of the IRS69–PUS Match

*Cohort Variables*
Type of tax return
Sex of respondent (single returns)
Race of head of household
Age of head of household

*X Variables*
Number of children
Owner occupied home or rental unit
Wage and salary earnings
Business earnings
Farm income
Total income

*Y Variables (PUS file)*
Education
Birthplace
Occupation
Industry of employment
Class of worker
Years married (married couples only)
Number of years at current address
Value of property (homeowners only)
Number of automobiles in household

for business and professional earnings. Because the definition of farm income differs so much between the PUS and the IRS files, we used a (0,1) dummy variable for farm income reported or not reported. For the total (personal) income variable, we started with adjusted gross income (AGI) on the IRS file and total income in the PUS file. The two concepts differ considerably. To reconcile them, we first added dividend exclusions and other adjustments to AGI to obtain personal gross income. The two concepts were still not identical, since gross income in the IRS file excluded Social Security and welfare income but included capital gains, whereas total income in the PUS included Social Security and welfare income but excluded capital gains. We therefore subtracted capital gains from gross income in the IRS file and subtracted social security and welfare income from total income in the PUS file.[28]

Six iterations were necessary for a satisfactory match. Table 6.A.5 shows the final matching levels and the number of matching intervals at each level for each X variable. In this match there was also a sharp fall-off in the number of intervals by matching level. The two most important X variables were wage and salary earnings and total income. Business and farm income both washed out at the second level of the match, number of children at the third level, and homeowner status at the fourth level.

Table 6.A.5    **Number of Matching Intervals by Matching Level in the IRS69–PUS Match**

| | Matching Level | | | | | |
| | 6 | 5 | 4 | 3 | 2 | 1 |
| X Variable | Corre-lation (.50) | Corre-lation (.70) | Corre-lation (.80) | Corre-lation (.90) | Corre-lation (.97) | Chi-square (.99) |
|---|---|---|---|---|---|---|
| Number of children | 1 | 1 | 1 | 1 | 4 | 8 |
| Homeowner status | 1 | 1 | 1 | 2 | 2 | 2 |
| Wage earnings | 3 | 4 | 5 | 9 | 20 | 36 |
| Business earnings | 1 | 1 | 1 | 1 | 1 | 13 |
| Farm income | 1 | 1 | 1 | 1 | 1 | 2 |
| Total income | 2 | 2 | 3 | 6 | 16 | 36 |

Before the match was executed, both business and professional income and total income required alignment. The fact that the distribution of business and professional income differed in the two files was due to differences in concept and in reporting error. The distribution of total income also differed in the two files, even after the adjustments described above were made. This was probably due to differences in reporting error. The alignment was done on the basis of percentile rank. Selected correspondence points at given percentile ranks are shown in table 6.A.6.[29]

IRS values were consistently higher than the corresponding PUS values in the bottom eight deciles of total income and slightly lower in the top two. This may be due to underreporting by low income recipients in the Public Use Sample. The percent difference between the two files declined steadily through the first eight deciles, and corresponding values were quite close in the top four deciles. For business and professional earnings, the PUS values were consistently higher than the corresponding IRS values. This may be due to the fact that costs are offset against earnings in computing business and professional profit or loss in the tax returns but not as a rule in the census questionnaire. The percent difference increased up through the fourth decile and declined thereafter.

Table 6.A.7 shows the distribution of matches by matching level in the final iteration of the match. There were no nonmatches, and only three percent of the records matched at the cohort level. Of the 89,705 tax returns in the IRS69 file, 15,406 (or 17.2 percent) were used in the match. The low percent of IRS records used is not surprising, since the IRS file is heavily stratified toward the upper income levels.

Table 6.A.8 presents some additional statistics used to evaluate how close the match was with respect to three of the X variables. The cor-

Table 6.A.6    Selected Correspondence Points in the Alignment of Total Income and Business and Professional Income in the IRS69–PUS Match

| Percentile | PUS Value | IRS Value | Percent Difference[a] |
|---|---|---|---|
| | *Total Income* | | |
| 12 | $    750 | $  1,145 | 52.7% |
| 22 | 1,550 | 2,311 | 49.1 |
| 31 | 2,550 | 3,495 | 37.1 |
| 42 | 4,150 | 5,029 | 21.2 |
| 50 | 5,750 | 6,409 | 11.5 |
| 60 | 7,550 | 8,013 | 6.1 |
| 71 | 9,750 | 9,882 | 1.4 |
| 81 | 12,150 | 12,119 | − 0.3 |
| 90 | 16,150 | 15,602 | 3.4 |
| | *Business and Professional Income (recipients only)* | | |
| 12 | $    550 | $    430 | 21.8% |
| 21 | 1,150 | 814 | −29.2 |
| 31 | 2,150 | 1,444 | −32.8 |
| 41 | 3,550 | 2,242 | −36.9 |
| 53 | 5,150 | 3,655 | −29.0 |
| 60 | 6,550 | 4,763 | −27.3 |
| 70 | 8,550 | 6,619 | −22.6 |
| 80 | 11,350 | 9,732 | −14.3 |
| 90 | 18,150 | 16,322 | −10.1 |

*Note*: [a]Percent difference is defined as (IRS–PUS/PUS) × 100.

Table 6.A.7    Final Calibration of the IRS69–PUS Match

| Matching Level | Percent of Matches |
|---|---|
| 1. Chi-square (.99) | 16.0% |
| 2. Correlation (.97) | 18.8 |
| 3. Correlation (.90) | 30.6 |
| 4. Correlation (.80) | 14.3 |
| 5. Correlation (.70) | 12.2 |
| 6. Correlation (.50) | 6.2 |
| 7. Cohort | 3.0 |

Table 6.A.8    Measures of Closeness of Fit by Matching Level for Selected X Variables in the IRS69–PUS Match

| Matching Level | Wage and Salary Earnings | | Business and Professional Income | | Total Income | |
|---|---|---|---|---|---|---|
| | Correlation Coefficient | Percent Difference | Correlation Coefficient | Percent Difference | Correlation Coefficient | Percent Difference |
| 1. Chi sq. (.99) | 0.95 | 0.8% | 0.92 | 7.3% | 0.96 | 1.4% |
| 2. Correl. (.97) | 0.94 | 4.1 | 0.43 | 17.9 | 0.96 | 2.5 |
| 3. Correl. (.90) | 0.96 | 3.1 | 0.36 | 40.2 | 0.96 | 3.1 |
| 4. Correl. (.80) | 0.92 | 9.5 | 0.23 | 265.1 | 0.92 | 9.2 |
| 5. Correl. (.70) | 0.89 | 4.7 | 0.07 | 384.9 | 0.91 | 8.0 |
| 6. Correl. (.50) | 0.75 | 11.8 | 0.04 | 423.1 | 0.74 | 20.3 |
| 7. Cohort | 0.41 | 19.2 | 0.01 | 485.8 | 0.57 | 54.7 |
| Total file | 0.96 | 3.5% | 0.50 | 72.9% | 0.97 | 4.1% |

*Notes*: The correlation coefficient is defined as the correlation of $X_A$ and $X_B$ for matched records occurring in the specified match level, where subscript $A$ refers to the IRS value and subscript $B$ to the PUS value.

Percent difference is defined as $100 \times (\overline{X}_A - \overline{X}_B)/\overline{X}_B$, where the bar indicates the mean value of the $X$ variable in the specified match level.

relation coefficients measure how close the individual $X$ values in the matching records were by matching level, and the percent differences measure how close the mean values of the $X$ variables were in each of the matching levels. As to be expected, the matches were closer in value for matches at higher levels of statistical confidence than for matches at lower levels. Wage and salary earnings entries in the IRS file were quite close to their corresponding entries in the PUS file in the first five match levels, which accounted for 91 percent of the matches. The correlation coefficient was 0.96 for the entire file and the percent difference was 3.5. The same pattern was recorded for the total income variable. The matches were quite close for the first five matching levels and the overall correlation coefficient was 0.97. The fit for business and professional income was decidedly poorer, with an adequate fit occurring only at the first match level.

The following variables were transferred to the PUS file from the matched record in the IRS 69 file: adjusted gross income; wage and salary earnings; interest income; long-term capital gains; short-term capital gains; rental income; dividends; farm income; royalty income; trust income; business and professional income; pension income; property sale gain; income adjustment; mortgage interest expenditure; and other interest expenditure.

## The 1970 5% Public Use Sample–1970 15% Public Use Sample Match

The third match was between the 1970 census 1/1000 5% and 15% Public Use Samples (PUS5 and PUS15). The designations 5 and 15 refer to the percent of the population receiving the respective questionnaires. Approximately 80 to 90 percent of the variables are the same in the two samples. Our interest in matching the two files was to transfer consumer durable information present in the 5% sample but not in the 15% sample to the now augmented 15% sample.

The 5% and 15% samples are identical in structure. Since consumer durable ownership is assigned to the household, we used the household as the unit of the match. The cohort, $X$, and $Y$ variables used are shown in table 6.A.9. Since there was a wide choice of overlapping variables in the two files, we chose for the cohort and $X$ variables those we felt would be significantly related to consumer durable ownership. The $Y$ variables, which were drawn from the PUS 15% sample, consisted of additional demographic and income information, as well as data on automobile ownership.

**Table 6.A.9     Structure of the 1970 Public Use Sample 5%–15% Match**

*Cohort Variables*
Marital status (married vs. single)
Age of head of household
Sex of head of household (if single)
Race of head of household (white vs. nonwhite)
Owner occupied home vs. rental unit

*X Variables*
Number of children in household
Value of property or gross monthly rental
Wage earnings of head of household
Wage earnings of spouse of head of household (if married)
Total family income

*Y Variables* (PUS15 File)
Education of head of household
Education of spouse of head of household (if married)
Industry of employment of head of household
Occupation of head of household
Place of birth of head of household
Farm income (yes or no)
Professional income (yes or no)
Social Security income (yes or no)
Welfare income (yes or no)
Place of residence five years ago
Place of work of head of household
Number of automobiles owned by the household

Table 6.A.10        Number of Matching Intervals by Matching Level in the
                    PUS5–PUS15 Match

| | Matching Level | | | | | |
|---|---|---|---|---|---|---|
| | 6 | 5 | 4 | 3 | 2 | 1 |
| X Variable | Corre-lation (.80) | Corre-lation (.90) | Corre-lation (.93) | Corre-lation (.97) | Corre-lation (.98) | Chi-square (.99) |
| Number of children | 1 | 1 | 3 | 3 | 3 | 7 |
| Value of property | 2 | 5 | 5 | 7 | 9 | 11 |
| Gross rental | 1 | 1 | 1 | 1 | 4 | 6 |
| Wage earnings (head) | 4 | 6 | 10 | 16 | 20 | 26 |
| Wage earnings (spouse) | 1 | 1 | 1 | 3 | 7 | 12 |
| Total family income | 3 | 5 | 8 | 12 | 18 | 41 |

Three iterations were necessary for a satisfactory match. Table 6.A.10 shows the final matching levels and the number of matching intervals for each $X$ variable at each matching level. The dominant $X$ variables in this match were total family income and the wage earnings of the head of household. Property value was also an important $X$ variable. The other variables washed out after the first few matching levels.

Table 6.A.11 shows the distribution of matches by matching level in the final iteration of the match. There were no nonmatches, and less than 2 percent of the matches occurred at the cohort level. Moreover, of the 63,490 households in the PUS 5% file, 34,623 (or 55 percent) were used in the match.

Table 6.A.12 presents the correlation coefficients and the percent differences for total family income, wage and salary earnings of the head of household, and wage and salary earnings of the spouse. For total family income, the correlation coefficients are quite high for the first five levels but low for the bottom two. For wage and salary earnings of the household head, the correlations are high at all levels except the cohort

Table 6.A.11        Final Calibration of the PUS5–PUS15
                    Match

| Matching Level | Percent of Matches |
|---|---|
| 1. Chi-square (.99) | 18.3% |
| 2. Correlation (.98) | 19.4 |
| 3. Correlation (.97) | 25.8 |
| 4. Correlation (.93) | 17.6 |
| 5. Correlation (.90) | 13.5 |
| 6. Correlation (.80) | 3.9 |
| 7. Cohort | 1.5 |

Table 6.A.12    **Measures of Closeness of Fit by Matching Level for Selected X Variables in the PUS5–PUS15 Match**

| | Total Family Income | | Wage and Salary Earnings | | | |
| | | | Head | | Spouse | |
| Matching Level | Correlation Coefficient | Percent Difference | Correlation Coefficient | Percent Difference | Correlation Coefficient | Percent Difference |
|---|---|---|---|---|---|---|
| 1. Chi-sq. (.99) | 0.96 | −0.2 | 0.95 | 0.5 | 0.99 | − 1.1 |
| 2. Correl. (.98) | 0.96 | 0.4 | 0.98 | 0.2 | 0.96 | 0.7 |
| 3. Correl. (.97) | 0.95 | 0.3 | 0.93 | 0.2 | 0.88 | 2.1 |
| 4. Correl. (.93) | 0.87 | 0.2 | 0.88 | −1.4 | 0.16 | − 2.9 |
| 5. Correl. (.90) | 0.70 | 0.8 | 0.76 | 2.3 | 0.34 | − 3.3 |
| 6. Correl. (.80) | 0.31 | −6.5 | 0.71 | 3.5 | 0.32 | 12.1 |
| 7. Cohort | 0.19 | −4.6 | 0.14 | 17.8 | 0.26 | −10.1 |

*Notes*: The correlation coefficient is defined as the correlation of $X_A$ and $X_B$ for matched records occurring at the specified match level, where subscript $A$ refers to the PUS5 value and subscript $B$ to the PUS15 value.
Percent difference is defined as $[(\overline{X}_A - \overline{X}_B)/\overline{X}_B] \times 100$, where the bar indicates the mean value of the $X$ variable at the specified match level.

level. The correlation coefficients for wage and salary earnings of the spouse are high at only the top three levels. The mean values of these three $X$ variables are quite close in the two files at all matching levels except for the cohort level for wage and salary earnings of the head and the bottom two levels for wage and salary earnings of the spouse.

The following variables were transferred to the PUS 15% file from the matched record in the PUS 5% file: washing machines; clothes dryer; dishwasher; home food freezer; television set; radio; and second home ownership.

# Notes

1. This was only one of several major data bases developed as part of this project. Others included extended national income, product, and capital accounts (R. Ruggles, N. Ruggles, J. Kendrick, R. Eisner, and R. Goldsmith); a micro–data base for the government sector (J. Quigley); a micro-data base for the enterprise sector (R. Lipsey and M. Gort); and an environmental pollution account (H. Peskin).

2. This information is not normally included in the tax return, except when the filer is 65 years of age or older.

3. Since the overlap in demographic information between the two samples was so substantial, this match provided an ideal opportunity to test the reliability of

the matching technique. To do this, we ran two sets of regressions, the first with variables from the 15% PUS and the second with a mix of variables from the two files. In 90 percent of the cases, the regression coefficients in the two sets were not statistically different (see Ruggles, Ruggles, and Wolff [1977] for more details).

4. We expected some upward bias, since the MESP sample is a sample of *households,* which may file more than one tax return.

5. This procedure probably resulted in a slight downward bias in the percent of households receiving the respective income items (see note 7).

6. We determined the percent of positive entries to keep $(p_1)$ *and* the percent of negative entries to keep $(p_2)$ by solving the following simultaneous system:

$$p_1P + p_2N = T$$

$$p_1q + p_2r = s$$

where $P =$ total positive income in the MESP file;
$\quad N =$ total negative income in the MESP file;
$\quad T =$ total income from the IRS file;
$\quad q =$ percent receiving positive income in the MESP file;
$\quad r =$ percent receiving negative income in the MESP file;
$\quad s =$ percent receiving the income item in the IRS file.

7. Technically, we might have performed a $t$-ratio test for the difference in means for choosing the pattern of aggregation for each durable. However, from table 6.4, income, age, and residence seemed by far the predominant determinants.

8. An alternative technique would have been to use logit regression to estimate the probability of purchase of each durable as a function of all nine demographic characteristics. Time and cost constraints prevented us from pursuing this course.

9. This procedure introduces two offsetting biases. First, since real income grows over time, the probability of purchasing for a given household will increase between 1960 and 1969. However, the probability of purchasing a durable declines with the age of the head of household (table 6.4), since stocks of durables tend to be acquired early in the life cycle and then gradually replaced (and perhaps upgraded) as the household ages.

10. This is, of course, a very rough assumption. We could have assumed that the decision to purchase durable $i$ is independent of ownership of $i$ to allow multiple purchases. The distribution of the number of times durable $i$ is purchased in a given span of years would then be given by a binomial distribution.

11. These are the durables already included in the PUS inventory.

12. In the case of automobiles and televisions, where the PUS inventory indicates the household owns more than one, the age of each was estimated.

13. This would overstate the probability of purchasing each in a given year, since the decision to purchase the item is treated as independent of the ownership of that item.

14. Regression results are available on request from the author. Our major findings were: (1) Income is a positive determinant of the amount spent on each durable, while the percent of income spent on durables is negatively related to the income level. (2) The amount spent on durables is positively related to the rate of dissavings, particularly for the more costly durables. (3) Homeowners spend more on durables relative to income than renters. (4) Larger families have smaller expenditures on durables.

15. The only restriction was that if $p_i$ was less than zero, $p_i$ was set equal to zero.

16. We ignore the problem of differences in capital gains for different portfolios in the case of financial securities, as well as stocks. We also ignore the problem of both capital and ordinary gains in the case of the other assets. See Lebergott (1976) for a discussion of this problem.

17. The average yield by AGI class was as follows:

| AGI CLASS | AVERAGE DIVIDEND YIELD |
|---|---|
| Under $5,000 | 2.77% |
| 5,000–9,999 | 2.76 |
| 10,000–14,999 | 2.78 |
| 15,000–24,999 | 2.75 |
| 25,000–49,999 | 2.65 |
| 50,000–99,999 | 2.56 |
| 100,000 + | 2.51 |

18. There is the additional problem that not all investment real estate is rented. This will result in an overstatement in the concentration of investment real estate ownership, though there is no apparent systematic bias with respect to income or wealth.

19. The costs include such items as utilities, repairs and maintenance, mortgage interest, property taxes, and depreciation.

20. The Gini coefficient measure includes both holders and nonholders. The Gini coefficients were considerably lower for owners alone in most asset groups.

21. Households with negative AGI must be rich enough to own stocks and bonds, which they can sell at a loss, or to own a business that can report a (book) loss.

22. This conforms with the predictions of many life cycle models. See Modigliani and Brumberg (1954), for example.

23. The Gini coefficient, which we use to measure the level of inequality, is defined as twice the area between the Lorenz curve and the 45 degree line of perfect equality.

24. This information was added in a special run by the Social Security Administration, which used the actual Social Security numbers on the sample of tax returns to transfer this information.

25. This method of alignment was deemed superior to a simple inflation of 1969 AGI levels by the average increase in AGI between 1969 and 1970. The reason is that different parts of the AGI distribution shifted by different percents between 1969 and 1970.

26. The particular sample used was the "state 15%" sample.

27. This will somewhat understate the level of homeownership in the IRS file, since some homeowners do not have an outstanding mortgage and some do not itemize their deductions.

28. One additional adjustment was made. Because the income entries in the PUS file were truncated at $50,000, we truncated IRS income entries above $50,000.

29. No alignment was necessary for wage and salary earnings, since their distributions were almost identical in the two files.

## Comment    Vito Natrella

This paper concerns a new synthetic microdata file containing information on wealthholdings of consumers in the U.S. together with income data and a considerable amount of information on demographic characteristics. Edward Wolff describes the methods used to put the data base together and presents comparisons with other files and estimates.

Wolff indicated that there are three data bases containing information on individual wealth. These are the 1962 Federal Reserve Board Survey of Financial Characteristics of Consumers, the 1967 Survey of Economic Opportunity, and the estimates of personal wealth based on Internal Revenue Service estate tax data. The first two of these are one-time surveys based on samples of 2,500 and 30,000 households, respectively. The third is based on a sample of about 50,000 estate tax returns (Internal Revenue Service 1975). This latter file is available approximately every four years and has been used by the Internal Revenue Service to estimate the wealth of the living. Estimates of wealth have also been prepared by Smith and Franklin based on the same data files using somewhat different multipliers (Smith and Franklin 1974). Estimates based on estate tax data cover the population of top wealthholders—those with assets of $60,000 or more—and in 1969 accounted for almost 50 percent of total wealth. As Wolff mentions, the estimates are created under critical mortality rate assumptions which affect significantly the level of the estimates. However, it should be noted that the various mortality assumptions have considerably less effect on the distributions.

There are two other current estimates of household wealth based on aggregate data rather than microdata sets. One consists of the residual estimates from the annual flow of funds data of the Federal Reserve Board. This, together with the modified version developed by Helen Tice and R. W. Goldsmith, was used by Wolff as the source of control aggregates. The other set of estimates was prepared by Stanley Lebergott (1976) on the basis of aggregate income flows obtained from *Statistics of Income* for 1970. These were used to distribute national wealth estimates also developed from the flow of funds. In effect, both Wolff and Lebergott use flow of funds national balance sheet data as a basis for capitalizing income flows, one on a micro basis, the other as applied to aggregates, in order to develop estimates of the distribution of wealth.

Vito Natrella is director of the Statistics Division of the Internal Revenue Service, Washington, D.C.

These comments are based on the original paper presented at the conference in Williamsburg, December 1977. Many of the suggestions made have been incorporated in the revised version published in this volume.

The data file developed by Wolff and known as the MESP file has certain significant advantages over each of the above. For one thing, it covers the whole distribution of wealth, not just the segment of the population with more than $60,000 in assets. It is aligned with national wealth totals and includes data on holdings of consumer durables. Most important, it contains a wealth of demographic data which can be used for analyses not possible up to this time.

## Creation of MESP Data File

The sample frame for the MESP file is the 1970 PUS 15 percent Census 1/1000 file and contains approximately 63,400 households. Since this file consists of information for 1969, it was desired to have a 1969 Tax Model file which included data on itemized deductions not ordinarily included in the odd years and all Social Security demographic data. The construction of such a file starts with the 1970 IRS Tax Model, containing data from about 90,000 returns augmented with Social Security demographic data which is matched on a simulated basis with the 1969 IRS Tax Model so that the demographic information and itemized deduction information can be introduced. The tax model file also contains, of course, all income flows as reported on individual tax returns.

Another simulation match is then made between the modified and augmented 1969 Tax Model and the 1970 PUS 15 percent file. This latter file, which contains all housing, durables, overall income, and basic demographic information, comprises the final sample frame. Estimates of income flows and certain itemized deductions based on the 1970 PUS file are compared with published IRS *Statistics of Income* aggregates for 1969. The PUS file is aligned to the *Statistics of Income* totals by reducing the number of households and reducing the aggregate amounts for the remaining households. In this way, the *Statistics of Income* totals constitute the control figures on income flows.

A further match is made with the 1970 5 percent PUS Census file in order to bring in additional information on durable goods. Values for automobiles and other durables are imputed from data contained in the 1960–61 BLS Consumer Expenditure Survey. The totals are then aligned with Bureau of Economic Analysis aggregates.

The final step in the preparation of the file consists of converting income flows to asset holdings. This is done by capitalizing the income flows appearing in the microfile on the basis of the relation of aggregate income from *Statistics of Income* to aggregate assets held by households as developed in national balance sheets. The tangible assets data on holdings were obtained from estimates prepared by R. W. Goldsmith, while the financial assets came from the flow of funds of the Federal Reserve Board.

The paper presents estimates of the income-size distribution of wealth in the form of percent distribution of portfolio at each size level. Estimates of percent portfolio distribution are also shown for various demographic categories. In addition, data are presented on the mean holdings of total assets and net worth by the various demographic categories and by income levels. An analysis of inequality within the various income levels and demographic groups is presented in a table of Gini coefficients. Comparisons are also made with estimates of personal wealth based on estate tax data using information on the percent of total wealth held by the top 1 percent of the population.

The MESP data file makes a distinct contribution to the body of information available for analyses of wealth and its distribution. It contains more demographic characteristics than any other wealth file. It makes it possible to construct size distributions of various kinds, such as by income or by asset holdings. It shows the composition of wealth and includes holdings of consumer durables which generally have been rather meagerly detailed. The file can also be used in analyses of the life cycle accumulation pattern and in simulation for various purposes.

Problems and Deficiencies

There are a number of troublesome shortcomings in the presentation, some of which can be taken care of easily. One is the absence of dollar figures for the population by the various classifications. The data presented in the tables are in the form of percents or means. Since the dollar figures are easily available, I feel that the estimates should be presented in that form so that it is possible for the reader to make comparisons with other similar estimates.

I also think that more information should be included on what was actually done. For instance, it was difficult to determine what was done to align estimates from the MESP file with aggregate income flows from *Statistics of Income*. On the other hand, a considerable amount of detail is presented on the methods used to arrive at the durable goods imputations. Categories used should also be better defined as to what they include, particularly with respect to the various combinations of assets. Finally, I think it is very important that asset size distributions of the new data be presented as well as income size distributions. At present, personal wealth estimates based on the estate tax data of the IRS can be distributed only by asset size. It should be pointed out that in the 1976 personal wealth estimates by the IRS income size distributions will be presented, since income of the decedents for a prior year is being introduced in the file.

In addition, there are some problems with the data base of a more basic nature. In constructing a national balance sheet to which income flows are capitalized, data from "Flow of Funds Accounts, 1965–73," published in September 1974, were used for financial assets in spite of the fact that revised figures were published in 1976. Also, the Consumer Expenditure Survey for 1960–61 was used in connection with the estimates of durable goods. Although probably not available at the time the paper was first prepared, the 1972–73 Consumer Expenditure Survey could be used in a revision, improving the estimation procedures considerably.

Besides out-of-date sources, a number of the sources used appeared to be inappropriate to their purpose. The aggregate household balance sheet which was used as the benchmark for asset holdings comes from a mixed source. Financial assets are from the flow of funds of the Federal Reserve Board. These figures include both nonprofit organizations and trusts. Tangible asset data in the balance sheet are obtained from estimates prepared by R. W. Goldsmith and appear in Richard Ruggles's "Statement for the Task Force on Distributive Impacts of Budget and Economic Policies of the House Budget Committee" (1977). In the same statement appear estimates of financial assets developed from the flow of funds data eliminating nonprofit organizations and treating trusts as a separate form of wealth. In addition, the estimates are more up to date than the flow of funds data used by Wolff. It would, therefore, have been more consistent as well as more accurate to use the Goldsmith data for the financial assets as well as for the tangible assets.

Mortgage interest available from the 1970 individual tax model was used as a proxy for home ownership. Using this item, of course, has an inherent understatement since individuals owning homes with no mortgage would be underrepresented. A better approach would be to use the itemized deduction for real estate tax which is also available in the 1970 Tax Model.

In connection with the capitalization ratios used by Wolff, he rightly indicates that it would be desirable to use differential yields according to demographic and income characteristics. Research in this area was reported for corporate stock by Blume, Crockett, and Friend (1974). For 1971, they indicate yields of 2.2 percent for persons with adjusted gross income of $50,000 or more compared with yields of about 2.7 percent for persons with lower income and 2.5 percent in total. In view of these data, Wolff's figure of 2.3 percent does not appear to be as out of line as he indicates.

In developing the estimates, Wolff used only business and professional income both in the tax model files and in the *Statistics of Income* alignment procedures. However, I believe that the PUS file includes partnership income in its total income while equity in partnerships is also included in the aggregate assets shown in the household balance sheet. As used by Wolff, therefore, the capitalizing process implies that equity in partnerships is distributed in the same way as equity in sole proporietorships. This could have been avoided by including partnership income from the tax model in the matching procedure and also in *Statistics of Income* totals for alignment.

Comparisons with Other Wealth Data

As previously mentioned, comparison with other wealth estimates are rather difficult because of the lack of money amounts and the failure to include a distribution of wealth according to size of assets. However, Wolff makes some comparisons with the personal wealth estimates based on estate tax data using the proportion of total wealth held by the top 1 percent of the population.

The indications are that the estate tax data give estimates of higher concentration than do the MESP data. Estimates from the MESP data show the top 1 percent holding 14 percent of tangible assets, 42 percent of financial assets, and 25 percent of total assets. These compare with 21 percent, 46 percent, and 37 percent, respectively, for wealth estimated from estate tax data.[1] These differences were ascribed by Wolff to the truncated house values used in the MESP file and the inclusion of durables. I feel that they could also reflect a basic distortion in the distribution of asset holdings as shown in the estimates derived from the MESP data. In effect, too little wealth may have been allocated to the upper income brackets.

A comparison which Wolff did not make is with the estimates for 1970 prepared in a basically similar way using, however, aggregate data. The Lebergott estimates show a greater proportion of total held in financial form, assets which persons in the upper income brackets are more disposed to hold. These estimates also indicate substantially higher holdings of total assets in the upper income brackets. Total assets held by persons with incomes over $50,000 were 75 percent higher than those shown for the same group by Wolff. On the other hand, for persons with incomes under $50,000, the holdings were about the same in both sets of estimates. On the basis of income size distributions, the Lebergott estimates indicate considerably greater inequality in wealth than the Wolff estimates. Since the asset size distribution is not available for the Lebergott estimates, it was not possible to compare Gini coefficients.

Wolff indicated a Gini coefficient of .66 for the estimates of total assets developed from the MESP file. For that part of the population subject to the federal estate tax, Smith estimated the Gini coefficient at .50. Extending this to the full population could imply a Gini coefficient close to Wolff's figure. However, in view of the comparisons with other data, I would like to know more about the Wolff computation.

Alignment with SOI Income Flows

The simulated match of the 1970 PUS file with the 1969 modified and augmented IRS Tax Model produced a first approximation of the MESP file with the PUS file as the sample frame. Estimates of population income flows were prepared and then compared with similar data from *Statistics of Income*. The results for adjusted gross income and salaries and wages were reasonably close. However, dividends and interest estimated from the MESP file were more than twice, while business and rental income was about one and one half times, the SOI aggregates.

Wolff ascribes these results to oversampling of high income returns in the IRS file. Alignment to the controlling SOI totals was made by reducing the number of imputed returns and reducing the dollar amounts in the remaining returns. I find adjustments of the magnitudes involved particularly disturbing and feel that the findings of comparatively low concentration could have resulted from this alignment procedure. Forcing by such large amounts substantially weakens the differences in the distribution of those assets more likely to be held by persons in the upper brackets. The result is a data file with a serious deficiency in the upper levels.

I feel that the distortion in favor of the lower brackets may reflect the use of the 1970 PUS file as the sample frame. This file consists of an across-the-board random 1-in-1,000 sample. Such a sample is excellent for estimating demographic characteristics. It is very poor for estimating money amounts which are unequally distributed. The sampling variability of such estimates would be quite high. I suggest that the final sample frame should be one whose sample selection rates are higher the higher the income level.

In conducting the match of the 1969 Tax Model with the 1970 PUS file, Wolff indicated that only 17 percent of the Tax Model file was used. This rather low rate is also an indication of possible undersampling in the PUS file. One solution may be to use the 1969 augmented tax model as the sample frame for tax return filers while the 1970 PUS file could be used as the sample frame for nonfilers. This could be achieved by dividing the PUS file into those required to file and those not required to file, using requirements in effect for 1969. Data from the file of 1970 PUS return filers would be merged into the 1969 augmented tax model. Data for non-filers from the 1970 PUS file would be imputed. Estimates of money aggregates would be prepared using the stratified weights from the tax model for filers and the random 1,000 weight for nonfilers.

This procedure should result in income flow estimates needing only small adjustments to align with SOI. They should have much smaller sampling errors and be distributed more accurately to reflect holdings in the upper income levels.

Conclusion

A data file of the MESP type meets a definite need for wealth data associated with income and demographic characteristics. However, as indicated, improvements are needed. Inconsistencies need to be resolved. More of the basic estimates should be presented so that the file can be better evaluated. Distributions should show actual dollar estimates instead of just ratios. Asset size distributions should be presented as well as income size. More careful use of both definitions and sources should be made in regard to balance sheet aggregates.

In spite of these problems and deficiencies, I feel that this approach has great promise for development of an excellent analytic tool.

**Note**

1. Based on IRS estimates used by Natrella (1975). The more recent aggregate household balance sheet data developed by Goldsmith were used as the base. These ratios are not too different from those used by Wolff based on the Smith estimates if corrections are made to keep them comparable. Cash and deposits (including time deposits) must be included in the Smith figures, while demand deposits and currency must be included in the aggregate assets.

# References

Blume, Marshall; Jean Crockett; and Irwin Friend. 1974. "Stockownership in the United States: Characteristics and Trends." *Survey of Current business* 54, no. 11.

Friedman, Milton. 1939. "Discussion on Income Capitalization." *Studies in Income and Wealth* 3. New York: National Bureau of Economic Research.

Internal Revenue Service. 1975. "Statistics of Income, 1972: Personal Wealth Estimated from Estate Tax Returns." Washington, D.C.: U.S. Government Printing Office.

Lebergott, Stanley. 1976. *The American Economy*. Princeton: Princeton University Press.

Modigliani, Franco, and Richard Brumberg. 1954. "Utility Analysis and the Consumption Function: An Interpretation of Cross-Section Data." In K. K. Kurihara, ed., *Post-Keynesian Economics*. New Brunswick, N.J.: Rutgers University Press.

Natrella V. 1975. "Wealth of Top Wealthholders, 1972." Proceedings of the American Statistical Association, Washington, D.C.

Projector, Dorothy, and Gertrude Weiss. 1966. *Survey of Financial Characteristics of Consumers*. Washington, D.C.: Federal Reserve Board.

Ruggles, Richard. 1977. "Statement for the Task Force on Distributive Impacts of Budget and Economic Policies of the House Committee on the Budget." Mimeograph.

Ruggles, Richard, and Nancy Ruggles. 1974. "A Strategy for Matching and Merging Microdatasets." *Annals of Economic and Social Measurement* 3, no. 2.

Ruggles, Richard; Nancy Ruggles; and Edward Wolff. 1977. "Merging Microdata: Rationale, Practice, and Testing." *Annals of Economic and Social Measurement* 6 no. 4.

Smith, James D. 1974. "The Concentration of Personal Wealth in America, 1969." *Review of Income and Wealth,* series 20, no. 2.

Smith, James D., and Stephen Franklin. 1974. "The Concentration of Personal Wealth, 1922–1969." *American Economic Review* 64, no. 2.

Stewart, Charles, 1939. "Income Capitalization as a Method of Estimating the Distribution of Wealth by Size Group." *Studies in Income and Wealth* 3. New York: National Bureau of Economic Research.

U.S. Internal Revenue Service. 1971. *Statistics of Income 1969.* Washington, D.C.: Government Printing Office.

Wolff, Edward. 1978. "The Effect of Alternative Imputation Techniques on Estimates of Household Wealth in the U.S. in 1969." Paper presented at the C.R.E.P.-I.N.S.E.E. International Meeting on Wealth Accumulation and Distribution, Paris.

Young, Allan and John Musgrave. 1976. "Estimation of capital stock in the United States." Paper delivered at the Conference on Research in Income and Wealth, Toronto.

# 7    The Intergenerational
Transmission of Wealth:
Does Family Size Matter?

James D. Smith and Guy H. Orcutt

The progeny of small families are likely to inherit more wealth than are
children with greater numbers of siblings for two rather simple reasons:
parents of smaller families can save more, and they have fewer heirs
among which to leave their accumulated wealth. If subpopulations such
as Catholics and blacks have larger than average families and Jews tend
toward smaller families, this simple demographic fact may have a substantial impact on the distribution of wealth which is unrelated to any
overt or subtle discriminatory behavior of the dominant population.

How large are the effects of family size likely to be? An adequate data
base to answer the question directly does not exist. We therefore created
a synthetic population with the characteristics of the 1962 U.S. population and used a microsimulation system (MASS) to explore the importance of family size on inherited wealth.[1]

## 7.1    An Initial Population for Simulating
the Transmission of Wealth

An analysis of the limited information on inherited wealth provided
by the *Survey of Financial Characteristics of Consumers* suggests that
social-economic variables usually measured in field surveys explain very
little of the variance in the probability of inheriting, or of the value of
inherited wealth (Projector and Weiss 1966). Age, sex, marital status,
income level, and occupation are very poorly associated with the dependent variables. The most important and rather obvious predictors of
inheritances are the wealth, age, and marital status of one's surviving

James D. Smith is senior project director, Institute for Social Research, University of Michigan. Guy H. Orcutt is professor of economics at Yale University.

parents and the number of one's siblings. We are unaware of a data base in which these variables are associated with inheritance.

Although a population has never been measured in a field survey with genealogical links among the units of observation, enough information existed to build a synthetic population. We started with a sample representation of the 1960 U.S. population which was 'grown' from the 1860 U.S. Census of Population by Peabody.[2] The 1960 Peabody population has a limited set of characteristics. These include age, race, sex, and marital status. The population consists of 1,115 families, and each person in each family carries the identity of his mother, father, and children. These relatives either exist within the same family, are members of other families in the population, or have died. Thus, it is possible to identify at least three generations of relatives within the same sample population. When the population was grown Peabody did not have operating characteristics to generate values for economic variables such as income, assets, and labor force participation. This would have required historical information at the microlevel which was and is not available. The important and unique value of the Peabody population is its genealogic links.

To utilize the links it was necessary to superimpose them on a contemporary U.S. population sample containing a sufficiently large set of personal characteristics to simulate economic activity such as earning and saving, and social behavior such as marriage, birth, divorce, and death. All of this, of course, was for the purpose of generating the accumulation of wealth by individuals in the social context of families and its disbursal upon their death to their heirs. For this purpose we chose the 1/10,000 1960 Census Public Use Sample which had had wealth variables imputed to it.[3]

We imposed the genealogical links in the Peabody population on the 1960 Public Use Sample in a manner which preserved the covariance between relatives of the key variables age, sex, race, and marital status. The Public Use Sample contained about 7,500 families, while the grown 1960 population consisted of only about 1,100 families. Consequently, the genealogical links of each family in the grown population were used an average of about seven times.

We proceeded as follows:

1. Each *family* in each data base was classified by the age, sex, race, and marital status of its head.[4]
2. Heads and wives in families in each data base were all classified according to their own age, sex, race, and marital status.
3. All families in the Peabody population were arrayed into groups according to their age, sex, race, and marital status of their heads.
4. All *heads* and *wives* in the Public Use Sample were grouped by age, sex, race, and marital status characteristics.

5. Each family in turn was selected from the Public Use Sample. A family was drawn from the appropriate group of Peabody families so that the characteristics of the heads of the two families matched. The age, sex, race, and marital status of the head's father and mother and the wife's father and mother in the Peabody family were then used to select individuals from the Public Use Sample to be the parents of the head and wife in the Public Use Sample.

At the end of this process we had a file in which each person in the 1960 Public Use Sample "knew" who were his mother and father or child (up to 10 children), whether they lived together or in another family.

## 7.2   Driving the Initial Population Forward

The simulation system MASS, for Microanalytic Simulation System, was developed as a broad gauged model with an emphasis on economic behavior. For the work reported here we incorporated a "post office" into it which permits individuals to send one another messages during simulation runs.[5]

In a MASS simulation, marriages, divorces, births, and deaths take place; individuals participate in the labor force and receive income from labor, transfers, and wealth. Consumption takes place out of income and family saving occurs (See Orcutt and Glazer 1976). When a death occurs, relatives of a decedent are notified of the event by messages sent through the post office.[6]

In the real world death and transference of ownership of a decedent's wealth impose certain costs upon an estate and/or surviving relatives. The most important of these are are associated with last illness, burial, executors' and lawyers' fees. Cost functions for each of these were estimated using data from federal estate tax returns and incorporated into the simulation model. The estimated parameters for these operating characteristics are are shown in appendix 1. Many decedents' estates have little wealth to distribute after payment of these costs of dying. This is particularly true of the very young and the old. When death costs are fully accounted for, some decedents leave negative estates.[7]

Wealth transferred from one generation to another may also be eroded by death taxes. At the federal level, about 5 percent of estates are taxed. A rough representation of the pre-1972 estate tax statute is used in the simulations.[8]

The simulated events which take place each year are outlined in figure 7.1. They take place at the individual level. Events and changes in status which take place during a simulation year are, for the most part, stochastically determined using annual probabilities of occurrence. A few changes, such as age incrementation, are purely mechanical.

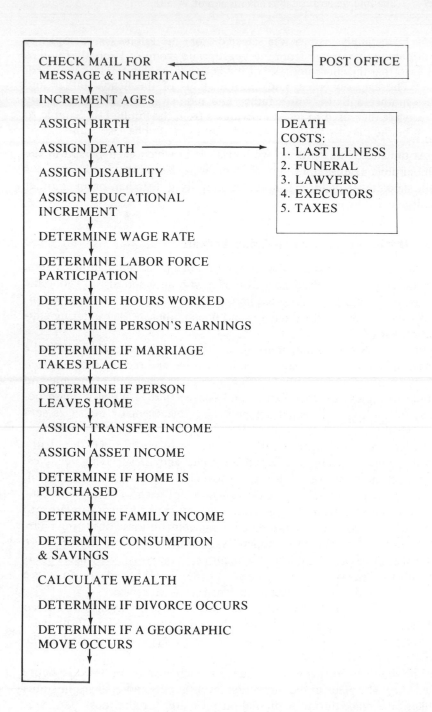

**Fig. 7.1**        Sequence of MASS Operations

In a simulated year the first thing which each person in each family does is to check his "post office box" for messages. In this particular application the messages are limited to information that a relative has died or a relative has died and left him assets.

This information is used in two ways. First, since every person in the population keeps a record of the names of his living kin, messages about the deaths of relatives are used to update their records, which we can think of as electronic family bibles.[9] Secondly, when one finds a relative died and bequeathed him wealth, he takes it and adds it to his own assets and to those of his family if he is the head or wife in a family. (All wealth owned by married persons in our simulated world is shared equally with their spouses.) Wealth inherited by children living at home is kept by them and not considered as part of the family's wealth. By the same token, when a child leaves home he takes only his own wealth.

After checking his post office box for information, a person's age is incremented. He or she is then given a chance of giving birth, dependent upon sex, marital status, age, race, education, number of children born, and parity (see Orcutt, Glazer, Jaramillo, and Nelson 1976).

The next step in the simulation is the assignment of death. If death occurs, a message is put into the post office box of "known" relatives of the decedent. An estate is set up and probated. The estate begins with the decedent's net worth at the time of death. From this the cost of last illness is subtracted (see appendix). The estate of each decedent is charged with the cost of a funeral, and the fees of executors and lawyers are calculated and charged against it as well.

Finally, an estate tax is levied. It provides for a $100,000 personal exemption after the above costs have been subtracted. The value of the estate after the exemption is treated as the taxable estate. The tax rates used are a function of the size of the taxable estate and are computed as follows:

$$\text{ESTRATE} = .05 + .015(\text{TXBLEST}'/10,000)$$
$$+ .02(\text{TXBLEST}''/100,000)$$
$$+ .03(\text{TXBLEST}'''/1,000,000)$$

where TXBLEST' is the value of the taxable estate under $100,000; TXBLEST" is the value of the taxable estate from $100,000 to $999,-999 and TXBLEST ''' is the value of the estate in excess of $999,999. For example, a taxable estate of $1,200,000 would have a tax rate of 40.6% (.05 + .15 + .20 + .006).

After the taxable estate has been reduced by the estate tax, the remaining estate is distributed to heirs according to the following devolution rules.

1. If there is a surviving spouse, the entire distributable estate de-
   volves to the spouse.
2. If there is no surviving spouse, the distributable estate is divided
   evenly among surviving children.
3. If there are neither children nor spouse surviving, the distributable
   estate passes equally to the decedent's surviving parents.
4. If there are neither children, spouse, nor parents surviving, the distributable estate goes into the kitty.[10]

We will not describe the remainder of the general simulation of MASS
outlined in figure 7.1. The reader is referred to Orcutt et al. (1976) for
a complete description of the other operating characteristics.

Our hypothesis that children with fewer siblings receive larger parental wealth bequests than do children with more siblings follows from
the reasoning that other things being equal, parents with fewer children
save more, and wealth is passed to surviving children in equal shares.
Although this proposition has face and some empirical validity, it is sel-
dom noted in the wealth distribution literature, and its importance vis-
à-vis other factors is unknown.

In table 7.1 the simulated amounts bequeathed and received by persons with different numbers of siblings is shown for twelve years. We
denote the period of the simulation as 1960 to 1972. The interpretation
of the simulation, however, is not dependent upon its alignment with
some historical period. The results are most appropriately thought of as
belonging to an interval of lapsed time, rather than a period of history.

It should be noted in table 7.1 that the results of the first simulation
year (1960) show the value of bequests to be several times greater than
the inheritances received. In a society in which wealth is increasing and
there is a lag between the time when a person dies and the time his heirs
inherit, there is a tendency for inheritances in a year to be less than bequests. The great difference shown for 1960, however, is largely mechanical, reflecting the fact that in the first year of the simulation everyone
in the population had a chance of dying and bequeathing an estate, but
no one had a chance of inheriting from a relative who died in year $t$-1.
Once the simulation is underway, the amounts bequested and inherited
begin to converge.

The most striking information provided by the table is the concentration of inheritance in persons with no more than three siblings. The
values shown are in billions of dollar amounts of the inheritance. There
are, of course, bequests to persons with greater numbers of siblings, but
bequests with positive values are offset by negative bequests. A negative bequest comes about because a decedent leaves little or no wealth
and the costs of last illness and funeral expenses are "inherited" by his
kin. This is clearly the real world situation for decedents who are young
children and for a reasonable number of decedents who are unmarried

**Table 7.1**    Value of Annual and Cumulative Bequests and Inheritance by Number of Siblings of Benefactors and Inheritors over a Simulated 12-Year Period (amounts in billions of dollars)

| No. of Siblings | 1960 | | 1961 | | 1962 | | 1963 | | 1964 | | 1965 | | 1966 | |
|---|---|---|---|---|---|---|---|---|---|---|---|---|---|---|
| | Year | Cum. | Year | Cum. | Year | Cum. | Year | Cum. | Year | Cum. | Year | Cum. | Year | Cum. |
| *0–1 siblings* | | | | | | | | | | | | | | |
| Bequests | 19.0 | 19.0 | 14.6 | 33.6 | 24.9 | 58.5 | 11.1 | 70.0 | 24.5 | 94.0 | 23.0 | 117.0 | 23.1 | 140.2 |
| Inheritance | 3.3 | 3.3 | 14.8 | 18.1 | 11.9 | 30.0 | 17.4 | 47.4 | 11.5 | 58.9 | 16.5 | 75.4 | 14.4 | 89.8 |
| Kitty | 1.0 | 1.0 | 0.8 | 1.8 | 5.9 | 7.6 | 0.1 | 7.7 | 6.0 | 13.6 | 8.6 | 22.3 | 2.3 | 24.6 |
| *2 siblings* | | | | | | | | | | | | | | |
| Bequests | −0.1 | −0.1 | 0.0 | −0.2 | −0.1 | −0.3 | −0.2 | −0.5 | −0.1 | −0.6 | −0.1 | −0.7 | −0.1 | −0.8 |
| Inheritance | 0.0 | 0.0 | 0.5 | 0.5 | 0.3 | 0.8 | 0.8 | 1.7 | 0.5 | 2.2 | −0.1 | 2.1 | 0.7 | 2.8 |
| Kitty | 0.0 | 0.0 | 0.0 | 0.0 | 0.0 | 0.0 | 0.0 | 0.0 | 0.0 | 0.0 | 0.0 | 0.0 | 0.0 | 0.0 |
| *3 siblings* | | | | | | | | | | | | | | |
| Bequests | −0.1 | −0.1 | −0.1 | −0.2 | 0.0 | −0.2 | −0.2 | −0.3 | −0.1 | −0.4 | −0.1 | −0.4 | −0.1 | −0.5 |
| Inheritance | 0.0 | 0.0 | 0.1 | 0.1 | 0.7 | 0.8 | 0.5 | 1.3 | 0.0 | 1.3 | 0.1 | 1.4 | 0.0 | 1.4 |
| Kitty | 0.0 | 0.0 | 0.0 | 0.0 | 0.0 | 0.0 | 0.0 | 0.0 | 0.0 | 0.0 | 0.0 | 0.0 | 0.0 | 0.0 |
| *4 siblings* | | | | | | | | | | | | | | |
| Bequests | −0.1 | −0.1 | −0.1 | −0.2 | 0.0 | −0.2 | 0.0 | −0.2 | −0.2 | −0.4 | −0.1 | −0.5 | −0.1 | −0.5 |
| Inheritance | 0.0 | 0.0 | 0.0 | 0.0 | 0.0 | 0.0 | 0.0 | 0.0 | 0.0 | 0.0 | 0.2 | 0.2 | 0.0 | 0.2 |
| Kitty | 0.0 | 0.0 | 0.0 | 0.0 | 0.0 | 0.0 | 0.0 | 0.0 | 0.0 | 0.0 | 0.0 | 0.0 | 0.0 | 0.0 |
| *5 siblings* | | | | | | | | | | | | | | |
| Bequests | −0.1 | −0.1 | 0.0 | −0.1 | 0.0 | −0.2 | 0.0 | −0.2 | 0.0 | −0.2 | 0.0 | −0.2 | 0.0 | −0.2 |
| Inheritance | 0.0 | 0.0 | 0.0 | 0.0 | 0.0 | 0.0 | 0.0 | 0.0 | 0.0 | 0.0 | 0.0 | 0.0 | 0.0 | 0.0 |
| Kitty | 0.0 | 0.0 | 0.0 | 0.0 | 0.0 | 0.0 | 0.0 | 0.0 | 0.0 | 0.0 | 0.0 | 0.0 | 0.0 | 0.0 |
| *6 siblings* | | | | | | | | | | | | | | |
| Bequests | 0.0 | 0.0 | 0.0 | 0.0 | 0.0 | 0.0 | 0.0 | 0.0 | 0.0 | 0.0 | −0.1 | −0.1 | −0.1 | −0.2 |
| Inheritance | 0.0 | 0.0 | 0.0 | 0.0 | 0.0 | 0.0 | 0.0 | 0.0 | 0.0 | 0.0 | 0.0 | 0.0 | 0.0 | 0.0 |
| Kitty | 0.0 | 0.0 | 0.0 | 0.0 | 0.0 | 0.0 | 0.0 | 0.0 | 0.0 | 0.0 | 0.0 | 0.0 | 0.0 | 0.0 |
| *7 or more siblings* | | | | | | | | | | | | | | |
| Bequests | 0.0 | 0.0 | 0.0 | 0.0 | 0.0 | 0.0 | 0.0 | 0.0 | −0.1 | −0.1 | 0.0 | −0.1 | 0.0 | −0.1 |
| Inheritance | 0.0 | 0.0 | 0.0 | 0.0 | 0.0 | 0.0 | 0.0 | 0.0 | 0.0 | 0.0 | 0.0 | 0.0 | 0.0 | 0.0 |
| Kitty | 0.0 | 0.0 | 0.0 | 0.0 | 0.0 | 0.0 | 0.0 | 0.0 | 0.0 | 0.0 | 0.0 | 0.0 | 0.0 | 0.0 |

**Table 7.1**—*continued*

| No. of Siblings | 1967 Year | 1967 Cum. | 1968 Year | 1968 Cum. | 1969 Year | 1969 Cum. | 1970 Year | 1970 Cum. | 1971 Year | 1971 Cum. | 1972 Year | 1972 Cum. |
|---|---|---|---|---|---|---|---|---|---|---|---|---|
| *0–1 siblings* | | | | | | | | | | | | |
| Bequests | 21.7 | 161.9 | 11.1 | 173.1 | 35.7 | 208.7 | 18.9 | 227.6 | 26.6 | 254.3 | 14.8 | 269.1 |
| Inheritance | 19.7 | 109.5 | 17.3 | 126.9 | 14.5 | 141.3 | 24.6 | 165.9 | 12.9 | 178.8 | 21.6 | 200.5 |
| Kitty | 2.9 | 27.5 | 0.3 | 27.8 | 7.1 | 34.9 | 1.4 | 36.4 | 5.4 | 41.7 | −0.2 | 41.5 |
| *2 siblings* | | | | | | | | | | | | |
| Bequests | −0.1 | −0.9 | −0.4 | −1.3 | −0.1 | −1.4 | −0.2 | −1.6 | −0.2 | −1.8 | −0.3 | −2.1 |
| Inheritance | 0.3 | 3.1 | 0.7 | 3.8 | 0.1 | 3.9 | −0.1 | 3.8 | 0.3 | 4.2 | 1.7 | 5.9 |
| Kitty | 0.0 | 0.0 | −0.2 | −0.2 | 0.0 | −0.2 | 0.0 | −0.2 | −0.1 | −0.2 | −0.1 | −0.3 |
| *3 siblings* | | | | | | | | | | | | |
| Bequests | −0.1 | −0.6 | 0.0 | −0.6 | −0.1 | −0.7 | −0.4 | −1.2 | −0.6 | −1.8 | −0.1 | −1.8 |
| Inheritance | 0.0 | 1.3 | 0.0 | 1.3 | 0.0 | 1.3 | 0.2 | 1.5 | 0.5 | 2.0 | −0.1 | 1.9 |
| Kitty | 0.0 | 0.0 | 0.0 | 0.0 | 0.0 | 0.0 | 0.0 | 0.0 | −0.1 | −0.1 | 0.0 | −0.1 |
| *4 siblings* | | | | | | | | | | | | |
| Bequests | −0.1 | −0.7 | −0.1 | −0.7 | −0.1 | −0.8 | 0.0 | −0.8 | 0.0 | −0.8 | −0.3 | −1.1 |
| Inheritance | 0.1 | 0.1 | 0.0 | 0.1 | 0.0 | 0.1 | 0.0 | 0.1 | 0.1 | 0.1 | −0.2 | 0.0 |
| Kitty | 0.0 | 0.0 | 0.0 | 0.0 | 0.0 | 0.0 | 0.0 | 0.0 | 0.0 | 0.0 | 0.0 | 0.0 |
| *5 siblings* | | | | | | | | | | | | |
| Bequests | −0.2 | −0.4 | 0.0 | −0.4 | −0.1 | −0.4 | −0.3 | −0.8 | 0.0 | −0.8 | 0.0 | −0.8 |
| Inheritance | 0.0 | 0.0 | 0.0 | 0.0 | 0.0 | 0.0 | 0.0 | 0.0 | 0.1 | 0.1 | 0.0 | 0.1 |
| Kitty | 0.0 | 0.0 | 0.0 | 0.0 | 0.0 | 0.0 | 0.0 | 0.0 | 0.0 | 0.0 | 0.0 | 0.0 |
| *6 siblings* | | | | | | | | | | | | |
| Bequests | 0.0 | −0.2 | −0.2 | −0.4 | 0.0 | −0.4 | −0.1 | −0.4 | 0.0 | −0.4 | −0.1 | −0.5 |
| Inheritance | 0.0 | 0.0 | 0.0 | 0.0 | 0.0 | 0.0 | 0.0 | 0.0 | 0.0 | 0.0 | 0.0 | 0.0 |
| Kitty | 0.0 | 0.0 | 0.0 | 0.0 | 0.0 | 0.0 | 0.0 | 0.0 | 0.0 | 0.0 | 0.0 | 0.0 |
| *7 or more siblings* | | | | | | | | | | | | |
| Bequests | −0.1 | −0.2 | 0.0 | −0.2 | 0.0 | −0.2 | −0.1 | −0.3 | −0.3 | −0.5 | −0.2 | −0.7 |
| Inheritance | −0.1 | −0.1 | 0.0 | −0.1 | 0.0 | −0.1 | 0.0 | −0.1 | 0.0 | −0.1 | 0.0 | −0.1 |
| Kitty | 0.0 | 0.0 | 0.0 | 0.0 | 0.0 | 0.0 | 0.0 | 0.0 | 0.0 | 0.0 | 0.0 | 0.0 |

*Note:* The initial population has characteristics which have been aligned with that of the U.S. population in 1960, but the intent here is not to track historical time.

children living away from home. In the simulation, when these individuals died the negative value of their distributable estate was sent to their surviving parents. Elderly persons who died during the simulation were also frequently poor. The negative value of their estates was bequeathed to their surviving spouse or children. As noted above, life insurance contracts are not included in the model at this time. Their inclusion is likely to make considerable difference in the value and distribution of intergenerational transfers. The same would be true of health insurance, and to a much smaller extent, Social Security death benefits.[11] To further illustrate the importance of number of siblings on the level of inherited wealth, we produced a simple cross-tabulation, shown here in table 7.2. In the table there is a definite inverse relation between number of siblings and amount of inherited wealth. Ninety-four percent of persons who inherited $15,000 or more over the twelve-year period were either only children or had one sibling. Only about one percent of those who had three siblings inherited $15,000 or more in the same period. For practical purposes, virtually all persons with four or more siblings, i.e., from families with five or more children, inherited less than $1,000 in the twelve years of simulation. It should be kept in mind that the probability of inheriting anything in a given year is not very great. In a given year about one percent of the population dies. If each decedent had an average of four survivors unrelated to any other decedent, only about four percent of the surviving population would receive an inheritance (including a negative or zero-valued inheritance). One would like to look at lifetime inheritance to better understand the importance of of family size for ultimate wealth status. Work is progressing to run simulations of one-hundred-years' duration to further the exploratory efforts presented here.

**Table 7.2**    **Percent Distribution by Value of Inheritance and Number of Siblings after Twelve Years of Simulation (row %/column %)**

| No. of Siblings | < $1,000 | $1,000 < $3,000 | $3,000 < $5,000 | $5,000 < $15,000 | ≥ $15,000 |
|---|---|---|---|---|---|
| | | | Amount Inherited | | |
| 0–1 | 92.6/59.7 | 1.2/87.1 | 0.7/87.2 | 2.6/93.9 | 2.9/94.2 |
| 2 | 98.4/10.5 | 0.1/ 1.4 | 0.1/ 1.2 | 0.7/ 4.1 | 0.7/ 3.9 |
| 3 | 98.6/10.8 | 0.7/ 8.2 | 0.1/ 2.3 | 0.3/ 2.0 | 0.3/ 1.8 |
| 4 | 99.5/ 9.0 | 0.0/ 0.0 | 0.5/ 9.3 | 0.0/ 0.0 | 0.0/ 0.0 |
| 5 | 99.4/ 4.7 | 0.6/ 3.4 | 0.0/ 0.0 | 0.0/ 0.0 | 0.0/ 0.0 |
| 6 | 100.0/ 2.4 | 0.0/ 0.0 | 0.0/ 0.0 | 0.0/ 0.0 | 0.0/ 0.0 |
| 7 or more | 100.0/ 2.8 | 0.0/ 0.0 | 0.0/ 0.0 | 0.0/ 0.0 | 0.0/ 0.0 |

## Appendix

### Cost of Last Illness

Nearly all deaths impose medical costs on the estates of decedents. Where there is a prolonged terminal illness, the medical costs may be substantial. The deductibility of these costs for purposes of calculating taxable estate on the federal estate tax return provided a data base to estimate the relation of the cost of last illness to other characteristics of decedents. The cost of last illness was estimated using AID-III.[12]

In figure 7.A.1 the result of the AID analysis is shown. The five final groups explain 5.4 percent of the variance in the cost of terminal illnesses as reported on federal estate tax returns. One would not expect to explain a great deal of the variance with the variables available to us, but there is a systematic, positive relationship between net worth and cost of last illness. The only other variable which contributed significantly to reducing the original variance was age of decedent. Thus, only these two characteristics of decedents were used in the attribution of last illness costs. The actual attribution of the cost was unsophisticated; the expected value was assigned within each characteristic class.

### Attorneys' Fees

Attorneys' fees are a deductible item in the federal estate tax. Consequently, they are available from the estate tax return. When AID was used to split the population into groups such that a regression of attorneys' fees on gross estate within groups would produce the greatest reduction of variance relative to a regressions on the total set of observations, 51.1 percent of the variance was explained. Age and marital status of decedent were the only other variables which were able to provide a basis for splitting the population with a significant reduction in variance. In figure 7.A.2 it can be seen that a simple regression of attorneys' fees on gross assets (measured in thousands of dollars) would produce coefficients of $a = \$549$, $b = 15.66$. The predicted value $\$3,645$ is the expected attorneys' fee when the mean value of the group's gross assets ($\$198,000$) is plugged into the equation.

### Executors' Fees

The cost of executors' fees was estimated using two regression equations and data from the 1962 federal estate tax file.

$$\text{EXCOM} = a + b_1 \text{ (NETWORTH)} + b_2 \text{ (MS1)} + b_3 \text{ (MS2)} + b_4 \text{ (MS3)}$$

where net worth is measured in thousands of dollars, MS1 is a dummy for married decedents MS2 is a dummy for never married decedents, and MS3 is a dummy for all other marital statuses. The equation was fitted separately for decedents with net worth under $200,000 and those with net worth of $200,000 or more. The estimated coefficients for the two equations are given in table 7.A.1:

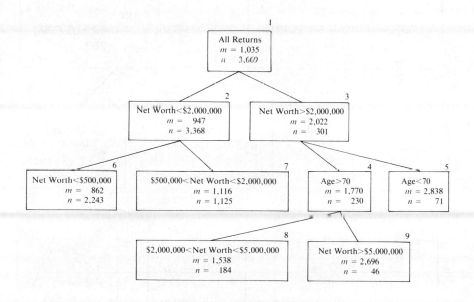

**Fig. 7.A.1**     Medical Expenses of Last Illness ($m$ = mean cost in dollars). Variation $e$ explained equals 5.4%. Sex was an eligible in variance.

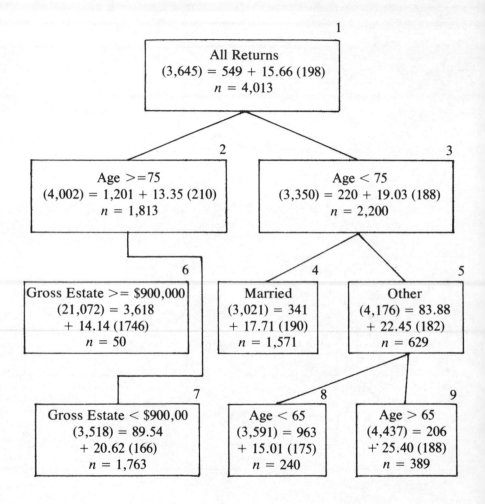

**Fig. 7.A.2** Attorneys' Fees AID with Regression on Gross Estate (dollars). The overall regression $R^2$ equals 46.8%. Marginal variance explained by subgroup regressions equals 4.3%. Total $R^2$ equals 51.1%. Sex was also an eligible variable but could not produce a significant reduction in variance. The predicted value of the equation in each group is the value of attorneys' fees estimated when gross estate measured in thousands of dollars was at its mean for the group.

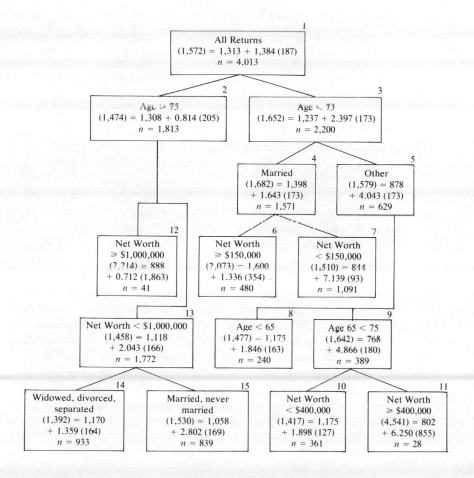

**Fig. 7.A.3** Funeral Expenses AID with Regression on Net Worth. The overall regression $R^2$ equals 9.3%. Marginal variance explained by subgroup regression equals 9.9%. Total $R^2$ equals 19.2%. The dependent variable in parentheses is the estimated value of funeral expenses when the independent variable in parentheses, net worth measured in thousands of dollars, is at the mean for the group.

| Table 7.A.1 | Estimated Cost of Executors' Fees | |
|---|---|---|
| | Net Worth | |
| | < $200,000 | ≥ $200,000 |
| $a$ | $172.50 | $2,517.80 |
| $b_1$ | 14.8 | 17.3 |
| $b_2$ | −843.5 | −3,575.0 |
| $b_3$ | 575.5 | 4,223.4 |
| $b_4$ | 268.0 | − 648.1 |
| | $R^2 = 17.9$ | $R^2 = 32.2$ |

Funeral Expenses

In the simulation, funeral expenses are attributed to decedents' estates on the basis of eight regression equations fitted in the process of an AID run on the 1962 estate tax file. The combined splitting of the population into eight final groups, and the simple regression of funeral expenses on net worth within each final group, explained 19.2 percent of the variance of funeral expenses. In figure 7.A.3 we show the results of the AID run with group regressions.

In some cases, the total costs of dying exceed the assets of the decedent. This is frequently the case with children. Although their estates will not generally incur legal or administration fees of any significance, the cost of last illness and funeral will diminish them as well as those of adults. Whether for a child or for an adult, the costs of last illness, administration fees, lawyers' fees, and funeral expenses are all deducted from the estate in accordance with the AID analyses above. When these costs result in a negative estate, it is transferred to the decedent's heirs in the same manner as a positive valued estate. This conceptualization is consistent with the actual process of cost bearing for decedents.

# Notes

1. MASS (Microanalytic Simulation System) was developed through the joint efforts of a number of researchers over a longer period of time than we have had funds to simulate. The principal contributor and father of the model is Orcutt. Smith designed and implemented the "post office" software which permits individuals to send messages to one another while the system is running and in the application presented here to bequeath wealth to their heirs. The basic MASS software system was designed and implemented under the direction of Amihai Glazer. See Orcutt and Glazer (1976) for a general description of MASS, and Orcutt, Glazer, Jaramillo, and Nelson (1976b) for a programmer's perspective.

2. The growth of the 1860 sample population to 1960 was carried out several years ago by Gerald Peabody at the Urban Institute using DYNASIM. For a description of DYNASIM see Orcutt, et al., 1976a.

3. Using the *1962 Survey of Financial Characteristics of Consumers* to estimate income-wealth relationships by demographic characteristics, Smith and Franklin had imputed to a 1960 Public Use Sample a set of asset and liability variables. See Smith, Franklin, and Orcutt 1977.

4. We also attempted to use measures of family size and numbers of children, but these proved to be ineffective.

5. The post office is technically an array with elements for storing messages. The element subscripts are the IDs of all persons in the initial population plus all IDs for children born during the simulation period.

6. In the work presented here messages are sent only to parents and children. We have also limited the distribution of bequests to parents and children. The model is capable of transmitting messages and bequests to siblings, uncles, aunts, grandparents, great grandparents, and cousins, but the evidence suggests that very little bequeathed wealth moves beyond the radius of spouse, children, and parents.

7. We have not incorporated life insurance contracts into the model at this time. It is expected that including life insurance policies will reduce the rather large number of decedents we find with negatively valued estates.

8. Implementing death costs and taxes into the model represents work in progress. In the present application of the model, alignment of these observable costs is not critical so long as our approximations do not distort the relationships we wish to measure, namely, the importance of number of siblings and inherited wealth.

9. In the current implementation each person in the population carries with him the names of up to ten persons who are related to him as mother, father or child. With this amount of information it is possible to find his brothers and his sisters and his uncles and aunts.

10. The kitty represents all other heirs including both collateral relatives, charitable organizations and governments.

11. In an earlier simulation experiment by Smith, Franklin, and Orcutt 1977 using a one-year period, life insurance was modeled as part of the financial characteristics of persons. In a simulation model which runs over many years, not only must the initial distribution of insurance risk be modeled, but the operating characteristics which generate purchases, lapses and cash surrender value must also be implemented. This work is on our research agenda, but is at least a year away from completion.

12. AID-III is a data-searching algorithm which sequentially splits a population into pairs such that the sum of the variance around the mean of the pair or the expected value of a regression is the smallest possible proportion of the variance around the expected values of the group from which the pair was derived. The technique has the advantage over regression in not requiring an additive set of independent variables. It also imposes no linearity restrictions on relations between variables. For a detailed discussion of AID-III see Sonquist, 1971.

# References

Orcutt, Guy H.; Steven Caldwell; Richard Wertheimer II; Stephen D. Franklin; Gary Hendricks; Gerald Peabody; James D. Smith; and Sheila Zedlewski. 1976a. *Policy Exploration through Microanalytic Simulation*. Washington: The Urban Institute.

Orcutt, Guy H., and Amihai Glazer. 1976. "Research Strategy, Micro-analytic Modeling, and Simulation." Working paper 793. Yale University: Intitution for Social and Policy Studies.

Orcutt, Guy H.; Amihai Glazer; Helena Jaramillo; and Phil Nelson. 1976. "Microanalytic Simulation." Working paper. New Haven: Institution for Social and Policy Studies of Yale University.

Projector, Dorothy S., and Gertrude Weiss. 1966. *Survey of Financial Characteristics of Consumers*. Washington: Board of Governors of the Federal Reserve System.

Smith, James D.; Stephen D. Franklin; and Guy H. Orcutt. 1977. "The Intergenerational Transmission of Wealth: A Simulation Experiment." In F. Thomas Juster, ed. *The Distribution of Economic Well-Being*. Cambridge, Mass.: National Bureau of Economic Research.

Sonquist, John A.; Elizabeth Lauh Baker; and James M. Morgan. 1971. *Searching for Structure*. Ann Arbor: Institute for Social Research, University of Michigan.

# 8    Relevance in Economic Measurement: Public Inheritances

Nelson McClung

In recent years questions have been raised about the substitutability of pension and other wealth. Reviewing research on this issue, one must conclude that statistical analysis has rather more than exhausted the potential of available data to supply answers to these questions.[1] The new Survey of Income Program Participation (SIPP)[2] could be designed to collect the data required for answering better these and other questions of family decision making in a lifetime planning context.

In this paper I use the substitutability of pension and other wealth as an example of data collection capabilities which SIPP should have. Policy analysts in estimating or testing postulated theoretical relationships should not be forced by unnecessary data limitations into such tortured reasoning and farfetched estimating expedients that the interpretation of their research results is too doubtful to admit of definite conclusions. We need a survey vehicle which is responsive to policy analysis requirements, whatever these may be at any time. I would hope that SIPP will be designed to collect data such as those which I identify in this paper. But I emphasize that mine is merely one of many examples of data requirements that SIPP should be able to satisfy.

This paper is a constructive criticism of economic measurement, not of economic analysis. Three comments may be made on that statement. First, the set of measurements criticized and for which I propose

Nelson McClung is Assistant Director (Personal Taxation), Office of Tax Analysis, U.S. Treasury.

As I use the term, the distinction between public and private activities is not synonymous with any distinction between government and private activities. The presumption that government activities produce only public goods, that is, goods which for one reason or another are consumed in common, and that other activities produce only private goods never was accurate and is less so now than formerly.

reforms is defined by the data requirements of models of family lifetime savings plans. There are many models of the family lifetime savings process. A simple and easily accessible one is that of Laurence Kotlikoff (1979). Mordecai Kurz (1980) has developed a model which is more complete and is better formulated for estimation. Second, no implication is intended that these or any other economic models are beyond criticism; it is just that I choose not to critique models in this paper. Third, the set of economic measurements considered is not necessarily that most deserving of criticism.

## 8.1   Concept of Transfers

Pensions are transfers. To appreciate their economic significance we need to distinguish transfers from transactions which are not transfers. There are two concepts of transfers: the theoretical and the institutional.[3] Only the institutional has been measured at all well. However, for behavioral analysis, only the theoretical is of any interest.

In the National Income Accounts, Disposable Income differs from Personal Income by the net of transfers out over transfers in. The transfers out are mainly taxes and the transfers in are mainly grants through government programs. In equations which purport to explain consumption, saving or transfers, available micro equivalents of Personal Income or of Disposable Income are not correct nor are they the best concepts of income that we could construct from family surveys. Personal Income does not include current period accruals of capital gains and Disposable Income does not include taxes which may be voluntary allocations of income and does include charitable contributions and other outlays which may be as involuntary as any taxes. The Federal Personal Income Tax concept of Taxable Income does not include state and local tax outlays or charitable contribution outlays even though they may be in either case purchases of services for personal use. What we require for behavioral analyses is a measure in each period for each family of just that income over which it has a degree of control. There is no one measure that will satisfy all analysts in all applications. But, while analysts must choose, statisticians need not; they should collect income and outlay data in sufficient detail that analysts have appropriate choices of measures.

### 8.1.1   Transfers as Transactions

Transfers are transactions ultimately between persons. In common with all transactions, transfers engage two classes of actors: payors and payees. We want to distinguish transfer transactions from other transactions between persons, transactions in consumption goods (consumption) and transactions in assets (saving) or transactions in labor services and transactions in property rentals. With suitable definitions, income

$(Y)$ equals output $(O)$. Consumption $(C)$, saving $(S)$, and transfers out $(TO)$ may be an exhaustive classification of income allocation transactions. Wages $(W)$, rentals $(P)$, and transfers in $(TI)$ may be an exhaustive classification of income receipts transactions. Thus, aggregating without netting across units: $Y = C + S + TO$ and $O = W + P + TI$. An alternative and for certain analyses preferable interpretation of this budget identity is that uses of funds $(Y)$ equal sources of funds $(O)$. On this alternative interpretation, $S$ may be either a use or a source of funds, depending upon the sign of the net transactions on capital account. In these identities there are some difficulties which I will try to resolve.

### 8.1.2 Direct and Mediated Transfers

One person may transfer resources (or command over resources) to another directly through bequest or gift. Or the transfer may be arranged through an intermediary. These intermediaries may be business firms, governments or, of course, other persons. Debt forgiveness is an example of a transfer through a business firm. Tax financed grants are transfers mediated by governments.

As transfer intermediaries, business firms fall into two classes: those which do a little and those which do a lot. Firms organized for profit do little transferring relative to gross income. Insurance companies, pension funds, charitable foundations and universities do much more. However, the meanest governments do relatively more than all but a very few firms. Among governments, the federal is preeminent. The aggregate mediated transfer through all intermediaries is very large, perhaps a quarter to a third of the national output, but much depends upon how one counts.

### 8.1.3 Transfers as Unrequited Transactions

Most transactions, what we may call economic transactions, leave both transactors with a value after the transaction that is the same as or greater than before. Transfer transactions are noneconomic, are not genuine exchange transactions, because they leave grantors with less value, although they may leave grantees with greater value, after the transfer than they had before. In general, there is no way to determine in any one instance or in the aggregate whether the gain to grantees is greater or less than the loss to grantors. The rule in statistical practice is to value transfers at apparent cost to grantors. But, as we shall see, apparent cost to grantors is not actual cost to grantors; actual cost is equal to or less than, possibly much less than, apparent cost. That it may be less weakens the case for measuring the institutional concept, for the valuation rule may be no more correct for grantors than for grantees.

The institutional definition of transfers is merely a list of transactions which are presumptively gratuitous on at least one side of the exchange. But in these putative transfers there may be substantial elements of compensation or consumption. On the other hand, transactions not on the list in fact may have large gratuitous elements. Thus, we may see people cheerfully paying taxes; potential AFDC recipients questioning whether they should take up the trade, given the meagerness of the rewards; and electric rate payors complaining that they are being ripped off. The question, then, is what to do. We could apply more imagination than we have in the past to measuring the theoretical concept of transfers but, to the extent that we must use measures of institutional concepts in behavioral analyses, we should be very careful in the interpretation of our results.

### 8.1.4   Asymmetry in Transfers

A transaction which may be a transfer to one transactor may not be a transfer to the other. A person in paying his utility bill may think that he has received full value; yet, if the utility company would have supplied in a negotiated deal the same amount of electricity for half the price, half of the bill is a transfer in to the utility company, although it is not a transfer out to the person. Similarly, taxes paid by a person may be a transfer out to him but, if the tax receipts are used by a government to purchase the labor services of persons who but for the compensation would not supply them, the amounts received are not transfers. The services provided by government employees may be transfers in to users of the services. This asymmetry holds for both the theoretical and the institutional concepts of transfers.

At this point, we need to modify the expressions above in section 8.1.1. They become

$$Y = C + S + TOD + TOM$$

$$O = W + P + TID + TIM$$

where $TOD$ is direct transfers out, $TOM$ is mediated transfers out, $TID$ is direct transfers in and $TIM$ is mediated transfers in. The argument is that $TOD \neq TID$ and $TOM \neq TIM$. More generally, $TO \neq TI$, whether at the unit level or in the aggregate. Measures of transfers thus depend upon whether we add up the receipts $(O)$ side or the allocation $(Y)$ side of family budgets.

### 8.1.5   Transfers as Involuntary Transactions

There is a presumption that transfers out are involuntary. But grantors taking into account all indirect benefits may not always be dissatisfied with their role in transfer transactions. A person paying his taxes may reason that in being able to continue living inside the country and outside of jail he is better off than if he did not pay. The person giving to charity may be really buying the approval of his neighbors. On the other hand, the child, who, having said grace, must now confront the vegetables may consider himself worse off for the Lord's beneficence. Nevertheless, he may be better off eating the vegetables than forgoing dessert. There are good reasons, as the Trojans discovered, for giving a gift horse an examination before accepting it. Proceeding along these lines, we make transfers vanish, and all transactions become economic exchanges.

There is something to be said for preserving a distinction between those transactions which a person enters into for personal advantage, absent external influences, and those which he acquiesces in from social coercion. The distinction, however, is one not easily preserved in statistical measurements. A family's disposable income properly may be defined as family total income, somehow defined, minus involuntary transfers out or minus the sum of involuntary and voluntary transfers out, depending upon one's interest or confidence that the transfers out identified as voluntary or involuntary in fact really are so. Statistical measurements should be conducted so as to give analysts as much freedom as is feasible either to classify only involuntary payments as transfers out and only gratuitous receipts as transfers in or to include voluntary payments among transfers out and, illogical as it may be, include receipts which in fact are compensation among transfers in.

### 8.1.6 Transfers and Consumption

Primarily because they appear so much to be involuntary, taxes commonly are considered transfers out. We distinguish between benefit and equity taxes, but even with respect to benefit taxes, we recognize that generally some form of coercion is necessary, else people would take the benefits and not pay the taxes. In enclaves of rich families, fortunate enough to have their own local government, people pay high property taxes to buy schools, swimming pools, tennis courts, and other amenities through their local governments and recognized charities, contributions to which are deductible under the Federal Personal Income Tax on a par with state and local taxes. All of these amenities are available at a price from private for-profit suppliers or through governments and nonprofit institutions at a user charge. Prices and user charges paid, however, are not deductible under the Federal Personal Income Tax. If the weighted average marginal Federal Personal Income Tax rate in a community is 0.50, then the people of the community can buy with local government property taxes tennis courts at half price. At that price, one may suppose that much of the taxes paid is voluntary, a supposition reinforced by the evident responsiveness of local political processes. Through its Personal Income Tax the federal government subsidizes socialism for the rich. In promoting socialism one sensibly might begin by coopting the rich.

The point for our purposes is that there is no clear distinction between equity and benefit taxes and, hence, no neat statistical distinction between transfers out and consumption expenditures. As a consequence, estimated elasticities of consumption with respect to income depend upon specific institutional arrangements. Imagine what would be the case were the oft-made suggestion adopted for setting the income tax rate equal to the ratio of federal expenditures to aggregate taxable income and allowing all taxpayers unlimited deductions for contributions to federal agencies for specified purposes, such as fish and wildlife conservation. Little or no tax would be collected and measured personal consumption outlays would increase by nearly total present income tax collections. The difference between Personal and Disposable Income that is accounted for by Federal Personal Income Tax would vanish. However, even though there is no precise demarcation between transfers and consumption expenditures, we need not abandon theoretical refinement at the low level of sophistication which we now do. The test should be whether payments buy a family things which it wants for its own personal use. On this test most local property tax payments would be classified as consumption outlays. There are, as we know, childless persons who pay local property taxes with the thought that government schools at least keep little rascals busy and may give them some marketable skills that offer them an alternative to growing up big rascals.

That brings up a related matter. In addition to personal consumption financed by tax and charitable contributions, we must recognize direct or mediated vicarious consumption. If A's consumption enters into the utility function of B, then it is usual to say that A's and B's utility functions are interdependent, although strictly speaking B's utility merely is dependent on that of A. It may be that some people pay taxes, make charitable contributions or direct transfers of income to others from motives purely of love. More commonly, perhaps, the payments made are intended to motivate and finance modifications in the behavior of the recipients which are agreeable to the payors. To the extent that payments are intended to change behavior and in fact do, they are compensation to receiving units for services rendered and consumption by paying units.

### 8.1.7  Transfers and Saving

We observe people paying insurance premia, Federal Insurance Contributions Act and Self-Employment Act taxes and employee pension plan contributions, if we accept that employer payments are distributed in some manner over employees and borne entirely by them. On the other hand, we observe people receiving insurance benefits, OASDHI benefits and employee pensions. In a strictly economic sense the payments and receipts are current period transfers. Those who produce the output of a period transfer command over some part of that output to those who have rights under these government and private programs. Yet, we have a problem with this view. In a period as short as one year, much wage income and perhaps most property income received are economic rents and, hence, transfers in. Even in a long run, some wage and much property income is economic rent: actual compensation for supplying labor and capital services is above owner supply prices. With respect to property income, this is true if people hold wealth for the control of businesses or, as implied by lifetime saving theory, for income averaging and, although sensitive to relative rates of return, would engage in these activities almost irrespective of the level of returns.

In making advance preparation for the financial consequences of some bad outcome, such as death and survivorship, disability, sickness, unemployment, fire, theft, a person has a choice: he may save or he may insure. All insurance is a scheme for averaging bad outcomes over more families than suffer bad outcomes in any period. It is not always apparent whether people are insuring or saving. Saving, in a lifetime net zero saving model, is self-insuring and that is the root of the difficulty. In simple term casualty insurance, a person buys coverage in each period which presumably is worth the premium. This is a consumption (or business) outlay. Insurance proceeds received in the event of a loss are merely an involuntary asset conversion; in the normal case, apart from gain (or loss) on a conversion, the insurance proceeds net against the loss to zero. Contributions to employee pension plans may be regarded by the persons covered as saving for retirement (and perhaps other events which result in a loss of income). But, if the plan is fully funded, all plan members, both those active and those retired, neither save nor dissave: plan contributions and interest receipts each period just match plan benefit payments and administrative expenses each period. The arrangement looks much like term insurance.

There are two consistent treatments of family pension saving. One is to classify certain family income allocations as transfers or saving from a knowledge of the extent to which the pension plans that they participate in are not only advance funded but funding. The other is to classify all contributions and interest earnings as savings by families and net out the benefit payments in aggregation. Either we measure family income (1) inclusive of transfers out and allocations to saving and exclusive of transfers in and withdrawals of saving or we measure income (2) exclusive of transfers out and allocations to saving and inclusive of transfers in and withdrawals of saving. The first is a Haig-Simons concept of income; the second is a Fisher-Kaldor concept. Basically, the choice is one between accrual and realization accounting for income, although Fisher measured income by accruals. The basic complication is in distinguishing between transfers out and saving. We would like to preserve a concept of saving such that allocations of income to saving by all families sum to the amount that is available for capital accumulation. However, an individual family may regard payment of FICA taxes as purchasing a future interest not significantly different from that which could be acquired through personal saving. But FICA taxes finance no capital accumulation while personal saving does.

### 8.1.8    Transfers and Wages

In the administration of federal tax laws, cases come up commonly in which the issue is whether a payment is subject to gift tax payable by the payor or to income tax payable by the payee. Decisions in these cases turn on whether the transaction is a transfer or compensation. If the recipient modified his behavior in some significant manner with the expectation of receiving the payment, the presumption is that the receipt is compensation. In fact, much of inheritances and gifts received is earned income; a larger fraction is earned than one would infer applying the rules which the courts use.

In a more romantic age, Robin Hood took from the rich and gave to the poor. Modern day robbin' hoods take from rich and poor and keep it all. In suits for restitution initiated by persons who have been swindled, for example, the IRS may interpose a tax lien, asserting that the value of the property appropriated is earned income of the swindler on which income tax is payable. The courts are rather inclined to regard the transaction as a transfer on which neither gift nor income tax is due.

From time to time suggestions are made for including AFDC payments in the Personal Income Tax base. The Personal Income Tax essentially is a tax on factor incomes before tax. Thus, unless one is proposing a fundamental redefinition of the tax base, inclusion of AFDC payments must rest on an argument that they are a factor income. If the children are regarded as wards of the state and the mothers as hired caretakers, then one may argue that AFDC payments are wage income. If we assume that the mothers enjoy their children as do other parents, no deductions for outlays on the children would be allowed and the entire grant would be taxable compensation. From this perspective AFDC does not necessarily reduce compensated work effort; it may increase the total. But it changes the form; the mothers, instead of supplying labor outside the house, work at home. The taxes which finance AFDC payments may not be transfers. Present generation income tax payors may be investing in exemptions from military service for their children or in additional FICA taxpayers to pay the taxes which will assure that

OASI grants will be maintained when the present active generation retires.

These examples are intended to suggest that wages and transfers cannot be distinguished with much precision. I have mentioned economic rents as a component of wage income. These economic rents do not affect decisions to work a little more or less except through their effect on total income. But the neglect of accruals of wage income through the accumulation of pension rights may distort estimates of the relationships of labor supply, consumption and saving to total income or to wage income because either the dependent or independent variables or both have been mismeasured. To assume in behavioral analysis that what is usually called wage income is earned (has an opportunity cost) and what is usually called transfer income is unearned is to invite confusion. Estimated labor supply responses will be in error if the measured marginal wage income in fact is nonwage income or if the true marginal wage income is erroneously classified as transfer income.

### 8.1.9   Transfers and Property Income

Old-fashioned socialists asserted that property income is theft. New-fangled socialists recognize that the old conclusions remain as valid as ever if property income is subsumed under the more general heading of transfers. In the period in which they are received, property incomes are economic rents and, hence, transfers.

In one essential respect property incomes cannot be distinguished from deferred compensation. Both are legally enforceable rights to command over the outputs of future periods. These rights are acquired ultimately through saving out of current period income. But they are enforceable only under law. Thus, both those who expect property incomes and those who expect to receive current period earnings in future periods must look to government for their assurances. Their claims are never any better than the guarantees which government provides. Their claims indeed may be worth very little if the government is irresponsible with the money supply or is overturned by redistributing revolutionaries, who are given to viewing all property income as "earned" by capitalists only through the efforts made by capitalists to maintain control of government.

### 8.1.10   Income and Wealth Transfers

Transfers of income are transfers of present interests, that is, rights to dispose over current period output. In statistical practice, the period usually is the calendar year. Transfers of wealth are transfers of future interests. Future interests may be classified with respect to transferability and contingency. The right to receive property income typically is transferable and noncontingent. Property income receivable under a trust may be qualified with respect to transferability and may be contingent upon the satisfaction of certain conditions. The right to receive pension income typically is contingent upon attaining an age at which pensions are payable, being disabled, becoming unemployed or dying (in the case of a survivor pension) and may be contingent upon other circumstances, such as quitting employment with a firm or industry or, as with OASDI, leaving the wage labor force. Pension rights typically are not directly transferable.

Present interests can be converted into future interests at some rate of interest and future interests can be converted into present interests at some rate of discount. The rate at which any particular interest can be converted is a market rate for that interest and that conversion. In any period, a family may convert present interests to future, future interests to present, both or neither. A family converts present interests to future interests by buying physical or financial assets or own debt held by others; it converts future interests to present interests by selling physical or financial assets or own debt. Subject to certain qualifications, if all families in any period sought to convert all of their future interests to present interests, market discount rates would rise until the value of all future interests fell to zero. However, usually some families are converting one way and others another and indeed most families in any period are converting both ways.

What is interesting for our purposes is that the structure of asset markets is quite complex and not all families have equal access to all markets. To simplify, assume that rates of return on real assets for each family are equal to some lending rate to which it has access. We may relate family lending and borrowing rates to family permanent income as in the illustrative graph in figure 8.1. Federal and state tax treatment of property income and interest expense affects the shape of these curves. Their location for any family is affected by age and sex of head, race and other factors.[4]

The curves shown in figure 8.1, with the indicated and other qualifications, describe families' opportunity cost of funds. Suppose that a family has occasion to raise funds in some period. If it is rich, it should borrow; if it is poor, it should sell assets. Alas, poor families have few assets to sell and the lending curve tends to become undefined below an income which I have indicated as $Y_1$. Thus, poor families borrow but at higher rates than do rich families.

The point is that the cost (positive or negative) of shifting funds between periods varies from one family to another, depending upon family income and other circumstances. Given that a family has some expected flow of future income, we cannot know what the present value to the family is of that flow until we know its opportunity cost of funds, the

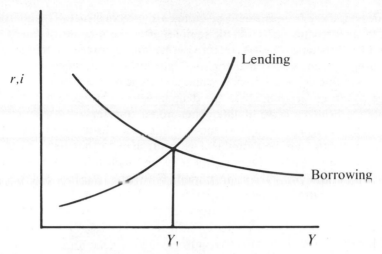

**Fig. 8.1**          The Relation of Family Lending and Borrowing Rates to Permanent Income

lower of its accessible lending or borrowing rates. It is incorrect to use an interest or discount rate that may be appropriate for another family or even for the average of all families unless one has an effective way of controlling for implicit weighting. Furthermore, rates which are appropriate for transferable interests are not necessarily appropriate for nontransferable interests. One would suppose that the transferable are lower because generally transferable interests are more valuable than nontransferable. By the same token, noncontingent interests are worth more than contingent.

### 8.1.11   Intragenerational and Intergenerational Transfers

Transfers may be within or between generations. Generations may be defined in terms of relationships or of age cohorts. Defined in terms of relationships, there may be at any time a generation of grandparents, a generation of parents and a generation of children. Defined as age cohorts, there may be the class of all persons aged 65 or more, those aged 18 to 64 and those under 18. We can specify age cohort generations such that there is not a significant number of two relational generations in a cohort. Fifteen years certainly is adequate and twenty might do.

The problem with relational generations is that they require the collection of data on a large number of possible relationships of persons in one household to persons in other households. Samples must be sufficiently large that the relationships among persons in the sample are representative of the relationships in the total population. The sample could be smaller if they were drawn from frames which had all of the relationships but these frames would be quite costly to construct. The alternative is the construction of synthetic samples after the manner of Guy Orcutt and his associates (1976). Otherwise, we are restricted to an age cohort concept of generations and for some purposes this is adequate.

Given that there are transfers and that some of these could be between age cohort generations, then the diagram shown in figure 8.2 may indicate the primary flows of intergenerational transfers.

In this scheme, $S$ is support and $G$ is gifts. The distinction between support and gifts may be thought of as equivalent to that between income and wealth transfers. Support is a transfer which normally is consumed within an income accounting period. Gifts are transfers not normally consumed entirely in one accounting period. Gifts in this usage include bequests. Bequests, of course, are made by living persons and differ from other transfers only in having in each individual case an indeterminate although determinable effective date.

The flows of transfers are between minors $(K)$, nonaged adults $(A)$ and aged adults $(O)$. If we regard persons under 18 as minors and persons 65 years of age and older as aged, then the nonaged adults are 18 through 64. Within the age range 18 through 64, there may be three relational generations; in the open ended class of aged, there may be two; in the under 18 class, there may be one, if for each class we ignore statistically insignificant higher orders. Transfers between relational generations within an age cohort are treated as intragenerational transfers in the three-cohort classification suggested.

For the most part, the flows $A$ to $K$ are completed within nuclear family groupings and those $O$ to $K$, $A$ to $O$ and $O$ to $A$ within extended family groupings. These direct flows primarily of provision of goods and services are intergenerational flows. They are mainly income flows. The allocation of total flows between income and wealth transactions depends upon how one chooses to treat education and health expenditures by parents on their children. Assuming an accounting period as long as one year, doubtless no one would treat expenditures for children's food and

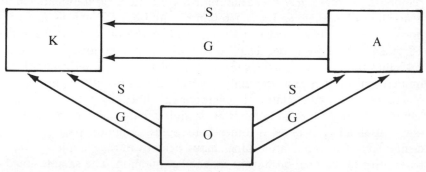

**Fig. 8.2**          Flows of Intergenerational Transfers

clothing as wealth transactions. The basic analytic problem in transactions within families is what part should be regarded as transfers from adults to children and what part should be regarded as consumption by the adults. In contrast to direct flows, mediated flows do not raise so serious an issue of adult consumption, except in the flows $A$ to $O$. Nonaged adults, in paying Social Security and income taxes to support aged adults through OASI and SSI, may be substituting mediated for direct intergenerational transfers. If having the old folks in the house is a nuisance but the old folks would prefer to live with their children, the transactions are compensation for the abatement of a nuisance and all gain.

## 8.2    Transfers and Saving

In this section I want to consider an issue in government policy: does the availability of transfers, particularly intergenerational transfers, reduce saving. The questions that come up are the following. (1) Does the promise of AFDC, legally enforceable if eligibility is established, discourage poor young women and perhaps poor young men from making the human capital investments which could make them self-supporting? (2) If OASI discourages saving, do not SSI and Veteran Pensions also? (3) If OASI reduces saving, would not employee pensions do so equally when plans have become fully funded? (4) Should not bequests be taxed at a 100 percent rate in order to avoid the discouraging effect of inheritances on saving? In each case, we are concerned with the relationship of transfers, direct or mediated, to saving. The general case is this: if a person has a reasonably well defined consumption ambition (or standard of living), any income expectation will contribute to the satisfaction of that ambition. An expected increase in income from private or public inheritances or an expected reduction in transfers out will enable the person to maintain his standard of living with less saving or lesser earnings from sales of labor services or capital rentals. In this paper, I am considering effects on saving of only one form of public inheritance, a pension.

### 8.2.1    Saving Models

There are two general classes of family saving models: the extended family model and the nuclear family model.

*Extended Family Model*

An extended family usually is thought of as a multigenerational household in which the nonaged adults support the old and the young in a succession of age cohort duties to support and rights to receive support. In practice, each person in a family is expected to do his best; the young who receive full support are very young and the old are very old. Some persons in the family, the disabled, the not so old and not so young, make partial contributions to their support. However, members of an extended family need not all live together in one household. Genuine extended families from antiquity have maintained members in distant abodes for long periods as traders, branch bankers, missionaries, students, and so on. The essential condition for a family to be an extended family is that the association of persons include at least three generations with substantial transfers of income within some relevant time frame between the nonaged adults and the aged adults and from the adults to the children. There are other associations of persons, such as associations of adult siblings, which may be referred to as extended families but they do not have the same analytic implications as the multiple generation family and should be called perhaps communes. Doubtless in almost all extended families the members are related by blood or marriage. Furthermore, the economic relationships among the members in the main are quid pro quo exchanges. For short periods of time, such as one year, it is recognition of duties and rights to support and not actual transfer transactions which define the association as an extended family.

If an extended family is large enough or has brought over adequate resources from the past, it need not save for consumption averaging purposes. It may, of course, save for estate building purposes. Now, if a family is self-insuring against the risks of unemployment and disability due to illness, injury or old age and perhaps does not need to insure against an unfavorable shift in the age composition of its membership, the introduction of a compulsory comprehensive scheme of social insurance will leave it overinsured. It cannot compensate by reducing its saving. If it is saving for estate building or human capital formation, it can build faster by reducing or changing the direction of intrafamily transfers but, in any event, it can reach its desired level of risk-protection only through reducing or redirecting intrafamily transfers. Indeed, the overinsured argument was that made by certain religious sects in protesting coverage under OASDHI and, were we sure that they could keep their close-knit extended families from coming unraveled, the argument would be sufficient for leaving them out.

Robert Barro (1977) has attempted to infer indirectly the effect of Social Security transfers on intrafamily transfers. The data used were macro time series constructed by BEA or others using similar methods. With all variables measured in annual real per capita units, he regresses consumer expenditures on (a) disposable personal income, current and lagged one year, (b) net corporate retained earnings, (c) surplus of the government sector, (d) net stocks of capital or net wealth, (e) consumer durables and (f) Social Security (OASI) wealth or Social Security

(OASDHI) benefits. To these independent variables he adds (g) an average annual unemployment rate. He finds that the effect on consumer expenditure of either Social Security wealth or benefits using either the stock of capital or net worth is not significantly different from zero. Thus, the effect on saving is not significant and family adjustments over the period since the 1920s to the introduction of Social Security must have been substitutions of mediated for direct transfers. The substitutions could have been made through (a) reduced transfers from non-aged to aged adults, (b) larger transfers (gifts and bequests) from aged to nonaged adults that compensate them for the negative wealth effect of FICA taxes or (c) larger transfers from nonaged adults to children in order to enhance their earning capacity and thus reduce the burden of FICA taxes which they will pay when grown to finance the benefits their parents will receive.

There are observations which lend credence to Barro's inferences. For example, with the growth of OASI grants, old people have tended increasingly to live in their own rather than their children's households. That is presumptive evidence of a reduction in intrafamily exchange and transfer transactions. One would expect adjustments to the introduction of OASI to take the form partially of family reorganizations and it should be possible to identify these reorganizations in part from Current Population Surveys since the late 1940s and from the consumer expenditure survey at about the time that OAI went into effect. However, it is the amount and direction of transfer flows that define adjustments and these cannot be identified in the microdata. Implicit evidence now is all that we shall ever have for the past. Not even retrospective surveying could capture these distant past adjustments now. Nevertheless, the Barro evidence, although highly implicit, is support for his conclusions. It does not eliminate a third alternative: that people made no adjustments either to direct transfers or to saving.

Uncertain evidence as the Barro estimates are, there are problems of specification. Barro regresses consumer expenditure, a realization accounting concept, on BEA disposable income, also basically a realization accounting concept. But Barro then mixes realization and accrual accounting by introducing corporate retained earnings as a proxy for the current period accrual of capital gain on corporate shares. Accrual of gain on noncorporate real estate is reflected in the capital stock or net worth variables. The Barro model in common with all models estimated on macro time series data is quite sensitive to specification error, as he recognizes. Dropping the unemployment variable, he gets results comparable to those of Feldstein when estimating a similar model on similar data; that is, Social Security wealth reduces saving. Keeping the unemployment variable, he gets estimates for the Social Security wealth coefficients that are not significant. The basic problem is the data. In the

National Income Accounts there are the misclassifications of transactions and other measurement errors which I consider in section 8.1 and suggest in section 8.3 could be avoided in suitably planned microdata collection. But, in addition, the techniques of estimation used in the construction of BEA and related macro time series introduce such high orders of autocorrelation in each series and serial correlation between series that the data give a researcher little help in choosing among competing hypotheses. Within each of Barro's several sets of equations, the $R^2$s differ only in the third and fourth places and, for two sets, round to 1.0 at the third digit. No one can believe that the world is really that thoroughly determined.

### Nuclear Family Model

A nuclear family includes at most two generations and one but no more than two adults. If there are two adults, they are related by marriage, somehow defined. The family may or may not include minor children. One adult living alone is a nuclear family. This definition of nuclear family together with the extended family definition of the previous section leaves some persons in limbo. If minors living alone are considered adults, all in limbo are living in associations of two or more persons and, as suggested in the previous section, these associations might be called communes. Communes would include persons living together in group quarters and in institutions. The reason for not putting these associations of persons in either of the classes of extended or nuclear families is the uncertainty about whether such units can be considered reasonably to have a lifetime consumption plan.

Extended families have consumption planning horizons which may be indefinite but at least are not bounded by the life expectancies of adult members at any time. Nor is the time path of income conditioned by the earning capacities of any one family member, if the family is sufficiently large and/or well-heeled. For nuclear families, saving (positive or negative) is a necessary device for averaging consumption over time. When income is higher than the cost of maintaining its standard of living, a family saves; when income is below the cost of the standard, it dissaves. If the standard is set realistically or the family suitably adjusts its work effort, it just breaks even over its life span, barring surprises. A typical pattern is for a family to save during its active years, but perhaps only after a child rearing period, and dissave in retirement.

For nuclear families, transfers are of no small consequence. There are, of course, the intrafamily transfers from parents to children. When the children leave the parent unit and go out to form nuclear families of their own, they do not go naked and alone. They begin their adult life with a complement of skills, attitudes and connections which can be converted into a stream of income. An intriguing idea in taxation is substitution of a lifetime cumulative inheritance tax for the present federal estate tax. The value of the initial endowments which children take from home would be the first term in the inheritance tax base. To avoid driving people back into extended family associations we might value the endowments at an arbitrary age, say 25. Keeping the Personal Income Tax, we would value the endowments at cost to the parents. Data on the cost of rearing children suggest that the Treasury would be enriched even at modest rates and an exemption equal to mean estimating error. Direct transfers between nuclear families are far from insignificant. They are merely grossly underestimated, in effect ignored, in available micro-data. If we are concerned about the effect of transfers on saving, we should pay some attention to direct transfers. Attention thus far has been directed only toward mediated transfers and not even to all of them.

There are two interesting sets of estimates of the effects of mediated transfers on saving. Both are in an implicit nuclear family context and both sets of estimates were made using microdata, a fact which by itself would make them interesting. The first study, by Martin Feldstein and Anthony Pellechio (1977), measures the effect of OASI on saving. The second, by Alicia Munnell (1976), measures the effect of employee pensions on saving, along with the impact of OASI. The models in both cases are variants of the Ando-Modigliani lifetime consumption (or saving) model. Current period saving by each family is regressed on the family's current period labor income, its expected future labor income and its holding of net wealth. Wealth enters the equations in two (or three) components: (a) noncontingent, transferable wealth, (b) OASI wealth and (c) employee pension wealth, Munnell only. With respect to OASI, the two studies come out at about the same place. OASI grants substitute for personal saving approximately dollar for dollar in lifetime planning models. Private pension grants apparently substitute somewhat less well.

At first glance, these results are something of a mystery. They suggest that people regard contingent and nontransferable future interests as almost or equally as good as noncontingent and transferable future interests. Yet, when a young man receives an inheritance we do not observe him in the typical case running off to a life insurance company to buy a life annuity beginning at age 65 and subject to the restrictions to which company or OASI pension rights are. The results, thus, would seem to require some interpretation. Perhaps, for the purposes for which income averaging saving is undertaken at all, contingent and nontransferable wealth serves essential purposes. Allowing for asset management expenses and temptations to fritter away the estate, it may be even better than noncontingent and transferable wealth. We know next to nothing about people's attitudes toward holding assets of various types. Relative market rates of return give us average opinions but only for traded assets.

Every family, we may suppose, has certain saving objectives. One of these may be maintenance of a standard of living in retirement (or, more generally, in the event of any interruption in wage income). A family may be able to satisfy this objective by holding assets specialized to the purpose, that is, pension rights. To the extent that this is so, we may observe both lifetime net zero and lifetime positive savers trading the accumulation of other types of claims on future output for pension rights. This merely recognizes that the purchase, for example, of a life annuity beginning at age 65 may make satisfactory provision for contingencies which are of consequence only as long as one lives after age 65. We might expect, as the Feldstein and Pellechio and Munnell estimates suggest, that lifetime net zero savers would hold only pension wealth and that lifetime positive savers would hold at least some. For either to hold pension wealth, they must have access to these claims. Given access, the choice of how much pension wealth a family can hold typically is severely constrained. It is likely that there are families some of whom hold less and others more of this wealth than they would were they able to choose without constraint.

For some families, and perhaps for most families to some extent, the nontransferability of pension claims may give pensions an advantage over other claims. Pension claims, thus, are not unlike spendthrift trusts. Restrictions on dissipation may be not only accepted but welcomed by persons covered by pension plans, as they often are by spendthrifts, as protection from their own too generous dispositions. It may be convenient but certainly it is unnecessary to assert that the persons holding pension claims care nothing for their potential heirs. This is not necessarily true even of those persons who hold only pension wealth. These people may make *inter vivos* donations of human and nonhuman capital to their children and others which satisfy any reasonable bequeathing motive. And holders of other claims may do so for motives of control or of social status and in fact care nothing for potential heirs.

A final advantage is the tax treatment of pension relative to other saving. Where the option is available, a given financial contingency can be provided for with less sacrifice of current consumption through pension than through other saving. In the case of OASI, half of contributions and all of implicit earnings on total contributions are in effect saving out of before-tax income and benefits are received tax free. For employee plans, some and typically all of contributions and all of earnings are saving out of before-tax income and benefits are taxable as received. Allocations of income to personal saving, in contrast, are out of after-tax income and earnings are taxed as they accrue; spending from accumulated balances is tax free. Thus, as compared with personal saving, saving through employee plans permits tax deferral and through OASI exemption of income from tax. Implicitly, the Feldstein and Pellechio and the Munnell measured substitution elasticities reflect these relative tax treatments. Taking into account explicitly and accurately the relative tax treatments would require better data than are now available.

### 8.2.2    Generalizing the Estimates

Both Feldstein and Pellechio and Munnell generalize their results to the estimation of the effects of pension plans on aggregate national saving. The generalizations are of doubtful validity. The question raised by Barro remains unanswered: do pensions substitute for personal saving or for transfers? The issue is not easily resolved because the substitution of pensions for direct transfers is confounded with changes in family organization and the participation of individuals in the wage labor and nonwage labor forces. For extended families without pension plans, entry into the labor force and retirement are less well defined than for nuclear families with pension plans. In a lifetime planning model for nuclear families, labor supply decisions and savings decisions are related through the effect of labor supply decisions on the amount of income which may be allocated to consumption averaging in any period and through the length of time over which savings may be accumulated. For extended families, one substitutes transfers for savings in these relationships. The relationship between labor supply and consumption decisions is recognized by Barro, Feldstein and Pellechio and Munnell but none accounts adequately for the likely variation in the relationship that is associated with differences in family organization. Feldstein and Pellechio and Munnell recognize that there is a problem and the problem is the whole point of Barro's analysis but available data will not permit an explicit treatment.

A second limitation on generalization is that both the Feldstein and Pellechio and Munnell estimates are for only subsets of the population. From the total Survey of Financial Characteristics of Consumers sample, Feldstein and Pellechio screen out high and low income units, young and old, the self-employed and units with female heads. They run their regressions on middle income units with middle-aged male heads who indicated in the survey that they planned no bequests. Munnell introduces a variable into her equations for National Longitudinal Survey men aged 45-59 in 1966 to indicate whether they did or did not intend to make bequests. Either procedure is a way, although crude, of classifying survey respondents into lifetime savers and nonsavers. Munnell probably had an inadequate representation of lifetime nonzero savers in her sample; she casts out five rather obvious nonzero savers. The bequesting variable is significant in all equations and, thus, if a unit intends a bequest, its saving will be greater, other things equal. Nevertheless, however good the estimates may be for families with middle-aged male heads, they may not accurately reflect the behavior of other families.

A third limitation is that substitutions among forms of saving have differential effects on flows of funds to loan markets. One dollar saved by a family in the purchase of a noncontingent, transferable future interest adds one dollar to the flow of funds available to finance capital accumulation. One dollar saved through an employee pension plan may add much less than one dollar to that flow of funds. Pension capital markets saving is done not by families but by pension plans. Not all pension plans are advance funded; some other than OASDHI are current funded and, hence, save nothing. A plan that is advance funded will not save if (a) it has funded all past service obligations and (b) it has a stable membership. Strictly, there are a few other conditions on zero saving but the point is that plans make funds available to capital markets only when they are striving to satisfy a funding standard. Were plans to adopt an endowment standard of funding, as Feldstein has suggested for OASI, that would set off a new saving process even for plans now fully advance funded. Thus it is that a family may substitute one dollar of pension saving for other saving but the pension plan drop less than one dollar into the capital accumulation kitty.

Fourth, we must recognize that apart from the degree of funding, pension plans are a more efficient device than personal saving for insuring against interruptions in wage income. If each family is self-insuring, each will feel impelled to provide for something approaching the worst case. But a group plan can play the odds and finance payments to those of its members who suffer the most costly experience (for example, live the longest in retirement) from the excess contributions made by those members of the group who have the least costly outcomes. So a shift in provision for interruptions of income from individual to group plans will reduce national saving even in a lifetime zero saving model.

In principle, we need to account independently for changes in family organization and the substitution of saving for transfers, the inherent efficiency of group income averaging plans and the degree of plan funding of accruing liabilities. The amount which plans save even if they are funding properly will not be equal to the increase in the present value of pension assets as viewed by families. What we can expect is that growth of pension coverage will reduce aggregate saving, for a given level of income security. The question is, how much? Estimating merely the effect of accruing pension claims on other saving by families overstates the effect. Measuring the offsets to this effect is not easy. If we had the data, we could construct and estimate a model which would show what substitution elasticity is compatible with no change in the aggregate saving rate. Then if we should find that we can affect the substitution elasticity through tax policy, we would have a rule for the optional taxation of pension saving.

## 8.3   New Data

In sections 8.1 and 8.2 I have attempted to define a policy analysis problem. The results of section 8.2 reveal an unsatisfactory state of knowledge. Actually, we do not know what is the effect of pension saving on total saving. The purpose of this section is to suggest a remedy.

Like all arguments, this one starts from an axiom: if you want to know what people have done and why, go out and ask them. The Census Bureau survey program, merely deficient on the what, is hopeless on the why. Yet survey questions on motives are not hypothetical nor are respondents without readily retrievable information. Because it is possible to ask meaningful questions on motives, policy analysts need not be forced to fit behavior into always oversimplified rational action models. What we need is a responsive survey vehicle. It should be a flexible instrument which permits appropriate respondents to be selected and the right questions to be asked of them for any of a wide range of intensive data collection efforts. Routinized data collection for the construction of time series is the bane of policy analysis. This paper tries to make persuasive the case for a job order survey program by developing one of many examples of policy problems whose resolution requires a one-time data collection effort.

### 8.3.1   Interfamily and Intrafamily Transfers

In the analysis of the effects of pension saving on total personal saving our most basic data requirement is for information on transfers of income between or among persons. The larger are interview units (the more inclusive the concept of the family), the more these transfers will be intrafamily, and the smaller are interview units (the more exclusive the concept of the family), the more these transfers will be interfamily. Interfamily or intrafamily, the transfers to be measured are those which serve the purpose for a family of averaging consumption over time or, more accurately, reducing the variance in the consumptions of a series of time periods. It is these transfers which substitute for pension and other saving. What we want are cross-section data on transfers and pension and nonpension saving for persons with and without pension coverage. We can measure accurately the effect of pension saving on total saving only if we can control for transfers. The extended family is not extinct and a useful survey would enable an analyst to control for degrees of extendedness through measured interfamily and intrafamily transfers. It may be that the transfer effect is not significant but it is better scientific procedure to measure the effect than merely to assert that it is of no consequence.

At the least, we must control for family organization. Without this, there is no way to measure accurately an entirely appropriate concept of transfers. We would find ourselves attempting to measure the value of the consumption of a live-in grandmother net of the value of the child care and other services which she provides. But we must recognize that a more inclusive family normally will have a smaller savings requirement than a less inclusive one. The more inclusive family has more degrees of freedom in averaging income over family members. It has a lower level of uncovered risk. Other things, such as age, sex composition and self-employment being equal, we would expect large families to save less, at least per head, than small ones. The rates at which large and small families substitute pension and other saving likely differ. If large families can more nearly meet their requirements for income averaging through direct as opposed to mediated transfers, they should be less willing to trade pension for other saving; their other saving will be prompted more strongly than for small families by considerations other than reduction of the variance in consumption over time.

But we can collect some information on the financial relationships of members of a household and the financial relationships between those persons and persons in all other households in the world. If persons in one household are making transfers to a person in another household, it is the transfer that is significant. The fact that the recipient is the wife's third cousin, twice removed, whatever that may mean, is of subordinate importance. There is no doubt that eliciting accurate responses to questions on interpersonal transfers will not be easy. Payments made for the upkeep of paramours or of love children kept out of sight may not be known to the respondent or, if known, a source of some embarrassment. Of course, one would not ask of each respondent, "Do you keep a paramour?" One might ask (a) "Did this family last year make any payments directly to persons in other families?" (b) "If so, what was the amount of payment to each person?" (c) "What is the relationship of that person to persons in this family?" (d) "What was the reason for the payment?" This suggested approach no doubt would miss much of the payments to paramours, which in the main, perhaps, are consumption and not transfers. It should yield reliable data on transfers and purchases of services which are free of moral taint and those surely are most of such payments.

### 8.3.2    Transfers Out and Consumption

Payments made by a family and not otherwise classifiable are either transfers or consumption expenditures but it is not always apparent which. However, questions may be asked in a survey which will assist in a proper classification. Thus, for example, one might ask about the frequency of church attendance. If attendance is frequent, payments to the church might be classified as consumption expenditures (purchases of church services); if infrequent, as transfers. Property taxes paid by families which have children in elementary or secondary government schools might be classified as consumption expenditures; by other families, as transfers. This is, of course, too simple because property taxes buy government services other than schooling.

Questions can be asked which would enable us to make inferences with some confidence as to whether an apparent transfer transaction was in fact an exchange transaction or not. Although these inferences cannot be made with high confidence, any improvement over present practice would be welcome. In current tax and statistical accounting, transfers out through taxes are overstated and consumption expenditures are understated and, in the treatment of contributions of many sorts, consumption expenditures are understated in tax accounting and overstated in statistical accounting. Consumption expenditures, of course, include consumer surpluses (transfers in) and monopoly rents paid (transfers out possibly but not necessarily) but the failure to identify these transfers does not have so great a distorting effect in analyses of family economic decisions as the arbitrary classification of all taxes as transfers out, even though they buy personal consumption goods and services; all charitable contributions as consumption outlays, even though they are made under duress and buy only peace of mind; and all outlays by a family on consumption goods and services as consumption expenditures, even though the family is making in-kind contributions to the support of persons in another family.

Classifying what are properly consumption expenditures as transfers out, we understate family disposable income and understate family consumption. If the classification errors were uniform over all families, the errors introduced into estimated behavioral parameters would not be serious. But the classification errors are not uniform. The transfer element in payments to churches probably is substantially greater for the rich than for the poor. But it is in the misclassification of state and local taxes that the confounding of effects in the data is a major impediment to statistical analysis. In present practice, the family with a child in a private school has a larger consumption outlay than another otherwise the same with a child in a government school. The proportion of a family's state and local taxes which is properly a consumption outlay depends upon a number of attributes but the variation over families otherwise similar is quite large.

### 8.3.3   Transfers Out and Saving

The first problem is whether employee pension contributions should be classified as taxes or saving. If a person as a condition for employment must allocate a part of his wage income to a pension plan and the pension credits which he purchases with his contributions are worth nothing to him, the payments in effect are taxes and not saving. That he may later revalue the credits is another matter. The valuation of pension credits I take up in section 8.3.6, although valuation of the credits is the prior issue. The classification problem arises in the treatment of employee pension contributions where a person does not have effective access to jobs not entailing employee contributions and, in certain circumstances, employer contributions. In the simplest case, the issue is whether FICA contributions are taxes or saving. It is possible that for the young worker they are taxes, for mid-career workers partly taxes and partly saving and are fully saving only for older workers, such as those included in the Munnell data base. It may be, of course, that the contributions are in fact transfers out which substitute for other transfers out (the support of aged parents) which need not be made because FICA contributions are being made. For either case, the crucial question is each person's attitude toward the payments made. In an analysis of family spending decisions we want to know whether pension contributions are an allocation of income or a constraint: does the budget to be allocated include income before pension contributions or after pension contributions? This need not remain a conundrum. We can ask survey respondents questions which reveal their attitudes toward pension contributions.

A second but not unrelated problem is whether saving should be measured on an accrual or realization accounting. Pension saving has little meaning outside an accrual accounting framework. Pension saving may be measured in one or the other of two ways. As a first measure, we may take plan contributions by employer and employee plus current period earnings on accumulated funds that are attributable to an employee. An alternative measure which may yield quite different results is to take the difference between beginning and end of period valuations which a family makes of its accumulated pension credits. Both are accrual concepts. Relating pension saving measured either way to realized income, total budget allocations may exceed or fall short of the budget to be allocated. So we require measurements of incomes and outlays which are consistently on accrual accounting. This isn't impossible; merely difficult. Adding to employee income employer plan contributions and plan earnings, two major elements of accrual income neglected in a realization accounting, would entail two-stage surveying. We would administer a questionnaire to families and, for those with plan coverage, send a questionnaire to their employers asking for employer contributions on behalf of the covered worker and the worker's share of plan earnings. From an interest in evaluating employee attitudes toward pensions we might ask the employer (or the insurance company) for the value of the employee's pension accumulation, although as I point out in section

8.3.6 it is the employee's valuation, not the plan's valuation of the pension accumulation, that is relevant in any explanation of employee saving behavior.

### 8.3.4    Transfers In and Wages

In the estimation of a lifetime saving equation, one introduces a current period wage income variable in order to sort people into comparable stages of their lifetime income paths. One introduces an unemployment variable to sort people into those who are on their paths from those who are off their paths in the current period. Another variable, expected lifetime wage income, sorts people into path levels. The current and expected income variables together identify the path in "normal" cases. Expected lifetime wage income for most families determines their lifetime consumption plan. The income pattern together with the consumption plan determines current period saving. What has been left out thus far is the influence of wealthholdings and property income, which I take up in section 8.3.5, and whether a family is or is not a lifetime net zero saving unit, which I take up in section 8.3.7.

Estimated relationships depend upon the accuracy with which wage income is measured. Current survey data enable us to make certain reclassifications. We can, if we wish, reclassify AFDC as wage income. We would do less well reclassifying alimony and child support as wage income. Only by arbitrary rules can we reclassify wage income as property income. Reclassifications can be improved by collecting income data in sufficient detail. For the rest, it is a matter of collecting data which give us a basis for inferring whether an income receipt is wages, a transfer or a participation in profits.

Current survey data give us very little information for valuing and adding to family wage income the wage income of members that is earned in home production. An obvious expedient is to classify families into units of (a) one earner, one adult; (b) one earner, two adults; and (c) two earners, and estimate for each class separately. Imputing home wage income to family income is a preferable procedure but only if it can be done with reasonable accuracy. The basic problem is valuation. There are two valuation rules: opportunity cost (what the home worker could earn in the best alternative employment) and replacement cost (what it would cost to hire persons outside the home to perform each of the several tasks). With relevant information on the home worker, the opportunity cost valuation is feasible. It might be possible to make replacement cost valuations by using data collected for families which hire much help to impute costs to families which hire little.

Current survey wage income fails to include quite a bit of realized market wage income, such as employer contributions to life and health insurance plans and the value of employee consumption paid for by employers. If these errors of measurement were distributed uniformly over all employees, estimated relationships would be wrong only by a constant. The distribution, however, is far from uniform and policy prescriptions are likely to go astray on implicit weighting effects. But, not only is there missing realized income; data now collected do not enable us to construct an accrual concept of wage income for families. The main missing element is employer contributions to and earnings of pension plans, including OASDHI, or, alternatively, the change in the present value of pension rights less own current contributions. To combine a wealth variable or variables which include pension wealth with a current wage income variable which does not include employer contributions to plans will bias the effects on saving both of wealth currently held and of labor income. But only better data will make it possible to correct the error.

From current survey data we have no information on expected income. For estimating lifetime savings models, the practice is to infer expected income from recent past income and other information. The inferred expected income may vary widely from family expectations because the family has information and attitudes toward the future which are not taken into account. Yet it is not unreasonable to ask people questions about their income expectations. There is nothing hypothetical in such questions. What we want is each family's expectation. That is the relevant information. What we may guess is their objective expectation is not relevant. They act on the basis of their expectations however inaccurate or even logically inconsistent those expectations may appear.

### 8.3.5   Property and Property Income

Property income usually does not enter explicitly into lifetime saving models. Net wealth currently held enters as an element of total resources available to support the consumption plan. A family, of course, cannot spend both principal and interest but it can spend the interest as long as the principal is held and spend the principal at the sacrifice of the interest. In the extreme case, there may be a few families which finance their consumption plans entirely from property income. If they neither add to nor subtract from the capital, they are lifetime net zero savers. In the design of lifetime saving models there seems to be some uncertainty about the proper treatment of property income. If it is to be included explicitly, then it needs to be measured.

In family survey data now available property income is seriously underreported and apparently in a very nonuniform manner (McClung, Koenig, Barkerding 1973). We have two usable surveys of wealth in the past two decades, the latest over ten years old. Apart from their age, both surveys, but especially the Survey of Economic Opportunity, have major shortcomings. Except for the Surveys of Financial Characteristics of Consumers and of Changes in Family Finances, the survey sample frames were or are inappropriate. Because of that and nonresponse, the surveys miss the rich and much of their income and wealth. The samples should be drawn from lists of persons whose income at least is known. It may not be possible to reduce nonresponse very much but it is possible to use more effectively information collected from respondents together with information from administrative records to impute missing income and wealth to nonrespondents.

There is one very important source of income on which the surveys make no attempt to collect data. This is the current period accrual of capital gains. Logically, in a savings model, the current accrual of capital gain appears on both sides of the equation: it is a component of income and a component of saving. Failure to include the current accrual of gain on both sides of the equation will yield an unbiased estimate of the parameter relating saving to income only if the true value of that parameter is 1.0. Accruals of capital gains are substitutable for other saving. A person may provide for his retirement or meet other savings objectives as well through accruals of gain as through other saving, allowance being made for uncertainty. Most families with substantial accruals of gain no doubt are not lifetime zero savers, but the Treasury at least, good shepherd that it is, is more concerned with those which are outside that fold than with those which are safely within. To measure current accruals of capital gains we need observations on beginning and end of period market values and current period net transactions. With gross transactions we could relate gain realizations to accruals. This does not necessarily imply two interviews. Two interviews might improve the quality of the responses, but if two interviews improve the second response more than the first, one interview may measure changes in values better.

### 8.3.6    Valuation of Future Interests

There are two rules for valuing assets (or debts). The first is to use current market values. The second is to discount to the present the stream of future net incomes (or outlays). These two rules would yield identical results were capital markets perfect. Capital markets not being perfect, a choice must be made. Regarding assets (or debts) as positive (or negative) resources for financing consumption plans, one encounters a logical problem in aggregating market values; not everyone could sell his assets without driving prices to zero or call his debts without causing prices to rise very high. In microanalysis, there is no problem because we consider the affairs of but one family; the affairs of all others are assumed to remain unchanged. In the case of discount values, there is a question of whether streams of net income would continue if no one were willing to pay anything for them. In real terms, some streams would continue. Only the stark empiricist would insist that a flower is less fragrant because it wastes its fragrance on the desert air. Nevertheless, metaphysics aside, the custom in analysis of saving decisions is to use discount values primarily because certain forms of wealth, not being traded, have no market value.

The difficulty in using present values of future interests is finding the correct rates of discount. Theoretical analyses run in terms of time rates of discount weighted by various risk factors. A person's rate of discount for time and risk is not directly observable but in equilibrium it is equal to a market yield. Market yields are observable but vary from one lender and borrower to another. An obvious solution and one which avoids any assumptions about the perfection of capital markets and errors of implicit weighting is to ask survey respondents what they paid for funds raised recently. If they borrowed, that is the borrowing rate; if they sold assets, it is the lending rate sacrificed. If the family both borrowed and sold assets or borrowed at several rates or sold assets with different sacrificed yields, we might take a weighted average of the rates as the measure of its opportunity cost of funds. Having asked these questions, we could then discount future incomes and outlays at rates which are appropriate to each family.

That is one way out. There is another. It is simply to ask families to value their assets and debts. Now we will worry of course that the families will not get the values right; that is, they will not assign the value to an asset that we would assign or that the market has assigned to it. But a family is as rich as it thinks it is and makes its consumption and savings decisions with reference to its subjective wealth, not its objective wealth. Taking this way out, we get values directly and discount rates only implicitly. Since we have no interest in discount rates at least in this context, we lose nothing. We would still require rates for discounting expected wage income, unless we asked families for present values. The major difficulty with the procedure is assuring ourselves that the family decision makers are in fact agreed on subjective values. It will not do for the wife to think that the family has a net wealth of $100,000 and the husband to think that its wealth is $200,000. And this is true whether we interview husband or wife unless the one interviewed is a thoroughgoing autocrat. When we weight these subjective wealths, we will discover discrepancies between the resulting national estimates and estimates derived by other methods. However, we will not be able to say that the survey results are wrong, at least for behavioral analyses.

It is likely that people in general value noncontingent, transferable future interests at near their market value. The measurement problem there is that the respondent is not fully informed about the number of units in the stock held. But, with respect to contingent, nontransferable future interests, subjective valuations may differ markedly from objective valuations. The young possibly value retirement pensions, for example, at a fraction of their objective worth while persons close to the end of their working lives may overvalue them. A perfectly satisfactory reason for asking survey respondents for their valuations and, in addition, collecting data for making objective valuations is that we do not know how people value their assets and debts. We may be substantially in crror if we assume that they are well informed and completely objective.

### 8.3.7   Estate Building Plans

Presently we have very limited data on transfers by gift and bequest. The principal sources of these data are tax returns, on which the transfers are underreported. The Federal Gift Tax may be regarded as not a tax on gifts but a gift of tax to the federal government. The matching of Federal Estate Tax returns with decedent and heir Personal Income Tax returns, now being made by the IRS Statistics Division, will improve significantly our understanding of transfers by bequest for the approximately 7 percent of the population which leaves significant estates. It would be helpful to have more complete data on bequests and gifts.

However, for estimating a lifetime saving model, actual bequests and gifts paid are irrelevant. What we require is information on current plans for transferring wealth by gift and bequest. Essentially, it is plans for wealth transfers by bequest and gift which separate lifetime positive savers from lifetime zero savers. To the extent that gifts substitute for bequests, information on gifts assists in the classification. Again, much depends upon motives. Only from a knowledge of motives can we sort gifts from support. And the knowledge of motives can be acquired. A survey can ask respondents if they plan to make transfers in the future and, if so, whether the transfers are intended as consumption support or capital grants. Asking respondents about their transfer plans is a lot better than guessing that gifts made after some advanced age are an alternative to bequests and, hence, are capital grants and that transfers made prior to that age are consumption support or capital grants depending upon the size of the transfer. The fact is that each respondent has more relevant information than an analyst is likely to have. A person at age 30 who expects to die in a few years may make gifts which, however IRS auditors may later decide, in fact are in anticipation of death, and an 80-year-old who expects to live for 10 years more may not make gifts because he thinks that he has time remaining before the burden of proof shifts.

While we are asking respondents for their planned transfers out, we should ask them for actual and expected transfers in through inheritance, gift and support. Expected inheritances should affect current period saving in much the same way as expected wage income but, in any case, we make a mistake in supposing that they have no effect. Any effect, of course, applies only to that small fraction of the total population which expects to receive inheritances. However, that small population accounts for much of family saving. More generally, we should try to identify the sources of a family's acquisition of its current holdings of future interests. Future interests acquired through gift and inheritance and through current funded and mature advance funded pension plans contribute nothing to aggregate saving. Only accumulations out of current income have a full effect; accumulations through immature advance funded plans have a partial effect. In explaining family saving, we should try to separate out that saving which adds to the supply of funds available for capital accumulation from that saving which does not. Saving through a current funded pension plan, OASI for example, is genuine saving to a family paying FICA tax but, to a family in receipt of a pension, the transaction may be and possibly should be regarded as a transfer in. From the viewpoint of the national economy the transaction is entirely a transfer. If this macrotransfer reduces macrosaving through its effect on microaccumulations out of current income, then there is a cause for concern. That concern should find its first expression in the collection of better data for analysis of the issue.

## Notes

1. Martin Feldstein (1977) reviews research prior to 1978 and considers its implications for economic growth.

2. The survey program is being developed jointly by the Census Bureau and the Department of Health and Human Services. Under current plans, the survey program will become operational in 1982.

3. In U.S. Treasury Department 1977, there is an extended treatment of institutional concepts of income.

4. For an empirical analysis, see Eugene Steuerle 1975.

## References

Barro, Robert. 1977. "Social Security and Private Saving—Evidence from the U.S. Time Series." Mimeograph. University of Rochester.

Feldstein, Martin. 1977. "The Social Security Fund and National Capital Accumulation." In Federal Reserve Bank of Boston, *Funding Pensions: The Issues and Implications for Financial Markets*.

Feldstein, Martin, and Anthony Pellechio. 1977. "Social Security and Household Wealth Accumulation: New Microeconometric Evidence."

Discussion Paper no. 530. Cambridge Mass.: Harvard Institute of Economic Research.

Kotlikoff, Laurence. 1979. "Testing the Theory of Social Security and Life Cycle Accumulation." *American Economic Review* 69, no. 3.

Kurz, Mordecai. 1980. "The Effects of Pensions on Capital Formation: A Framework for Sample Analysis." Menlo Park, Calif.: SRI International. Xerox draft.

Munnell, Alicia. 1976. "Private Pensions and Saving: New Evidence." *Journal of Political Economy* 84, no. 5.

McClung, Nelson, Lou Koenig, and Charlotte Barkerding. 1973. "Editing Census Survey Files for Income and Wealth." Washington, D.C.: The Urban Institute.

Orcutt, Guy, Steven Caldwell, Richard Wertheimer III, et al. 1976. *Policy Exploration through Microanalytic Simulation.* Washington, D.C.: The Urban Institute.

Steuerle, Eugene. 1975. Expected Rates of Return on Savings Portfolios: The Variance Across Socio-Economic Classes." Ph.D. thesis, University of Wisconsin.

U.S. Treasury Department. 1977. *Blueprints for Basic Tax Reform.* Washington, D.C.: USGPO.

# Contributors

Allen, Michael P.
Department of Sociology
Washington State University
Pullman, WA 99164

David, Martin H.
Department of Economics
University of Wisconsin
Madison, WI 53706

Gallman, Robert E.
Department of Economics
University of North Carolina
Chapel Hill, NC 27514

Lindert, Peter
Department of Economics
University of California, Davis
Davis, CA 95616

McClung, Nelson
Assistant Director Econo-
    metric Analysis
Office of the Secretary of the
    Treasury
Room 4225, Main Treasury
Washington, DC 20220

Menchik, Paul L.
Department of Economics
Michigan State University
East Lansing, MI 48824

Mirer, Thad W.
Department of Economics
State University of New York
    at Albany
1400 Washington Avenue
Albany, NY 12203

Natrella, Vito
1718 North Hartford Street
Arlington, VA 22201

Newell, William H.
125 Peabody Hall
Miami University
Oxford, OH 45056

Orcutt, Guy H.
ISPS, Yale University
70 Sachem Street
New Haven, CT 06520

Smith, James D.
Department of Economics
Pennsylvania State University
University Park, PA 16802
            or
1221 William Street
State College, PA 16801

Williamson, Jeffrey
Department of Economics
University of Wisconsin
Madison, WI 53706

Wolff, Edward
Department of Economics
New York University
8 Washington Place, Room 700
New York, NY 10003

Wolfson, Michael
Treasury Board
Ottawa, Ontario
Canada K1AOR

# Author Index

# Subject Index